Library of
Davidson College

Perspectives
in the
Sociology of Science

# Perspectives in the Sociology of Science

*Edited by*
**Stuart S. Blume**

JOHN WILEY & SONS
Chichester · New York · Brisbane · Toronto

Copyright © 1977 by John Wiley & Sons Ltd.

All rights reserved.

No part of this book may be reproduced by any means, nor translated, nor transmitted into a machine language without the written permission of the publisher.

*Library of Congress Cataloging in Publication Data:*

Main entry under title:
Perspectives in the sociology of science.

    1. Science—Social aspects—Addresses, essays, lectures. 2. Science and state—Addresses, essays, lectures. I. Blume, Stuart S., 1942–
Q175.55.P47    301.5    76-30827
ISBN 0 471 99480 4

Text set in 11/12 pt Photon Times, printed by photolithography, and bound in Great Britain at The Pitman Press, Bath

# CONTRIBUTORS

| | |
|---|---|
| MARCEL FOURNIER | *Department of Sociology, University of Montreal, Quebec, Canada.* |
| STEPHEN C. HILL | *Department of Sociology, University of Wollongong, Australia.* |
| LOUIS MAHEU | *Department of Sociology, University of Montreal, Quebec, Canada.* |
| ELZBIETA NEYMAN | *Institute of Organization and Management, University of Warsaw, Poland.* |
| LOUIS H. ORZACK | *Department of Sociology, Rutgers University, USA.* |
| RADHIKA RAMASUBBAN | *School of Planning, Indian Institute of Management, Ahmedabad, India.* |
| PETER WEINGART | *Faculty of Sociology, University of Bielefeld, Federal Republic of Germany.* |
| RICHARD D. WHITLEY | *Manchester Business School, University of Manchester, England.* |
| | |
| STUART S. BLUME (Editor) | *Cabinet Office, Queen Annes Chambers, Tothill St., London, SW1.* |

# CONTENTS

Introduction: Sociology of Sciences and Sociologies of Science   1
*Stuart S. Blume*

1 The Sociology of Scientific Work and the History of Scientific Developments   21
*R. D. Whitley*

2 Science Policy and the Development of Science   51
*Peter Weingart*

3 Scientific Career, Scientific Generation, Scientific Labour Market   71
*Elzbieta Neyman*

4 Competing Professions and the Public Interest in the European Economic Community: Drugs and their Quality Control   95
*Louis H. Orzack*

5 Nationalisms and Nationalization of the Scientific Field in Quebec   131
*Marcel Fournier and Louis Maheu*

6 Towards a Relevant Sociology of Science for India   155
*Radhika Ramasubban*

7 Contrary Meanings of Science—Interaction between Cultural and Personal Meanings of Research in a Developing Country Scientific Research Institution   195
*Stephen C. Hill*

Index   231

# Introduction

## SOCIOLOGY OF SCIENCES AND SOCIOLOGIES OF SCIENCE

### Stuart S. Blume

It is becoming increasingly difficult to offer any brief characterization of the scope, orientation, and priorities of the sociology of science, as I think the diversity in the contributions to this volume will make clear. In this introductory essay I hope to give at least an indication of what seem to me to be currently the principal orientations (or preoccupations) which have emerged from a sort of conceptual dissatisfaction over the past few years. I shall conclude by suggesting that the time may be ripe for consideration of the question 'what should the sociology of science be about?', while recognizing that there may be arguments in favour of current diversity, and indeed against the meaningfulness of the question itself.

Surveying the scope of the sociology of science in 1970, Ben-David's task was relatively straightforward (Ben-David, 1970). He noted that comparison of the literature of the 1960s with writings of the 1930s and 1940s (one might add, at least those writings which in retrospect one would like to claim as of the sociology of science) showed the disappearance of attempts to explain the content and theoretical development of science in terms of broad social structures or values. (It will be recalled that just such attempts had characterized the work of the Marxist historian of science Boris Hessen, of the British Marxist scientists such as J. D. Bernal who had been influenced by him, and of the early Robert Merton.) Ben-David went on to suggest that two major orientations could be distinguished: 'interactional' and 'institutional'. Under the former heading could be subsumed studies of relationships within research (i.e. primary) groups, and of their effects on scientific production; communication networks within science; and of the nature and structuring of relationships within specific fields of science. Ben-David concluded that a recent shift of interest 'from laboratory work groups to networks encompassing distinct fields of research was greatly influenced by the emergence of a view of science as the work of a community in the sociological sense'. A major manifestation of this shift in emphasis was surely Hagstrom's pioneering empirical study of the values and social structure of American science, *The Scientific Community* (1965). By contrast, the institutional approach was seen as focusing, more macroscopically, upon the broader social, economic, and religious influences upon scientific organization, and upon definition of the scientist's role in society. Much of this work was of a purely descriptive kind (produced, for example, by international organizations) and lacking any systematic sociological perspective, though one would have to except studies such as Barber (1952) and Merton (1957). Joseph Ben-David himself gave impetus to this approach with his *The Scientist's Role in Society* published in 1972. Here, he sought essentially to explain changing relative levels of scientific activity between major industrialized nations. In particular, Ben-David wanted to explain the migration of the 'centre' of world science ('centre' being the nation scientifically preeminent at any one time) from England, to France, to Germany, and ultimately to the United States. Two kinds of explanatory variables were adduced. First, a precondition, was initial establishment of the scientific role, explicable in terms of 'the changing constellation of social values and interests among the population as a whole' (Ben-David, 1972, p. 169). Second, determinant after initial establishment of scientific activity, was 'the organization of scientific work which was more or less effective in marketing the products of research and encouraging initiative and efficiency in it' (p. 169). This 'market' model of scientific excellence/productivity is, needless to say, in striking contrast to studies conducted within the context of Socialist planning of science, to which I shall refer below.

Despite Ben-David's work, despite some work of Marxist inspiration (whether theoretical, or within a 'planning' context), despite the (retrospectively) clear interrelation of institutional and interactional factors (and questions), it was a specific form of the interactional approach which until recently provided the sociology of science with a dominant paradigm. It need hardly be said that I am referring to that articulated and developed in an impressive series of books and papers produced by Robert Merton and his students and colleagues through the 1960s and early 1970s. This of course was the result (though one supposes not the end result!) of an evolution in Merton's thinking about science, from his earlier concerns with science in a broad social context, towards a detailed concern with the social processes accompanying scientific discovery and evaluation. Though, as we shall see, a good deal of criticism is now levelled at this approach there is no doubt that Merton's own insights as well as the cumulative empirical studies of Crane (e.g. 1972), J. R. and S. Cole (e.g. 1973), Gaston (e.g. 1973), Zuckerman (e.g. 1967) *et al.* have much enhanced and deepened our understanding of science as a social activity.

It is surely generally known that this approach focuses (focused?) upon the social processes within the scientific system, conceiving these principally as controlled functional interactions. These interactions are (were?) said to be governed by a set of norms of a moral (descriptive–prescriptive) kind, themselves functional for the advancement of science (or, as some would now argue, for application of the scientific method). The social institution of science can then be said to reward contributions to publicly certified knowledge, that is fulfilment by the individual of the requirements of the scientific role, by various forms of recognition. The commitment of the scientist is maintained by institutional control of these rewards. It might be noted at this point that a distinction can be made between the 'pure' Mertonian approach, which saw scientists as individually motivated by commitment to advancement of knowledge, and an approach derived from exchange theory (e.g. Hagstrom, 1965; Storer, 1966) which saw scientists as inherently motivated by the search for professional recognition. As Whitley (1972) puts it, 'In exchange theory the goal of advancing knowledge is institutional, not individual.' It is not necessary here to give an account of the achievements of the Mertonian approach: this has been done by Storer (1973).

Merton's view of the normative structure of science is fundamental to this functionalist approach. At one level this may be seen from the extent to which his colleagues' empirical studies have sought specifically to examine systematic departure from prescribed normative behaviour: for example, studies of the extent to which ascriptive factors influence the reception of a scientist's work. Second, concern with normative structure is a necessary component of analysis of the exercise of legitimate social control. This is reflected, for example, in Hagstrom's discussion of the differentiation of scientific disciplines: the control of 'deviancy' (Hagstrom, 1965, chapter 4). Rather differently, King (1971) and Whitley (1972) have suggested that Merton's emphasis on moral norms derives from, and is a means of defending, his positivist epistemology: this is shown, for example, by treatment of scientific controversies not in cognitive terms ('who discovered what?') but as a dispute over priorities ('who made *the* discovery first?'), explicable in terms of commitment to a norm of originality.

Recently, on the basis of considerable empirical research, Mitroff (1974) has sought to develop the Mertonian conception of normative structure in science. This he has done by arguing, on the basis of interview material, that there exists also a set of norms exactly opposing those of Merton which may, on occasion, more properly govern (and represent) knowledge-advancing behaviour. (For example, it may sometimes be wiser to judge, or select from, the research literature on the basis of one's knowledge of men; emotional commitment, not detachment, may sometimes be essential if a line of research is to be pursued in the face of general scepticism.)

Finally Mulkay has developed a radical critique of notions of normative structure which provides a useful continuity between the Mertonian functionalist approach and the 'antagonistic' approaches which I shall discuss below. There are two strands to Mulkay's thesis (Mulkay, 1969, 1976b). The first is the suggestion that scientists' normative commitment is not to rules of social behaviour (universalism, communality, etc.) but rather to cognitive structures, technical procedures. This is demonstrated on the one hand by the extent to which empirical research has in fact failed to demonstrate actual commitment to the social norms, and in fact shows overwhelming departure from it. Mulkay is then led to question the meaning of a notion such as 'universalism'. Commitment to evaluation of scientific contributions by 'universalistic criteria' implies no more and no less than that researchers 'assess the results of others mainly in accordance with the cognitive and technical standards current within their research network. In other words, the notion of "universalistic criteria" has no content until we formulate it in terms of specific bodies of scientific knowledge, practice and technique'. At that point, however, the notion of universalism becomes redundant. Mulkay's second concern is with the reassessment of evidence adduced by Merton, Mitroff and others in support of a 'behavioural' normative structure. Mulkay suggests that the scientific community in fact draws upon a 'repertoire' of possible accounts of its own actions, selecting on the basis of perceived self-interest: Merton and Mitroff have then partially categorized this repertoire. In fact, 'scientists have tended to select ... those formulations originally taken by the functionalist interpreters to be the central norms of science ... because [they] served the social interests of scientists. It follows that the original functional analysis did identify a genuine social reality, but one better conceived as an ideology than as a normative structure'.

In attempting to account for functionalist stress on the autonomy of science it is possible also to perceive the impact of science ideology upon sociologists:

> since the end of World War II, scientists themselves have argued strongly and successfully that science must be left alone if it is to succeed. On a philosophical plane the major exponent of this view has been M. Polanyi. Scientists were successful in convincing policy-makers on this, and it seems that they may have been equally successful with sociologists. In other words, in constructing their ideal type model of the scientific system, sociologists may have been greatly influenced by the 'propaganda' of the scientists. (Blume, 1975)

These remarks form part of an attempt to justify abandonment of the assumption of autonomy, and thus a sociology of science which deliberately focuses upon interactions between science and other domains of social action (for example, the political). It is significant that Mulkay, beginning from a concern with the normative structure of science and the exercise of social control, should have been led to so complementary a view of scientists necessarily manipulating an external socio-political environment with the aid of an abstracted ideology. To accept this argument is surely to see the role of sociologists in subsequently legitimating, 'scientizing' this ideology as an ironic exercise in dupery.

I want to move on now to consider separately two explicit reactions against the Mertonian paradigm for the sociology of science, both now well established, and both represented in the present volume. The first, which I call the 'externalist' approach, is based upon just such an abandonment of notions of the autonomy of science. The second 'cognitive' approach is based upon a radical critique of the (for critics) logical positivist epistemology underlying functionalist sociology of science, and seeks to develop a sociology of scientific knowledge. These two critical approaches are not in any necessary opposition to each other: the former being in a sense a critique of the *explanans* of Mertonian sociology, the latter of its *explanandum*.

## The Externalist Approach

Though a partisan of the externalist approach, I do not at this point want to offer any elaborate defence of the view that there is value in seeking to understand the social structures and processes associated with the practices of science, against those who see value only in the consideration of knowledge-structures and meanings. Herminio Martins may well be correct when he suggests (not boasts!) that we are today living through a 'cognitive revolution' in sociology (Martins,

1974). It is still the case, in my view, that much of (at least potential) sociological interest in science is not (at least not yet) usefully analysable from any of the current multiplicity of cognitive perspectives. Rather more explicit in the indications which follow will be the related notion that the sociology of science need not, should not, limit itself to a single dependent variable (to adopt an inappropriate formulation!): developing scientific knowledge.

That science, and here I include both social and cognitive aspects, is to be understood wholly or largely through the influence of factors outside itself is a view of venerable lineage. It unites those sociologists who would root such understanding in general socio-economic structure (including Marxists) with those who would root it in culture, general social norms, or in ideology (including Parsons, early Merton, some neo-Marxists). It allows for the possibility of insights, and perhaps more, from adjacent disciplines such as economics and political science. The latter, after all, will necessarily share a view of science as being influenced by political factors (or else will have no concern with science at all). The former may even 'prove' the dependency of science (or 'invention', the economists' transformation of the concept) on economic forces, as in the work of the neo-classical economist Schmookler (1966). Moreover, an externalist perspective must underpin *any* practical concern with science policy, since government programmes and interventions cannot be assumed without effect on (the rate and/or direction of) science by their propagators.

There is a variety of other reasons for admitting the influence of extraneous social and cultural factors into one's sociological framework. One, in my view, is provided by the increasingly apparent unreality of the assumption of autonomy. For example, in the 1950s and 1960s, governments of industrialized countries largely delegated to the scientific community the influence which they could have exerted on science through their control of financial resources. This is much less so today, and research sponsors in such countries reflect economic and social priorities in increasingly *dirigiste* policies, rather than as previously allowing the hegemony of purely scientific considerations.

Another reason, and in my view a sociologically compelling one, is provided by the diffusion of interest in the sociology of science itself. The speciality in its functionalist manifestation developed very largely in the United States, focusing upon a scientific community (more precisely on certain disciplinary communities such as physicists) which to a greater degree than elsewhere accorded with its (nonepistemological) assumptions. Such studies of science in other societies as were carried out were limited to totalitarian states, in which external ideologies and structures were indeed seen as impacting: but this was an uncommon pathological situation with deleterious consequences for science. Today much science is carried out in societies (developing countries, culturally distinct regions of industrialized countries) in which little autonomy has been achieved. Indeed, as Fournier and Maheu point out in their contribution to this volume, the scientific domain then tends to be doubly dependent: upon structural and cultural factors within the host society, and upon the scientific priorities and influences of the large industrialized countries. To deny the relevance for sociology of science of, for example, accounts of the institutionalization of science in a developing country (on the grounds that this is 'insignificant' science—which has its parallels in Popper's strictures against Kuhn's 'normal' science) is surely indefensible on sociologists', as distinct from philosophers' criteria. To admit to the sociology of science those questions which sociologists of, or in, developing countries wish to ask about science is both to admit the relativeness of notions of autonomy, and also the existence of a very different set of research priorities for the speciality (see the contributions of Fournier and Maheu, Ramasubban, and Hill to this volume. See also Gomezgil (1975) for a discussion of sociology of science in a Latin American context).

To turn now from the justification of an externalist approach to its exemplification is naturally to change the level of argument from the meta-theoretical to the theoretical level; from the sphere of background assumptions to the sphere of evidence. Yet of course the distinction is not so clear-cut. In the following paragraphs I propose to outline some of the empirical evidence relating to the social structure of science which supports (since some is the reinterpreted findings of Mertonian sociology of science) and illustrates (since some is newly admitted as evidence relevant to sociology of science) an externalist approach. (What I shall have to say here is a very brief résumé of (Blume, 1974, chapters 3–6), which was intended to justify, and to demonstrate the scope of an externalist sociology of science. A rather different treatment, though from a similar perspective, is to be found in Salomon (1970, 1974).)

One focus is upon the reward system in science. As already indicated, there is a good deal of evidence from studies in the Mertonian tradition to the effect that the *recognition* of *scientific achievement* (the former institutionalized through election to honorific academies, invitations to travel, appointment to advisory committees, etc.; the latter usually operationalized by sociologists through, for example, weighted indices of publications, citations, etc.) departs very substantially from Merton's norms. One interpretation of this American and British evidence (e.g. Cole and Cole, 1973) is to recognize the resulting constitution of a stratification system in science, itself regarded as essentially functional. A second (Mulkay) is to see in it evidence for the functional irrelevance of the norms, which then become part of a 'repertoire of accounts'. My own interpretation of evidence for the influence of, for example, sex bias, status-consciousness, political bias, personal preferences upon the rewarding of scientific achievement, is in terms of 'permeability'. Such findings may be viewed as the permeation of those values, prejudices, loyalties, affiliations characteristic (to use no more precise a term) of the environing society, into the social processes of scientific activity.

A second focus for inquiry is represented by the *diversity* of social demands made of the scientist, *qua* scientist. Consider, for example, those linking him with the working of the political system. Among the 'politico-scientific roles' which have emerged in situations in which science is highly institutionalized are those associated with the operation of the complex networks of advisory bodies established by many administrations. Again, we may note the attempts made by scientists to capitalize on the symbolic power or authority of science in order to operate within the broader political system. This may be in *ad hoc* pursuit of some purely political goal (say, the election of a favoured Presidential candidate, or democratization of the political system (Blume, 1974, pp. 58–60)), or in the attempt to secure some major facility or resources for science itself (e.g. Greenberg, 1969, chapter 10). The latter case is in some way comparable to Mulkay's notion of the use by scientists of science ideology, outlined earlier, and the propagandizing efforts on behalf of science itself discussed in this volume by Fournier and Maheu. At the same time, many activities and indications previously regarded by sociologists as of purely internal importance are now seen as having also a political dimension. This would be true, for example, of election to an honorific academy (such as the National Academy of Science, the Soviet Academy of Sciences) where such bodies are closely linked with government. Election is then not only a recognition of scientific eminence, but has both symbolic and instrumental political significance.

A third focus is represented by evolution in the institutional structure of science. Apart from the institutional reflection of disciplinary change, or differentiation, which has been much discussed, one can note (related) processes of 'politicization' and 'unionization' (Blume, 1974, chapter 5). These processes can be ascribed to growth of concern with the ways in which science is used for antisocial purposes (or in whose interest it is used); to reduction in funds available for research and in the freedom of scientists to determine research priorities; to a deteriorating employment situation for scientists in the 1960s, etc. Politicization can be discussed, and demonstrated, by reference to the resurgence and emergence of bodies such as the Federation of American Scientists (initially a response to proposals for post-war control of atomic energy (Kimball Smith, 1970)) and Scientists and Engineers for Social and Political Action. A parallel development was represented by the politicization of the major professional associations of American science or the spawning by these of political or radical offshoots. Cahn (1974, pp. 41–120) shows that a large majority of scientists interviewed around 1970 considered that the professional societies to which they belonged were becoming politicized. (Nichols (1974, pp. 123–170) offers more detail on radical science bodies in the United States.) Unionization, more apparent in the United Kingdom, can be seen as also having proceeded by, on the one hand, attempts on the part of white collar unions to recruit from among scientists and allied personnel, and on the other (in part a reaction against the first trend) an increasing 'unionateness' (Blackburn, 1967) among professional associations. All this may be seen as a response to socio-economic environment quite similar to that which (sometimes with considerable disruption) had much earlier led to professionalization of learned societies (such as the Chemical Society) originating in the nineteenth century. It is my view that an understanding of such institutional responses to social, economic or political change is as significant for the sociology of science as is an understanding of the processes by which the socio-economic transformations of seventeenth-century England led to the foundation of the Royal Society.

The approach to the sociology of science which I am outlining has been criticized not only by those who consider that only appreciation of the changing intellectual structure of science merits attention (other matters presumably then being relegated to other sociological specialties), but also by Mertonians. Storer (1974), for example, has argued that it lacks a clear focus. By rejecting emphasis upon the way in which the scientific community is organized 'to produce certified empirical knowledge' this approach is stripped of the principal sociological criterion by which 'the scientific community is to be identified and its functioning assessed'. This comment provides a useful stimulus to an (admittedly necessary) clarification. The fact is, as Ravetz (1971) has shown, that science has been, is, and could be, many things. Views of what science most importantly 'is' will, among other criteria, determine both 'identification' and 'assessment' of the scientific community. Storer's position then becomes a special case of the more general problem: what views of science are held by what social actors within a given society (i.e. interaction of ideologies and social structure) and with what effects? Others might formulate the problem differently by attaching determinant weight to class structure or organization of means of production, or to cultural characteristics of society. The response can still be made, however, 'effect upon *what*?' My own answer would be: effect first upon the boundaries, structure, values, and operation of the scientific community, and second upon the social functions of science (which will be varyingly emphasized from one society to another) and the ways in which these are discharged. 'Effectiveness' then is only meaningfully considered (if it is to be considered) by reference to a specific function. There is no reason why sociologists should not (as do economists) concern themselves with the relations between science (whether conceived as a body of beliefs or as a productive process), technological change, and economic development; or (as do political scientists) with the relations between science, expertise, and the exercise of power. (Indeed I shall go on to suggest that this seems to be one of the major growth points of externalist sociology of science.) Such a model is of course complicated by feedback loops. As indicated earlier, the scientific community itself may influence views of what science 'is', what its principal function is, what it can achieve (drawing upon Mulkay's 'repertoire of accounts'). Moreover, through its connections with technology (whether we choose to perceive these causally or dialectically) science can influence social structure and (though in other ways also) the potential for social change.

Exploration of such relationships and effects in a variety of societies (allowing for possible disciplinary differences) seems to me to offer a fruitful research programme for the sociology of science. Within it there is, certainly, room for a variety of approaches and priorities which have not been considered together at the theoretical level. In the West, for example, it seems to me that particularly useful work has been done on the borderlines between political science and political sociology, and the sociology of science. One might cite, for example, Schroeder's work on the government of science in Weimar Germany (Schroeder, 1970); Graham's on the political links of the Soviet Academy of Sciences (Graham, 1967); work on the politics of expertise (e.g. Benveniste, 1972; Flash, 1965) and on the role of experts in technical controversies (e.g. Sapolsky, 1968;

Nelkin, 1971, 1975); and Mulkay's work on the roles of scientific elites (Mulkay, 1976a). All relate to the exercise of power in, and through, science. The situation is quite different in Eastern European countries.

In the first place, as Mikulinski (1974) has pointed out, sociological studies tend to be subsumed under a general 'science of science' approach, whose major intellectual task is the formulation of laws of scientific development (structural and cognitive) which might yield more 'scientific' planning of science. The Marxist view of the proper form of such laws is of course quite different from the views underpinning most Western debate in the philosophy of science (and hence the 'cognitive' approach to the sociology of science which is described below). Thus Kröber has written:

> The developmental laws of science are laws of connections, between science and the other vital spheres of society, particularly of the material production process as their fundamental basis. The nucleus of this hypothesis is the assumption that the developmental laws of science are not science-intrinsic. This assumption is a Marxist alternative to the immanent conceptions of the development of science. Its consequence by no means consists in any denial of the existence and significance of relationships internal to science but in the assumption of its secondary character which is derived from these fundamental laws of development. (Kröber, 1974)

In practice, most of this 'science of science' seems to focus directly upon the planning and management of science and innovation. Rabkin has recently stressed also the relative dominance of such work by physical rather than social scientists, and its quantitative non-ideological nature. (He notes (Rabkin, 1976) in this context the paucity of references in the science of science literature to the work of Marx, Engels, and Lenin, compared with typical articles in journals of history, economics, and philosophy.)

How much common theoretical ground there is between Marxist sociologists of science and those non-Marxists who would either stress cultural and other non-economic factors, or invoke productive processes also, in developing an externalist sociology of science, I do not know. There is certainly need for more theoretical reflection in developing this (or these) approach(es).

**The Cognitive Approach**

Following Martins once more, it is indeed true that many contemporary movements in sociology (phenomenological sociology, ethnomethodology, structuralism, etc.) are inspired by a desire to place 'meaning', 'knowledge', 'cognition' at the centre of the sociological stage. If, as Martins (1974, p. 252) points out, 'one wanted to unify conceptually the post-functionalist schools so as to periodise the recent history of sociological theory in a neat way one could hardly do worse than speak of a Cognitivist Revolution'. This revolution finds its echoes within a number of the subdisciplines of sociology. The sociology of education is one where, as Bernstein (1974, p. 152) has said, interest has shifted from 'how social class entered into, maintained and repeated itself in the organizational structure of education' to 'similar analysis on the contents of education'. The sociology of science is another. The influence of general cognitivist trends is problematic here, since for many, though not all, cognitively inclined sociologists of science, the task is not the replacement of sociologists' by participants' accounts but almost the reverse: replacement of the scientists' tradition of systematic historical reconstruction by sociological accounts. Indeed revolutionary inspiration has derived more directly from debate within the philosophy of science. Most briefly put, it was the critique of logical empiricist philosophy of science developed in the work of, for example, Popper, Kuhn, Lakatos, Feyerabend (and in the debates between these, and others) which led a few sociologists to examine, and to reject, the epistemological assumptions implicit in Mertonian sociology of science. At the same time the work of Kuhn in particular not only suggested a new focus for the sociology of science, but in a sense offered external legitimation of a place for sociology in the understanding of science.

The logical empiricist tradition in the philosophy of science (exemplified in the work of, for example, Carnap, Hempel, Nagel) was concerned with the delineation of scientific knowledge from metaphysics, and with the elaboration of timeless logical rules according to which (scientific) knowledge claims are to be assessed or validated ('the' scientific method). How scientists actually tended to behave, and in particular how 'discoveries' were made, was not relevant: the latter could happily be abandoned to a sociology of knowledge (Dolby, 1971). Such a perspective had no use, no place, for a sociology of science and little for a history of science (which might only provide supporting illustrations). Kuhn's (1962) *Structure of Scientific Revolutions* represented a transformation in the relations between the history and the philosophy of science. It suggested that scientific methods, theoretical formulations, criteria for the evaluation of problems and for the definition of solutions were not universal, but varied over time. As is now well known, Kuhn went on to suggest that scientific paradigms (of which these seem to be aspects) were subject to occasional breakdown and thence revolutionary transformation. Moreover, Kuhn accepted that theories, standards, criteria, were subject to public negotiation within, and the consensus of, a community of scientists: opening up, thereby, the sociological dimension. It was against the background of currently existing communal beliefs that knowledge claims were evaluated. At least sometimes (and especially in revolutionary periods leading to paradigm changes) the views of scientific communities were open to general cultural and institutional influence.

The extreme relativism of Kuhn's initial formulation, which denied that there was any means by which developments within succeeding paradigms could be compared, or any language of comparison, has been the subject of intense debate among philosophers. Lakatos, for example, sought to discredit what he saw as the 'mob psychology' of Kuhn's position, and to re-establish over-arching criteria necessary for a general notion of scientific progress. The publication of *Criticism and the Growth of Knowledge* in 1970, which contained a major paper by Lakatos, other criticisms of Kuhn, and a rejoinder, brought this debate before a wider public (Lakatos and Musgrave, 1970).

The cognitive sociology of science more or less dates from that time. Dolby

(1971), King (1971), Barnes and Dolby (1970), and others, noted the (only occasionally explicit) notion of science as a simply linear, cumulative process of intellectual development, based on reliable, non-problematic observation, underpinning Merton's work. Whitley (1972) attacked the reduction by Merton, Hagstrom and others of intellectual disputes to disputes over property rights or problems of control. Whereas Lakatos saw conflict between competing research programmes as a stimulus to scientific progress Hagstrom (Whitley pointed out) had seen conflict as essentially 'deviant', a problem in the exercise of social control. King (1971), Martins (1972), Whitley (1972, 1974), Weingart (1974) and others wished for a sociology of science which sought to explain intellectual changes in sciences in terms of interacting social–structural and intellectual/cognitive factors. Whitley in particular specifically rejects explanation purely in social terms (for example, the exercise of authority by a scientific elite: the relativism of the early Kuhn given sociological form) and stressed the place of cognitive factors in *both explanans* and *explanandum* of sociological accounts of scientific progress. Thus Weingart (1974) develops a distinction between 'cognitive orientations' and institutional structures. A hierarchy of cognitive orientations—ranging from 'paramount values' (general conceptions of the value, nature of science) down to 'conceptual schemes' (used by scientists in specific problem-solving activities)—is distinguished. To this a parallel institutional hierarchy corresponds (discipline—speciality—research area), each element of which corresponds to, or is integrated around, one level of cognitive orientation. Different levels of the institutional structure are institutionalized to different extents, and it was recognized that change could originate in each, though necessarily with impact on others. In the light of these classifications, it is suggested that the major task for the sociology of science is examination of the correspondences between cognitive and institutional orders, and of the (interactive) dynamics of change. However, Weingart sees the principal focus for sociology of science as being at the lower end of his hierarchy ('research areas'—'conceptual schemes') since it is here that 'the important substantive processes of problem-solving and decision making take place'. The more 'metaphysical orientations' are more properly the province of a 'sociologically informed history of science and culture'.

Whitley's approach (Whitley, 1974) is broadly similar. His first concern is to clarify concepts of 'social institutionalization' (encompassing both internal organization and societal integration) and 'cognitive institutionalization' (encompassing both degree of consensus, and similarity/predictability of research activity). Whitley goes on to consider the forms of social and of cognitive institutionalization corresponding to 'research areas' and to 'specialities'; the conditions under which research area or speciality functions as the source of social and cognitive identity for scientists; and the relations between his theoretical concepts and observables of scientific activity such as communication processes.

It is clear that case studies of scientific change (including the emergence of what become new specialities or research areas) are to provide the essential arena for both testing the feasibility and for elaborating this approach. In contrast to those who, like Mullins, had sought separately to characterize, and to correlate, theoretical problematic and social structure at various stages of speciality development (Mullins, 1972, 1973) this cognitivist approach demands consideration of the interaction between these two aspects of scientific change. Attempts are being made to produce case studies along these lines. However, because (it seems to me) disagreement exists over the proper nature of a cognitive sociology of science, case studies are not strictly comparable. Collins, for example, has studied the nature of the cognitive consensus in a number of research areas, and the implications of different forms of consensus for the explanation (or explicability) of experimental success and failure (Collins, 1975). But his emphasis upon the centrality of 'negotiation' (for example 'about what is to count as the same experiment') shows an espousal of interpretivist or phenomenological notions shared with a few other British sociologists of science (see for example Law and French, 1974). This interest in the relevance for science of such processes of 'accounting', 'negotiating', 'reconstruction' by scientists may provide the basis for a distinct tradition in the cognitive sociology of science. At the present time this approach, though profiting from a good deal of reflection, seems often overdependent upon debates in the philosophy of science (and of social science) and upon the well known general confrontations within sociology at large. This may follow almost inevitably from an implicit view (made explicit by Bourdieu, as I point out below) that perhaps the sociology of science is not quite a speciality like all others.

**The Cognitive Domain in Social Context**

The externalist perspective, discussed earlier, focuses upon the institutionalization, social relations, and social functions of science in different societies and upon the relevance of political, economic, and other social factors for the functioning of the scientific system. Work of this kind lacks (perhaps inevitably) a clear epistemological base, and is highly eclectic in its notions of science. By contrast the cognitive perspective includes a high degree of concern for the internal structure and development of scientific knowledge though not, it seems, for the classical problems of demarcating scientific knowledge from metaphysics or 'pseudo science' (Popper). Understanding of cognitive change is generally to be in terms of (interacting) cognitive and (internal) social structural factors.

Very broadly, in the first case focus is upon the relations between internal and external structural factors, in the second upon the relations between internal structural and cognitive factors. What possibility is there of a still more general approach, perhaps also involving cultural elements of explanation, but broadly bringing together the cognitive, internal, and external social factors discussed above? This, of course, is to see in the sociology of science the roots of a new approach to the classic problems of the sociology of knowledge. A number of authors seem, more or less ambitiously, to be attempting something along these lines.

Perhaps the most ambitious effort, though a controversial one, is represented by the 'finalization' thesis of Böhme, van den Daele, and Krohn (1973). This thesis suggests that when a scientific speciality has reached maturity its subsequent theoretical development is susceptible to external goal-setting: i.e. is externally determined. Mature specialities are characterized by possession of a 'fundamental theory' which can then be developed in alternative ways and which is seen as non-improvable, 'closed' (following Heisenberg), potentially 'transcendental'. The legacy of such a theory lies in its 'concretization' in its 'transition to special theories' (for example, general Newtonian mechanics leading to the theory of the planetary system, hydro- and aero-dynamics, etc.). Such special theories go through similar developmental processes, while being in some sense less 'restricted' by the 'logic of inquiry'. Such a process of theoretical differentiation, or specialization, is seen as leading ultimately to situations in which the internal potential for theoretical development is exhausted: development and application (to practical problems) in a way coalesce. This is finalization. A practical implication is that finalized specialities must be open to a kind of planning (science policy) which cannot be in any fundamental conflict with the developmental needs of the speciality itself. A subsequent paper by van den Daele and Weingart (1975) suggests that at different stages of cognitive development (of which finalization is the ultimate) sciences are capable of responding, or are 'receptive', to different levels of external demand. For example, the social sciences are seen as effective in offering 'assessments/descriptions' but not in developing means of intervention. A theory such as this clearly seeks to identify the conditions under which external factors (which are not themselves considered in detail) influence the development of scientific knowledge. The finalization theory seeks for these conditions exclusively in the pre-existing theoretical structure of science(s).

Controversies in science seem to offer a research focus permitting concurrent exploration of cognitive and broad social structural factors. Bourdieu has argued that epistemological conflicts always, inevitably, have a political aspect (Bourdieu, 1975). In trying to understand epistemological conflicts, therefore, exclusive focus either (as is common) upon the cognitive dimension, or upon the political dimension, is seen as inherently wrong. This follows from Bourdieu's notion of the scientific field as 'the locus of a competitive struggle in which what is specifically at stake is the monopoly of *scientific authority*, inseparably defined as technical capacity and social power ...'. Scientists are seen as competing to impose those definitions of science, those paradigms, those theories which are likely to bring them individually the maximum 'symbolic profit'. It would not be difficult to show that in such struggles recourse is had to all available resources of power (not necessarily excluding political power or influence in its traditional sense). It follows, in my view, that there is no clear distinction between 'purely internal' cognitive disputes, and disputes in the public domain (for example, between technical 'experts').

Robbins and Johnston (1976) have provided a very useful account of the cognitive and social bases of just such a 'technical' conflict. Their focus is upon a recent dispute over the acceptability of levels of environmental lead pollution, conducted largely between medical scientists (for example, toxicologists) on the one hand, and physical scientists (for example, geochemists) on the other. In cognitive terms, the geochemists criticized the medically crucial concept of a 'threshold', which depends upon the identification of clinical symptoms of lead poisoning only at higher body level concentrations. Lower (typically occurring) lead levels were then considered 'natural' and acceptable. By contrast, entirely different geochronological techniques showed that biospheric lead levels in the pre-industrial era had been about 1 per cent of those common today: suggesting a very different 'natural' concentration. Robbins and Johnston write: 'The controversy bore all the marks of a conflict between self-contained systems of belief: lacking concepts and terminology in common, the protagonists tended to "talk through" each other.' But the dispute is shown also to have a social, or status dimension. The medical toxicologists responded by denying the chemists' and geologists' competence, or right to pronounce, in what they insisted was a purely medical problem area.

In a subsequent paper, Robbins and Johnston (1976–1977) argue specifically that separation between the externalist ('science and society') approach and the cognitive approach is 'artificial and unproductive. The concepts and modes of analysis used in the "science and society" literature are themselves called into question by theoretical developments within neo-Kuhnian sociology of science, while the latter is concentrating upon an increasingly idealized non-existent science'. They go on to offer an analysis of knowledge production in terms of occupational control which depends for its relevance upon a conceptualization of science as a profession.

**Present and Future of the Sociology of Science**

I have tried to show that dissatisfaction with the once fruitful Mertonian paradigm for the sociology of science has resulted in the emergence of multiple (I will not yet say competing) research programmes. Extent of agreement over priorities in research, over what is to be explained, in terms of what, and how, seems to be slight, and is certainly unclear. This volume is an attempt to illustrate some current approaches.

Richard Whitley pursues his concern with the interrelation of cognitive and social structures of scientific fields. In his chapter he demonstrates how the kinds of 'objects' with which different fields of science work, which they 'transform', necessarily influence the organization of scientific work within each. These 'objects' (systems of phenomena) are of varying degrees of complexity, are varyingly theory and technique dependent (cf. high energy physics and geology): this serves to determine the range of scientific tasks which can usefully be carried out. Whitley goes on to show how an ideal–typical distinction between 'restricted' and 'unrestricted' sciences, made on this basis, can be shown to relate to such aspects of work organization as the scope for division of labour, agreement over research priorities, competition, hierarchization of authority; to the nature of doctoral training; and to the emergence of different systems of stratification within disciplines.

Peter Weingart takes up the very broad problem, linking sociology of science with political sociology and political science, of 'the relation between scientific information, or more generally systematic knowledge, and political action'. His approach is through examination of the way scientific knowledge influences, and is in turn influenced by, emerging political programmes. What is the relative significance of political goals and commitments on the one hand, scientific knowledge on the other, to widespread concern with an emergent politico-scientific issue? Through consideration of the origin of environmental protection programmes in the Federal Republic of Germany in the light of changing problem perceptions in both political and scientific systems, Weingart is able to throw light on the classic dilemma of external versus internal views of the sources of scientific change.

Elzbieta Neyman's contribution tackles a number of questions of importance both for the sociology of science specifically and for sociology in general. Through formulation of a research programme aimed at understanding the development of different types of scientific career she maps out a rather different approach to the integration of cognitive and social structural (and indeed broad cultural) factors. The comparison and evaluation of individual careers (conceived as processes of choice and adjustment) is to be done with the aid of concepts of 'scientific generation' and 'scientific labour market' elaborated in the paper. Ahistorical concepts of generation, used in much work on age in science, are seen as of limited utility: an historical concept permits essential relativization of 'the history of individual successes and failures to the chances which objectively existed at that time'. 'Chances' are seen as reflecting not only the influence of the market (the structure of opportunities), but additionally the paradigmatic structures of sciences existing at a given time. Neyman's approach deliberately raises the much broader problems of the relations between micro and macro levels of analysis in sociology, and between synchronic and diachronic analyses, within a sociology of science framework.

Louis Orzack's paper is firmly within an externalist framework, and indeed adopts implicitly a view of science-as-a-profession which may prove the most fruitful paradigm for that framework. The paper is concerned with an interprofessional dispute which, as in the Robbins and Johnston paper discussed earlier, is conducted within the public domain and again relates to the delineation of professional competences or jurisdictions. The issue in this case is the validation of the quality of pharmaceutical products, required by law, and the responsibility of a variety of professions (pharmacists, chemists, etc.) in different European countries. Responses to a proposal to harmonize these responsibilities throughout the nine member states of the European Economic Community show, among other things, the emergence of an internationalism in the science-based professions more akin to developments in the trade union movement than to the traditional 'internationalism' of science.

The remaining papers are also externalist in orientation, and though all are concerned with evolving or developing societies, differ in the specific problems examined as well as in the specific conceptualization of 'external influence'. All focus upon what Fournier and Maheu, in their paper, call 'peripheral scientific systems': peripheral in the senses both that their scientific activities are not, on the whole, of major importance to international scientific production, and also in that scientific activity is marginal to the societies in question.

Marcel Fournier and Louis Maheu argue that study of peripheral scientific systems allows one 'to expose more clearly the social conditions of scientific progress'. Their essay in historical sociology is an account of the development and process of institutionalization of science in francophone Quebec. These processes are seen as a consequence both of changing cultural and ideological perspectives in society and of a (related) transformation in the Quebec social structure. Fournier and Maheu show how an early scientific popularization/propagandization movement led to confrontation with the traditional intellectual elite (in which the clergy played a major role) notably over questions of educational curriculum. Since this debate was seen as a challenge to the legitimacy, the authority, of the existing intellectual elite, it was rapidly politicized. The alliances formed by scientists with an emergent technical/professional bourgeoisie are discussed, and shown to depend upon common interest in transformation of the educational and administrative systems. Growth of nationalism, access to power of this new bourgeoisie, led to major transformation and expansion of the university system, through an extension of state control. Complete institutionalization of science is now seen as dependent on transformation of a still highly 'colonized' economy: a focus of nationalism today.

After comparing the Mertonian approach to the sociology of science with the Marxian one (which she defines as 'the investigation of the combined impact of the mode of production and the corresponding superstructure of ideas at each stage of history upon the development of science') Radhika Ramasubban offers an analysis firmly within the framework of the latter. It is her view that only from such a perspective can worthwhile questions concerning science and technology (these two being incapable of precise demarcation: exemplifying the dialectic of theory and praxis) in a developing country be posed. The task she sets herself is to show how the organization of productive relations influences the utilization of science and technology in India, and thus their effect on the nation's development. A major part of the chapter deals with the effects of the research-initiated 'green revolution' on Indian agriculture. The socio-economic structure of the agricultural sector is shown to determine the availability of the new high yield crops developed by scientists (usually abroad). A second aspect of underdevelopment discussed is the exploitative technico-economic relations existing between indigenous and foreign firms, which are shown to repress the development of industrial research in India. The whole is both a profound essay in Marxian sociology of science and one of relatively few strictly sociological accounts of science and technology in India.

Finally Stephen Hill's chapter is also externalist in orientation, also focuses upon a situation of 'implanted' science, and yet offers a very different analysis. Partly this is a consequence of level, for Hill discusses changes in the working of a single research organization (in Thailand) over a period of 10–15 years. Like Ramasubban, Hill criticizes Western ('international') notions that science organization can or must be everywhere the same. His view is that 'science organization may be influenced by the specific history of research institutions in [a] country, by cultural, religious and wider administrative values and practices, by ... backgrounds of researchers, and by interaction of these with international perspectives and meanings ...'. However, the dynamics of science organization cannot be understood, as others have suggested, in terms of a process of accommodation between scientific norms and values (expressed by international experts in establishing a research organization) and those of the local culture. Hill shows that foreign expert behaviour is not clearly rooted in scientific norms, and local participants are not equally committed to traditional cultural values. The case study demonstrates the variety of meanings which actors attached to the organization studied, and the consequences of their interaction for its development. The chapter is an interesting example of the use of an 'interpretivist' perspective within an externalist framework.

What is one to conclude from this *tour d'horizon*? The vigour of the sociology of science is not to be doubted. The variety of conceptual schemes gives rise to processes of extension (yet more sociologies of science) and of intension (sociology of yet more sciences). When so much attention is given to detailed articulation of those commonalities which bind scientists in research areas and specialisms, perhaps some equivalent questioning of the sociology of science itself is apposite.

A number of fundamental questions rapidly become apparent. What should be our considered attitude to the diversity of approaches (research programmes and nascent research programmes) which varyingly compete with, and develop in (studied?) ignorance of, each other? Within the philosophy of science Lakatos considers competition between research programmes to be an important source of development in the natural sciences. For sociology also, where perhaps competitions are played by different rules, Robert Merton stresses the benefits of theoretical pluralism: 'To the extent that the paradigms are intellectually disciplined and not merely an adventitious assortment of personal interests generating little cognitive power, diversity leads to the illuminating of quite distinct aspects of human action and society, including aspects that a single paradigm would leave unnoticed' (Merton, 1976, pp. 49–50). Others, for example Gouldner, may disagree. Bourdieu, whose views I have already quoted, presumably believes that the programmatic (and proto-programmatic) competition characterizing sociology of science must be seen as a (political) struggle for intellectual authority. Clearly, whether one sees this current heterogeneity (competition) as good, bad, or inevitable, is a fundamental aspect of one's philosophy and sociology of sociology itself. The question of how, over what, and to what extent, any theoretical *rapprochement* might be brought about then becomes subsidiary.

However, even setting aside (whether as meaningless, valueless, or fruitless) the search for theoretical monism, it seems to me that an intellectual process akin to such a search has much to offer. Such a debate must be partly metasociological (for example, how can one justify according or denying attention to the development of science(s) in peripheral societies?), partly about the relevance of philosophy of science (for example, of discussion of the delineation of science from non-science). What should be the role of history in sociology of science? (Case studies of the development of scientific specialisms are historical in only a very narrow sense. A truly diachronic sociology of science demands much more.) What has sociology of science (or, have sociologies of science) to contribute to/learn from sociological analyses of other forms of cultural (or symbolic) production? From this follows perhaps the most fundamental question of all. What in fact is, or should be, the relation of the sociology of science to sociology over all? It is no accident that many disputes which currently vex the sociological community (for example, theoretical pluralism versus theoretical monism) are matters which, manifest in other disciplines, are within the province of the sociology of science. Bourdieu expresses clearly the view that sociology of science is not simply one speciality among others: 'The official sociology of science ... has the function not only of providing a justificatory ideology for [the sociological community] but also, and above all, of imposing on it a respect for the norms and models borrowed from the natural sciences—though at the price of a positivistic reinterpretation' (Bourdieu, 1975). Bourdieu, it is clear, sees sociology of science as encompassing the sociology of sociology itself. If this is to be so, then it must be recognized that application of the Mertonian paradigm (for example, in studies of acceptance/rejection of articles by sociology journals) has made a very minor contribution to the debate. What is entailed by requiring an approach which can encompass this debate in its full complexity? Indeed, to go further with Bourdieu, the requirement must be for a sociology not merely of alternative sociologies (strategies)—in which case it is itself no more than a political strategy—but of 'the complete system of strategies', 'the game as such'. Is this challenge to be taken up?

## References

Barber, B. (1952), *Science and the Social Order*, New York, The Free Press.
Barnes, S. B., and R. G. A. Dolby (1970), 'The scientific ethos: a deviant viewpoint', *European Journal of Sociology*, **11**, 3–25.
Ben-David, J. (1970), 'Introduction', *International Social Science Journal*, **22**, 1, 7–27.
Ben-David, J. (1972), *The Scientist's Role in Society*, Englewood Cliffs, Prentice-Hall.
Benveniste, G. (1972), *The Politics of Expertise*, Berkeley, Glendessary Press.
Bernstein, B. (1974), 'Sociology and the sociology of education: a brief account' in J. Rex (ed.), *Approaches to Sociology*, London, Routledge and Kegan Paul.
Blackburn, R. M. (1967), *Union Character and Social Class*, London, Batsford.
Blume, S. S. (1974), *Toward a Political Sociology of Science*, New York, The Free Press.
Blume, S. S. (1975), '"Realismo" y "alcances" en la sociología de la ciencia moderna', *Revista Mexicana de Sociología*, **37**, 1, 35–53.
Böhme, G., W. van den Daele, W. Krohn (1973), 'Finalisierung der Wissenschaft', *Zeitschrift für Soziologie*, **2**, 128–144 (published in English as 'Finalization in science', *Social Science Information*, **15**, 2/3 (1976) 307–330).
Bourdieu, P. (1975), 'La Specificité du champ scientifique et les conditions sociales du progrès de la raison', *Sociologie et Sociétés*, **7**, 1, 91–118.
Cahn, A. H. (1974), 'American scientists and the ABM: a case study in controversy' in A. H. Teich (ed.), *Scientists and Public Affairs*, Cambridge, Mass., MIT Press.

Cole, J. R., and S. Cole (1973), *Social Stratification in Science*, Chicago, Chicago University Press.
Collins, H. M. (1975), 'The seven sexes: a study in the sociology of a phenomenon, or the replication of experiments in physics', *Sociology*, **9**, 2, 205–224.
Crane, D. (1972), *Invisible Colleges*, Chicago, University of Chicago Press.
Daele, W. van den, and P. Weingart (1975), *The Utilization of the Social Sciences in the Federal Republic of Germany*, Report no. 2, Forschungswerpunkt Wissenschaftsforschung, University of Bielefeld.
Dolby, R. G. A. (1971), 'The sociology of knowledge in natural science', *Science Studies*, **1**, 1.
Flash, E. S., Jr. (1965), *Economic Advice and Presidential Leadership*, New York, Columbia University Press.
Gaston, J. C. (1973), *Originality and Competition in Science*, Chicago, University of Chicago Press.
Gomezgil, M. R. S. de (1975), 'La sociología de la ciencia en México: motivos para su estudio', *Revista Mexicana de Sociología*, **37**, 1, 9–34.
Graham, L. A. (1967), *The Soviet Academy of Science and the Communist Party*, Princeton, Princeton University Press.
Greenberg, D. S. (1969), *The Politics of American Science*, Harmondsworth, Penguin.
Hagstrom, W. O. (1965), *The Scientific Community*, New York, Basic Books.
King, M. D. (1971), 'Reason, tradition, and the progressiveness of science', *History and Theory*, **10**, 3–32.
Kröber, G. (1974), 'On the problem concerning the objective laws and stimuli of the development of science' in I. S. Spiegel-Rösing and J. J. Salomon (eds), *Science Policy Studies*, Tokyo, International Commission for Science Policy Studies, IUHPS.
Kuhn, T. S. (1962), *The Structure of Scientific Revolutions*, Chicago, Chicago University Press.
Lakatos, I., and A. Musgrave (eds) (1970), *Criticism and the Growth of Knowledge*, Cambridge, Cambridge University Press.
Law, J., and D. French (1974), 'Normative and interpretive sociologies of science', *Sociological Review*, **22**, 581–595.
Martins, H. (1972), 'The Kuhnian "revolution" and its implications for sociology' in T. J. Nossiter, A. H. Hanson, and S. Rokkan (eds), *Imagination and Precision in the Social Sciences*, London, Faber.
Martins, H. (1974), 'Time and theory in sociology' in J. Rex (ed.), *Approaches to Sociology*, London, Routledge and Kegan Paul.
Merton, R. K. (1957), *Social Theory and Social Structure*, New York, The Free Press, chapters 15–19.
Merton, R. K. (1976), 'Structural analysis in sociology' in P. M. Blau (ed.), *Approaches to the Study of Social Structure*, London, Open Books.
Mikulinski, S. R. (1974), 'La science de la science: problèmes et recherches des années 1970' in I. S. Spiegel-Rösing and J. J. Salomon (eds), *Science Policy Studies*, Tokyo, International Commission for Science Policy Studies, IUHPS.
Mitroff, I. I. (1974), *The Subjective Side of Science*, Amsterdam, Elsevier.
Mulkay, M. J. (1969), 'Some aspects of cultural growth in the natural sciences', *Social Research*, **36**, 1, 22–52.
Mulkay, M. J. (1976a), 'The mediating role of the scientific elite', *Social Studies of Science*, **6**, 3.
Mulkay, M. J. (1976b), 'Norms and ideology in science', *Social Science Information*, **15**, 415, 637–656.
Mullins, N. C. (1972), 'The development of a scientific specialty: the Phage Group and the origins of molecular biology', *Minerva*, **10**, 51–82.
Mullins, N. C. (1973), 'The development of specialties in social science: the case of ethnomethodology', *Science Studies*, **3**.

Nelkin, D. (1971), *Nuclear Power and Its Critics*, Ithaca, Cornell University Press.
Nelkin, D. (1975), 'The political impact of technical expertise', *Social Studies of Science*, **5**, 1, 35–53.
Nichols, D. (1974), 'The associational interest groups of American science' in A. H. Teich (ed.), *Scientists and Public Affairs*, Cambridge, Mass., MIT Press.
Rabkin, Y. M. (1976), '"Naukovedenie": the study of scientific research in the Soviet Union', *Minerva*, **14**, 1, 61–78.
Ravetz, J. (1971), *Scientific Knowledge and Its Social Problems*, Oxford, Oxford University Press.
Robbins, D., and R. Johnston (1976), 'The role of cognitive and occupational differentiation in scientific controversies', *Social Studies of Science*, **6**, 3.
Robbins, D., and R. Johnston (1976–1977), 'The development of specialties in industrialized science', *Sociological Review*, to be published.
Salomon, J. J. (1970), *Science et Politique*, Paris, Editions du Seuil.
Salomon, J. J. (1974), *Science and Politics*, publication in English of *Science et Politique*, London, Macmillan.
Sapolsky, H. M. (1968), 'Science, voters, and the fluoridation controversy', *Science*, **162**, 3852, 427–433.
Schmookler, J. (1966), *Invention and Economic Growth*, Cambridge, Mass., Harvard University Press.
Schroeder, B. (1970), 'The argument for self-government and public support of science in Weimar Germany', *Minerva*, **10**, 4, 537–570.
Smith, A. Kimball (1970), *A Peril and A Hope*, Cambridge, Mass., MIT Press.
Storer, N. (1966), *The Social System of Science*, New York, Holt, Rinehart and Winston.
Storer, N. (1973), Introduction, in R. K. Merton, *The Sociology of Science*, Chicago, University of Chicago Press.
Storer, N. (1974), Review of S. S. Blume: *Toward a Political Sociology of Science* in *Science*, 12 July, 137.
Weingart, P. (1974), 'On a sociological theory of scientific change' in R. D. Whitley (ed.), *Social Processes of Scientific Development*.
Whitley, R. D. (1972), 'Black Boxism and the sociology of science', *Sociological Review Monograph*, no. 18, 61–92.
Whitley, R. D. (1974), 'Cognitive and social institutionalization of scientific specialties and research areas' in R. D. Whitley (ed.), *Social Processes of Scientific Development*, London, Routledge and Kegan Paul.
Zuckerman, H. (1967), 'Nobel Laureates in science: patterns of productivity, collaboration and authorship', *American Sociological Review*, **32**, 391–403.

# 1

# THE SOCIOLOGY OF SCIENTIFIC WORK AND THE HISTORY OF SCIENTIFIC DEVELOPMENTS

R. D. Whitley

## Introduction

Traditionally the history of science has not concerned itself much with the organization of the sciences and the structure of research in different fields. Similarly, most studies of scientific research organizations have not considered the type of knowledge produced to be relevant to their purposes and have not usually incorporated a historical perspective. Indeed, they have rarely examined the actual work done in laboratories but have usually focused on productivity, scientists' attitudes, and authority structures (e.g. Pelz and Andrews, 1966; cf. Whitley and Frost, 1972, 1973). Work patterns of scientists in different fields have rarely been studied and attention has usually been focused on organizational success and individual career paths (cf. e.g. Glaser, 1964). Case studies of individual laboratories (e.g. Swatez, 1970) or groups of scientists (e.g. Holton, 1974; Mullins, 1972) have not usually seen the organization of work as being relevant to the nature of the knowledge produced in the sense that scientific development would have been different if the structure of research—broadly conceived—had been different. In this paper I want to argue that the sociology of scientific work is an essential aspect of accounting for scientific change and development and to briefly indicate various relations between patterns of work organization and intellectual structures of the different sciences.

The view taken here is that scientific knowledges vary and these variations are linked to differences in the way scientific work is organized. Intellectual structures are social products and differences in their organization reflect and affect systems of knowledge production. The understanding of how particular sciences developed involves, I suggest, an appreciation of how the organization of scientific work developed. Certain systems of knowledge production are commensurate with certain forms of knowledge and not with others. Different sciences are compatible with particular ways of organizing work and it is these relations which are the focus of this paper. This approach can be contrasted with the emphasis on scientific 'communities' in many sociological accounts of science which has led to numerous studies of 'research areas', 'specialities' and 'subdisciplines' (cf. e.g.

Crane, 1972; Mulkay *et al.*, 1975). These are seen as the motors of scientific development (cf. Mullins, 1975) while 'networks of association' (Mullins, 1968) are relegated to 'normal' science and considered residual to scientific change. The inherent difficulties of the Kuhnian (1970, 1974) notion of scientific change through 'revolutionary' conversions of paradigm bound communities have been fully discussed by Herminio Martins (1972) and do not require further analysis, but the notion of revolutionary groups as key phenomena in the sciences still maintains a powerful hold on sociologists (Mullins, 1975). Viewing the sciences as essentially communities of scientists governed by the CUDOS norms is, of course, a key facet of Merton's approach to the sociology of science which was extensively developed by Hagstrom in his revealingly titled *The Scientific Community* (1965). This facet has not been vanquished in the 'post-Kuhnian' sociology of science and the extent to which a 'revolution' has occurred in the field is rather dubious.

I emphasize the power of the notion of scientific communities because it has focused attention on the 'free floating' scientist who is relatively unattached to any work organization, free to choose his research problem and motivated by the lust for recognition and/or by the desire to extend certified knowledge. Now the epistemological implications of the Mertonian view have been extensively discussed and I will not pursue them here (cf., for example, King, 1971; Whitley, 1972), but the sociological side effects have been less often analysed. The search for solidaristic communities of like-minded scientists has become seen as the 'real' task of the sociology of science so that the ideal Ph.D. thesis would be to isolate a key group in a given field either by citation analysis or by using 'official histories' reified in textbooks and review articles and then to study how the group was formed and changed its membership as the area developed. This sort of study is then used to construct 'models' of scientific change, such as that by Crane (1972), which 'fit' the output of an area to a logistic curve. Intellectual development is reduced to the rise and decline of discrete 'communities' which effortlessly produce certified knowledge. The task of the sociologist is to trace the many and various migrations of 'free' individuals which, in aggregate, lead to changes in direction and new developments. The possibility of differences in knowledge structures being connected to the structure of work in the sciences is rarely countenanced.

Aside from the methodological and technical problems of isolating distinct communities, which have led some authors to call for an 'interpretative' or 'interactionist' approach to the study of scientists (Law, 1974; Law and French, 1974; McAlpine and Bitz, 1973; McAlpine *et al.*, 1974), a major consequence of this conception of the sociology of science has been the lack of attention paid to how the research situation is structured and scientists' choices limited. Science as a form of work occurring in employing organizations has been almost entirely ignored in sociological studies of the sciences except for some discussions of the 'industrialization' of research (Ravetz, 1971, pp. 44–57) and the 'incorporation' of science (Rose and Rose, 1975). The ideological conception of the scientist as an independent searcher after truth unfettered by mundane, everyday concerns may be overtly rejected by sociologists but is curiously reflected in their emphasis on autarchic communities as the key social component of intellectual development. Even if scientists are basely motivated by the desire for recognition and related rewards, so that the traditional notion of community is inapplicable to their associations formed for purely individual interests (Klima, 1974; Mulkay, 1972), they are still assumed to be free of organizational constraints and to be able to move into the most 'profitable' field. 'Perfect' labour and product markets seem implicit in this approach so that aside from the benevolent state providing adequate facilities and staff there are no collective entities impeding the free flow of information, men and materials. This idyllic state of affairs apparently is expected to continue indefinitely. If, on the other hand, it is held that scientists' actions are not those of a profit maximizing entrepreneur in a perfect market or of disinterested supermen then the conditions under which they act and produce knowledges become relevant to the 'real' sociology of the sciences instead of being relegated to the sociology of organizations, of education or even to non-sociologists, as some staunch upholders of the established tradition have been heard to murmur.

Thus formulated, this view may seem anodyne. However, the simple injunction to examine the conditions of scientific work does suggest a rather different form of sociological analysis to that sketched above. In situating scientists in their organizational context the ways in which knowledges develop and change are being connected to their manner of production. Where knowledge is conceived to arise from scientists simply applying the tools of their trade in a sociologically non-problematic way then the main task is to understand how scientists choose their work topics, since whatever their choice, certified knowledge will follow and so scientific change is simply the result of changing interests. If, though, scientists' choices are structured by their conditions of work and of training—again, broadly conceived—then it seems reasonable to argue that so too are the ways they implement those choices. If a scientist is solely motivated by profit maximization or by the search for truth it does not seem quite so important to enquire how he will proceed, somehow the production of knowledge is subservient to its exchange or certification, whereas the structure of scientific work as conceived here incorporates topic formulation, approach and evaluation. Focusing on the organization of research leads to the consideration of conditions of knowledge production and, once this process is taken to be problematic, of their relations to changes in knowledges. Once the scientist is seen as working in an ordered environment which limits and constrains his actions and ideas then it is not too great a step to consider science as an ordered phenomenon which is connected to its conditions of production. Changes in the structure of scientific production can be expected to affect the structure of knowledges produced just as the organizational arrangements in a science are linked to the organization of knowledge. The structure of scientific production here includes the day-to-day organization of work, the intellectual background to research and processes of recruitment, training and elite formation.

Rather than assuming the ubiquity of scientific communities and their crucial importance in scientific development, the particular conditions under which community type patterns of association occur and the form of knowledge they produce would be taken as problematic in the view being stressed here. Specialist communities may well turn out to be the exception rather than the rule in the sciences and occur only when existing organizational arrangements are inadequate for the development and maintenance of particular cognitive and social identities. Certainly the difficulties encountered in obtaining clear identities based on distinctive intellectual structures which direct current work among scientists in a variety of fields suggest that they are not overtly obvious (cf. Bitz et al., 1975). Indeed, for many scientists educational experiences and current tasks provide the basis for intellectual identity. The day-to-day exigencies of research direct their actions and views far more than any 'research programme' or community paradigm (Bitz et al., 1975).

It could, of course, be argued that although communities are uncommon in the sciences and consist of only a small minority they are crucial to understanding paths of development, and in any case this minority is the elite and hence of outstanding importance. Even if both of these points were, and always will be, correct that is no reason for assuming their validity *a priori*. Furthermore, the conditions under which such communities did emerge and produce startling developments still require specification. Similarly, elites require non-elites to act as such and once it is granted that work is structured for the non-elite then it is difficult to see how this structure is irrelevant to the work of the elite. For an elite to be an elite it must be part of some system which contains the non-elite; the existence of a structured, organized situation among the latter suggests it would be bizarre to insist on the lack of work organization among the former. The relations between any elite and the rest are not random and any elite community cannot be analysed without reference to the general framework within which it acts as an elite and produces knowledge. In fact, I think that a major point of studying scientific elites is precisely to ascertain how they influence the organization of scientific production and control recruitment processes because it is through these means that they affect scientific development as an elite. Without impinging on the general production system they can only exercise individual and limited influence. If they are indeed an elite, community processes of exclusion, boundary maintenance, and recruitment are of interest as is the form of knowledge produced and the ways further developments are directed by the guardians of the tradition.

If self-sustaining communities are not necessarily the key to understanding scientific change, and intellectual change itself is not to be reduced to patterns of scientists' migrations, the sociology of scientific development needs alternative approaches to the study of social and cognitive structures which allow for differences between the organization of intellectual structures (cf. Whitley, 1975) and between the ways knowledges are produced. A major constituent of such approaches is the way scientific work is organized in different sciences because this both reflects current interests and capacities and affects future directions through encouraging and discouraging particular patterns of collaboration, allocating resources for some approaches and problems and not others and through the organization of recruitment structures and employment opportunities. In a sense the organization of work in the sciences reproduces existing social and cognitive relations but, like all reproduction systems, not strictly homomorphically. Exactly what is covered by the organization of work here requires further specification because it is used in a broader sense than is common.

## Scientific Work and the Nature of Scientific Objects

By talking of the organization of work in sciences I mean to emphasize the need to direct analysis to what work is being done, how it is being conducted, and for what purpose. Work is conceived in the general sense of transforming objects with tools for some goal and so its organization includes procedures for producing and understanding objects, their transformation, and the development and application of some set of objectives. Scientific work shares these general features with other varieties but differs in its capacity to produce novel and theoretically infused phenomena in particular circumstances. The degree to which these phenomena are novel varies from science to science but they are recognizably distinct from commonsense cultural objects. The important point to be noted here is that scientific activity is characterized by its search for intransitive, in the sense of functioning independently of men, natural mechanisms which produce phenomena in closed systems, i.e. those in which a constant conjunction of events obtains (Bhaskar, 1975, p. 69). These phenomena are not the same as everyday experiences which occur in 'open' systems but are socially constructed for the investigation of natural structures. As Bhaskar puts it, they are 'artificially established as a means of access to the enduring and continually active causal structures of the world' (1975, p. 118). Scientific work consists of the transformation of these socially produced objects.

This very brief sketch of a rather global and general point of view requires further specification if it is to be sociologically useful. In viewing work as a transforming activity attention is focused on what is being transformed and how. In many respects it is differences in these features which distinguish the sciences and in terms of which we can examine differences in work organization. Pantin (1968, pp. 18–23), for example, differentiates 'restricted' and 'unrestricted' sciences in terms of the simplicity and complexity of the systems analysed, the 'richness' of the constitutive phenomena. The use of mathematical models and manipulations is more common in restricted fields precisely because their objects are less 'rich' and are what Georgescu-Roegen calls 'arithmomorphic' (1971). Differences in the way objects are constructed are linked to the ways they are transformed. Furthermore, as Pantin points out, these variations are connected to styles of work in that geological work—or the 'unrestricted' parts of it—often consists of field observation whereas most work in the natural sciences focuses on laboratory constructions, and consequently different forms of work organization occur. A key part of the organization of work in the sciences is, then, the sort of activity required to 'correctly' transform scientific objects. The nature of the objects affects the type of work done and its organization.

In viewing the sciences as production systems, we can distinguish three important aspects of work organization. First, there is the day-to-day organization of tasks and resources to accomplish them. This requires some arrangement of facilities, technical assistants and formulation of priorities. It also incorporates the specification of tasks and their relation to more general problems and issues. Second, there is the organization of the field, whether discipline, speciality, or research area (Whitley, 1974). This refers to the arrangement of intellectual and social structures 'within' a particular domain of activity (cf. Whitley, 1975). It covers the characterization of the boundaries of the proper objects of interest and legitimate approaches to them. General priorities, concepts of science, disciplinary principles, hierarchies of problems, the structure of journals and conferences are all aspects of this form of work organization. The third one is the arrangement of employing organizations, both the number and type—for example teaching departments or full-time laboratories funded by yearly appropriations—and the authority structures within and between them. These three aspects are interconnected and are related to training systems and the operation of elites in different sciences. In order to illustrate their mutual relevance and their importance to paths of scientific developments the rest of this paper will sketch forms of work organization commensurate with different scientific objects and means of transforming them. By developing Pantin's (1968) distinction between the 'restricted' and 'unrestricted' sciences I hope to show how particular sciences are associated with particular ways of organizing scientific work, training recruits, and elite operation. In some sciences, events and phenomena are embedded in a highly esoteric theoretical structure which requires elaborate technical facilities for their production. In fact, the understanding of these objects is impossible without the use of particular techniques which are themselves theory impregnated and not amenable to everyday commonsense understanding. As I understand him, this view corresponds to objects in Pantin's 'restricted' sciences. In other fields, scientific objects are constructed in a less theoretically specific manner. They are not so narrowly conceived and incorporate a range of attributes and properties. The transformation of objects occurs in a number of ways which are not necessarily mutually incompatible nor are they object specific. At any particular point it is not clear in these 'unrestricted' sciences which direction future work should take or how current developments should be evaluated. The 'richness' of the objects that Pantin sees as a major difference between the sciences means that there are a number of possibilities in, say, geological sciences and there is no obvious, unambiguous way we can select the most promising one or decide, *post facto*, which was the more important development. In 'restricted' fields the objects are so finely specified that only a small number of techniques are appropriate and while there are choices, these are not so many and are much narrower in their range of assumptions and outcomes.

Formulated in this way, a simple continuum of objects varying in their precision of conceptualization may seem all that is meant and so the development of the sciences will lead to greater precision for all. However, geological objects may be just as precisely defined as any other set of scientific objects, but 'richness' distinguishes objects in solid state physics from those in geology and physiology by their degree of theoretical closure, in the sense that the variety of meaningful operations that can be performed on the former is less than of those relevant to the latter. The nature of work in physics is constrained by the ways objects are conceived and related to appropriate manipulations much more than in other fields. Furthermore the type of manipulations that are relevant is restricted to a smaller set. For a novel technique to be adopted, more criteria need to be met and conditions fulfilled in a fairly coherent way. This is not to say that any technique can be used indiscriminately in other fields but the 'relevance criteria' will not be so clearly defined, nor so restrictive. Precision of conceptualization is not so much, then, the relevant factor here as the theoretical specificity of the objects such that possible ways of understanding and transforming them are clearly very limited. Where the theoretical specificity of objects is not so great, their theoretical universe will not be so clearly delineated and potentially 'fruitful' ways of working not clearly identifiable or easily evaluated. The difference being discussed is not one of definitional precision but of how narrowly and specifically conceptual closure is made. Following the specificity of objects the domain boundaries are more or less clearly drawn.

I should perhaps point out here that theoretical closure is never complete in the sciences and scientific work is not reducible to algorithmic progression. Choices of task and theoretical strategies remain in 'restricted' sciences but they are more constrained and object specific than in others. Existing intellectual frameworks delimit admissible developments more firmly and the likelihood of ranking—or at least tacitly ordering—promising ways of proceeding is stronger in 'restricted' fields. The degree of pre-selection of permissible concepts and ideas is considerable and theoretical presuppositions filter potential developments in a much stricter manner than in 'unrestricted' fields. The construction and transformation of objects have to adhere to a considerable number of interrelated rules and procedures to be counted as part of the field, whereas the comparative lack of theoretical specificity in other sciences means that the number of potentially 'fruitful' approaches is greater and there is no integrated set of criteria for judging 'fruitfulness' in an unambiguous manner. Because the objects are not tightly theoretically constricted there is considerable flexibility in evaluating novel developments. While not quite intellectually anarchic, this situation is more fluid than that obtaining in the more 'restricted' sciences.

Now this sort of distinction is only one that can be made for differentiating the sciences but it is a major consideration in the analysis of the organization of scientific work because different work patterns are appropriate in the two cases and different forms of social organization emerge. One obvious point is that research tasks and strategies are more easily specified and systematically interrelated in 'restricted' sciences. A fairly clear division of labour, or at least differentiation of research, should be 'rationally' possible in situations of high theoretical specificity, whereas in 'unrestricted' fields there is little theoretical justification for any one particular arrangement of tasks and priorities being preferred because the 'richness' of phenomena means that a wide range of tasks are possible and equally 'rational'. Organizational strategies (cf. Lemaine *et al.*, 1975, pp. 10–13)—and those of national funding agencies—should therefore differ across the sciences and so will personal reconstructions of career paths and patterns of collaboration and mobility.

It is perhaps worthwhile here to emphasize that although the terms 'restricted' and 'unrestricted' sciences are being used as a form of shorthand, I am not claiming to follow strictly Pantin's usage nor are these 'types' meant to be dichotomous. Rather they refer to certain clusters of attributes which vary on continua. Additionally, I am not suggesting that any particular science exhibits all the characteristics discussed but that a science dealing with particular sorts of cognitive objects will be organized in a way which is distinct from one that deals with other sorts of objects. It is the limits to forms of organization which are set by the nature of a science's concerns which are the focus here.

**Work Organization in 'Restricted' Sciences**

As already noted, a high degree of theoretical specificity restricts the range of meaningful developments in a science. It also delineates the type of task which can be usefully carried out and the sort of inferences which can be legitimately made. High specificity of objects, techniques, and purposes implies a considerable degree of clarity about task formulation and interrelationships. Separation of tasks and the differentiation of research topics and approaches are also facilitated. Interrelations between tasks should be fairly clear and their mutual implications traceable. Indeed, within the restricted sphere of phenomena and events considered characteristic of the field a developed division of labour between tasks and research areas could occur. However, differentiation of tasks need not imply their mutual interdependence in the sense that one cannot be completed without others. Indeed, it may not be clear what the result of a number of tasks might be, in terms of some theoretical goal, such that we could say that each was necessary for its accomplishment. The more specific objects become, the more easily they are separated and can be organized as the foci of distinct tasks but, equally, the more difficult it may be to relate them coherently and make sense of some more general phenomenon, as Bitz suggests is happening in particle physics (Bitz, 1975a). Processes of specification and refinement of instruments may outrun the development of integrative theories or models, especially if work does become organizationally distinct so that cognitive boundaries are reinforced by social ones. Rather than research tasks being derived from distinct aspects of a single problem, they may develop in a very *ad hoc* manner from everyday organizational and technological exigencies. What may be regarded as 'efficient' in the sense that work can continue in ever narrower directions may lead to 'inefficiency' in terms of making sense of increasingly disparate topics and procedures.

The increased 'efficiency' of sciences which permit, if not encourage, the packaging of research topics in ever narrowing limits may be enhanced by particular forms of work organization which inhibit consideration of general questions and purposes. The 'rationality' of the 'restricted' sciences may focus attention on highly specific tasks and lead to the development of organizational structures which institutionalize such research because it manifestly 'works', i.e. produces results which make sense in terms of the current framework, but this is likely to hinder attempts at integrating research topics. Indeed, a dual structure of work organization may result in that a small group of scientists—who may or may not constitute an elite—focus on more general problems while the majority concentrate on highly constrained topics.

Traditionally, clear definition of work tasks and appropriate procedures has been associated with a high degree of formalization and hierarchization of authority in work organizations. Clear lines of authority and formal specification of highly routinized work practices have been emphasized by many writers on organizations (e.g. Pugh and Hickson, 1968). Now, I am not suggesting that scientific laboratories or university departments are organized in a similar way to car factories or department stores, but pointing out that where research tasks can be relatively closely specified and appropriate ways of proceeding are clearly constrained, the possibility of formal control systems and authority structures is enhanced in comparison to sciences where objects are less 'obviously' specified.

The equivalent structure of work at the day-to-day level found in formal bureaucratic organizations occurs, perhaps, in the use of Ph.D. students in university departments. Often in the United Kingdom the bulk of research in established fields is done by apprentices who are organized by a scientist on the teaching staff and, sometimes, by post-doctoral fellows. As one scientist described the process in a large physics department, the beginning students are offered a 'package' which they then examine. If they are not particularly interested then another is suggested. By the time a third 'package' is requested time constraints—and associated financial pressures—ensure that students select one of the suggestions. A single supervisor may have up to 14 students under his tutelage, as well as four post-doctoral fellows, and it was obvious to us in the course of interviews that the only way this large number of research topics could be controlled and integrated was, on the one hand, to define each task very specifically and narrowly and, on the other hand, rely on the more experienced students to show the new ones how to construct the instruments and run experiments. This degree of task specialization is perhaps unusual but the point being made here is that it is possible to organize scientific work in this way if objects and techniques are specific enough.

The restricted nature of objects and techniques might be expected to lead to a highly developed division of labour between research topics focusing on distinct but mutually relevant aspects of a fairly well defined problem throughout whole disciplines. Some general but clearly bounded concern would be divided into 'packages' which would, when completed and integrated, result in its understanding. Work organization in this case would simply be a matter of dividing up the general problem, allocating tasks to appropriate workers, ensuring the work was conducted correctly and then putting the products together so as to resolve the initial problem. This resolution would lead to a further problem being generated and the process would be repeated. Assuming an availability of workers and facilities and an appropriate system of control and a framework for delineating problems, this production system could continue for some time. The ability to control large numbers of researchers is dependent upon the precision and narrowness of formulation of tasks, and in highly 'restricted' sciences they can be structured in a formal manner. Control can, therefore, be decentralized to other students and post-doctoral fellows, at any rate on a day-to-day basis. When 'oddities' or 'deviant' results occur, though, the supervisor often has to be brought in to decide whether they are to be taken seriously, as happened with the discovery of pulsars (cf. Woolgar, 1976).

This system of research production may well work at the Ph.D. level, and the analogy of factory batch production is worth pursuing (cf. Kynaston Reeves and Turner, 1971), but it is less clear that it represents whole fields in the sense that, say, solid state physics exhibits a fully functional division of labour with the bulk of researchers working on narrow topics which are mutually interdependent. In fact, it is doubtful if any cognitive structure in any science is so coherent and clearly organized that major problems can be formalized and broken down into separate components of a production line. Fully fledged division of labour between tasks in the sense of mass production systems is, therefore, unlikely, as is the associated control system in the sciences, but there are aspects of this approach which can be usefully developed.

Even if the factory analogy is fraught with difficulties—and it is noteworthy that few of the writers on the 'industrialization' of science have actually shown how it might be pursued (cf. e.g. Ravetz, 1971)—general problems are broken down into researchable topics and, sometimes, results are integrated to 'solve' them. Without necessarily positing some monolithic and omnipotent elite which allocates pre-structured work tasks, standards of relevance, adequacy, and importance are maintained by authority figures in all fields and topics are selected and formulated in the light of these criteria. Tasks are chosen and worked on by individual scientists—or collaborative groups—in line with current conceptions of what, say, a physics problem is and what appropriate techniques for tackling it are. Also, there seems to be a tendency to carve out an area which does not encroach on others' and, equally important, is not likely to be directly worked on by other scientists. An example here might be the division of topics between the Manchester and Cambridge groups in radio astronomy (cf. Mulkay and Edge, 1973). Another one occurs in anthropology where each writer appropriates his 'own' tribe or, coming nearer home, in the sociology of science where there is a feeling that since X and Y has already 'done' scientists working in a field or topic area, no one else should 'poach'. This sort of mutual distancing does not constitute division of labour in the sense that each result or product is necessary for some overall goal, but rather the differentiation of tasks so that competition is mitigated. However, while competition over the provision of answers to the 'same' question may be avoided by such differentiation, it still arises over the importance and primacy of areas to a science and hence over resources and personnel (cf. Whitley, 1977). Furthermore, the more restricted are possible alternatives the more intense this competition becomes. In so far as alternative foci of attention claim to represent the primary problems of a field and so define important work in it, they compete (cf. Whitley, 1976a). Also, of course, there are instances where competition occurs over the same problem as in the Double Helix (Watson, 1970) and the Omega minus particle (Gaston, 1973, pp. 83–93), but this, I think, is apparent only in highly 'restricted' fields because it is only there that objects are defined with sufficient precision for it to be possible to say there is, in fact, only a single discovery to be made.

Separation of topic areas in 'restricted' sciences implies some, however informal, framework which delineates legitimate problems. It may also order problems according to their relevance to current understandings of the nature of the field so that more notice is taken of work in one area than in another. Differentiation of tasks, then, need not imply equivalence of tasks, and while it may be 'rational' to select an area which is not being pursued by many, there are only a limited number of legitimate areas in these sciences, and by picking a minor topic a scientist may be ignored. It could be argued that the differentiation in radio astronomy was only possible because of the small number of groups, of roughly equivalent status and resources, involved and the high entry costs in terms of technological apparatus. If scientists pursue 'hot' fields, task differentiation becomes narrower and narrower and yet there is no necessary division of labour in the sense that the field is parcelled out among individuals in a coherent fashion with each part contributing towards the whole. Also, of course, there is no guarantee that pursuit of ever narrowing tasks will produce an acceptable solution to the general problem. Hierarchies of problem areas and restriction of legitimate tasks in 'restricted' sciences are likely to lead to concentration on increasingly specific tasks in a small number of areas. While increasing the 'restricted' nature of the objects considered and refining appropriate manipulatory techniques, this process may well result in general problems being bypassed except, perhaps, for a small elite who have the facilities, confidence, and 'capital' (Bourdieu, 1975) to tackle major problems and/or currently unfashionable ones.

The organization of fields in 'restricted' sciences is much more structured than in relatively open-ended ones. The restriction of legitimate objects and approaches orders scientists' perception of possible topics and ways of tackling them so that only a highly limited number of tasks are perceived as 'relevant' or 'interesting'. Intellectual structures are firmly bounded in the sense that permissible types of work are clearly distinguishable from 'irrelevant' or even 'non-scientific' concerns. The more 'restricted' a field, the clearer these distinctions become and the more 'relevance' criteria are institutionalized so that 'hot' areas are identifiable and work is directed towards them. Research priorities become 'rationalized' so that important topics and 'fruitful' models, etc., are firmly separated from 'marginal' or 'uninteresting' ones. Because legitimate problems and techniques are highly specific and restricted, work becomes much more patterned and ordered than in fields where the dominant intellectual structures are not so tightly bounded. The restriction of available problems and approaches results in a relatively small number of issues being pursued by a relatively large number of scientists as long as these fields are prestigious and can reproduce the labour force. This results in ever growing specialization of tasks, though not necessarily a high degree of division of labour, to reduce competitive pressures and create individual expertise and property rights. Consequently, everyday tasks become further removed from the general concerns which lie at the centre of the disciplinary identity and sub-groupings, such as specialties and research areas, emerge. The bulk of scientific work performed in highly 'restricted' fields develops in ever more refined ways so that purification of instruments becomes a task area in its own right.

These pressures towards specialization and narrowing of tasks and procedures can of course be ameliorated by emigration to, and colonization of, 'underdeveloped' areas such as less prestigious and 'unrestricted' fields in the geological and biological sciences (Fleming, 1969; Hallam, 1973; Mullins, 1972) or by infanticide, i.e. the exportation of neophytes to other social institutions such as industrial laboratories. Even so, their impact on the social and intellectual organization of the sciences is considerable. A major result is to enhance and reinforce existing patterns of stratification between individuals and organizations. The more refined and differentiated the mass of research tasks become, the more attenuated is the disciplinary identity. Fundamental concerns and principles are remote from the day-to-day tasks of most scientific workers, and may become the preserve of a distinct group. The objective of integrating and reconstructing the efforts of researchers develops as the distinct purpose of a separate collection of scientists. Since the way in which work in a field is 'made sense of' or 'rationalized' reflects and institutionalizes research goals and priorities, this group is obviously influential in directing interests and allocating rewards. However, it does not follow that anyone can set himself up as the arbiter of others' work without considerable resources. Because the interpretation of a topic's relevance and importance to the field has major repercussions on personal careers, attempts to synthesize current research are likely to be the focus of considerable dispute in which personal and institutional prestige will play a major part. Once a particular view of the discipline has become institutionalized and legitimate topics and approaches specified, reformulations and novel developments will be strenuously opposed since they imply a reordering of priorities and threaten the existing distribution of expertise and property rights. It follows that to undertake innovatory activities and successfully develop new ideas so that they become accepted, in other words to exercise intellectual leadership, considerable cultural and social capital (Bourdieu, 1975) is required. This, in turn, suggests that successful, major, developments in highly 'restricted' sciences are likely to be concentrated in those institutions in a position to bestow such 'capital'. An important aspect of these organizations is their tendency to focus on the more general problems and issues of the discipline and hence to employ the majority of these scientists engaged on 'reconstructive' tasks. These tasks constitute the basis for the construction of 'official histories' (Bitz, 1975a) of scientific fields and hence for the history of science.

In addition to the differentiation of the intellectual structures of 'restricted' sciences, a parallel differentiation of social structures occurs. As well as organizational prestige being differentially distributed, journals, conferences and seminars form a hierarchy. The existence of 'core' journals in physics has been extensively documented (cf. e.g. Bitz, 1975b; Gaston, 1973, pp. 138–139), similarly select meetings are often organized on particular topics which often play an important role in developing new approaches (cf. e.g. Mullins, 1972). The proliferation of research areas dealing with highly specific tasks and techniques encourages the proliferation of highly specialized media for disseminating results and establishing property rights but these are rarely examined by specialists in other areas. Consequently, broader intellectual concerns which ultimately 'make sense of' and legitimate this highly specific work in terms of disciplinary principles or the dominant specialty concerned become the focus of distinct media which, because of their general relevance and legitimatory function, are seen as central to the field and hence of greatest prestige. Current conceptions of the basic problems and fruitful ways of approaching them are reflected in their editorial policies and they structure scientists' identities and intellectual concerns throughout the field. Research priorities and orientations are exemplified in the allocation of space in 'core' journals. They serve as foci and identities for whole disciplines and specialties in highly 'restricted' sciences.

The third aspect of work organization is the arrangement of employing organizations which affects the way research priorities are institutionalized. The main means of organization control, especially in universities, is often by recruitment and promotion decisions. Generally speaking, only scientists specializing in 'worthwhile' or 'important' problems or techniques will be appointed. Control can, however, also be exercised through the provision of technical apparatus and technicians, if only negatively, as when necessary facilities are simply not available, and filtering of grant applications. Additionally, collaborative patterns can be encouraged or discouraged by various organizational decisions. More directly, of course, departmental seminars and informal discussions can ensure that younger scientists don't waste their time with 'boring' or 'peripheral' problems as well as preventing them from using incorrect techniques. In some departments, papers are screened before submission and, equally, fast publication for some can be secured by personal contacts. In general, patronage remains an important means of control and influence over work choice and styles. While, then, task allocation procedures are not formalized and each individual is a 'free' agent, in practice organizations can, and do, constrain work patterns so that research focuses on particular problems and is approached in particular ways. The more 'restricted' the science, the easier it is to enforce standards and ensure that proper objects are worked on in appropriate ways.

In full-time research laboratories which are not directly involved in undergraduate teaching, formal controls are more likely because of the pressures of financial accountability even if these only lead to largely fictitious project descriptions. While in theory university scientists are able to work on whatever they wish, most laboratories have fairly specific purposes and work is meant to be related to these. Additionally, the director tends to have more formal authority over scientists' work than do university department leaders and is sometimes able to intervene in everyday research. Attempts may be made to develop some division of labour between tasks, most notably with regard to large scale experimental apparatus, but, as already suggested, there are limits to this. More likely is some attempt to rationalize organizational boundaries and groupings around particular tasks and functions. Often, however, little evidence of mutual dependence and collaboration between groups is forthcoming (Bitz, 1975a, 1975b). In many ways, the main effect of organizing research in laboratories with particular equipment and skills is a negative one. Because the organization is established, it tends to constrain research in particular ways which are consonant with existing resources and it is difficult to pursue novelties or potentially rewarding but risky developments. This also occurs in universities, especially where there is a complex and expensive—both in terms of capital and recurrent costs—technological facility, but it is, perhaps, especially marked in special purpose research laboratories.

**Work Organization in 'Unrestricted' Sciences**

It is probably worth emphasizing here that 'restriction' is a matter of degree and while Pantin (1968) saw much of biology and geology as exemplifying 'unrestricted' sciences, he did consider meteorology as comparatively 'unrestricted' and botanical taxonomy as 'restricted'. Similarly, we might say that orthodox economics is 'restricted' while much of sociology is 'unrestricted'. Obviously, though, sociology is not the same as biology and there are degrees of 'restrictedness'. In talking in this section of 'unrestricted' sciences, I shall primarily be referring to biological and geological fields.

Given the broader specification of objects and techniques in these sciences we would not expect to find such a developed differentiation of labour as in 'restricted' ones. Although supervisors may still direct a number of Ph.D. students, and the research process may rely extensively on technical assistants, the openness of the problems and variety of potential solutions will make any attempt at allocating interdependent 'packages' difficult. The nature of Ph.D. research will differ in the sense that it incorporates a wider range of possible approaches and hence requires a deeper understanding of the basis of the science than is needed in more 'restricted' sciences. Because work is more open-ended, more general considerations have to be taken into account when engaging in everyday research. Formalized procedures are not so prominent in these sciences and acts of personal judgement are more commonplace. This need to rely on judgements rather than on relatively specific 'technical' decisions for 'successful' research practices means that supervisors have to control the work more directly and over wider aspects than in 'restricted' sciences. Judgement calls for experience and hence cannot be left to other students. While a large amount of research may be largely technical in 'unrestricted' fields, a substantial component of learning how to conduct work correctly cannot be reduced to purely technical criteria. Experienced advice is necessary to ensure students do not waste their time and this experience covers theoretical and technical areas. In this situation there is a low limit on the number of students any individual scientist can adequately supervise. Furthermore, because research is less highly structured, the student, although a neophyte, has to deal with general issues and cannot simply wait until writing his thesis to consider them. This means that each Ph.D. interprets the nature of the basic problem as well as deals with one aspect of it and so they cannot be guaranteed to 'add up' in an integrated manner. 'Packages' can still be constructed and offered, but they are less structured, are more open-ended and are not mutually interdependent.

Similarly, the work of technicians is less formalized than in more 'restricted' sciences. More reliance is placed on the individual's understanding of the purpose of the work and it is more important to integrate it into the overall research process. Because the problem is relatively unstructured, it is important to be certain about how tissues, for example, have been prepared and apparatus set up. This, in turn, calls for more direct contact between workers than may be the case in 'restricted' fields. Differentiation of tasks in research is less clear and multiple skills are often required. Of course, technicians may be organized in a similar way in biological fields as in physics or chemistry but they will need to exercise their own judgement more in the former and this requires experience and being cognizant of more aspects of the broader problem than the immediate requirements of the task.

If tasks are less structured within a set of research practices controlled by an individual, what are the implications for whole fields and disciplines? How are problems selected and legitimated if cognitive boundaries are ill-defined and a variety of approaches are possible? First of all, I think it is important to recognize that, although problems are more open-ended in 'unrestricted' sciences, there are definite procedures and techniques for conducting research peculiar to each science. These are not specifically tied to, or defined in terms of, particular objects of analysis, but they do act as fairly coherent guides to research practice and produce 'correct' results in the current framework. Work in a science has to minimally conform to these procedures if it is to count as scientific, so boundaries are not entirely absent, but they do not firmly constrain problem definition and selection.

The relative lack of closure in these sciences indicates considerable difficulties in relating research topics to one another and reconstructing 'logical' developments. The open nature of a field means that there are no 'obvious' ways of proceeding and of assessing alternative research strategies. Scientists sharing a background in a common discipline may rely on substantially the same techniques and general ways of conceiving researchable problems, but their current research may quite 'rationally' develop along divergent and conflicting lines without any clear way of integrating the results being available. Starting from a common problem, scientists can quite legitimately pursue widely divergent approaches and conclude in disparate ways. Whereas in 'restricted' sciences it is meaningful to talk of scientists concentrating on different aspects of the same problem, and hence there is some implication of the whole being reconstituted from the separate parts, in 'unrestricted' ones the tendency is to interpret the nature of the problem in divergent ways which makes any attempt at finding *the* solution doomed to failure. Division of labour in the strict sense is, therefore, impossible.

How, then, are tasks differentiated in these fields? This can be discussed at two levels. First, there is task differentiation within some disciplinary framework and, second, as occurring between disciplines. The second level is important here because it is a feature of 'unrestricted' sciences that problems, e.g. sleep (Lemaine *et al.*, 1975), are often studied by scientists from a variety of backgrounds, and it is not nearly so clear to which discipline a problem 'belongs' as it is in physics. Initially, though, I shall briefly analyse the situation where a single discipline is involved. However the term 'discipline' is interpreted (cf. de Certaines, 1977; Whitley, 1976b), there would seem little doubt that there are a number of differences between those in the physical sciences and those in the biological ones. At least a major one is the greater fluidity of conceptual boundaries and theoretical approaches in the latter sciences. Whether a scientist considers himself a biophysicist, or a biochemist or a molecular biologist varies across countries and, often, across time (cf. de Certaines, 1977). Social and cognitive identities are much vaguer in the 'unrestricted' sciences and mean much less in relation to scientists' current research (cf. McAlpine and Bitz, 1973; McAlpine *et al.*, 1974). Within disciplines there are more possible approaches to problems, more alternative interpretations of problems and less clear boundaries between than in 'unrestricted' sciences. Work is less obviously 'within' or 'outside' a given discipline and permissible limits are broad. Differentiation of tasks within a discipline is likely to occur along lines of acquired skills and expertise on the one hand, and along divergent theoretical approaches on the other. The lack of a clear institutionalized cognitive framework for the discipline which defines its dominant approach and sets standards to permissible work is likely to lead to an emphasis on technical criteria of adequacy and hence reliance on technical skills. It is also going to encourage, or at any rate not seriously discourage, the proliferation of alternative models and approaches to a variety of problems. Scientists will select and characterize tasks according to their own expertise and personal theoretical predelictions. Since there is no one overall integrated cognitive structure which defines problems and restricts legitimate approaches, the main integrative function in these disciplines will be performed by work organizations and organizational elites to a greater degree and in a more direct manner than in 'restricted' sciences.

Since the cognitive structure of disciplines is not so firmly bounded or coherent as in 'restricted' sciences, problems are not necessarily directly interconnected and 'rational' developments and extensions of previous work are less obvious. Scientists will not be able to clearly relate their work to that of others and the choice of topics is less structured by what has gone before. In turn, this means that highly institutionalized procedures for assessing the relevance of problems and their solutions are absent and research priorities are not clearly derivable from the central disciplinary cognitive structure. The open-ended nature of the field means that 'hot' areas are not unambiguously distinguishable and a clear hierarchy of problems is unlikely to become established. Where an integrated structure does not dominate and define an area of science so that work is legitimated and assessed solely in those terms, research is more contingent upon organizational, education, and technical exigencies. These factors are not unimportant in understanding work activities in 'restricted' sciences as Bitz has shown (1975a,

1975b), but they become even more relevant in sciences where boundaries are vague and the basic disciplinary assumptions do not greatly restrict legitimate problems or approaches.

Task differentiation in areas where a number of disciplinary backgrounds are involved tends to follow educational experiences in terms of the techniques used and how tasks are conceptualized. In a study of a cancer research laboratory, McAlpine and Carr (1975) found little or no collaboration between scientists with different skills which covered more than highly specific, brief, and limited provision of assistance. Generally, scientists developed their research skills to deal with problems which could be related to cancerous growth but this was an extension of existing expertise rather than the acquisition of a new approach which could be termed 'cancer science'. Analytical techniques and conceptual approaches were nearly always the same as those acquired in educational institutions and interdisciplinary work was highly unusual. Additionally, it should be noted here that the weakness of disciplinary boundaries and lack of cognitive closure enables a set of technical approaches and skills to be applied to a wide variety of problems. The relative lack of specificity of cognitive objects in these sciences enables scientists to work on a wide range of topics without necessarily changing their expertise. Problems such as cancer can be redefined and interpreted to fit the particular skill acquired and work can continue along similar lines to that on other problems. As a result, not only is the problem fragmented between disciplinary approaches, but it is redefined and reinterpreted in terms of available skills. There is, therefore, no single problem in the sense that a common view of its nature is held so that work can be interrelated in terms of that view (cf. Lemaine *et al.*, 1975, pp. 44–49). As Sadler points out (1976), there is no cognitive structure in the cancer field which delineates the problem in a way that leads directly to scientific practices. Similarly, McAlpine (1974) suggests that skin pathology is a medico-socio-legal concept rather than a scientific one.

The organization of scientific fields in these sciences differs from that in relatively 'restricted' ones. While it is doubtful if a 'Chinese box' model (McAlpine *et al.*, 1974) of disciplines, specialities, and research areas is accurate in describing the physical sciences, it is certainly inadequate for analysing the biological, geological, and social sciences. As Bitz (1975c) clearly shows in his discussion of geological specialities, based on a study of a very large geological research organization, problem areas do not unequivocally 'belong' to single specialities and these in turn to subdisciplines. As I have already suggested, disciplinary boundaries are simply not clear enough in these sciences to enable a 'tree' type classification of intellectual structures to be constructed. Any particular problem in, say, palaeontology involves not only stratigraphy but also leads to biological considerations. Given this fluidity of cognitive boundaries and the comparative ease of movement between problem areas, it is not surprising that scientists find it difficult to firmly identify 'their' major speciality or research area (Bitz *et al.*, 1975). There are a number of criteria which could be used for labelling one's work in, say, geology, such as location, rock type, geological formation, time period, techniques used, and so on, and it is by no means clear that any one of these is always prior to the others. In fact, if we look at how organizations categorize work units we tend to find a variety of criteria being used to identify them and these often reflect organizational pressures rather than current research work (McAlpine and Carr, 1975; Bitz, 1975c). However, it would be a mistake to simply assume that these are 'mere' conventions and are irrelevant to scientific practices or that there is in some 'third world' a clear, coherent, and consistent arrangement of cognitive structures which expresses the 'essence' of a science.

Even if work organizations were merely the social manifestation of some overarching 'paradigm' in the 'restricted' sciences this is clearly not the case in other sciences simply because there are no developed, closed, specific cognitive structures which unequivocally allocate research priorities. The idea of a highly institutionalized set of community norms, which firmly delineate legitimate problems, and order solutions so that scientists simply have to be given facilities to solve the pre-packaged puzzles for knowledge to accumulate, is inapplicable to 'unrestricted' fields. Work organizations therefore are highly involved in the setting of research goals and establishing priorities. Recruitment and promotion decisions, the provision of particular facilities and services, are even less 'obvious' or 'rational' in these sciences than in 'restricted' ones, and organizational strategies impinge directly on the sort of work done and how it is conducted. This impact is augmented by the comparative diversity and plurality of elites in these sciences. Given the cognitive pluralism we would not expect a high degree of social cohesion among organizational leaders from different areas and with distinct interests even when they are ostensibly working on the 'same' problem, for example cancer or sleep. While they may combine to promote the support of research into this field, they may not concur on the relative priority of particular approaches, for example radiobiological, virology, immunology, molecular biology, and each will probably tend to give priority to his 'own' field in 'his' laboratory although this may be mitigated by a desire to 'represent' the major disciplinary contenders, at least as long as it is financially possible (cf. Sadler, 1976). Elite pluralism is likely to reinforce and extend cognitive pluralism especially if organizational boundaries and barriers coincide with skill and technique differences.

I suggested earlier that integrative functions would be largely performed by work organizations in 'unrestricted' sciences. By this I mean the structure of a field is constituted by the topics and approaches emphasized in research organizations. If there is only a relatively tenuous and weakly articulated disciplinary identity then cognitive commitments and foci of concern become particularized in organizational priorities and policies as distinct from 'core' journals. The intellectual structure of a science is composed of the problems and approaches in organizational programmes to an extent which is not so directly the case in more 'restricted' sciences. Integration therefore occurs largely through organizational coherence and inter-organizational commonalities and implications. For a scientific field to be distinct and to have an identity, organizations have to legitimize its status and encourage work which is distinguishable from that in other areas. In many ways, if a field is not 'represented' in work organizations' programmes for more than one generation of workers, it ceases to exist as a scientific area. Of course this is true of 'restricted' sciences too, but whereas in those there is some integrated intellectual structure which identifies the field and to which organizations need to pay heed if work conducted by their members is to be seen as being 'in' it, in 'unrestricted' sciences organizations are not so bounded because the disciplinary identity is vaguer and not so socially institutionalized as a distinct unit in the form of journals, conferences, and teaching curricula. Criteria of legitimacy, relevance and adequacy are not so specifically drawn, and hence organizations, and individuals, are less restricted in their policies and decisions. 'Core' journals, crucial conferences, and 'the' educational curriculum of fields are not clearly identified and, indeed, there may be considerable overlap in these between fields. As a result, any distinct organizational strategies and connections become even more important in 'unrestricted' sciences if a distinct social and intellectual identity is to emerge and be maintained so that a particular 'knowledge' is to be constructed. This is especially so in educational organizations where the bases for career decisions are often laid. The importance of the training system for reproducing particular skills and interests and so affecting work organization has already been mentioned. Variations in this system between 'restricted' and 'unrestricted' sciences will now be discussed.

**Scientific Training in 'Restricted' Sciences**

As already remarked, work in these sciences is focused on highly specific objects and techniques which require extensive training for adequate task performance. Educational organizations have to ensure that the neophyte scientist is knowledgeable about the basic principles of the discipline and defining intellectual structures which may well be highly esoteric; they also have to make sure he or she is capable of conducting work on appropriate topics in the approved manner. The more specialized and refined are these topics and instruments, the longer will be educational experience and the narrower the range of tasks the scientist is capable of undertaking. From the point of view of reproducing the labour force for a particular area, this narrowness is advantageous because it ensures sufficient recruits to continue working in it, and the highly specialized skills, once acquired, represent an investment which is not easily transferrable to different concerns. It is likely therefore that, provided enough scientists can be attracted to the area at the Ph.D. stage, it will continue to develop. Similarly, if an area cannot obtain many Ph.D. students it may contract because the training is so specialized that scientists are unlikely to move into it once they have been trained in another one. The structure of Ph.D. education becomes, then, important for continued work in specialties and research areas.

It is also important because, as already pointed out, much of the research conducted in the contemporary sciences is performed by Ph.D. students. If a problem can be divided into 'packages' then obviously it is going to be resolved quicker by someone who has access to a number of apprentices than by someone who is primarily working on his own. The more 'restricted' the science the easier it should be to 'package' parts of a problem and the easier it should be to control a large number of students because procedures are highly specific and relatively formal. Ph.D. education therefore both has the intellectual capability and social impetus to become narrower and narrower in highly 'restricted' sciences. The more important a part Ph.D. research plays in knowledge production and the more easily it can be formalized and narrowed, the greater are the pressures to 'rationalize' the educational process by allocating students particular 'packages' which can be adequately dealt with in the two to three years of the state studentships. It is positively unhelpful to this process of factory-like production for students to interest themselves in the theoretical purposes underlying the research since it would take time—both theirs and their supervisor's—and, in any case, it is not necessary for them to conduct the work correctly. Of course, this is not to deny that some students in some departments do develop wider horizons but the logic of the situation, I am suggesting, leads away from general educational objectives towards training the mass of students for production of highly specific packages.

The consequence of this sort of training for the organization of work in 'restricted' sciences is to reproduce existing priorities and skills in such a way as to reduce individual and collective flexibility. If Ph.D. students are trained to carry out an experiment correctly they become highly skilled in the use of particular technical apparatus for very specific purposes. They do not necessarily develop the capability to conduct research using other instruments or for other purposes. In particular, they are not educated to develop new purposes or novel ways of conceiving problems. As a result they are most useful in team research where a problem is divided among scientists and each concentrates on a small part as occurs in large scale experiments in high energy physics. So the training process produces skills which are best applied in, again, factory-like production conditions. Once team research is developed—either on a single experiment or on a number of experiments derived from a single problem—and relies, at least partially, on students then it reproduces itself by ensuring that Ph.D.s are best suited for such work. Even where extensive collaboration is not necessitated as it is in particle physics, the products of the training system in effect collaborate by dividing up problems into narrow tasks and concentrating on these. They are able to do this because objects and approaches are highly specific in 'restricted' sciences and the range of possible, legitimate alternatives is highly restricted. In other words, the nature of the science enables, and even encourages, such specification of tasks and, of course, this process is reinforced by the educational system.

However, if this process was universal throughout a science major, general developments would be unlikely to occur since scientists would simply burrow deeper and deeper into increasingly narrow topics, and broad problems would become completely ignored. How, then, do some Ph.D.s develop the capacity for formulating problems and integrating the results of factory produced research tasks? First of all I think it is important to acknowledge that not all Ph.D. training is as narrow and limited as I have suggested in the 'restricted' sciences. Certain types of work in a few departments may encourage a more general educational approach, for example theoretical physics in a highly prestigious university. However, the major factor is the expansion of post-doctoral research fellowships.

The increasing routinization of much Ph.D. work in highly 'restricted' sciences means that obtaining a doctorate is no longer enough, on the one hand, to distinguish potential professional scientists from merely competent practitioners of doctoral research or, on the other hand, to develop a capacity for defining problems as distinct from solving pre-packaged tasks. It teaches the student how to work on highly specific tasks with a very narrow range of prescribed techniques but not, usually, how to characterize worthwhile problems and organize them into distinct tasks. Additionally, the large numbers of doctoral students leads to a requirement for some intermediate level of supervision between the academic staff member and the 'shopfloor'. As a result, a distinct category of research worker arises, the post-doctoral research fellow.

These fellows, judging from observations of work in a large physics department in the United Kingdom, work more closely with the supervisor than do the doctoral students and are also responsible for monitoring the latter's work. Usually they specialize in one aspect of the overall problem the staff member is interested in and assist him in breaking it down into 'packages' for the Ph.D. students. They gain experience in organizing problems and workers while being under the tutelage of a more experienced scientist. During this period they become sensitized to the dominant theoretical concerns of the field and appropriate ways of approaching them. Being less oriented to the immediate, practical exigences of research they are able to consider broader issues and the major problems of their field. It is probably at this stage that a distinct scientific identity, an awareness of disciplinary and speciality boundaries and foci are developed as well as an ability to assess career prospects and possibilities. Also, they begin to publish papers and generally contribute to their area in a way which was difficult, if not impossible, as a Ph.D. student.

The importance of this, usually brief, stage in the educational process for the recruitment and socialization of the labour force reinforces the influence of the large organizations in so far as they have more, longer term, fellowships available to exercise considerable discretion in whom is selected—indeed a pronounced bias towards the institution's own products is sometimes observable—and often have the prestige and contact to 'place' their fellows in reputable organizations. A number of fellowships also increases a department's flexibility by allowing it to switch resources from one topic to another fairly quickly because of the short term nature of the employment contract. The reproduction of skills and interests in 'restricted' sciences, then, occurs at two levels, Ph.D. and post-doctoral, and control is exercised at the entry points to both stages. In fact, for the professional scientists, the latter stage is more important and more dependent on personal relations than the former. Increasing routinization of doctoral work, and of standardization of entry criteria to it, mean that post-doctoral fellowships become the crucial selection stage for new scientists.

**Scientific Training in 'Unrestricted' Sciences**

It is much more difficult to routinize doctoral research in these sciences because cognitive objects and techniques are not so specific and highly bounded. Adequate research requires more attention to non-technical issues and difficulties in that, as already suggested, personal judgement is more important in day-to-day matters because potential alternatives are not clearly specified or ordered. To produce results which are of doctoral standard the student has to develop judgemental skills involving broader issues and problems than in a 'restricted' field. This means that control procedures are more personal, direct, and less standardized. It also suggests that tasks cannot be prepackaged to quite the same extent and that each student has the potentiality of going beyond his or her supervisor's expertise if the problem broadens out. Obviously, 'packages' are offered to students but the outcome is much more uncertain and if the work is to be completed in the period of the state studentship—a major factor, incidentally, in selecting all Ph.D. topics in the United Kingdom—the supervisor may have to become much more involved in the student's work than originally intended.

The open-ended nature of these sciences and, to some extent, of doctoral research means that, potentially, students may work much closer to current concerns and issues in the field than would usually be the case in highly 'restricted' sciences. Even if the research is deliberately narrowed down to a simple application of a single technique to a single object in order to reduce uncertainty, the comparative lack of specificity of the object and its interaction with the technique may create substantial difficulties. The use of electron microscopes in the analysis of tissues resulted in efforts to restrict the relevant area of interest and narrowly specify the object such that the effects of chemically destroying cells, so that the technique could be used, were generally ignored. Many geological and biological objects are simply not amenable to tightly 'restricted' approaches without considerable alteration and development of new observational theories. The complexities and lack of closure of these objects means that it is extremely difficult to package tasks so that the student can be safely left to get on with the job. The technical aspects of work in these fields are not so separate from broader problems and hence the successful completion of a task requires non-technical skills. Ph.D. training therefore incorporates a wider range of skills in these sciences than it does in highly 'restricted' ones.

This has two major consequences for the organization of work. First, it cannot be assumed that working with a large number of students necessarily provides an advantage over scientists without students because the outcome of the research is less certain. This in turn means that competition for students is mitigated and large organizations do not, in this respect at any rate, have a great advantage over smaller ones. When students are recruited for particular projects they are likely to be more thoroughly selected than in 'restricted' fields because the work is less routine and qualities other than an ability to do well in examinations become relevant. Also the link between the supervisor and students is likely to be more intense and personal involving a higher degree of commitment to the basic problem and approach adopted. Second, the broader range of skills and the less object specific nature of the techniques acquired mean that Ph.D.s will be flexible in their choice of future work areas and training in a single problem area need not restrict him or her to continue to work there. Mobility between topics is greater in these sciences and hence the reproduction of a given set of skills and interests is less likely over generations of scientists. Discipline and specialty boundaries are fairly fluid, and cognitive identities develop during doctoral work around the skills and interests acquired then which are not tied to a particular specialty concern. The significance of post-doctoral fellowships is less because the newly qualified Ph.D. has already acquired some understanding of general issues and interpretative difficulties. Equally, the relevance of undergraduate education increases and we would expect it to be closer to the realities of everyday research practices than it is in 'restricted' sciences. This, in turn, means that the choice of special subjects during undergraduate education affects the sort of work undertaken at Ph.D. level and so the choice of speciality. Correspondingly, stronger interest should be manifested in undergraduate education in 'unrestricted' sciences than in highly 'restricted' ones because it more directly influences the recruitment of doctoral students and the reproduction of particular skills and interests and hence the future development of a speciality.

The selection of Ph.D. students is the crucial stage in the training and directing of new scientists since it is this which determines what particular expertises and modes of problem formulation will be reproduced. Also students would be expected to publish more during this process than their counterparts in the 'restricted' sciences because they deal with more aspects of the research process and need to become known during their doctoral work. Again, personal contacts and prestige are relevant here, but because the fields are less structured a strict hierarchy of institutions and problems is unlikely so that concentrations of 'capital' are less obvious. Equally, access to 'core' journals for making a reputation is less crucial than in 'restricted' sciences because the intellectual structure of the field does not separate manifestly dominating media. Organizational requirements for particular skills are likely to play a considerable role in the selection of new recruits, as distinct from disciplinary renown in the 'hot' field. These points lead to a consideration of stratification within the sciences and the role of elites in the organization of work and production of knowledge.

**Elites and the Organization of Work in the Sciences**

I will focus here on how the restricted nature of a science is related to the emergence of particular stratification structures and the functioning of elites in the organization and control of research rather than on patterns of elite formation and forms of authority (cf. Whitley, 1976b). The more 'restricted' a science is, the more specific are the objects worked on and the more refined and circumscribed are the instruments used. I have suggested that work becomes progressively narrower and more tightly contained for most scientists in such fields. General issues and problems become reduced to highly specific tasks which are carried out within a narrow range of possibilities. But this may be true for the bulk of practitioners in a discipline without being the case for the elite. In fact, it is precisely the ability and confidence to tackle 'important' problems which characterize the intellectual elite in a discipline. While the risks attached to such endeavours render them beyond the majority of researchers, substantial 'cultural capital' is available to members of the elite to enable them to undertake major tasks (Bourdieu, 1975). As guardians of the basic principles of the discipline, the elite is able to control the definition of 'important' problems and to interpret the adequacy of proposed resolutions. Intellectual leaders can undertake difficult problems confident that their work will continue to be influential and that, whatever the outcome, it will have an input to others' work.

The more 'restricted' a science becomes, the more this distinction between the many who work on highly specific tasks and the few who work on synthesizing and integrative tasks—who, in other words, put the work of the majority together into a coherent framework and make sense of it for posterity—becomes apparent and sharper. Differentiation of tasks occur not only between objects and techniques but also between types of task in that elite scientists focus on combinative or general concerns; they formulate the major, 'important' problems—or at least interpret the disciplinary identity so that criteria for assessing a topic's importance are clear—so that they can be broken down into specific component parts for non-elite workers to focus on. The more routinized and highly structured the bulk of research in a science becomes, the more some group is needed to integrate the results and order priorities. This is not to say that Meisel's 'three Cs' apply to scientific elites in the 'restricted' sciences (cf. Parry, 1969, pp. 31–32)—although they might under certain circumstances—but to point out that if a science is not to disintegrate into an unco-ordinated set of narrow research tasks which cognitive and social barriers combine to separate, integrative tasks have to be undertaken and these require confidence and prestige. By focusing on this sort of work, elites are able to maintain their authority and superiority. They renew and expand their 'cultural capital' by risking it on major problems. Furthermore, by working on different sorts of tasks they emphasize their distinctiveness and this is often accentuated by adopting certain work styles. Some theoretical physicists, for example, make a virtue of working on a number of different problems at any one time and change topics with much greater frequency than experimentalists. As interpreters and reconstructors of experimental data, they are able to criticize others' work and produce 'official histories' of a field in a way that the 'journeyman' scientist cannot (cf. Gaston, 1973, pp. 59–68). The role of distinct groups of theoreticians in prestigious physics departments in constructing 'official histories' of contemporary developments requires more attention than it usually receives. Hierarchies of prestige based on the degree of abstraction of the work in physics would also repay further study. The lip service paid to von Neumann's 'impossibility' proof by eminent physicists can only be accounted for, it seems, by the ritualistic prostration before mathematical reasoning (Pinch, 1976, 1977).

Intellectual leadership in highly 'restricted' sciences is exercised more in terms of interpreting and developing the underlying assumptions and approach than through direct organizational control, although this latter aspect is not negligible. Because the field is highly constrained and possible alternatives are limited, influence is exercised through applying the 'rules of the game' to specify legitimate goals and strategies. It is through the delineation of appropriate domains and approaches that elites control research priorities and validate work. The scope of a discipline is defined by the restriction of its objects so that guardians of the disciplinary tradition can structure perceptions of worthwhile topics and tasks by specifying the 'core' phenomena in a highly restricted manner. The way in which objects are specified and approaches delineated determines 'fruitful' research and 'important' work. A disciplinary elite that monopolizes this process controls the direction of the production system. Its authority can also, of course, be increased by extending the scope of the disciplinary boundaries by, for example, reducing problems of other fields to phenomena amenable to 'restricted' analysis. This can be seen in the various attempts that have been made to 'arithmomorphize' parts of chemistry and biology (cf. Colvin, 1977; Georgescu-Roegen, 1971; Jenkin, 1976; Whitley, 1977a).

A crucial aspect of elite control is the reproduction of the labour force and, in particular, the selection and training of post-doctoral fellows. By attracting the 'best' neophyte scientists, educating them in the fundamentals of the discipline and then 'placing' them in major departments or research laboratories, the diffusion of a particular view of the discipline is encouraged. The organization of work is controlled by ensuring the domination of a particular conception of the discipline which orders problems and approaches in terms of their 'centrality' and appropriateness. Once a certain view of the discipline is institutionalized the field is structured, not completely unambiguously, but sufficiently to determine priorities and general orientations. Such institutionalization is usually the prerogative of large organizations with considerable prestige because they have the resources for fellowships and full-time research posts and the reputation to attract the 'best'. Once a position of institutional dominance has been reached it tends to reproduce itself through controlling the training process and bestowing cultural and social capital upon its products and members. The more 'restricted' the science the more such capital becomes centralized and concentrated because the discipline becomes more closed and highly structured so that prestige is clearly ordered and 'centres of excellence' and 'core' journals are foci of attraction and attention. The narrower a field is and the more closed its boundaries the easier it is to differentiate centres of prestige and influence which respresent and dominate the field.

In contrast, relatively 'unrestricted' sciences do not have highly institutionalized boundaries and their internal structure is less differentiated and graded. The central ideas of the discipline do not so circumscribe research topics and legitimate approaches, they do not so clearly define work areas and identities. Tasks may quite legitimately lead to the crossing of disciplinary boundaries, and a dominant cognitive structure which orders and constrains work is less evident in these sciences. This relative lack of a central, defining set of ideas which controls research priorities and strategies mitigates the influence of potential elites over work organizations. Or, at least it means that control in these sciences cannot be exercised in the same way. In particular, patterns of work are more likely to be influenced by organizational considerations and societal 'problems' than by a central, dominant cognitive structure. A single elite dominating a discipline through the development and application of a single set of ideas is less likely than a plurality of groups representing distinct tendencies and problems who influence work directly through organizational positions. Because the intellectual organization of these sciences is more fluid than in the 'restricted' fields, a single unitary elite based on a few highly central institutions is less likely than a differentiated set of high status scientists working on distinct problems with different approaches.

The organization of work in these sciences will be structured as much by organizational priorities and possibilities as by disciplinary principles. The relatively open-ended nature of problems and fields means that the identification of 'hot' areas and marginal ones is comparatively uncertain so that central direction of research by reference to a dominant set of assumptions is difficult. Instead, within some very general perspective a number of approaches will be developed and represented in most work organizations. Particular emphases in each will depend largely on the inclinations and experiences of organizational leaders who will exercise influence and control more by virtue of their position within the organization than by their disciplinary status. Of course, the acquisition of organizational authority is predicated upon some more general recognition, but influence is exercised more within organizations than over the whole discipline. Individual institutions do not dominate and represent the discipline to the same extent that they do in the 'restricted' sciences.

The relatively non-routine nature of much work in these sciences means that the stratification between tasks and groups performing different sorts of jobs noted in 'restricted' fields is less likely to arise. Distinct groups of 'theoreticians' who integrate and synthesize research to create some coherence and, thus, legislate the 'correct' view of a field will not emerge to the same extent. Instead, influence will be exercised through the reproduction of skills and interests at the Ph.D. stage and the subsequent control of job opportunities. Where scientists are trained in a set of techniques and approaches which are relatively non-object specific and transferrable the choice of problem area will be influenced by the labour market as well as by the nature of the acquired skills. The labour market is affected by general perceptions of 'important' problems as well as by organizational elites' views on major topics. While elites may mediate societal demands so as to claim resources for, say, cancer research while ensuring that current medical understandings of the problem do not dominate research practices (cf. Sadler, 1976), social views and perceptions of 'problems' intervene in the pattern of work in a more direct manner than they do in the more culturally autonomous 'restricted' sciences.

Because the differentiation of tasks and research areas is not so developed in 'unrestricted' sciences, the everyday organization of work is likely to be more directly related to general concerns and problems. Organizational policies which structure work and expertises in particular ways may have a considerable effect on disciplinary principles and identities. Decisions taken by organizational leaders—and by grant-awarding bodies—have a greater flexibility than in highly 'restricted' sciences and are more liable to feed back on to current presuppositions. This suggests that views of what constitutes the core of a discipline or specialty, are likely to change faster and in more uncertain ways than they do in, say, many parts of physics or chemistry. The potential impact of organizational elites, and their collective decisions on Research Council panels, is, then, considerable. Changes in the structure of work in research organizations are potentially highly relevant to reconstructions of 'official' histories.

## Conclusions

Starting from a rather broader view of scientific work and its organization than is usual, I have attempted to show how differences in the nature of objects and approaches in the sciences are likely to be related to variations in work structures. Assuming the type of production process affects the objects produced, the way that process is organized is relevant to an understanding of how scientific knowledges are developed and changed. Certain forms of scientific production are consonant with variations in the 'restricted' nature of cognitive objects and these have been outlined. The characteristics of the organization of scientific research in 'restricted' and 'unrestricted' sciences sketched above are not necessarily to be found in any individual discipline or speciality but represent the sort of properties which are consistent with the intellectual objects of those sciences. There are, of course, other ways of describing the foci of scientific work and they will be related to different forms of research organization. The point here is to show how differences between the sciences imply differences in work organization, and the latter, once established, are not suitable for producing alternative types of knowledge. Radical changes in the direction of a science and in the type of knowledge produced imply radical alterations in the organization of work. Similarly, changes in scientific production systems will alter the intellectual structures held to represent a field of knowledge. Instead of seeing scientific development as occurring in some ethereal 'third world', I suggest it is firmly rooted in organized practices, beliefs and activities which need to be examined if we are to understand it. The sociology of the sciences needs, therefore, to examine the organization of broad intellectual structures in conjunction with the way everyday research is structured and the organization of employing institutions in the sciences. These three aspects of work organization are interrelated and together constitute scientific production systems.

The history of scientific developments requires consideration of such production systems because the latter impinge upon the individual and collective decision-making process so that certain developments are followed and others are not. What is seen as 'rational' by workers in any science is related to the way their work is organized and legitimated. The ways in which previous research is made sense of affect current perception of worthwhile problems and appropriate techniques and adequate solutions. They also affect the development of 'official histories' or reconstructions which become institutionalized in textbooks and reviews so that they direct the efforts of new recruits. Historical reconstructions of developments have to take account of how these accounts were formed, if only to transcend them, and the organization of work in its broadest sense is an essential part of this process. In this paper I have suggested how scientific work can be conceived so that the development of intellectual structures can be understood in relation to differences in scientific production systems. The sociology of scientific work, in this view, incorporates the reconstruction of cognitive structures as part of the study of work organization and its consequences. It is, therefore, directly involved in the history of scientific developments.

## References

Bhaskar, R. (1975), *A Realist Theory of Science*, Leeds, Leeds Books.
Bitz, A. (1975a), 'History, division of labour, and the information process in fundamental particle physics' in A. Bitz *et al.*, *The Production, Flow and Use of Information in Research Laboratories in Different Sciences*.
Bitz, A. (1975b), 'Scientific research and the information process in a nuclear physics laboratory' in A. Bitz *et al.*, *The Production, Flow and Use of Information in Research Laboratories in Different Sciences*.
Bitz, A. (1975c), 'The social and cognitive organisation of geological specialties' in A. Bitz *et al.*, *The Production, Flow and Use of Information in Research Laboratories in Different Sciences*.
Bitz, A., A. McAlpine, and R. D. Whitley (1975), *The Production, Flow and Use of Information in Research Laboratories in Different Sciences*, British Library Report Series.
Bourdieu, P. (1975), 'La Spécificité du champ scientifique et les conditions sociales du progrès de la raison', *Sociologie et Sociétés*, **7**, 91–118.
Certaines, J. de (1977), 'L'Example de la biophysique en France, critique de la validité actuelle de la notion de discipline scientifique', in R. Macleod *et al.* (eds), *The Emergence of Scientific Disciplines*, Paris, Mouton.
Colvin, P. (1977), 'Ontological and epistemological commitments and social relations in the sciences: the case of the arithmomorphic system of production' in E. Mendelsohn, P. Weingart, and R. Whitley (eds), *The Social Production of Scientific Knowledge*, Dordrecht and Boston: Reidel.
Crane, D. (1972), *Invisible Colleges*, Chicago, Chicago University Press.
Fleming, D. (1969), 'Emigré physicists and the biological revolution' in D. Fleming and B. Bailyn (eds), *The Intellectual Migration*, Cambridge, Mass., Harvard University Press.
Gaston, J. (1973), *Originality and Competition in Science*, Chicago, Chicago University Press.
Georgescu-Roegen, N. (1971), *The Entropy Law and the Economic Process*, Cambridge, Mass., Harvard University Press.
Glaser, B. G. (1964), *Organisational Scientists: their Professional Careers*, Indianapolis, Bobbs Merrill.
Hagstrom, W. O. (1965), *The Scientific Community*, New York, Basic Books.
Hallam, A. (1973), *A Revolution in the Earth Sciences*, Oxford, Oxford University Press.
Holton, G. (1974), 'Striking gold in science: Fermi's group and the recapture of Italy's place in physics', *Minerva*, **12**, 159–198.
Jenkin, P. (1976), 'Structure and contradiction in scientific development: the case of N. Georgescu-Roegen and the entropy law', Manchester University, unpublished M.Sc. thesis.
King, M. (1971), 'Reason, tradition and progressiveness in science', *History and Theory*, **10**, 3–32.
Klima, R. (1974), 'Scientific knowledge and social control in science' in R. Whitley (ed.), *Social Processes of Scientific Development*, London, Routledge and Kegan Paul.

Kuhn, T. S. (1970), *The Structure of Scientific Revolutions*, Chicago, Chicago University Press, 2nd ed.
Kuhn, T. S. (1974), 'Second thoughts on paradigms' in F. Suppe (ed.), *The Structure of Scientific Theories*, Urbana, Illinois, University of Illinois Press.
Kynaston Reeves, T., and B. A. Turner (1971), 'A theory of organisation and behaviour in batch production factories', *Administrative Science Quarterly*, 16, 81–98.
Law, J. (1974), 'Theories and methods in the sociology of science: an interpretative approach', *Social Science Information*, 13, 163–172.
Law, J., and D. French (1974), 'Normative and interpretative sociologies of science', *Sociological Review*, 22.
Lemaine, G., M. Clemençon, A. Gemis, B. Pollin, and B. Salvo (1975), *Stratégies et choix dans la recherche*, Paris, GERS.
McAlpine, A. (1974), 'Information flow and use in a "skin pathology" research unit', Manchester University, unpublished paper.
McAlpine, A., and A. Bitz (1973), 'Some methodological problems in the comparative sociology of science', paper presented to a workshop on the 'Comparative study of scientific specialties', London, 7 December. Also in A. Bitz *et al.*, *The Production, Flow and Use of Information in Research Laboratories in Different Sciences*.
McAlpine, A., and I. Carr (1975), 'The information process in a cancer research laboratory' in A. Bitz *et al.*, *The Production, Flow and Use of Information in Research Laboratories in Different Sciences*.
McAlpine, A., A. Bitz, and I. Carr (1974), 'The investigation of patterns of social and intellectual organisation in the sciences', paper presented to a PAREX Conference, York, June, and in A. Bitz *et al.*, *The Production, Flow and Use of Information in Research Laboratories in Different Sciences*.
Martins, H. (1972), 'The Kuhnian "revolution" and its implications for sociology' in T. J. Nossiter, A. H. Hanson, and S. Rokkan (eds), *Imagination and Precision in the Social Sciences*, London, Faber and Faber.
Mulkay, M. J. (1972), *The Social Process of Innovation*, London, Macmillan.
Mulkay, M. J., and D. O. Edge (1973), 'Cognitive, technical and social factors in the growth of radio astronomy', *Social Science Information*, 12, 25–61.
Mulkay, M. J., G. N. Gilbert, and S. W. Woolgar (1975), 'Problem areas and research networks in science', *Sociology*, 9, 187–203.
Mullins, N. C. (1968), 'The distribution of social and cultural properties in informal communication networks among biological scientists', *American Soc. Rev.*, 33, 786–797.
Mullins, N. C. (1972), 'The development of a scientific specialty: the phage group and the origins of molecular biology', *Minerva*, 10, 51–82.
Mullins, N. C. (1975), 'Aspects of a sociological theory of revolutionary science' in K. Knorr, H. Strasser, and H. G. Zilian (eds), *Determinants and Controls of Scientific Development*, Dordrecht, Reidel.
Pantin, C. F. A. (1968), *On Relations Between the Sciences*, Cambridge, Cambridge University Press.
Parry, G. (1969), *Political Elites*, London, Allen and Unwin.
Pelz, D., and F. M. Andrews (1966), *Scientists in Organisations*, New York, Wiley.
Pinch, T. (1976), 'Paradoxes and impossibilities: a study of the cognitive and social roles played by paradoxes and "impossibility proofs" in non relativistic quantum theory', Manchester University, unpublished M.Sc. thesis.
Pinch, T. J. (1977), 'What does a proof do if it does not prove? A study of the social conditions and metaphysical divisions leading to David Bohm and John von Neumann failing to communicate in quantum physics' in E. Mendelsohn, P. Weingart, and R. Whitley (eds), *The Social Production of Scientific Knowledge*, Dordrecht and Boston: Reidel.
Pugh, D. S., and D. J. Hickson (1968), 'The comparative study of organisations' in D. Pym (ed.), *Industrial Society*, London, Penguin.

Ravetz, J. R. (1971), *Scientific Knowledge and its Social Problems*, Oxford, Oxford University Press.
Rose, H., and S. Rose (1975), 'The incorporation of science' in M. Langer, and D. K. Miller (eds), *Institutions and Science Public Policy*, Annals of the New York Academy of Sciences, 260.
Sadler, J. (1976), 'Elites in science: a study of elites in relation to the cognitive structure and social organisation of cancer research', Manchester University, unpublished M.Sc. thesis.
Swatez, G. M. (1970), 'The social organisation of a university laboratory', *Minerva*, **8**, 36–58.
Watson, J. (1970), *The Double Helix*, London, Penguin.
Whitley, R. D. (1972), 'Black boxism and the sociology of science', in P. Halmos (ed.), *The Sociology of Science*, Sociological Review Monograph 18, September.
Whitley, R. D. (1974), 'Cognitive and social institutionalisation of scientific specialties and research areas' in R. D. Whitley (ed.), *Social Processes of Scientific Development*, London, Routledge and Kegan Paul.
Whitley, R. D. (1975), 'Components of scientific activities, their characteristics and institutionalisation in specialties and research areas' in K. Knorr, H. Strasser, and H. G. Zilian (eds), *Determinants and Controls of Scientific Development*, Dordrecht, Reidel.
Whitley, R. D. (1976a), 'Konkurrenzformen Autonomie und Entwicklungsformen Wissenschaftlicher Spezialgebiete' in N. Stehr, and R. König (eds), *Wissenschaftssoziologie*, Köln u. Opladen, Westdeutscher Verlag.
Whitley, R. D. (1976b), 'Umbrella and polytheistic scientific disciplines and their elites', *Social Studies of Science*, **6**, 471–497.
Whitley, R. D. (1977), 'Specialty marginality and types of competition in the sciences' in P. Gleichmann, J. Goudsblom, and H. Korte (eds), *Human Configurations: Essays in Honour of Norbert Elias*, Amsterdam.
Whitley, R. D. (1977a), 'Changes in the social and intellectual organisation of the sciences: professionalisation and the arithmetic ideal' in E. Mendelsohn, P. Weingart, and R. Whitley (eds), *The Social Production of Scientific Knowledge*, Dordrecht and Boston: Reidel.
Whitley, R. D., and P. Frost (1972), 'Authority, problem solving approaches, communication and change in a British research laboratory', *Journal of Management Studies*, **9**, 337–361.
Whitley, R. D., and P. Frost (1973), 'Task type and information transfer in a government research laboratory', *Human Relations*, **25**, 537–550.
Woolgar, S. (1976), 'Writing an intellectual history of scientific development: the use of discovery accounts', *Social Studies of Science*, **6**, 395–422.

# 2

# SCIENCE POLICY AND THE DEVELOPMENT OF SCIENCE

## Peter Weingart

*in collaboration with G. Küppers, and P. Lundgreen*

## The Problem

The 1950s and 1960s experienced the revival of a theoretical tradition that is as old as political theory itself: the promise of technocracy. Authors such as Daniel Bell and Jacques Ellul as well as Helmut Schelsky believed that the 'end of ideology' had come and a 'technological society' or a 'technical state' emerged in which essentially all political problems would be reduced to scientific ones. The unequivocal scientific solution was to render the classical functions of political power superfluous (cf. Ellul, 1954; Schelsky, 1961).

These technocratic diagnoses of social development very probably were a reaction to changes that had occurred in the character of governmental functions, the configurations of political power and the public role of science. All analysts could agree on the evidence that more and more political problems had become scientific in character, more and more political decisions were based on expert advice, and the number of advisory bodies increased steadily. Perhaps most importantly, as the provident and planning functions of the central authorities had expanded considerably, pushing forward the time horizon of political decisions, the element of the 'political', being associated with the short term shifts of public support and power, seemed to have been discriminated as irrational.

The principal idea contained in the technocratic theories, that the ends of political action are derived from the system of certified knowledge, i.e. science and technology, the self-dynamics of which thus determine the socio-political development, is challenged by another school of thought. The Marxists or, for that matter, the 'critical' social theorists such as Marcuse and Habermas, have held that not only is the technocratic Utopia an ideology itself but that science and technology have become the chief productive force and therefore represent a stage of development of capitalism (cf. Habermas, 1968). The more vulgar version of this theoretical viewpoint is that the state, in having assumed the functions of the 'general capitalist', directs with its policies science and technology so as to provide the necessary infrastructure for the capitalist system. Science and technology are suited to the partial goals of capitalist enterprises.

Both these contradicting theses have implications the common denominator of which is the development of science. The technocratic thesis implies that the development of science and technology to a very large extent determines the problem-solving activities of the state. The 'Marxist' thesis (although this term does injustice to them) implies, to the contrary, that the development of science and technology is largely determined by the structural constraints of the political system and the interests and policies that result therefrom.

If we take the government as the frame of reference we rediscover the analogous dichotomy which characterized the discussion in political science in the 1960s and early 1970s, when in all advanced industrialized nations in the West the discrepancy between elaborate reform schemes as an answer to increasingly complex systemic problems and the very tight socio-economic and political constraints to such policies became apparent. The policy sciences approach identified the deficiencies in the traditional structure of the decision-making and information system which could be overcome by technological improvements of these systems. The contrary approach identified the obstacles in the socio-economic constraints and the veto power of interests that are firmly institutionalized within the system (cf. Offe, 1969, 1972).

In these approaches, again, the relation between scientific information and problem-solving activities is the common denominator. They assign the exclusive priority either to scientific information or to the structural constraints of action as the chief determinants of social or political development. Although they are more differentiated than it appears in this presentation they are all nevertheless over-simplifying reality. It is hardly possible to disprove theories which are so global in nature, but it will be attempted, here, to present evidence of a more complex picture which may also provide a point of departure for a theoretical alternative.

The central problematic is the relation between scientific information or more generally systematic knowledge and political action. If viewed from the philosophy and sociology of science, by trying to approach this complex we touch upon the unresolved discussion over the internal versus the external determination of scientific development. We believe that it is impossible to come to final answers with respect to that problem as countless incidents can be found supporting either the conviction that science develops autonomously or that external constraints determine its development. In fact, we proceed from the assumption that the relation between scientific development and practice is not unidirectional but multilateral and that it is necessary to leave the macrotheoretical level and to attempt to identify different configurations of the relation between 'internal' and 'external' factors as well as the factors themselves. We, therefore, limit ourselves to the analysis of the process of programme formulation and implementation in the political system and try to account for the various factors that determine that process, i.e. the use that is being made of scientific knowledge and the changes that occur in the perception of problems. Thus, we ask two questions:

(1) How do certain science policy programmes or political programmes with a conspicuous relation to science evolve and what is the respective role of scientific information and political goals?

(2) How are such programmes implemented into research and what are the factors that determine the success or failure of this implementation?

The empirical evidence which is presented along with the argument is mostly of an illustrative nature rather than systematic. The reason for this is that it represents material assembled in the course of a research project which at the time that this essay is written had not been completed. For the time being our chief purpose, therefore, is to provide a problem analysis and develop a more fruitful theoretical framework and support it with the data we have at hand.

**Problem Perception and Problem Solution in Governmental Action**

Among political scientists, constitutional lawyers, and students of public administration it has become commonplace to characterize the functional change of the public administration which has taken place since the times of the liberal state of the nineteenth century as one from an ordering and service function to an active regulating and welfare function. This development is important in the context of our discussion as it implies a change in the nature of governmental action. Such action used to be mostly of a *reactive* character, i.e. reactive to the dysfunctional developments of an otherwise self-regulating economic and social order. Consequently, most problems could be and were defined in legal terms, as a malfunction of the order signalled the necessity to adapt the legal framework. For analytic purposes (for this ideal type of the liberal state was hardly ever realized) one can distinguish from that stage of development the modern state ('late capitalist' or 'post-industrial', as it may be), the regulative functions of which necessitate *active* interventions. These are, by definition, future oriented and complex. Isolated *ad hoc* measures no longer suffice. Instead 'comprehensive and co-ordinated political programmes have to be realized. This means that constructive public action is typically planning' (Mayntz, 1973, p. 99). To the extent that planning has become a function of public administration this also implies that the time horizon of action is extended, the execution of comprehensive programmes calls for the anticipation of first and second order consequences and this, in turn, makes it necessary to obtain as much systematic information as possible on those areas which are affected. Although governmental action assumes, in the last analysis, the form of a legal act, the information that is required by comprehensive programmes cannot be restricted to legal concepts but must include systematic knowledge of the material subject matters, be it through the natural and engineering sciences or the social sciences. The change in the nature of governmental function, therefore, implies an extention of the utilization of systematic knowledge. It remains an open question whether the increased utilization of scientific knowledge is a result of the functional change of governmental action or, vice versa, if the latter is a result of the development of science (and technology) which, first of all, opened up the possibility of an extension of regulative functions.

Two notes of caution must be added. First, this simplified sketch of an historical change must not conceal the fact that governments have utilized scientific knowledge at a very early point in time, and even a fairly systematic science policy existed (cf. Dupree, 1964; Pfetsch, 1974). Second, the utilization of scientific knowledge by governments need not be oriented towards the problem-solving capacity of science. Three possible functions of the utilization of science can be analytically differentiated, at least for the time since science became established as a major social institution.

(1) The utilization of science can be oriented towards the process value of science. This is the case when, for example, the establishment of a large research installation or a university is supported not because of the specific scientific results that are expected to accrue from it but for the side effects these installations have for the economic development of the region or for the increase in the qualification of manpower.

(2) Science can be used for legitimation purposes, i.e. to give greater credibility or power of conviction to a political decision scientific experts are called upon, commissions are established, etc. In this case, again, the use made of science is not dependent on specific results but on the prestige and status of science in society. (There are, of course, cases where the legitimation purpose is dependent on the results of research and the borderline to the next type becomes very thin.)

(3) Finally, the utilization of science may be oriented towards the product value of science. This is the case where science serves in its problem-solving capacity. Science is put to use with the aim to provide answers to certain problems, for example for the reform of the education system, the establishment of information and communication systems or the protection of the environment (cf. van den Daele and Weingart, 1975).

These analytically differentiated functions of science in political action are not necessarily mutually exclusive and in a concrete case it may be very difficult to identify whether a certain measure is designed to use science for legitimation purposes only or whether science is to solve a genuine problem. Nevertheless, it is important to make the distinction as only in those instances where the product value of science is in demand is an interference of political goals with the internal rules of scientific problem selection and the orientation of intellectual development implied. This is important when it comes to determining the factors that are responsible for the success or failure of the utilization of science (cf. van den Daele and Weingart, 1975).

Before that, however, we will look at the conditions of problem perception because it can be assumed that already the circumstances under which the public administration perceives and defines certain problems and attempts to formulate programmes to cope with them determine the function that science is to have in this process.

**The Conditions of Problem Perception**

Quite obviously only that is a problem which is being perceived as a problem. Thus, poor housing conditions among low income groups may appear to be an inevitable or negligible fact for a conservative government, a pressing problem for a progressive government, and a low priority problem for a poor government. In this instance the perception of the problem is dependent on the values and norms or, more generally, the basic ideologies of the assumed government. A second condition of problem perception is knowledge. Not very long ago educational policy proceeded on the assumption that the desired increase in the overall qualification level found its limitation in the natural distribution of talent. This belief rested upon the premises of a concept of genetic intelligence which prevailed in science, and the rationality of selection criteria in the educational system. That the distribution of talent is at least to a conspicuous extent socially mediated was discovered only after statistical analyses had revealed regional differences and a correlation with factors of social stratification. After that the level of educational qualification was no longer perceived as a limiting condition of social development but as a problem that could be attacked with appropriate policy measures, even though these measures themselves may not yet be known (cf. van den Daele and Weingart, 1975, pp. 146–164).

This example shows that problem perception is a function of systematic knowledge and, thus, indirectly a function of the development of science. But, here again, it is immediately apparent that both analytical types of determinants of problem perception are not mutually exclusive, the most compelling reason being that ideologies influence to an extent what knowledge is being perceived and how it is interpreted. Ideologies or norms and values act as selective mechanisms that structure the perception of knowledge. They act as intervening variables in the relation between the development of knowledge and the perception of problems.

Nevertheless it can be considered a general principle that only those 'obstacles' are viewed as basically solvable 'problems' which lie within the scope of science. If they do not they appear as quasi-natural limitations (cf. van den Daele and Weingart, 1975, p. 20). It could seem, now, that we want to imply, after all, that the development of systematic knowledge defines the problems that become the object of political action. In fact, however, there is not an identity of scientific and practical problem perception. Rather, the pertinent scientific knowledge is generated according to the internal rules of development and is rarely immediately suited to solve the problem in question. Thus, in the example given above, the evidence that the distribution of talent is determined also by social factors is a long way from being able to devise an educational system in which these factors are sufficiently controlled. The initial insight that some 'obstacle' can be considered a 'problem' that is, in principle, solvable, may be the starting point for the formulation of a political programme the realization of which depends, among other things, on the directed development of scientific research. The gap which, in many instances, remains between the initial identification of a problem and its solution through scientific research, can also be attributed to the fact that science is increasingly ascribed a 'generalized problem-solving capacity' so that a scientific solution is anticipated even though there is no basis for it in the body of knowledge.

One other distinction has to be added to that picture. Having assumed that, from a cognitive point of view, ideologies (norms and values respectively) and/or systematic knowledge determine problem perception from an institutional point of view, it has to be asked who perceives a problem: which implies the question which kind of actions are affected by the problem perception. We proceed from the assumption that a problem may be perceived either within the governments, i.e. the administration itself, or by the scientific community (in the wide sense of the word), or by the public (which we will operationalize for our purposes as the press).

**The Dialectic of 'Issue Formation'**

The relationship we have just described is where the dialectic between the development of scientific knowledge and political action originates. The first step in determining the relative role of scientific knowledge and political intent with respect to a given policy or programme is to identify the inputs from the institutional sectors that we have defined as relevant. For obvious reasons a government programme serves as a frame of reference. Its particular content is investigated for the likely causes that have led the government to formulate the programme and embark on the activities prescribed therein. For an example we turn to the evolution of the 'programme for environmental protection' of the German Federal Government, and we draw on some analyses from the United States as well, although presentation of the material must remain extremely sketchy.

Trying to trace the evolution of the 'programme for environmental protection' and the different inputs, one is faced with the complex history of the emergence of an 'issue'. In its programmatic address of October 1969 the new coalition government had declared that the protection of nature and animals as well as recreational areas would receive more attention. Shortly afterwards a cabinet committee for environmental problems was formed which presented a preliminary '*ad hoc* programme for environmental protection' ('Sofortprogramm') in September 1970 and suggested that the various departments under the co-ordination of the Ministry of the Interior present a draft for an 'environmental programme' ('Umweltprogramm') by March 1971. This programme was prepared with the help of scientist and technician advisers whose role will be discussed later. One of the central diagnoses of the programme and at the same time the explicit rationale for the activity in environmental protection was that industrialization had reached a level where the entire ecosphere began to be irreversibly affected, the resources got scarce, soil, air, and water as well as animals and plants had to be protected from human interventions into the natural balance. The programme formulated a number of goals and spelled out the appropriate measures by which they were to be attained. Among these goals were:

(1) Long term environmental planning by means of a legal framework which was to be continually adapted to the progress of science and technology, an effective scientific advisory process in order to ensure the considerations of scientific and technological findings in all decisions affecting the environmental, and the integra-

tion of environmental protection into all measures of structural and regional politics.
(2) The realization of a technology which presents no threat to the environment.
(3) The strengthening of international co-operation in environmental matters (cf. Bundesminister des Innern, n.d.).

Now it may be asked: Why was this problem taken up at this particular time and, more importantly, which inputs were decisive in determining the time and the particular form that the issue assumed when it was taken up by the political agencies. The possibilities are that the problem was either formulated autonomously by the government, or that it was expressed by public opinion because of the immediate experience of pollution, etc., or, finally, that it was publicized by the scientific community in the course of the ongoing research process.

These questions come immediately to mind because there are 'identical' precursors of problem formulation. To cite just one particularly astonishing example: in 1961 the Social Democratic candidate for chancellor, Willy Brandt, in his election campaign pointed to research results on diseases caused by air and water pollution and coined the slogan that the 'sky over the Ruhr must be blue again'. The science journalist Thomas von Randow took up this slogan and published a series of articles on air and water pollution in Germany citing the very same data and diagnoses that almost a decade later became part of the environmental issue (cf. von Randow, 1961a, 1961b). In other words, almost a decade before the environment became, in fact, a political issue (a year before Rachel Carson's influential *Silent Spring* appeared) the conspicuous facts were known and available to the public.

It is possible, however, that the problem assumed a new quality and that this new quality was brought about by scientific research. This explanation is suggested by a number of indications. First of all, departing for a moment from the German scene, an overall look at the environmental movement in the United States shows that there the issue developed from isolated measures, such as the preservation of wilderness (since 1924), outdoor recreation, highway beautification, the prevention of air and water pollution, to the proclamation of an environment 'that is pleasing to the senses and healthy to live in' as a 'prime national goal' by President Johnson in 1965. (Cf. Sundquist, 1968, chapter VIII. Most of the 'isolated' issues that arose in the 1950s and became the object of congressional debate were put into law under Johnson.) The 'new quality' of the issue also came out in President Johnson's message on natural beauty, when he distinguished the 'new conservation' from the 'classic conservation of protection and development' as being a '*creative* conservation of *restoration* and *innovation*. Its concern is not with nature alone, but with the *total relation between man and the world around him*' (quoted from Cooley and Wandesforde-Smith, 1970, our italics).

One new element evolving in this development is the realization that the environmental hazards are systemic and not isolated, global and not national in scope, and that they touch upon political, legal, sociological, biological, physical, chemical, and technological problems. We will have to qualify this later to some extent, but there can be no doubt that with respect to this aspect of the environmental issue the politicians—and primarily their administrative experts in the ministries—took note of and were influenced by scientific findings. The West German Minister of the Interior, Genscher, in answering the questions of a member of the parliament regarding environmental problems in his long statement (1970) referred to the analyses of Paul Ehrlich, the American biologist (cf. 'Stellungnahme von Bundesinnenminister Genscher zu Fragen der Umweltverseuchung', cited from Siebert, 1971, p. 23). In a statement (1970) by Helmut Kohl, the chairman of the opposition party, the Christian Democratic Union, one finds the rare reference to the 'interdisciplinary science' of ecology which that party wanted to be introduced at the universities (cf. Siebert, 1971, p. 20).

The second new element which is implied with the first seems to be that of the *active* intervention of the government in environmental affairs. This became a recurrent theme in the speeches of prominent German politicians at the beginning of the 1970s. Thus Chancellor Brandt stated that his government in having placed environment protection high on the priority list proceeded from the assumption that 'these problems can no longer be dealt with by defensively preventing dangers but that it is necessary to actively shape the environment through anticipatory and preventive measures' (speech before the 'Deutsche Naturschutzring', 29 November 1970, quoted from Siebert, 1971, p. 12).

These are singular pieces of evidence which suggest that beneath what seems to be a continuity of conservationism a new quality is apparent with the development of the environmental issue. This new quality, it is safe to say, is a consequence of scientific information and it, in turn, affects the shape of policies, namely the shift to *active*, anticipatory, and systemic planning in the area of what was formerly conservation policy. That does not fully explain, however, why the issue arose at the time it did as the information on and incidents of environmental damage were known some time before 1970. For an answer we will look at the public conscience and the awareness of the scientific community.

The very few public opinion polls on the public awareness of the environmental problem of which we know are of little help for our purpose because they do not trace the development of the dimensions of the problem. Also, due to the time the polls were taken they do not allow us to draw conclusions as to the effect public awareness may have had on the programme formulation of the government. We try to approach the problem by taking as an indicator the development and crystallization of the issue in the press. The articles by von Randow cited above show that singular reports on air and water pollution did appear long before 1970. A review of Rachel Carson's *Silent Spring* appeared in the same weekly paper *Die Zeit* and with it the term 'environment' ('Umwelt') in 1962 (cf. Hodgson, 1962). By that time, it must be concluded, the fundamental facts about the environmental issue were known and accessible. Also, particularly alarming incidents of pollution were reported such as a three day smog over the Ruhr district in December of that year (cf. von Randow, 1962).

A systematic analysis of the news magazine *Der Spiegel* for the years

1968–1974 conveys a good impression of the crystallization of the environmental issue. Throughout 1968 and the better part of 1969 there are isolated but recurrent reports on incidents related to environmental problems ranging from energy, health hazards in pharmaceutics, and city planning to noise pollution and DDT bans in Sweden and the United States. In October 1969 a series on the population explosion is started (no. 41), and six weeks later (no. 48), in a reprint of an article by Paul Ehrlich, the term 'environment' appears for the first time and with it Ehrlich's analysis (entitled 'The murder of the planet') which puts the environmental problem into the perspective of the new ecology. In 1970 the number of articles concerned with environmental problems increases until they become a major concern of the magazine in the latter half of that year. This is documented by the fact that from now on there are recurrent cover stories on environmental issues and that a special column entitled 'environment' ('Umwelt') is introduced (no. 38, 1970).

This allows us to conclude that as far as the development of the issue is reflected in the press (assuming that *Der Spiegel* is fairly representative in its function as the leading weekly news magazine):

(1) there is a realization of the problem, although remaining fractioned, a considerable time before it becomes a political concern;
(2) the crystallization of the issue occurs at about the same time that government activities start;
(3) this crystallization is initiated by and in terms of popularized scientific findings.

But again, it remains open why this did not happen eight years before when the problems were known, too, and when Rachel Carson's book contained many of the basic ecological principles (such as the dispersion of DDT through the foodchain) that may be considered the core of both the new conservationism and the type of *active* planning policy that ensues from it. Apparently, this question cannot be answered by looking at the evolution of public awareness and it must, therefore, be assumed that, putting it into very vague terms, factors in the political system are, in the last analysis, determining the 'appearance' of the issue. This is indirectly corroborated by looking, finally, at the input from the scientific community.

As of now we have only very incomplete information on the development of the environmental issue in the scientific community, especially with respect to the question whether it arose from the ongoing research process or whether it was 'imported' into the scientific discussion from outside. The evidence suggests that both is the case. On the one hand, as we have shown, the political agencies as well as the mass media take recourse to scientific diagnoses of the environmental crisis. However, these as well as the multitude of pertinent research findings precede the actual 'issue formation'. On the other hand, the issue was taken up in the scientific community in very much the same manner as in the public and assumed a fashion-like form. This is suggested, for instance, by the activity started by the AAAS in 1968 when at its annual meeting several symposia were devoted to the discussion of unanticipated environmental hazards of technology and to the global effects of environmental pollution. Also, the board of directors created a permanent committee on environmental alterations and with that supplemented the activities of many other groups 'because the problems are of such widespread importance that many groups *must* be involved' (Wolfle, 1968, p. 155). A similar development is suggested by a survey among German universities which revealed that beginning in 1971 every fifth university had developed concrete plans to deal with environmental problems in a concerted effort of the relevant disciplines instead of leaving it to small and isolated groups (cf. A. Siebert, 1971, p. 82).

In 1971 the Deutsche Forschungsgemeinschaft (the principal national science foundation) published a report on 'environmental research' presenting its own activities of the past 20 years under this title. It pointed out that although the individual problems of environmental protection were the object of research for a long time in the various disciplines it was now sensible to integrate the various aspects under the cover of 'environmental research' (cf. DFG, 1971, II). (An explanation why this did not happen earlier was not given by the DFG except that in the past the priorities were set differently.) Finally, a very similar impression is given by a substantial number of those experts who participated in gathering the scientific and statistical data for the government report on the environment. The unanimous opinion among those who were interviewed is that the relevant research has been going on for many years but that the government activities helped to provide an overall, coherent picture of the problem.

The apparent contradiction is, in fact, none at all. For scientists all over the world (primarily biologists) environmental problems seem to have been aspects of their research whether they were central to their work or only peripheral. When the issue arose in the public and in the political agencies it gained momentum and spread in very much the same way in the scientific community, except that the scientists may have felt a particular responsibility as a result of their competencies. With respect to the research process nothing had changed in any dramatic way. It was only the perspective that was new. In so far as we can see, this new perspective had originated in the writings of such scientists as Rachel Carson, Paul Ehrlich, G. R. Taylor, and others. (It would, of course, be necessary to support that argument with a dimensional analysis of their work which we cannot provide here, however.) At this point we are left to conclude that environmental protection crystallized as a *political* issue, in the public, and within the scientific community roughly at the same time and in the same way.

With respect to the theoretical problem to determine the extent to which a particular political programme and its translation into science policy is initiated 'autonomously' within the political sector or by the scientific community, we are left with a surprising answer and a methodological problem. It is surprising that the scientific community as a whole reacts simultaneously with the government agencies although the scientific findings that provided the rationale for governmental programme formulation came from a particular faction within the community at an earlier point in time. (In this context it would be worth looking at possible signs of resistance within the community both against 'ecology' in general and against the writings of Carson, Ehrlich, etc. in particular.) In other words, the community—or rather a smaller part of it—has an initiating function in the process of issue formation and is, at the same time, subject to a bandwagon effect as the issue crystallizes in the public and political sectors. The methodological problem that remains is how to identify the actual causes of the formation of the issue as such. (The 'empirical' explanation which is suggested in this context, such as an acute crisis or autonomous processes of 'politicization' and consensus formation, either fails altogether or is unsatisfactory (cf. Scharpf, 1973, p. 71).) In order to approach that problem we will now look at the structural conditions of political programme formulation.

## Structural Conditions and Mechanisms of Political Programme Formulation

Any administrative organization and the public administration in particular is designed to solve certain prescribed tasks or task complexes. Therefore, the structure and the boundaries of jurisdiction of government departments as well as their internal differentiation into task oriented sections are a function of problem perceptions. These have both developed over a long period of time and become tradition and are the result of shifts in the distribution of power and the representation of interests. While they are subject to continuous change as they are affected by a countless number of factors they also represent relatively inert structures. Thus, the inertia and flexibility of these structures can be explained not only in terms of political and organizational processes but, as these always have a cognitive substitute, they may at the same time be interpreted in terms of cognitive processes. By saying that a particular department is designed to deal with a certain problem or set of problems and is structured accordingly thus implies a specific configuration of problem perception and information processing. The substructures of a department have command over an accumulated stock of specialized expert knowledge, routinized procedures, and established contracts to 'external' communities of interested and expert parties. By this it is assured that the political agencies have a considerable 'environmental and problem sensitivity' (cf. Scharpf, 1973, p. 80). The ability to sense and identify problems and to devise measures to solve them is limited, however, to the problems of an environment for which the organizational unit was originally established. The problem perception of the respective unit is selective; it tends to ignore the problems that lie outside its jurisdiction (cf. Scharpf, 1973). It has become commonplace to speak of a growing complexity of the problems that face the public administration though, in fact, it is inconceivable that the administrative structure as a structure of problem perception ever matched the 'real' dimensions of the problems it was dealing with. The adaptation of the former to the latter is one reason for organizational change.

(In fact, one may ask if it is permissible to speak of the 'real' dimensions or the problem as it 'really' is, at all. Certainly, a problem is viewed differently by those who are affected by it, than by those who study it systematically but from a neutral viewpoint or by those who have to solve it under certain constraints of action. These different perceptions and definitions may be principally incommensurable and if the political system *alone* is in the position to deal with the problem *its* definition of it will, in the final analysis, be constitutive for the actions that ensue and the consequences they have.)

To some extent the same analytical considerations that we have developed for the relation of administrative organizations and their tasks (i.e. problems of action) also apply to the relation between the system of science and its subject matters (i.e. problems of analysis). Thus, the definition of the boundaries of a scientific discipline is the result of the conception of a subject matter which has become institutionalized in organizations (such as university departments). Due to their social self-dynamics they are relatively inert, structuring, as such, the perception of the subject matter and its study. And yet, they are subject to continuous change as the research process evolves and new findings affect the definition of the subject matter and the research problems.

The crucial difference between the political and the scientific systems with respect to the context we are dealing with is in the respective 'internal' criteria of relevance. Thus, it may be that the operation of these criteria leads to a disparate problem perception. It is then an empirical question how in the process of problem identification and the formulation of the political programme to deal with the problem the disparate notions of the problem among the administration and the scientific community are adapted to one another. This is the second step in determining the relative impact of political and scientific inputs into a political programme. We turn again to the case of the programme for environmental protection to illustrate this point by confronting different notions of environmental protection with one another. The basic notion of the environmental problem has become the concept of the 'ecosystem' which originated in the biological sciences. The crucial innovative element in the concept is its enlargement to the consideration of man's interference with the balanced forces of nature. By this the problem of environmental protection is expanded beyond the limits of the classical subject of 'ecology' which was only concerned with the interrelations between species of flora and fauna in certain biotopes. At the same time the systemic character of the ecosphere implies that interferences with the natural balance (which are inevitable) and the prevention of damages must be planned with a view to a whole complex of second order consequences. On the other hand the detailed research problems that have to be solved fall into the realm of various disciplines or subdisciplines such as biology, physics, chemistry or plant physiology, hydrodynamics, molecular biology, etc. These follow a reductionist research strategy which means that causal relations among those factors are sought which fall into their general subject matter. The selective perception of disciplinary boundaries tends to prevent or at least to impede the synthesis of the findings in an overall systemic view.

Turning back, now, to the process of programme formulation we can identify two structural mechanisms that are at work.

(1) The problem as it is perceived by the administration is divided into subproblems according to established departmental boundaries and political interests. Thus, while a cabinet commission was set up to co-ordinate the activities and con-

tributions of the various departments it was also decided that the Minister of the Interior was to have the chief responsibility in setting up the programme. Aside from contingent political reasons this was justified by the fact that environmental protection was considered an aspect of internal security, for example reactor security, or was traditionally a part of the regulation of commerce ('Gewerbeordnung')—as in the case of the regulation of waterways, emission control at large industrial plants, the setting of noise standards, etc. From this viewpoint the problem of environmental protection was one of deriving legal standards. (Of course, in the last analysis all political action takes the form of legal or quasi-legal provisions.)

Other ministries such as agriculture, health, and science and technology were to contribute to the programme according to their respective jurisdictions. This created problems of delineation especially with the Ministry of Agriculture which felt that environmental protection fell into its competency for conservation, and with the Ministry of Science and Technology which was to concern itself with technological innovations that would be of minimal harm to the environment ('Umweltfreundliche Technologien') but claimed that all research should be coordinated under its jurisdiction. These conflicts of delineation which ensued are not only an indication of conflicts of power among the departments but they could only evolve because obviously the issue itself could be viewed from different points of reference and extended across the jurisdiction of several departments.

Thus, the 'action programme' was divided into the traditional categories of nature and landscape, waste disposal, chemicals and biocides, water, high seas and coastal waters, air and noise. The concept of the ecosystem is fragmented into 'subsystems'. The overriding goal of the programme, then, is to define the upper limits up to which the 'sub-ecosystems' can be burdened with pollutants before their regenerative forces fail to operate. In this way the government is enabled to identify the secular limits of economic growth which can effectively be moulded into a legal framework and serve as an orientation for the economic subjects. A concern for the systemic interrelations that constitute the ecosystem as a whole is not apparent although there can be no doubt that the experts in the ministries are aware of this notion.

(2) The second mechanism determining the contents and structure of the programme is the process by which the expert advisers from the scientific community are chosen. (There is evidence that the programme was written before the various advisory groups had finished their reports collected in the 'materials on the environment' which was to provide the scientific foundation for the action programme.) Inevitably the administration falls back on the existing institutions and, thus, the established structure of disciplines and problem areas of research. The type of interdisciplinary concern that the notions of ecological crisis and man's interference with the ecosystem call for were not institutionalized when the issue crystallized.

The division of the expert commissions which had to give *status quo* analyses and research recommendations, therefore, reflects not only the conflict between the Ministries of the Interior and of Research and Technology (BMI and BMFT) but also the prevailing structure of subject matters. This shows that in so far as the political programme formulation takes recourse to scientific knowledge it is subject to two selective filters or criteria according to which knowledge is organized and problems are perceived, the criteria of political organization and administration and the criteria of scientific disciplinary organization and specialization. If, as we have reason to assume, the process of programme formulation is first organized by the administration before the scientific advisory capacity is tapped, the selective operation of the two filters accumulate. In other words, those aspects of the problem which fall through the first filter cannot be recovered by the second. This does not allow us to answer conclusively the question with which we started out except that the mechanisms operating in the process of issue formation and programme formulation permit conclusions as to the general character of this process. While some of those conclusions will concern us in the next section we may summarize here that although some problems of research remain open there is certainly no evidence for a clear-cut relation between political programme formulation and scientific development. In order to penetrate deeper into the complex dialectic of cognitive processes and institutional constraints it will be of crucial importance and at the same time a major methodological problem to perform a dimensional analysis tracing the changes in dimension that occur with the problem or the issue under study as it passes through the administrative and the scientific advisory stages in the process of programme formulation.

**Implementation of Programmes into Research Processes**

In a model presented elsewhere (van den Daele and Weingart, 1975) we assumed that any attempt to direct scientific development according to external goals, i.e. to utilize science for the solution of political problems, unless it is merely a question of the unproblematic application of existing knowledge, is faced with the problem of whether science is receptive or resistant to such attempts. It was hypothesized that one could categorize the type of political demand in terms of the implied technical function of science and relate that to the prerequisite level of theory development. Thus, it could be deduced whether, in the concrete case, a deficit in theoretical development and consequently a 'cognitive resistance' exists, which leads either to a reformulation of the problem or an extended problem-oriented theory development ('finalization'). Aside from the problem of categorizing distinct classes of technical functions and of theory development on which, of course, the concept of 'cognitive resistance' is based it also implies the ultimate disjunction of political programme formulation and scientific problem definition. Although the functional dependence of political programme formulation on science was considered it was believed to have only an initial effect. On account of the foregoing analysis and the limited empirical evidence we have, this model must be revised.

First, the phenomenon of cognitive resistance, which is assumed to determine the success of the translation of political problems into scientific research processes, must be located chronologically in the early phase of problem perception and programme formulation. Second, it is apparent that what we termed the 'deficit of theory development' does already affect the programme formulation. This is the likely consequence of the combined operation of the administrative and the scientific criteria of knowledge organization. The theoretical deficit that exists with respect to the integrative ecosystemic view is largely reduced by a fragmentation of the problem of environmental protection into subproblems according to administrative areas of jurisdiction and again according to disciplinary subject matters. The deficits which remain are primarily those that are identical with the already existing research problems. Instead of an external direction of science or a 'finalization' the implementation of political problems into the research process occurs as an 'anticipatory reduction of complexity'. Or in other words, in the process of problem perception and programme definition the 'external' political and the 'internal' scientific criteria of relevance are not allowed to clash.

This mechanism also operates with respect to the formulation of the political goals in so far as they imply a demand for scientific problem solutions. Here, the consequence is that the programmatic ideas, if any do exist, are reduced to relatively 'conservative' goals that do not reach very far beyond the existing potential of science.

In view of that one may ask if there remains any problematical difference between political goals (i.e. demands for scientific problem solutions) and the development of science at all or if we have posed an imaginary problem. Many more analyses have to be directed to this complex and a conclusive categorization is difficult. However, the little evidence we have at present in combination with the theoretical considerations suggests that such a difference does, in fact, remain and has certain consequences. Thus, the established specialities (as in our case) of biology such as molecular biology, botany, plant physiology, and others remain, as such, unaffected. (This will have to be determined conclusively in the research project under way and may not apply to other cases.) On the other hand, the effect of the government programme seems to be a thematic reorientation. Biologists of various specialities regularly claim that the government programme for environmental protection did nothing to change their immediate research but that the main effect was the integration of many isolated research activities and the creation of a thematic awareness of a common concern among scientists who until then thought of their fields in terms of the limited perspectives of their respective specialities only.

Besides this there seems to be yet a further effect of reorientation that can be located on two levels. The 'political demand' tends to focus attention on and thus enhance the exploitation of the scientific potential for purposes of application. This is the case not only because of the inherent constraints in the process of problem perception and programme formulation but also because of the required level of concreteness, i.e. the translation into legal standards to which the research must be downgraded. The closer a research area may be said to be to the development of 'technologies' the more apt it is to take up concrete problems of environmental protection. The problems themselves *may* in that case be largely identical with those in the 'basic field'. Thus, for example, the same problems that the limnologists consider as fundamental to that speciality and which they study in a given delimited ecosystem (i.e. river or lake) are treated by the 'applied' limnologists, the only difference being that for the latter the concern is for a particular ecosystem and its concrete problems. There can be little doubt, however, that as far as this 'applied' sector is concerned the treatment of problems remains fragmented in the way that the areas were differentiated all along.

On the other hand, as we have shown above, the crystallization of the issue of environmental protection also occurred in the scientific community initiating a sort of bandwagon effect. It is in this context that the issue is taken up in the systemic dimensions as they are spelled out by the 'new ecologists'. This, however, is first of all an institutional effect which may signify either of two things. Either, established research institutions jump on the bandwagon and claim—by using the name tag—to pursue environmental research while, in effect, continuing research programmes which existed before. This type of 'fraud' is explained and enhanced by government resource allocations. Or, there occurs an institutional differentiation, i.e. the problem area as it is defined by the 'new ecologists' is established institutionally such as by the formation of interdisciplinary university working groups or institutes, the construction of curricula, and the establishment of professional career patterns, for example the 'environmental engineer'. These two developments are not mutually exclusive, and the problem is to differentiate between one and the other. The crucial problem in this context is to determine if the institutional differentiation constitutes the framework of a new research area with its own theory development because only then is it possible to speak of a (re)direction of scientific development. What is true for social change in general may—within limits—be said for processes of change in science, as well, namely that new institutions emerge that bypass old ones and gradually replace them. Much of today's science policy—at least where it is product-value oriented—is implemented as an institutional policy in comparison to which the relative importance of allocative policies utilizing the established institutions of science, such as foundations, stagnates (cf. Weingart, 1975). The significance of this is that with the establishment of new institutions new criteria of relevance are institutionalized that structure the research process, i.e. problem selection, problem definition, and goal definition, all of which decide over direction, scope, and length of the process. This points to the study of the interrelations between academic science, applied science, and technology and between the respective institutional settings in which they take place. Cases such as that of fusion-oriented plasmaphysics where the realization of a certain technology requires the clarification of a number of 'fundamental' problems (cf. Küppers, 1975) suggest that it is necessary to look beyond the line of distinction between 'basic' and 'applied' research. Likewise, in order to adequately judge the effect of government programmes on the development of science, even though taking into account the adaptive mechanisms, it is evidently necessary to look not only at the community and institutions of basic research but also at those of problem-oriented and applied research. For, it may very well be that effects of direction of scientific development do not occur directly, but indirectly as a result of the demand for certain applied research, i.e. technology in the wider sense of the word. Of course, concluding that there is no direct external direction of science or intervention with the cognitive criteria of relevance within the existing institutions of science, but rather an institutional differentiation, does not eliminate one problem. Although the forms of institutional direction may assume primary importance they represent only a long term prerequisite for the establishment of subject matters and the organization of research focused on them. However, it is still a question of the delineation of the subject matter, i.e. its 'manageability', its relation to established fields of science, the availability of methods, and many other factors (cf. for some of these factors van den Daele and Weingart, 1975; Lemaine *et al.*, 1976).

**Conclusion**

In the preceding argument we have not given a definitive answer regarding the relation between systematic (i.e. scientific) knowledge and political action and it should have become clear that there cannot be any simple and definitive answer. On the one hand there are a number of open research problems such as the microanalysis of the emergence and crystallization of 'issues' and the relative weight of inputs of scientific knowledge and political interests. On the other hand the recourse to the cognitive dimension reveals a complexity of the process which—at least at this time—leaves little hope for neat generalizations. Instead, by taking the cognitive contents of information as a major determinant of action we are faced with an immense spectrum of process configurations and contingencies. And yet, although we have done little more than to give a problem analysis, a rough pattern becomes apparent in terms of which the process of governmental problem formulation and the utilization of science can be described (cf. Figure 1). From that it seems highly probable, notwithstanding further clarification of the open problems, that both the technocratic and the 'Marxist' hypotheses about the relation between scientific development and the state are misleading simplifications.

The 'Marxist' thesis fails to recognize that political goals, at least where they have an impact on or imply the utilization of science, are not formulated autonomously within the political arena and without some preceding and initiating developments in the research process. This does not affect the fact that structural constraints to which the state is subject do play a major role in determining *which* problems are taken up, how they are defined, and in which way they are solved.

The technocratic thesis, on the other hand, ignores just those 'political' ingredients which undoubtedly mediate scientific insights not only in the sense of deciding over their 'appearance' in the political sphere in the first place but also by shaping the configurations they assume once they have become the subject of the process of programme formulation. This is shown particularly by the discrepancies in time between a discovery in the research process, its crystallization as an

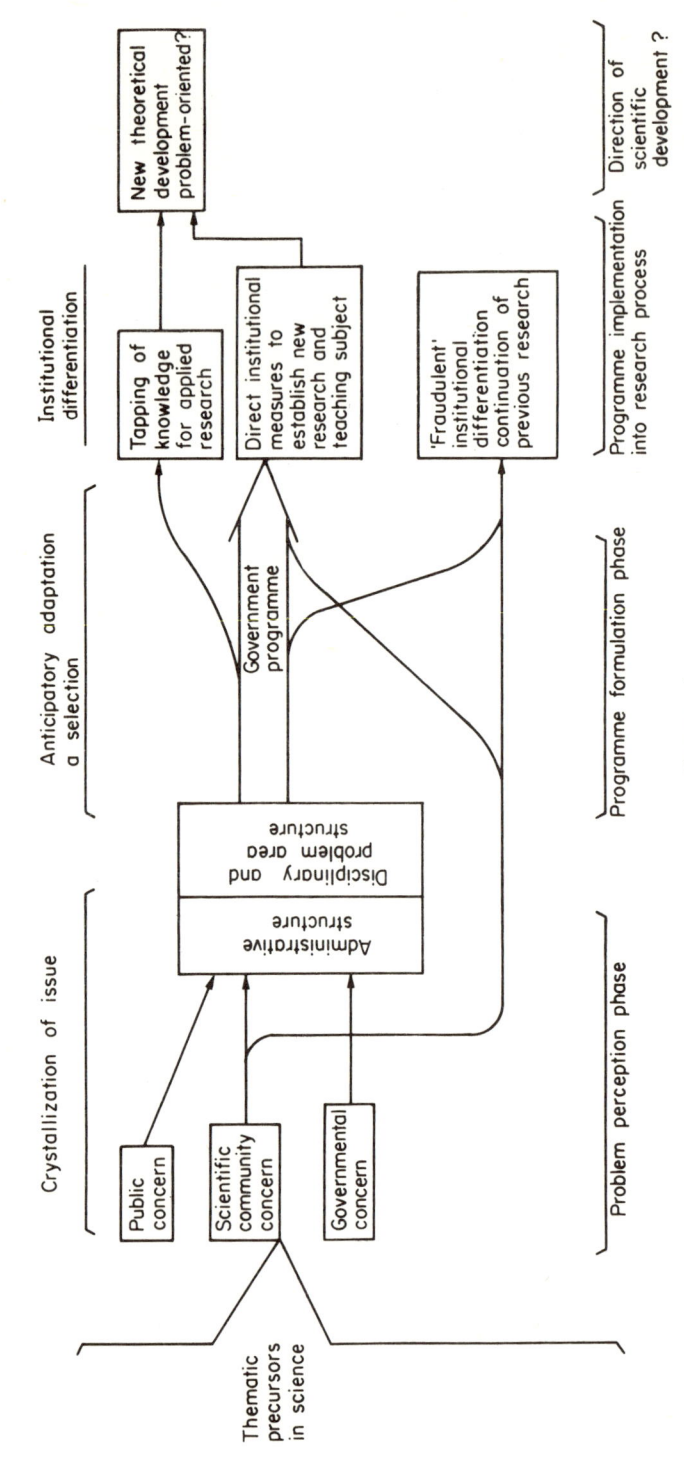

FIGURE 1

'issue' by the public, and its translation into problem-solving activities by the government. While it does not come as a total surprise that macrosociological theses about the relation between scientific development and political action have to be qualified considerably when they are confronted with microsociological evidence, the significance of it extends beyond a mere refutation of these theses. We believe that by this type of analysis we are able to approach the issue of 'external versus internal' determinants of scientific development in a more fruitful way than was the case before. By locating this analysis in a macrotheoretical context it becomes apparent that it has some potential for the explanation of scientific and social development as well.

### References

Bundesminister des Innern (ed.) (n.d.), *Betrifft: Umweltprogramm der Bundesregierung*, Bonn.
Cooley, R. A., and G. Wandesforde-Smith (1970), *Congress and the Environment*, Seattle and London, University of Washington Press.
Daele, W. van den, and P. Weingart (1975), 'Resistenz und Rezeptivität der Wissenschaft—zu den Entstehungsbedingungen neuer Disziplinen durch wissenschaftspolitische Steuerung' in *Zeitschrift für Soziologie*, vol. IV, 146–164. English version in G. Lemaine *et al.*, *New Perspectives on the Emergence of Scientific Disciplines*, Paris, Mouton.
DFG (1971), *Umweltforschung—Aufgaben und Aktivitäten der DFG 1950–1970*, Bonn-Bad Godesberg.
Dupree, Hunter A. (1964), *Science in the Federal Government, the History of Politics and Activities to 1940*, New York, Harper and Row.
Ellul, J. (1954), *La Technique ou l'enjeu du scièclé*, Paris, Libraire Armand Colin.
Habermas, J. (1968), *Technik und Wissenschaft als 'Ideologie'*, Frankfurt, Suhrkamp.
Hodgson, G. (1962), 'Vergiften wir unsere Umwelt?' in *Die Zeit*, 26, 7 September.
Küppers, G. (1975), 'Deutschland', Report 4, Universitätsschwerpunkt Wissenschaftsforschung, Universität Bielefeld.
Lemaine, G., R. MacLeod, M. Mulkay, and P. Weingart (eds) (1976), *New Perspectives on the Emergence of Scientific Disciplines*, Paris, Mouton.
Mayntz, R. (1973), 'Probleme der inneren Kontrolle in der Planenden Verwaltung' in R. Mayntz and F. Scharpf, *Planungsorganisation*, Munich, Piper & Co.
Offe, C. (1969), 'Politische Herrschaft und Klassenstrukturen' in G. Kress and D. Senghaas (eds), *Politikwissenschaft, Eine Einführung in ihre Probleme*, Frankfurt, Europäische Verlagsanstalt, pp. 155–189.
Offe, C. (1972), *Strukturprobleme des kapitalistischen Staates*, Frankfurt, Suhrkamp.
Pfetsch, F. (1974), *Zur Entwicklung der Wissenschaftspolitik in Deutschland 1750–1914*, Berlin, Duncker & Humblot.
Randow, Thomas von (1961a), 'Der veruntreute Himmel' in *Die Zeit*, 32, 4 August.
Randow, Thomas von (1961b), 'Das Wasser ist krank' in *Die Zeit*, 42, 13 October.
Randow, Thomas von (1962), 'Verhängisvoller Smog' in *Die Zeit*, 50, 14 December.
Scharpf, F. W. (1973), *Planung als politischer Prozeß, Aufsätze zur Theorie der planenden Demokratie*, Frankfurt, Suhrkamp.
Schelsky, H. (1961), 'Demokratischer Staat und moderne Technik', *Atomzeitalter*, 5.
Siebert, A. (ed.) (1971/1972), 'Materialien Umweltschutz und Raumordnung, Übersicht über Ziele und Bestrebungen in der Bundesrepublik Deutschland', Hannover,

Akademie für Raumforschung und Landesplanung, Heft 1, 4, 5 continued, from Heft 4, p. 82.

Sundquist, James L. (1968), *Politics and Policy*, Washington, D.C., The Brookings Institution.

Weingart, P. (1976), *Wissensproduktion und Soziale Struktur*, Frankfurt, Suhrkamp, Ch. 4.

Wolfle, D. (1968), 'The Only Earth We Have', *Science*, CLXIX, 12 January, 155.

# 3

# SCIENTIFIC CAREER, SCIENTIFIC GENERATION, SCIENTIFIC LABOUR MARKET

#### Elzbieta Neyman

Sociological inquiry seems to oscillate between the Scylla of macrostructural, global analyses and the Charybdis of the description of microstructural data. The schema of research set out in this paper tries to integrate those two different approaches to treating social data into a coherent conceptual framework.

### The Scientific Labour Market

The concept of 'scientific market' that I propose is very similar to the concept of 'labour market' widely understood. I define it as the permanently changing body of opportunities for the individual to enter the institutional–organizational system of science and to advance in it. From a different point of view we can define the scientific market as the whole system of selection and rewarding of individuals within scientific institutes.[1]

As in each profession, the personal opportunities depend not only upon some attributes of an individual (such as his mental abilities, attained skills, formal education, etc.), but they are also conditioned by macrostructural factors (cultural, demographic, political) as well as by institutional–organizational ones. By 'institutional' factors we mean those connected with the functioning of the scientific community as a social milieu—including its ethos and morality, tradition of intellectual atmosphere, etc. By 'organizational factors' we mean all factors secondary to the formal, legal organization of science. This category is of a special importance to those who are interested in practical, political purposes: active politics rely on intervening essential processes of social life (in this case—those of science) by reinforcement (or protection) of tendencies defined as desirable and by elimination (reduction) of tendencies viewed as undesirable, dangerous, etc. They are realized by manipulation of the organizational sphere. The problems concerning an organizational system of science viewed as means of politics, which seem to be of special interest, are as follows:

(1) Its degree of universalism and openness;
(2) Established 'rules of the game' regulating individual careers;

(3) Its degree of homogeneity;
(4) Its elemental processes and planned modifications;
(5) Its evolution and its relation to broad socio-cultural phenomena;
(6) Relation of its present state to the ideological assumptions and the explicitly formulated directives of the present politics.

We can obtain a picture of a national scientific market by the analysis of formal documents (for example, prescriptions, laws, conference reports, official correspondence, statistical data) and information from well informed persons (for example, interviews with scientific administrators or articles in newspapers). In such a way we can try to reconstruct the ideological assumptions and directives of a national politics of science, the means undertaken to their realization, and their results. But the impression received in such a way seems to be unsatisfactory—by showing the global effects we bypass the problem of how that system works. It is the analysis of the mechanisms of recruitment, selection, and rewarding/punishing (broadly understood) of people which seems to be crucial for our purposes. We can distinguish five levels of selection characterizing a scientific marketplace:

(1) The 'primary selection' contains all post-graduate students applying for employment or for doctoral fellowships. The moment of 'entry' into the scientific market is crucial for a scientific career in those organizational systems which are characterized by a weak rotation and as such it involves great competition. It is very interesting to observe what kind of students find the motivation to scientific work and are attracted by it. We think that encouragement by their academic teachers is of greatest importance, but also the influence of family tradition seems to play some role.

(2) The 'mechanisms of recruitment' determine what type of people aspiring to scientific work succeed and are submitted to the process of scientific initiation as assistants and fellows and what kind of young people fail. Studies of these mechanisms might begin with the answer to the question of what kind of factors determine personal success: is it only previous scientific achievement or not? We can cite several hypotheses concerning the importance of other factors, as for example the social origin of a candidate (which can facilitate his entry to the scientific institutions because of personal connections, etc.); institutional power or scientific prestige of his promotor; socio-psychological traits of a candidate, etc.

(3) The mechanisms of distribution of privileges and rewards concern 'adult scientists'—those who have already established a position within the academic market. To study these mechanisms properly we must begin from the anthropological analysis of the values of the scientific community. We define 'rewards' psychologically as all values whose attainment is desired by subjects and, in the case of their realization, as a source of their satisfaction. Of course they are of very different kinds as, for example, autonomy and satisfaction of work itself, scientific prizes, salaries, or travel connected with participation in international conferences, etc. Some of them are more coveted than others; there exists a hierarchy of them. The study of the allocation of all 'rewards' important

to scientists must be preceded by the identification of those rewards and the recognition of their 'strength'—in relation one to the other. The main problem here is the degree of their universality. It is interesting to observe if these values (rewards) are in practice cumulative, monopolized by a small group of scientists or dispersed. Is there any continuity or discontinuity in the winners' group; does the fact of being once rewarded multiply the chances of being rewarded in the future?

(4) The 'mechanisms of organizational promotion' we distinguish from the vast category of previously mentioned mechanisms of distribution of rewards. We mean by the 'mechanisms of organizational promotion' the factors which influence the distribution of those titles and functions which are dependent in a greater measure on the organizational and political authorities than on the efforts of the particular scientist. While the title of 'doctor' is an effect of concrete personal achievement, the position of 'departmental director' or 'president of a scientific institution' is a good example of success in organizational promotion. We treat these mechanisms independently because they seem to be the best indicator of national science policy and its ideological basis.

(5) The 'mechanisms of secondary selection' affect all those persons who abandon one scientific institution for another, and those who completely abandon the organizational subsystem of science. As the scientific institutes and also organizational subsystems of science form a prestige structure, it might be interesting to distinguish:

(a) scope of the horizontal mobility of scientists;
(b) scope of individual promotions connected with their institutional mobility;
(c) scope of individual demotions connected with their institutional mobility.

The scientific market so understood is, of course, a very complex and complicated social phenomenon, quite different in different countries, and continually evolving in particular countries. It seems necessary to postulate international comparative research, which could help to determine the criteria of effectiveness of differently orientated science policies. In this paper we propose a schema for research dealing with scientific phenomena on the national scene. Such research can only have a socio-historical character because of the dynamics of the scientific market. We can distinguish several factors influencing metamorphoses of those complex phenomena and organize them into two main groups:

(1) Macrostructural data: as, for example, political atmosphere, cultural system, socio-economic state of a given country which have a direct influence on the attitudes of science managers and on the attitudes of people aspiring to scientific careers and of scientists; on results of mechanisms of recruitment and rewarding, etc. We can mention as examples the following factors and events.

The internal political situation of a given country and the international situation. A trivial example is the enrichment of the scientific potential of the United States by the immigration of German intellectuals at the time of the Third Reich.

The Second World War had a direct influence in several countries on the profile of the scientific market. In that time Poland lost about 23 per cent of its total population and it was especially the intellectual milieu which was affected; so entry to the scientific market was relatively easy in the first post-war years.

Naturally each year it became more difficult, and a drastic change in the situation came in the middle of the 1960s when the generation of the demographic explosion entered the adult society. Demographic waves are of great importance in the functioning of the labour market.

The influence of economic factors on the scientific market is especially visible in a time of crisis. As science is not a 'directly profitable' institution, in the time of declining economic prosperity it is rapidly affected by restrictions of financial/institutional possibilities. The trouble of the American scientific market in the last years is a good example here.

Cultural factors also exert an influence on relevant phenomena. Usually we treat cultural data as stable. But in the modern world they very often play the important role of revolutionizing social phenomena. For example, in pre-war Poland, which had a social structure containing a mixture of feudal and capitalistic elements, there existed several models of worthwhile individual careers. Political events, change of political régime and of social class structure induced a cultural change and unification of views of personal success in life. As sociological research has shown, the scientific career has the greatest merit and seems to be without competition in the hierarchy of prestige. Knowledge has replaced wealth as *the* criterion of personal value. It is difficult to underestimate the social results of such cultural reorientation for the functioning of the scientific market (Wesolowski and Sarapata, 1961; Sarapata, 1965).

(2) Organizational data in science are in great measure dependent upon macrostructural factors. But especially in societies where science is included as an object of central planning, where science policy is the effect of conscious decisions and not the unpredicted result of spontaneous processes, organizational factors are relatively autonomous. In such societies general legislative prescriptions concerning science can give rise to profound reorientations of the scientific market. As an example we can cite here the change in the Polish system of selection caused by the special prescription of adding supplementary points to the marks achieved by workers' and peasants' children in examinations designed to select for entry to Higher Schools; or the change in the system of rotation influenced by so called 'rotation prescription' determining that time in which the scientific worker is obliged to prepare his Ph.D. thesis and, subsequently, *dozent* dissertation. The change of conditions (for example the rapid increase of salaries of scientific workers in 1972) also has an influence on the situation of the scientific market.

Up to this time we have spoken about *the* national scientific market, and assumed a homogeneous environment. It seems, however, that the most fruitful analysis of its functioning must focus on the level of the individual scientific discipline, because the general principles defining the membership of a given scientific community work in a different manner at that level, and individual chances to succeed and to make a career vary accordingly. For example, at the beginning of the 1950s Professor Leopold Infeld returned to Poland after several years of emigration. He founded the Warsaw school of modern physics which still retains its high prestige on the international scene. His first pupils became university professors when they were less than 30 years old; their professional careers advanced rapidly. The next generation no longer had such opportunities: the principles of recruitment became very severe and each year only three or four persons could be employed. As the faculty possesses a sufficient number of professors, each year it becomes more difficult to gain that title not only because of organizational factions but also because of the intellectual atmosphere. Great expectations and the severity of evaluations influence the tempo of an individual's career.

Sociology represents a quite different situation. The great pre-Second World War tradition declined in the 1950s; the faculties and chairs of sociology were closed, and it was impossible to study that discipline. Its revival in 1956 gave relatively great opportunities to the first students recruited after 1957 and also gave opportunities to the representatives of different disciplines to be employed in sociological institutions. But after a few years the first signs of stagnation touched new incoming students; the principles of recruitment were much more strict. On the other hand, the relatively autonomous development of sociology after 1956 soon acquired a 'social service' character. That transformation provides new opportunities to enter the scientific market: according to social needs several new scientific institutes were organized giving new possibilities for employment.

We treat the concept of scientific market as a social grounding of the phenomena crucial to our research into the individual career in science. The transformation of the scientific market and the continuing changes of an individual's chances in it make it very difficult to compare personal scientific biographies. That is why it is necessary to introduce the category of 'scientific generation', which makes possible the relativization of the history of individual successes and failures to the chances which objectively existed at that time. Such relativization makes possible further comparisons and evaluations.

**The Scientific Generation**

The concept of scientific generation permits us to 'mediate' between two extremes: that of the overarching sociological analysis of the scientific community and the scientific market on the one hand, and that of the socio-psychological, individualizing picture of the scientific career on the other. It permits us also to link the organizational and cognitive problems of science.

It is necessary to begin this section by noting that the concept of generation has in practice several meanings. In general it is utilized in one of two ways: ahistorical or historical.

*Ahistorical Concepts of Generation*

Ahistorical concepts of generation are based on an absolute consideration of the factor of time at the social or individual level.

*Generation as a measure of social time* This means of treating the category of generation is characteristic especially of genealogies and is connected with the succession of parents–children–grandchildren. It is a biological dependency: a schema of kinship which essentially determines the generation to which an individual belongs. According to this approach the approximate interval between the date of birth of one generation and that of the next generation serves as a measure of the periodization of the history of a family or tribe. The best example is the Old Testament (see Ossowska, 1963; Renouard, 1953).

Let us here digress briefly to consider treatment of the category of age by sociologists in their empirical research. Their tendency towards a desire for quantitative data has created a 'fetish of number' in handling the category of generation. It is generally assumed that—like sex, education, and social origin—an individual's age is also an important factor determining personal attitudes or other attributes of an individual. Typologies of age based on an absolute conception of time, secondary to mechanistic and arbitrary divisions (say 5, 10, 15 years), seem to be primitive and asociological. It is not age defined as the number of years lived which is important for sociological studies (as it is, for example, in medical ones); it is rather the quality of those years and membership of the relevant social group of peers which should be seen as of greater importance.

*Generation as a measure of individual time* Metrical understanding of a generation often directs the attention of sociologists from the succession of generations to their coexistence. So the social scene can be viewed as a set of roles performed by different individuals during their life. As J. Marias puts it:

> In each data there are four major human strata or generations coexistent in interaction, with precise and unsubsistable functions: (a) the 'survivors' of the previous epoch who indicate the origins of the present situation, that is, the man of 'another time' who nevertheless remains in this one; (b) those in power in all areas whose pretentions generally coincide with the actual state of the world; (c) the 'opposition' or active generation that has not yet triumphed and fights with the previous generations for the transfer of power and the realization of its own innovations, and (d) the young, who have new pretentions and look forward to a 'putsch' or downfall of the *status quo* (Marias, 1968, p. 91)[2]

Some authors treat the institution of science analogically. The Soviet author, G. M. Dobrov, writes for example:

> the harmonious connection between the rich scientific-methodological experience and the great knowledge of the older generation of scientists and the energy and courage in searching for new ways in science characteristic of a young generation of scientists is the golden mean in forming a structure of employment in Soviet science according to age. (Dobrov, 1966, p. 116)

It is possible also to treat generations inside any discipline or speciality in a similar manner. So Zuckerman and Merton showed that, depending upon the generation to which they belong, scientists of a speciality differ between themselves in their cognitive structures, in the problems they choose, and in the scientific works they cite (see Zuckerman and Merton, 1972).

It is easy to see the value of these approaches in comparison with those which mechanically divide 100 years into three generations. Generations are here relativized to a defined actuality, and differentiated according to the different roles each plays in it. On the social plane this analysis is of a synchronic character. It is diachronic when applied to the biography of a particular individual: as the attribute of age changes, so does his membership in a generation. Generation is here a synonym of stages in the life of the individual; we assume the universality of individual growth, treating it as 'a movement from amorphous plasticity through mature competence toward terminal rigidity' (Ryder, 1965). So age is treated as a surrogate for specific psychic and mental traits.

This attitude towards age is also very common in the field of science. It is generally assumed that the age of about 30 is the most creative period in the scientific biography. Psycho-sociological research does not confirm that sterotype.[3] Most scientists dealing with that problem prefer to characterize it not only in psychological–physiological terms, but also in socio-cultural ones. They show that it is not only age which characterizes intergenerational differences, but also positions acquired in the institutional structure, determined in great measure by the length of time worked. In the sociological notion of a generation (as a measure of time of the individual) that which is most important for its identification is the accumulation of organizational rewards, changing of roles, and the acquisition of higher and higher positions during the professional career. According to Berger the opposition of those who possess power and those who are deprived of it is crucial for defining generation (see Berger, 1960).

This means of treating generations is not very useful in the analysis of modern societies mainly because of the rapidity of changes taking place in them. The process of universalization of roles in modern societies does not, however, affect all of its domains equally. The spheres of science and politics, for example, seem to be insulated from the process. Nevertheless the ahistorical concept of generation is not inapplicable to the analysis of scientific institutions because of the evident gerontocracy within them. We find here a phenomenon parallel to that discovered by Marx in the field of economics: 'productive relations' in science seem to be dysfunctional for its development: scientific organization seems to be inadequate for its needs of growth. For several reasons the character of a science itself helps to sustain this gerontocratic tendency.

First, the important role of learning, of the social transmission of knowledge, inevitably divides the scientific community into teachers and pupils. The process of individual socialization in science is prolonged: the initiate must acquire more information and technical skills. The democratization of higher studies intensifies the process: the rhythm of teaching is determined by the abilities of the average student. In such circumstances the roles of teachers are performed by scientists of older generations. There are, however, facts working against this tendency: the growing co-operation of older and younger scientists in teams and the explosion of new disciplines and specialities.[4]

Second, as is often noted, the greatest input in science is that made by young generations: in contrast with the distribution of the prestige inside the scientific community. The latter is due to the long period necessary for recognition. It is also the bureaucratization of all social life, science included, which plays an important role. A. K. Davis has put it: 'Since social status and office are everywhere partly distributed on the basis of age, personality development is intimately linked with the network of social position successively occupied during life' (Davis, 1940).

Third, social relations inside the system of the production of science are very often based on a hierarchical structure with great distances between individuals occupying different status-positions. Those positions are available not only according to the scientific success (meaning the role played in the development of a discipline) but also to other factors, among which the category of age is of great importance. Ways of individual promotion are inherently connected with that system of organization—as in the hospital structure, where:

> Such a hierarchial pattern provides an exceedingly large number of steps for the new member of the profession. His progress through them symbolizes achievement in his personal career. For the administrator the hospital is a finely articulated status structure; the various positions represent a wide range of rewards to be conferred on the doctors attached to the hospital. (Hall, 1948)

An individual career depends upon the system of organization, but successful adaptation, achieving higher and higher steps, mainly depends upon the opinions of other scientists—especially those who hold the highest status positions. Generally they are older. In that social order of science the older generation seems then to play the role of executing the knowledge of the younger one. Such a situation is due to the assumption of the unity of scientific knowledge and of the intellectual omnipotency of the older generation.

All these facts support that self-fulfilling prophecy in the domain of science, criticized by Zuckerman and Merton (1972).[5]

*Historical Concept of Generation*

The historical concept of generation does not depend upon the assumption of their continuation and repetition, nor that of genealogy. Its attention is rather focused on change and discontinuity, on 'gaps' and conflicts between generations. The recognition of some regularities in psychological development of the individual does not necessarily lead to the definition of a generation according to the laws of developmental psychology, assuming the unity of human nature, or according to the 'iron laws' of vertical mobility. In the historical concept of generation that which is most important is its cultural specificity and uniqueness. The latter are dependent upon the historical events accompanying the experiences of primary socialization, the period of adolescence, and the beginnings of adult life. They create similar cognitive orientations, similar sensibilities, and a similar way of reacting. H. Peyré (1948) described the literary generation as follows:

> They studied the same schoolbooks, they acquired the same academic philosophical notions, as well as those of physics and history; they learnt by heart the same 'chosen texts'; they experienced the same political events; they secretly liked the

same actresses; they adored the same singers and the same champions; they visited the same coffee-bars; their eyes liked the same colours and they preferred the same pictures; together they discovered Wagner or Ravel.[6]

The measure of time here is relativistic, dependent upon the 'rhythm' of a given epoch. We can analyse it on different levels: that of a culture, of a science, of a discipline, of a speciality. The identification of any generation in science depends upon the generality of a given perspective; hence we can speak about sociocultural generations in science (for example, the rationalist one); about scientific generations (for example, the neopositivistic one); about generations within a discipline (for example, the generation of the quantum theory); or about one inside a school or theory (for example, the revisionist generation in the theory of evolution). Empirical research can show the interdependence of the generation within a theory, the scientific generation, and the socio-cultural one.

It is interesting to see how much the state of any theory (or more generally—of a paradigm) determines the character of an entering generation. According to Kuhn's version of the history of science we can speak about the succession of generations to successive paradigms. But we can also observe the succession of generations within a paradigm as the author identifies three main phases in the development of any paradigm: its beginning, its normal state, and its decline. The rhythm of the development of a paradigm, including crisis and normalization, 'creates' generations of 'revolutionaries' and 'believers', differentiated between themselves by their attitudes towards the theory and empirical base; by the character of problems interesting to them; by the criteria of judgement of individual scientific output and of innovativeness. In normal science scientists are concerned especially with facts and are orientated towards elaboration of the existing paradigm with further empirical data. The consistency of experimental results with those expected on the basis of theory determines how a researcher will be judged. His qualifications; his knowledge of the theory; his skills to operationalize it; his familiarity with methods and techniques, are the decisive factors. Research training is treated a bit as the transmission of secret knowledge. It is different in situations of crisis. Individuals who as young scientists confront this phase of the development of a paradigm, experience quite different standards of scientific activity. As it is a period of intensive and searching enquiry, attention is now paid to those facts, which are not 'natural' in the light of existing theory. Originality and nonconformity are the most valuable attributes of an individual—they permit him to be sceptical towards the paradigmatic *status quo* and to formulate new theoretical interpretations. It is no longer confirmation of theory which is the source of success, but rather the discovery of a new theoretical key explaining anomalies. Skills acquired in academic training and in a long research career can be useless or even dysfunctional for invention. The scientific generation so conceived is determined by the 'logic' and the 'tempo' of a paradigm: the 'revolutionary' generation is more innovative than the biologically younger generation of 'believers'. But that 'paradigmatic determinism', in spite of its usefulness, is not adequate for the sociology of science because it assumes the autonomous development of a paradigm. It *is* useful in the analysis of scientific revolutions, but is too narrow to cope with 'everyday science' because of its integration around specialities and schools rather than on the fundamentals of a given paradigm. Mulkay's research has shown, that in some circumstances the dynamics of a generation influence the tempo of the development of a paradigm (Mulkay, 1974).

There are some suggestions in Kuhn's own work which permit us to lessen the force of that 'paradigmatic determinism', in dealing with the problem of generation in science. Kuhn shows, for example, that the most successful ideas in creating a new paradigm are those formulated by 'newcomers': beginners in scientific work or those who have already some experience in the job, but from different fields. Thus it is 'relative youth' which is decisive for innovation. There are two aspects of this youthfulness which seem to be most important: the 'ignorance' combined with non-stereotypical thinking; and the contact with modernity. The lack of specialization so characteristic of newcomers means not only the lack of routine, but also greater universality of cognitive structure and more general knowledge. The initiate before making his choice of specialization is *au courant* with actual discoveries over a wide area in the discipline and often in other disciplines besides. The modern universities often employ scientists belonging to different scientific traditions and orientations, and this as well as the practice of publishing anthologies including discussions and comment make informed choice possible. We can say that, at any given time, different paradigms and different specialities are in competition for the approval of young people. The 'result' determines the influx of new researchers, and so also does the growth of 'turnover potential' of a speciality which in turn makes its development more rapid, and determines its entry to the normal state and its ultimate decline. So the strategies of the generations can influence the mechanisms of the development of paradigms either as stimuli or as obstacles.

The same fact is evident in the case of individuals who are mobile, changing specializations during their life. So Mulkay has reason to criticize Kuhn's model in that it does not include the fact of migration of individuals:

> Such processes of redefinition, although they occur in science, as Kuhn has shown, are far from being the predominant pattern of innovation. Thus many instances of scientific innovation are marked not by arduous intellectual redefinition but by intellectual migration followed by the modified application of existing techniques and theories within a different area. (Mulkay, 1972, p. 34)

Research activity in the humanities does not demand so deep a specialization as in the natural sciences, which fact has important consequences for the specificity of processes in generations. The individual need not make those choices which limit him to narrow specialization. That is why, especially in the domain of the social sciences, we can observe periods of very intense tendency to integration, when the common language of a generation devalues some traditions and brings together the different experiences of diverse and distinct schools. New aspirations and standards, common to the new generation, differentiate them strongly from their scientific ancestors. For example, neopositivism as an ideology and as a methodology has cut across all orientations within humanities: modern representatives of functionalism and of evolutionism have much more in common among themselves than with their predecessors within their theoretical traditions. The agreement of most sociologists (and of Kuhn himself) about multiparadigmatic disciplines permits one to demonstrate a source for the development of theory other than the growth of empirical knowledge: namely, the permanent dialogue between competing theories. It is especially evident in multiparadigmatic disciplines for the reason that generations representing different cognitive structures and even different cultural orientations are of a greater importance than in natural sciences. As Stehr (1973) concludes: 'It seems that one can tentatively assert that generational cognitive orientations and age as its structural complement assume significance at the point of transition from one cognitive perspective to another within a mature discipline and may be of continuous importance within multi-paradigm disciplines such as the social sciences.'

But the creation of new hypotheses and the crystallization of new interests in science, which are critical for the future direction (development) of science are not only the effect of the internal 'logic of discovery', nor only dependent on the actual state of knowledge. The remark of Zuckerman and Merton (1972), made in the context of their polemic with Kuhn, seems worthy of further study:

> Sociological interpretations of extra-theoretical influences upon the selection of problems for investigation in a science include more than its norms and institutional structure. They also include exogenous influences upon the foci of research adopted by scientists that come from the environing society, culture, economy, and polity: influences of a kind put so much in evidence these days in the heavily publicized form of changing priorities in the allocation of resources to the various sciences and to problem-areas within them as to become apparent even to the most cloistered of scientists.

These remarks are of great importance for our concept of the generation in science as they show the role played by the organizational criterion for its identification. Scientific work means not only intellectual activity but represents also, at the same time, a profession, a source of income. So actual science policy (the character of organization, the making and teaching of science in a given country) determines the differing chances of scientific employment available to different generations and influences the prevalence in each of career strategies and preferred models of the scientific career. Among such policy decisions important for the functioning of the scientific market we can include decisions changing distribution of money for research between disciplines and specialities, creating and reorganizing scientific institutes, etc. These can directly influence intellectual migration in science, which is not neutral for the development of paradigms and theories as Mulkay has shown. These conclusions show how much the organizational and cognitive problems of science are intimately connected—a fact underestimated by most authors in the sociology of science concerned with either its organizational or philosophical problems. We wish to include both of these aspects in our studies of individual careers, so we agree with Blume, when he writes:

> It is all too easy to underestimate the relevance, on the one hand, of socioeconomic

factors for development of new scientific disciplines, and, on the other, of intellectual factors for development of new professions.... A new disciplinary identity may have few implications outside the relevant area of science and external significance—though it may stimulate emergence of this identity—is no criterion of maturity. A scientific profession, on the other hand ..., is formed more directly by market forces emanating from the world-at-large, indeed, large-scale employment may provide the major stimulus to emergence of professional identity. (Blume, 1974, p. 116)

**The Scientific Career: a Scheme for Research**

Information on the effects of the functioning of the scientific market on individual biographies might be obtained with the aid of a sociological questionnaire which is being prepared. We would wish to obtain such information not only for the present scientific workers, but also for persons rejected through the mechanisms of selection at various stages. Information sought is mainly of an objective kind, the questions on attitudes concerning only: (1) the evaluation by the scientist of several aspects of scientific work; (2) his evaluation of his own career; (3) his assessment of the greatest achievements of his own discipline and of its scientific institutions. The schema of the individual career will be based on the following categories of information:

(1) Ascribed characteristics, for instance personal biography until the moment of the entry into the scientific market, for example:

(a) Age (and membership of a specific cohort);
(b) Family background—socio-economic status of parents and family; cultural status of parents: their education, profession; history and structure of the family. We would like to distinguish several kinds of interpretations of individual scientific careers: scientific job as social promotion, as continuation of family tradition, as compensation for family frustration and as a form of its adaptation to new socio-political conditions.
(c) Sex. This category seems to play a less important role in Poland than in Western countries.
(d) The nature of completed schooling and its location (metropolis, big town, little town, village, etc.). Primary hypothesis suggests that together with family background the character of secondary schooling plays a decisive role in the success or failure of the individual on the scientific market. Where the family seems to play an important role is in creating motivations and ambitions towards scientific work; schools seem to be the decisive instance of the intellectual preparation of a young man for higher and post-graduate studies.

(2) The second category of data is indicative of the tempo of a scientist's accomplishments.

(a) Institutional criteria—dates of receiving scientific degrees: *magister* (M.A.), *doktór* (Ph.D.), *doktór habilitowany*.
(b) Organizational criteria—dates of achieving positions in organizational struc-

ture of science: *asystent* (assistant), *starszy asystent* (higher assistant), *adiunkt docent* (lecturer), *professor* (the title of 'professor' is by nomination by the Polish government), and dates of achieving leading positions: leader of research group, head of department, director of institute, etc.

Crane and Mullins showed that the moment of achieving autonomy and independence is of special importance for intellectual development. We will seek to test this hypothesis in relation to the Polish situation. Taking advancement in the organizational hierarchy as the only indicator of an individual's success is common among Western authors. As Patterson (1971) states for example: 'Career advancement is measured by such organizational rewards as departmental affiliation and rank in the department, organizational variables that indicate the regard the organization has for the individual and that influence treatment of him in such areas of his daily work as teaching assignments.'

We propose to treat these organizational rewards as only one of several dimensions of a scientific career. The analysis of their allocation will be of importance to us not only to evaluate individual success or failure, but also as a measure for evaluating the efficacy of our organizational system of science. The main purpose of this organizational system is to encourage and help those scientists who influence the advancement of science the most.

(c) 'Essential career' relates to scientific productivity and to the prestige of scientists. The data we could wish to obtain include information about: number and character of publications (books, articles, review); the prestige of the publisher or the scientific journal (noting important publications in foreign countries), and number of editions, etc.; a graph of publications over time; number of citations in the basic journals of the discipline and the number of book reviews; the evaluation of scientific productivity by colleagues (perhaps only of the more eminent scientists). We would prefer to avoid the problem of estimating the creative potential of a scientist, agreeing with Kubie, who shows that all tests are based mainly on easily recognizable positive achievements, which can be quickly identified. In practice the individual contribution to a discipline's development may be of many different kinds: sometimes important and indirect at the same time.

(d) Other scientific activities and power include: membership in scientific associations (national and international) and functions held in them; membership in the editorial bodies of scientific journals and publishers; the number of collaborators (in the case of leading positions); the number of undergraduate and post-graduate students preparing their M.A. and Ph.D. theses under his guidance; participation in conferences and scientific meetings and lectures in other centres (Poland, socialist countries, Third World, capitalist countries); participation in the informal distribution of scientific information (exchange of papers, approximate number of Polish colleagues and foreigners); popularizing activities. Some of these are crucial to individual power on the scientific market (for example, membership on editorial boards or promotorship). Others are important for achieving privileges or as privileges themselves (for example, membership and crucial positions in scientific associations; participation in international meetings and membership in informal groups). They are also important in so far as they facilitate access to scientific information, which is crucial for purely scientific activity. Each of them, popularizing activity included, serves as a factor of individual visibility, which in turn influences the scientific career.

In our final analysis we hope to show the dialectic links between all the aspects of scientific careers, where each can play a role in gaining personal power, visibility or prestige, access to scientific information, or other help in scientific activity or even of scientific or more general privilege—and in many possible ways influence other aspects or dimensions of that career. At the same time it would be of special interest to observe all the divergencies between self-rewarding activities and the institutional–organizational rewards already mentioned. We would like to analyse especially those cases where there is a discrepancy between 'essential career' and 'organizational advancement', and also—if this proves possible—to trace what kind of scientific activity helps in career advancement as well as serves in reality as a façade for intellectual inertia.

(3) The third main category of information we intend to collect relates to the scientist's achievements and career *outside* the scientific market, as, for example:

(a) The standard of living and the style of life of the scientist and his family.
(b) The 'external' career—for example, in the political scene as expert or diplomat.

Usually the category of individual biography or career is not treated by sociologists as a dynamic concept. The stress is upon the individual's adaptation to, conformation with, the external conditions. It is implicitly assumed that there is only one possible form of success in it, and moreover that the process of individual adaptation is of a repetitive and timeless character. Thus Hall defines the medical career as 'a set of more or less successful adjustments to these [meaning medical] institutions and to the formal and informal organizations' (Hall, 1948, p. 327).

It is to be noted that he speaks of 'a set' and not about 'a series'. We would prefer to treat the individual career as the resultant of *continuing* efforts of adjustment to *changing* institutional–organizational conditions and to *changing* informal relations inside the professional group on the one hand, and of the individual's *strategy* in scientific work on the other hand. These continuing efforts can be observed by their external correlatives, including both the crucial and the less important choices constitutive of a career strategy. Each such choice is determined by the 'environmental pressures' as well as by the individual's desires and by his evaluation of his personal chances. This evaluation is a result of his potential abilities to be successful (his professional skill, status position, degree of participation in the formal scientific community, etc.); but also of his previous experiences, his satisfactions, and his past frustrations. Such a view identifies the individual's career with the effects of his personal strategy and does not assume a unilinear development. On the contrary, it insists on its dynamics, considering the possibilities of a change of utilized methods and also all modifications of personal aims, reorientations of value-structures and motivations. The process of adaptation is not wholly conscious: it concerns the sphere of external behaviour of the scientist as well as its inner characteristics. We hope that the analysis of such individual choices will permit us to typologize them, and thence to evaluate the effects of the changing scientific market by comparison of the extent to which different types of careers occur within different generations. We can present the form of such an analysis by indicating what we consider to be the crucial choices inherent in the scientific career, notably discipline, institution, and sponsors.

(1) The choice of the discipline (speciality, school) determines not only the general character of work (theoretical or in a laboratory, etc.), but also the possibilities for individual contributions to the science. Most important for 'essential' career, and also for the organizational promotion of the scientist, are—as it seems—the following attributes of the discipline chosen:

(a) Theoretical versus empirical, pure versus applied. We are aware of the difficulties in distinguishing empirically these kinds of scientific activity. But in spite of several objections it seems to us that the traditional distinction has not wholly lost its value. In some disciplines, especially those in which 'empirical' means 'experimental', the identification of each kind of scientific work does not seem so difficult—there are organizational factors which reinforce the distinction, as, for example, the particular nature of laboratory work contrasting with the relatively free work in 'academic' science. The consequences of the choice between those two kinds of disciplines seem to be as follows:

(i) In the field of prestige. Theoreticians seem to have generally higher prestige. As Gaston (1970) has shown, team work in a big laboratory is often virtually anonymous.
(ii) In the sphere of the dependency of an individual upon such organizational factors as availability of machines, resources, and collaborators. It is trivial but still worth noting, that a big laboratory has an effect upon the regularity of working habits, and requires co-ordination and planning.
(iii) In the sphere of satisfying personal professional ambitions. The possibilities of being 'a star' in science seem to be much greater in the theoretical fields—not only because of the more universal character of theoretical knowledge and the greater prestige of theoreticians in general, but thanks to the 'democratization' of science which often follows from the collective and hierarchical character predominating in organizations concerned with research on practical problems.

Despite the several processes in the organization of science, 'public science' still seems to remain characteristic of 'applied sciences', which are different from the 'private science' of theoreticians. As Weinberg shows, the interdisciplinary team is not a social characteristic of the basic sciences, as the problems the scientists try to resolve are usually internally generated (that is, they are derived from the 'internal logic' of the specific field), so 'basic science' is pursued within relatively narrow disciplines (Weinberg, 1970). It seems that some disciplines, because of their nature, cannot be pursued by team researchers, as for example mathematics. Even if these assumptions (which accord with the impressions of the majority of modern scientists) are not true, we hope to test them in an empirical way.

The general influence of team work upon the activities of a scientist will be of great interest to us. Is the inspiration by others, the rewarding and controlling role of the 'micro-environment', the collegiate fellowship, of greater importance for individuals than the 'alienation' which might typify collaborative team work? (We refer here both to the way in which division of labour may render impossible an appreciation of the whole enterprise in cognitive terms, as well as to the need to subordinate individual personal and professional preferences.) It would be interesting to compare the scientific activities of scientists belonging to different teams to know if they function differently in different disciplines or if there are accidental factors, as the personality of the group leaders, which are of decisive importance.

(b) Disciplines requiring a long initiation process versus disciplines with a rapid initiation. It is obvious that in some disciplines the period of education and of waiting for eventual rewards is extremely long. All disciplines based on learned skills belong to that category. Commonly it is medicine which is taken as an example. Hall speaks of a system of 'prolonged apprenticeship' in medicine and of 'long delays before being rewarded'. The research done by Manniche and Falk (1957) on the age of the Nobel Prize winners shows the great differences between physicists, chemists, and medical scientists in this respect. Authors try to explain them in two ways: by referring to the actual state of the organization of knowledge in each discipline under investigation, and by referring to the differences in their social organization.

(c) 'Autonomous' versus 'borrowing' disciplines. The qualification of a discipline as 'autonomous' or 'borrowing' has two aspects. First, the 'autonomy' of a discipline depends upon its present state of development. In each historical moment we find 'leading' disciplines, and disciplines following them. Science seems to provide a particular example of the general law formulated in anthropology: that of the descent of cultural elements. Becoming a scientist in the leading discipline gives more opportunities to be creative, to be a 'real' discoverer, but it requires greater innovational potential. Choice of a 'borrowing' discipline implies choice of the work of 'translator', of 'adapter' of categories, of theoretical systems and of methods elaborated in other sciences: it implies scientific work based on synthesis. The process of adoption of a waning paradigm by another discipline is presented by Keesing in his article 'Paradigm lost: the new ethnography and the new linguistics'.

The other aspect of my distinction between 'autonomous' and 'borrowing' disciplines has a national dimension. Sociologists seem not to interest themselves in the problem of 'aristocracy' and 'proletariat' within the world's disciplinary communities. They are mainly concerned with the prestige of concrete institutes. Speaking of 'proletarians' we mean those scientific workers who work in the background, without an effective tradition and in institutes without modern equipment. They are condemned for imitating patterns elaborated by their colleagues from other institutes, from other countries; with a consciousness of backwardness. This is frequently the situation of scientists from underdeveloped nations.

(d) 'Traditional' versus 'new' disciplines, specialities or theories. The choice of a traditional discipline contains the risk of a general competence and widespread competition, but on the other hand these disciplines (as Anne Roe has shown) offer more 'visible' rewards. The choice of a new discipline offers very often not only greater freedom in research, but also the need to struggle for the institutionalization of that discipline, for acceptance of it by the scientific community, and for organizational opportunities. Moreover the enthusiasts of a new discipline usually confront an overt social conflict in their institution before the process of differentiation takes place (see Hagstrom, 1965, pp. 222–226).

Perhaps of the greater importance is the choice of the field of research (speciality, theory, school). Here we enter into the problem of 'paradigm'. Apart from all the discussions of Kuhn's theory we can discover in each speciality 'creative epochs' and those of 'decadence'. The choice of a new, developing field gives greater opportunity for freedom in individual work, as also for originality. The scientist's situation seems here quite similar to that obtaining in the arts. In that field of human activity we also find different 'lines of development' and individual strategies within them: 'When one line of development appears to be exhausted, new ground must be broken in some entirely different direction. Wagner felt that Beethoven had carried his type of symphony as far as it could go, so decided to develop a new form—the music drama' (Faris, 1940). Very similarly Holton (1960) speaks about the mechanism of the development of science as about 'escalation of knowledge' and Mulkay about 'the exploration of new fields of ignorance'. We can look at these general phenomena not only from a 'macroscience' point of view, but also as at the scientist's search for intellectual independency, personal prestige or opportunity for personal career.

We have at our disposal the recollections of several eminent scientists who have touched on this problem. For example, Wilson, winner of a Nobel Prize:

> I was in the best of all possible positions for a student—I have a good problem, had fallen heir to a wealth of experimental equipment, and was entirely on my own. . . . I have studied enough by then to know, that the fundamental problems of gaseous discharge were essentially solved. I wanted to move on to what I regarded as being the basic problem of physics, the nucleus of the atom, which was then virtually unexplored. (Wilson, 1970)

Compare with another, less successful physicist:

> It was easier to do things in the old days because quantum theory was much newer—all virgin soil. Now it's terribly involved and complex and broad and diffuse. (Cited from Roe, 1965)

A biologist:

> I think it's very probable that all of the aspects of what we now call molecular biology will be found out in 25 years and that so much will be found out in 10 that what's left won't be so interesting, so I may have to turn to still some other field. (Cited from Roe, 1965)

It seems that the choice of a completely new research field, one not yet organized and structured, gives in modern times the greatest opportunity for creativity. The power of the modern laboratories gives rise to a much more rapid development of disciplines and exploitation of new ideas. Weinberg (1970), in describing the history of Neil Bartelett's hypothesis, concludes: 'A field that in earlier times would have remained fertile and exciting for a decade or more, was largely elucidated in little more than one year's time.

Diana Crane showed that productive scientists are those most sensitive to the potentialities for growth in a given field in making their selection of research projects. According to her the proportion of productive scientists sharply diminishes with the development of a field under study (see Crane, 1969). Similarly, but on the level of different disciplines, Manniche and Falk (1957) indicate the 'differences in the personalities (including intelligence and work habits) of the persons attracted and recruited into the various fields at different times' and thereby try to explain the phenomenon of differences in age of Nobel Prize winners from different disciplines.

(e) 'Cumulative' versus 'noncumulative' fields. It seems to us that in each discipline we can find cumulative mechanisms. It would be interesting to study the existing kinds of cumulation of knowledge within some of the disciplines and their influence upon courses of personal careers, though we are not sufficiently prepared to explore this topic yet. We wish only to mention Wigner's conception as an example of the approach we have in mind. He shows the mechanisms of the development of relativistic quantum theory and of fundamental research in physics, which takes place by 'deepening' the existing body of theoretical knowledge by replacing existing concepts by more refined ones. That kind of development requires a much more elaborate and detached study. And each time the results are much less of an event that the discovery of the theory of relativity itself. Wigner (1950) concludes that: 'It is not difficult to imagine a stage in which the new student will no longer be interested to dig through the already accumulated layers in order to do research at all frontiers.' The author anticipates 'the shift of the second type'—the appearance of a new discipline which will not embrace physics in the way that, for instance, quantum theory embraces classical physics.

Other choices, which are not directly connected with the structure of scientific knowledge, but which are important for a personal career and therefore relevant here, are as follows:

(2) The choice of scientific institution is important for the well known reason that the institutions have different statuses and different intellectual atmospheres: not only because of the problem of 'visibility', but also for other reasons, such as the type of work in which they tend to engage, etc. It is trivial to say that they give different opportunities for a future career. We will be especially interested in organizational subsystem, locality, and status of the universities attended by a respondent, his institution of first employment, and his present place of employment. (It will be important to preface this aspect of our investigations of careers

by a study of the 'sociometry' of institutions (see e.g. Crane, 1970).)

(3) The choice of sponsors and the type of collaboration with them (active or passive) can show a tendency towards scientific inspiration and help on the one hand, as well as towards 'visibility', prestige, and organizational opportunities on the other. Information about joint research, publications, and rewards of a respondent—and his M.A. director, Ph.D. director, his boss—will be of special interest for us. Naturally we must know, just as in the case of institutions, the scientific and organizational power of those sponsors. Merton's well known hypothesis of the Matthew effect generated a good deal of empirical work. We would hope to examine this by reference both to individuals and to institutions (Merton, 1968; Cole, 1970; Crane, 1969, 1965).

Here we may indicate that Polish empirical research on this problem (Cichomski, 1976) has shown a significant correlation between the prestige of Ph.D. directors and their style of collaboration with post-graduate students, and with the scientific value of Ph.D. theses prepared under their guidance.

(4) The tendency towards acquiring qualifications that are not strictly professional, such as studies undertaken in fields other than that of principal specialization, or learning of foreign languages, belong to the category of important choices because some skills can be of great utility in the scientific development of an individual. Some can help in obtaining different privileges whereas others may play a compensative role.

(5) We are also inclined to subsume under the category of personal strategies the frequency and intensity of the personal relations of a scientist with his professional colleagues. Likewise we wish to observe to what extent these relations help in scientific work (for example, as 'channels' in the system of informal information about actual studies and actual tendencies on the scientific market) and in what measure they help in the organizational career (invisible sponsors, solidarity of fellows, etc.).[7]

(6) The choice of administrative/organizational activities, which are usually in conflict with one's own research, can be an indicator of the tendency towards power and other organizational rewards sometimes dominating purely scientific ambitions.

(7) Finally, choices outside of science which can influence the course of a career can be of different kinds. To us the most important seem to be those connected with participation in political life (belonging to the Party, being a Party-activist, etc.), participation in public life (so-called 'social work' in Poland—activities in social organizations, in local neighbourhoods, etc.), and the familial situation (the profession and income of wife or husband, and the number of children seem to be of the greatest importance for a career).

These very different kinds of choice depict in each particular case an aspect of a specific career pattern. Here we should like to propose a preliminary version of a typology of individual careers in science, based on the following criteria:

(1) Continuity and change in the scientific biography and their influence on success. We want to observe in what circumstances continuity (or change) of the

(a) discipline (specialization), of the (b) institution of employment, of the (c) sponsor and collaborators, as well as in kind of scientific activity, helps one to be successful in the Polish academic market and to what extent it restricts the possibilities of advancement or growth in the 'essential career'.[8]

(2) The dominant motivation (value-orientation) in the course of a career. We want also to look for evolution of dominant motivations in the course of a career. The types of motivation especially interesting to us are the following: (a) the 'autotelic' motivation, which means the orientation towards satisfaction from creativity itself; (b) the wish to make an individual contribution to science and to be recognized by professional colleagues; (c) the narrowly professional attitude treating employment in the scientific institution as a means of stabilization (salaries, medical insurance, etc.); (d) the search for power, wealth, and social prestige (especially important in Poland, where the professor has a high position in the hierarchy of professional statuses); and (e) the motivation that considers scientific work as a prelude to some other kind of career. The last two motivations are similar in that they are faces of more a general orientation towards values external to the system of science.

We want to discover the dominating individual motivations and their changes by analysing the behaviour of the scientist and the type of rewards he acquires. This would not be done through direct questioning. The answers to such questions are very often neither spontaneous nor frank: frequently they have a compensative character and, as such, create confusion. For example, Pellegrin and Coates (1957) defined the primary purpose of their study as follows: 'to demonstrate that attributes and values which find expression in verbalized definitions of success disclose levels of aspiration which, in turn, affect a person's behaviour on the job, and function as a determinant of his career pattern'. But our general scepticism towards such an approach gives rise to the question: Are the responses of those being questioned really indicators of their past and present motivations or—and to us this seems more probable—are they simply indicators of self-defence or of personal mystification (especially in the case of supervisors who have not succeeded)?

We hope to find an opportunity to trace individual reactions to their successes and defeats: the mechanisms of reinforcement and enlargement of motivations as well as their reduction, compensation or even renouncement. Considering the temporal aspect of different kinds of rewards achieved by individuals will helps us to evaluate the strengths of different motivations of personal patience and of willingness to accept disappointment in one's work.

(3) We can elucidate not only the *kind* of rewards towards which scientists can be orientated. Let us assume that the tendency to be recognized is characteristic of each scientist at least at one moment of his career.[9] We can try to classify scientists according to the scope of the intellectual milieu from which they expect to receive recognition. The two main categories of scientists based on this criterion are 'cosmopolitans' and 'locals'. But this 'scientific milieu of reference' can vary in time. In some cases one can observe a continuing enlargement of the milieu; growing expectation of recognition both from the local community of colleagues

and from the national and international scientific community. In other cases—on the contrary—a scientist in reacting to his personal failure on the larger scale may restrict his 'scientific milieu of reference'. In cases like this, narrowing the scope of expectations and looking for recognition from the local community is of a compensative character. (Only in exceptional cases does looking for the rewards on the international scene follow upon personal failure in the nearest, local scientific milieu (see Gouldner, 1957; Glaser, 1963).)

(4) The fourth criterion of the proposed typology embodies the degree to which an individual fulfils his own aspirations and the degree to which he attains the values he believes in. We want to search for an answer by comparing all the rewards acquired by the individual with his actual preferences (known thanks to a methodological experiment) and also by analysing an individual's declared self-evaluation. Such knowledge will permit us to identify the categories of 'frustrated', 'moderately satisfied', and 'satisfied'.

On the basis of the four sets of criteria mentioned above we want to try to distinguish general types of scientific careers according to their course through time. We do not assume their 'unilinear' character; on the contrary, we want to observe their dynamics. We shall treat each of them as a process of changing patterns of adaptation as the result of changing external factors and of past experiences.[10]

(1) The vast category of 'active adapters' includes all scientists whose careers are characterized by a growing participation in the system of rewards in pure science. We can distinguish two subcategories. (a) The 'expansive career', which is the type of scientific biography that is unilinear; it is characterized by a homogeneity of motivations, activities, and of growing rewards in time. The 'expansive career' can be an attribute of the 'essential career'. In such cases it is a characteristic of those scientists who are orientated mainly towards purely scientific activities and who continually succeed in that field. Expansive career can also characterize those who are orientated towards organizational rewards and who continually advance in the hierarchy of positions. It can also be a trait of scientists orientated towards consumption as such, in which case it means a growing income and growing participation in the social division of goods. (b) 'Compensative career' is the second subcategory of 'active adapters'. It refers to a career that depends upon personal strategies of changing general value-orientations and changing kinds of acquired rewards. As it seems that the most common aspirations are towards the 'essential career' (very often realized only at the time of scientific socialization), we assume that what we will discover to be most common is the subcategory of those who abandoned their 'autotelic' motivations and the search for recognition in the scientific community, and made a reorientation towards 'organizational' or 'consumptional' rewards, or towards a career realizing both of these. But we can also discover other kinds of reorientations in the course of professional careers in the scientific community—as, for example, the changing of 'organizational' rewards for 'consumptional' ones.

(2) The second general type contains 'passive adaptation' to the scientific community. These scientists are excluded from relevant systems of distribution of power and privilege because (a) their scientific activities have a value, but they are

restricted to minimum levels of activity by organizational exigencies, or (b) they remain in the scientific institute for reasons other than intellectual activity.

(3) Finally we have the category of 'refugees': those who have left science as a profession. Here we can distinguish a category of those who experienced a degradation and those for whom scientific work led to another type of career (a diplomatic career, for example).

## Acknowledgements

An earlier version of this chapter was presented at a seminar of the Sociology of Science Study Group, British Sociological Association. I should like to thank Dr S. S. Blume for his help, and Dr R. Fafara for help with its translation into English.

## Notes

1. The approach presented here is similar to that of Theodore Caplow and Reece McGee, but whereas these authors focus specifically upon the university, I intend to consider the research career as it may develop in a variety of research settings. See Caplow and McGee, 1960; also Williams *et al.*, 1974; Freeman, 1971.
2. Eisenstadt (1966) treats the category of generation similarly:

    > It becomes understandable from the foregoing that age definitions and differentiation are of great importance both to the social system and to the individual personality. For the social system it serves as a category according to which various roles are allocated to various people; for the individual, the awareness of his own age becomes an important integrative element, through its influence on his self-identification. The categorization of oneself as a member of a given age stage serves as an important basis for one's self-perception and role expectations towards others.

3. From among a substantial literature on this, we may note: Carlsson and Karlsson, 1970; Roe, 1961; Zuckerman and Merton, 1972.
4. On the subject of co-operation in science and its significance for the individual, see especially: Bush and Hattery, 1956; Weinberg, 1970; Wilson, 1970; Zuckerman, 1967.
5. It is unfortunate that this, the most substantial discussion of the theme of the present paper, deals only with the absolute category of age in science, and does not relate it to changing conditions of the scientific market or to the cognitive structure of disciplines. In view of the importance which we attach to the problem of generation viewed historically, and of its neglect in recent sociological work, we have enlarged disproportionately the section of this paper treating this problem.
6. It is not coincidental that reference here is to an historian of literature. The historical notion of a generation has emerged mainly in that field, also in political studies and more recently in demography. It is somewhat paradoxical that the theme treated in Karl Mannheim's classic essay on generations in his *Sociology of Knowledge* has been taken up more in other disciplines. Other classical treatments are those of Dilthey, Pinder, and Ortega y Gasset. Among more recent sociological studies see especially Ryder, 1959, 1965.
7. The notion of 'invisible colleges' has been applied to consideration of the process of scientific development, and can be of use here in examination of the essential career (see Ziman, 1968; Crane, 1972). But we wish also to examine the influence of the intensity of an individual scientist's informal relations with scientific colleagues upon his organizational promotion.

8. Since in Poland employment contracts are generally of unlimited duration, this largely depends upon individual choice.
9. On the notion of 'recognition' see especially Hagstrom, 1965, 1968.
10. Newcomb's conception of two types of orientation towards obstacles will be of use here. See Newcomb, 1950, chapter 10.

## References

Berger, B. (1960), 'How long is a generation', *British Journal of Sociology*, 11, 1.
Blume, S. S. (1974), *Toward a Political Sociology of Science*, New York, Free Press.
Bush, G., and L. H. Hattery (1956), 'Teamwork and creativity in research', *Administrative Science Quarterly*, 1, 3.
Caplow, T., and R. J. McGee (1958), *The Academic Marketplace*, New York, Basic Books.
Carlsson, G., and K. Karlsson (1970), 'Age cohorts and the generation of generations', *American Sociological Review*, 35.
Cichomski, B. (1976), *Nauka joko Instytucja Spoteczna* (*Science as a Social Institution*, in Polish), Warsaw,
Cole, S. (1970), 'Professional standing and the reception of scientific discoveries', *American Journal of Sociology*, 76.
Crane, D. (1965), 'Scientists at major and minor universities', *American Sociological Review*, 30.
Crane, D. (1969), 'Social structure in a group of scientists', *American Sociological Review*, 34.
Crane, D. (1970), 'The academic marketplace revisited', *American Journal of Sociology*, 75, 6.
Crane, D. (1972), *Invisible Colleges*, Chicago, Chicago University Press.
Davis, K. (1940), 'The sociology of parent–youth conflict', *American Sociological Review*, 5.
Dobrov, G. M. (1966), *Wstep do Naukoznawstwa* (*Introduction to a Science of Science*, Polish translation from the Russian), Warsaw.
Eisenstadt, S. N. (1966), *From Generation to Generation*, New York, London.
Faris, R. E. L. (1940), 'Sociological causes of genius', *American Sociological Review*, 5.
Fogarty, M., R. Rappoport, and R. Rappoport (1971), *Sex, Career and Family*, London, Allen and Unwin.
Freeman, R. (1971), *The Market for College Educated Manpower*, Cambridge.
Gaston, J. C. (1970), 'The reward system in British science', *American Sociological Review*, 35, 4.
Glaser, B. (1963), 'The local–cosmopolitan scientist', *American Journal of Sociology*, 69.
Gouldner, A. (1957), 'Cosmopolitans and locals', *Administrative Science Quarterly*, 2, 281–306, 444–480.
Hagstrom, W. O. (1965), *The Scientific Community*, New York, Basic Books.
Hagstrom, W. O. (1968), 'Scientists' in *International Encyclopaedia of the Social Sciences*, New York, Free Press.
Hall, O. (1948), 'The stages of a medical career', *American Journal of Sociology*, 53, 5.
Holton, G. (1960), 'Modern science and the intellectual tradition', *Science*, 131, 3408.
Leslie, G. R., and A. Richardson (1961), 'Life cycle, career pattern and the decision to move', *American Sociological Review*, 26, 6.
Manniche, E., and G. Falk (1957), 'Age and the Nobel Prize', *Behavioural Science*, 2, 4.
Marias, J. (1968), 'Generations' in *International Encyclopaedia of the Social Sciences*, New York, Free Press.
Merton, R. K. (1968), 'The Matthew effect in science', *Science*, 159.
Mulkay, M. J. (1972), *The Social Process of Innovation*, London, Macmillan.

Mulkay, M. J. (1974), 'Conceptual migration and displacement in science: a preparatory paper', *Science Studies*, **4.**
Newcomb, T. (1950), *Social Psychology*, New York, Dryden Press.
Ossowska, M. (1963), 'The concept of generation', *Polish Sociological Bulletin*, **7,** 1.
Patterson, M. (1971), 'Alice in Wonderland: a study of women faculty in graduate departments of sociology', *American Sociologist*, **6.**
Pellegrin, R. J., and C. H. Coates (1957), 'Executives are superiors: contrasting definitions of career success', *Administrative Science Quarterly*.
Peyré, H. (1948), *Les Generations littéraires*, Paris.
Renouard, Y. (1953), 'La Notion de generation en histoire', *Revue Historique*, **209.**
Roe, A. (1961), 'The psychology of the scientist', *Science*, **134.**
Roe, A. (1965), 'Changes in scientific activity with age', *Science*, **150.**
Ryder, N. B. (1959), 'On the concept of a population', *American Journal of Sociology*, **64,** 5.
Ryder, N. B. (1965), 'The cohort as a concept in the study of social change', *American Sociological Review*, **30.**
Sarapata, A. (1965), *Studie nad Structura; Ruchliwoscia Spoteczna* (*Studies on Stratification and Social Mobility in Poland*, in Polish), Warsaw.
Stehr, N. (1973), 'Generations, age groups, and the development of scientific specialities, University of Alberta, mimeo.
Stehr, N. (1974), 'Paradigmatic crystallization patterns of interrelations among areas of competence in sociology', *Social Science Information*, **13,** 1.
Weinberg, A. (1970), 'Scientific teams and scientific laboratories', *Daedelus*, Fall.
Wesolowski, W., and A. Sarapata (1961), 'Hierarchia zawodów i stanowisk' ('The hierarchy of professions and positions', in Polish), *Studia Socjologiczne*, **2.**
Wigner, E. P. (1950), 'The limits of science', *Proceedings of the American Philosophical Society*, **94.**
Wilensky, H. (1961), 'Orderly careers and social participation', *American Sociological Review*, **26,** 4.
Williams, G., T. Blackstone, and D. Metcalf (1974), *The Academic Labour Market*, Amsterdam, London, New York, Elsevier.
Wilson, R. K. (1970), 'My fight against team research', *Daedalus*, Fall.
Ziman, J. (1968), *Public Knowledge*, Cambridge, Cambridge University Press.
Zuckerman, H. (1967), 'Nobel laureates in science: patterns of productivity, collaboration and authorship', *American Sociological Review*, **32.**
Zuckerman, H., and R. K. Merton (1972), 'Age, aging and age structure in science' in M. W. Riley, M. Johnson, and A. Foner (eds), *Aging and Society*, vol. III, New York, Russel Sage Foundation.

# 4

# COMPETING PROFESSIONS AND THE PUBLIC INTEREST IN THE EUROPEAN ECONOMIC COMMUNITY: DRUGS AND THEIR QUALITY CONTROL

Louis H. Orzack

Within the domain of a particular nation, acts in the context of work are performed by persons with occupational or professional designations and titles. The acts may be quite general at one extreme or highly specialized at another. In the former case, the persons performing them come from a variety of educational and experimental backgrounds and carry them out in diverse settings, ranging from self-employment to bureaucracy, and no claim to a monopoly of control, or to restricted access, is honoured by publics to the work. In contrast, highly specialized acts entail restriction in some degree at least of the kinds of persons deemed capable or competent. This ultimately implies what Jamous and Peloille (1970) describe as the 'legitimacy of monopoly' through which persons with restricted characteristics of education, experience, and membership in specialized associations assert technical and moral superiority in the performance of those acts.

Competing claims that arise from diversities in education, in experience, in ideologies, and in associational membership often exist. Challenging and ascendent groups contest monopolistic assertions previously pre-eminent; the tendencies for further specialization, and the formation and expansion of educational empires at universities and training facilities, technological development, the entry of new economic interests and new conceptions of public obligations are among the inducing conditions. Whatever the basis for the monopoly claims, they are subject to change or redefinition, to enhancement or destruction.

Cross-national comparisons of identical or similar acts may show diversities in both the monopolistic claims accepted as legitimate and challenges to them. Interesting in themselves, these variations remain isolated from each other under most circumstances, especially if the services, products or professional specialists from each national system remain separately within their own enclaves. When circumstances of international trade and exchange, migration, and alterations in political boundaries bring those elements together, the insularity is reduced and possibly attacked.

In the immediate case of the European Economic Community or Common Market, its international authority under the terms of an intergovernmental treaty specifically includes the charge and responsibility to facilitate integration across a broad expanse of territory covering the domains of signatory states (Hallstein, 1962). Their membership in the EEC has thereby supplied the basis for a critical challenge to pre-existing professional latitudes. The mutual recognition of diplomas, the right to migrate without barriers to professional credentials, and the right to offer services on a short term basis are subjects of specific articles of the Treaty of Rome. These provisions authorize the avoidance of discrimination due to diversities in either professional systems of member nations or nationality *per se*. All these arrangements would be implemented in due course by the Common Market member states after the central legislative body, the Council of Ministers, would pass the appropriate Directives.

The objectives for the Common Market impinge upon public policy in each national system and upon existing profession—policy relationships internal to each nation. Whatever the existing patterns of legitimation or illegitimation for claims to professional monopoly in each member state, the creation of a supra-national authority to induce integration of arenas of work and of the products of those arenas in Western Europe necessitates re-examination of institutional arrangements and professional ideologies within the now larger system. As a consequence, national professional groups intensify efforts to affect policy positions expressed by their government prior to and during international negotiations. The governments themselves seek consultation with internal professional and industrial groups, or, if such is the national pattern, secure confirmation for their negotiating postures from professional groups subordinate internally to public dominance. The inclusion or exclusion of certain sciences and professions, task definition, the equivalency, length and substance of educational curricula, standards for admissibility to practice, the nature of practical training and experience, and the acceptability of those already in practice, have all become incorporated in propositions that are subjects of debates among governmental delegations of the nine member states of the EEC. Those delegations express their governments' positions on those propositions and finally, in the setting of the Council of Ministers, place themselves on record and vote as governments.

Cross-national interest groups of professionals and of scientists come into existence under these circumstances. *Groupes d'études*, liaison committees, and *groupements*, as they are variously named, are created on an international scale by national associations acting to affect public policy in the new international sphere. For each scientific and professional field across the Europe of the Common Market, existing national bodies have supported the formation of such new entities in a co-ordinated search for the consensus and for influence upon the making of those decisions by the European Economic Community which directly concern scientific and professional mechanisms. Such newly established structures now exist in a wide spectrum of liberal professions, including medicine, architecture, engineering, accountancy, nursing, opticianry (optometry), pharmacy, veterinary medicine, and dentistry.

The arenas of these committees are political, as public policy in relation to sciences and professions in each of the nine member states of the EEC, for the most part separate in genesis from one to another, now has come to affect the formation of public policy on an international scale. The international committees aim to enhance the influence of scientific and professional bodies within national political boundaries, to strengthen the specialists' efforts to affect their own governments' actions, to co-ordinate from one nation to another the efforts and strategies undertaken by these national bodies, and finally to create a single conduit whereby each scientific and professional field can responsibly interact with administrative and staff units of the European Economic Community. In a number of instances, a centralized staff has been established, mainly in Brussels, the location of the Common Market's Council and Commission; in others, a rotation principle carries the central responsibility sequentially from one national association to another.

This paper attempts to examine in specific terms the effects of and responses to a supra-national tendency, a move towards harmonization, upon a situation in which a particular task, entailing a high degree of social responsibility and trust, has traditionally been the task of different professions and sciences in various national contexts. The task in question is a set of acts performed in factories that produce pharmaceutical drugs or medicaments for use on patients by professionals. These drugs are a vital part of modern health care, of vast importance to patients and to society. To assure that the drugs produced conform in fact to standards of quality required by public health authorities, each member nation in Western Europe has usually stipulated that some person in each producing enterprise must assume individual responsibility for the quality of the drugs produced. Conformity to national and international standards must be certified by that responsible person. Scientific chemists, medical doctors, pharmacists, and others can be found in those roles in the nine member states of the European Economic Community. As a result, the commitment to integration on an international scale has drastically affected the patterns of dominance for this role in these nations. Sciences, professions, and governments have had to respond to these imperatives through complex efforts to be reviewed below.

**Health Care and Drugs**

Rising health expectations related to treatment and to prevention have become a part of the culture of modern life which challenges the long-standing acceptance of disease and death as inevitable. A key part of the arrangements for the provision of health care concerns the use of highly specialized, scientifically tested, and rigorously manufactured medications appropriate for particular maladies. Such use of drugs extends beyond human beings to include pets, food animals, marine organisms, and wild animals which can carry diseases threatening both to humans and to their food supply. Specialists such as medical doctors and veterinarians directly or through ancillaries and other health workers evaluate the conditions deleterious to health, and prescribe medications considered appropriate to the programme of treatment or prevention. Subsequent to these initial steps, the health specialist or auxiliary either directly administers the medication or relies upon the patient or others responsible for patient care to administer the medication.

The choice of which medications are appropriate in a given situation rests with the health specialist whose knowledge, derived from education and experience, provides the base. Extensive scientific and technological experimentation as well as medical, biochemical, pharmacological, and veterinarian research precede the stages at which medications become available for public use. Field and laboratory testing by initiators of medications commonly occur: engineering and industrial considerations come into play to aid the determination of whether laboratory processes of fabrication can be effectively duplicated on the more massive scales of factory production.

The quality of drugs produced may be evaluated either at the point of manufacture or of distribution by scientific, technical, and industrial specialists for the purpose of ensuring that the medications conform to local, national or international standards, such as those of the *European Pharmacopoeia*. Manufacturers employ specialists to supervise production and to carry out the assessment of quality of drugs produced in order to ensure conformity to those standards, thereby assuring the public health officials and the professionals who utilize the products in patient care of their merits and safety. The evaluation of drugs produced can be, and often is, undertaken by public health authorities, to ensure quality, to develop and maintain restrictions on import or export of certain medications, to monitor side effects of drugs and to identify their origins, and to ensure reduction of risks from use to the lowest levels consonant with maintenance and improvement of the health of patients and of the public. Complicated processes are thereby associated with the movement of medications from laboratory to factory to professionals and health care providers and to the consuming public.

The production of medications and the monitoring of their quality during the productive processes in the factories are among the focal points of the health care systems of modern society. Appreciation of the many components of the production of these commodities leads to the following questions: Who is competent to monitor the quality of medications at the point of production? Is it a chemist? A pharmacologist? A medical doctor? A pharmacist? A veterinarian? An engineer? Which kind of scientific or professional expert is best utilized in this work? Which body of knowledge applies most appropriately to the problems of the evaluation of medications?

**National Patterns and the Common Market**

The answers to those questions are important, in as much as European health practice requires that some individual must finally assume personal responsibility for the quality of drugs produced in a factory by signing a document which attests that the drugs have been appropriately tested and do in fact conform to pharmacopoeia standards. In some instances, the person in charge of production and the person in charge of the testing of quality can be one and the same; in other instances, this is seen as a conflict of interest and the roles are separated. Practice regarding who can be the *responsible person* for the quality of drugs varies in the several member states of the European Economic Community or Common Market. Chemists, medical doctors, pharmacists, and veterinarians, as well as persons who have risen mainly through experience, merit, and seniority, are all to be found in these roles. Pharmacists appear to be in the majority of those positions in Great Britain, while chemists have similar dominance in Germany.

The various professions in the European nations of the Common Market thereby confronted a new challenge and a new threat to their particular national patterns of dominance. These arise from the Treaty of Rome which created the Common Market in 1957. That Treaty contains (1) provisions to facilitate the free flow across national borders of human beings with competence to engage in activities and, (2) provisions to facilitate the free flow of goods. Since 1957, the provisions concerning activities which may be termed professional have been discussed, reviewed and analysed by the EEC's Commission and its staff. That body has prepared Draft Directives dealing with pharmacy and with pharmaceutical products which propose improvement in the free flow of specialists and of commodities.

The threat and challenge arise in as much as the Directives which deal with the concept that a single 'qualified person' must assume responsibility for the manufacture of a pharmaceutical product specifically avoid naming any particular specialist as that person. The Directive finally approved by the EEC Council specifies four years as the length of education in theoretical and practical areas and identifies the fields of knowledge wherein the theoretical and practical education can be undertaken. Any one of the following fields of knowledge is considered to be an appropriate source or pool from which the individuals can be drawn: pharmacy, medicine, veterinary medicine, chemistry, pharmaceutical chemistry, and technology. Beyond this, the Directive lists particular scientific subjects which the individuals must have studied.

Thus, the way has been opened for the assertion of claims to competency by a variety of scientific and professional disciplines. No single field will be the pool or source from which the *responsible person* will be drawn; a number of fields can supply the *qualified person.*

To ward off what ultimately occurred, the scientific and professional bodies in the member nations of the Common Market asserted claims based on existing national practices. First, they sought to influence the policies of their own national governments. For example, the Pharmaceutical Society of Great Britain sought to persuade the officials of the United Kingdom who would be participating in the actual negotiations to argue for the position that pharmacy should be pre-eminent. Similar endeavours were undertaken by other scientific and professional societies in Great Britain and in the other member nations as well.

Second, the professional associations formed international committees or groups for the purpose of trying to arrive at within-discipline unanimity and thereafter to work jointly to influence the formation of international public policy by direct or indirect contact with the Common Market's Commission, its Council of Ministers, the Council's Committee of Permanent Representatives, and its Economic and Social Committee. National associations of scientists and of professionals also sought to exercise direct influence on their own governments.

Change in public policy at the level of an international governmental body has come to be essential for the control of administrative requirements for the flow of goods necessary for high quality health care provided by individual professions to their human or animal patients. In the Common Market, lengthy sequences of discussion and consideration by staff members of various international groups of technical experts, of hearings and conferences on economic implications, and of deliberative sessions by policy-making groups occur as the existing public policies become clarified.

During these various stages, groups or committees of scientists and professions drawn from the national scientific and professional associations in the Common Market's individual member nations were formed, in large measure as the result of awareness of the significance of the impending decision by the Council of Ministers and with the aim of trying to influence that decision. Further, these international consortia provided forums whereby representatives from the various countries sought to modify the positions taken by representatives of associations of the other nations and to develop concerted strategies whereby they could influence the policies of their own national governments in anticipation of the future international negotiations.

A complex set of overlays is necessary to understand the answers to the questions about what skills are necessary and of the manners in which answers to these questions were stated by the scientific and professional associations. Existing national practices concerning the degree of dominance of one or more scientific or professional fields over the role of the *reponsible person* were confronted by the necessity of seeking legitimation within the sphere of public policy formulation at an international level. Each field sought to bolster its own position, by seeking either to maintain pre-eminence or to acquire it at the expense of others. This required intensive lobbying and persuasion by particular scientific and professional bodies within their own countries to encourage their respective governments to take a position in the ongoing international negotiations which it favoured. Each sought further to influence public policy at the international level by working through the international committees or groups of representatives of the scientific and professional associations. Thus, the scientific and industrial chemists, pharmacists, pharmaceutical chemists, biologists, industrial pharmacists, veterinarians, and medical doctors sought to develop cross-national consensus within each of their particular fields, as a basis for the development of support and of pressure. This would have two aims: first, to permit a national body to strengthen its bargaining ability in its efforts to influence the policy of the government of its own nation by stressing the cross-national basis of its own position, and, second, to permit the international scientific committees and groups to exert an influence upon the various units of the European Economic Community during the periods of deliberation preliminary to the ultimate issuance of definitive Directives by the decision-making body, the Council of Ministers.

Each government of the original six member states of the EEC, and later nine member states of the EEC, is directly represented in the Community through representation on the Council of Ministers. The Council has final legislative authority to enact Directives which then become the obligation of the member states to enforce through passage of appropriate enabling legislation operative within their national borders. Any government acting through its representatives can take a particular position, consonant with its own national interests, on any matter being considered by the Council. For matters such as Directives, individual nationals or associations of nationals can seek to influence the position taken by their government during the deliberation processes until final Council action.

The Commission of the EEC prepares drafts for consideration by the Council. These drafts are widely circulated in advance of such consideration, and here also the individual scientific and professional groups have ample opportunity to affect public policy. If a particular Draft Directive is viewed as antithetic to the interests of an interested party, that group can express its views directly to the Commission or its staff. This frequently occurs, and provides a basis for refinement of such documents. If opposition is comprehensive, withdrawal and reconsideration of drafts by the Commission may occur.

The Economic and Social Committee of the EEC has the responsibility of supplying an *avis* or opinion concerning any material originated by the Commission for consideration by the Council. It is more of a representative body than either the Council or the Commission, and various occupational and social bodies have direct representation in this forum. Here also the particular scientific and professional groups can influence the drafting of the *avis* by the Committee and thus shape the subsequent discussion by the Council.

Another EEC unit associated directly with the Council plays a vital part in its actions. That is the Committee of Permanent Representatives, comprising direct representation from the member governments. Its reponsibility is to perform necessary staff evaluations and preliminary screening and review of materials received from the Commission. A good deal of the work undertaken by that Committee of Permanent Representatives, known as COREPER, entails negotiations among administrative representatives of the various governments. Discussions occur there 'on a nontechnical or nonprofessional level, where they just . . . have to make a decision on a bargaining basis. We'll go along with you on this one, and we expect that you'll go along on that one. But there was no question of reexamining the professional arguments'. COREPER established a Committee of Experts, a working group, in this instance, which focuses mainly on economic questions. This group was created, according to one participant, 'on an *ad hoc* basis with members sent out from various capitals. We met our opposite numbers from other countries and tried to hammer out an agreed line'. In this forum, the 'spokesmen were permanent civil servants with their professional advisers standing by to interject when necessary' (personal interview, 4 June 1975).

It was in this setting that the United Kingdom put forth a position regarding the 'responsible person' which opened the role to individuals from various scientific and professional specializations rather than limiting it only to persons with backgrounds in pharmacy. The previous Draft Directive limited the responsible persons, with the exception of a few specialized fields, to pharmacists. Various influences were brought to bear on most of the governments to modify or to sustain the earlier Draft, these representing at least in part the interests of or positions taken by the international committees of various scientific and professional groups.

The position of the United Kingdom was clearly expressed by a senior administrative staff member of the Department of Health and Social Security as early as 16 April 1973, shortly after Great Britain had joined the Common Market, as follows:

> In their discussions before the United Kingdom joined the Community, the Six linked together in a 'package' the directives relating to authorization to market proprietary medicinal products, the two draft directives relating to pharmaceutical manufacturers and the two relating to basic pharmacy qualifications and training. The link arises because it was considered necessary for both 'product licensing' and the manufacturing directives for the manufacturers to be licensed under coordinated conditions. One of these required each manufacturer to have a pharmacist to be personally responsible for control of production, quality control and the release of finished products to distribution. The pharmacist's qualifications must be acceptable by all member states. These discussions became deadlocked. . . .
>
> We believe that the person's experience may be more important than his basic qualification. A pharmacist might well be the best person for supervising the manufacture of formulated pharmaceutical products whilst for the chemical synthesis of a drug a biologist may be the most suitable person. For quality control a chemist with experience in the pharmaceutical industry would be at least as suitable as a pharmacist.
>
> The Six, however, appear to be very strongly in favour of a single 'responsible' person and for that person to be a pharmacist. In a transitional period they would recognize non-pharmacists at present employed in this work, but are urging strongly that all future persons undertaking this work should be pharmacists of 'European' standing . . . .. (Whittet, 1973)[1]

The import of these points can be summarized as follows:

(1) Health care includes use of medications produced in industrial plants, for which European practice requires designation of a 'responsible person' to ascertain the quality of pharmaceuticals in accordance with accepted standards.

(2) Member nations of the European Economic Community have diverse patterns for determination of qualifications of such a 'responsible person', and in the various countries these persons may be chemists, pharmacists, medical doctors, veterinarians, engineers, or others with in-plant experience.

(3) Common Market imperatives concerning harmonization of standards for products, the free flow of goods across national borders, the rights of establishment and of services for those engaged in certain activities, and the mutual recognition of diplomas, include the attempt to seek reconciliation of diverse standards among member nations.

(4) The implementation of these imperatives impinges upon existing national practices concerning a 'responsible person', to the extent that such practices are

conceived by various national associations of scientists and of professionals to be threatened and disrupted.

(5) Efforts in response by national associations include (a) formation of international committees of liaison to seek and develop consensus among the associations in each of the scientific and professional fields concerned, (b) the strengthening of consultation relationships with national governments by national associations where such consultation relationships exist, and (c) the development of pressure and the application of influence upon both national governments and appropriate units of the European Economic Community structure.

Controversies among various specialized sciences and professions have marked the processes which have occurred as the European Economic Community has moved to formulate Directives for the harmonization of arrangements for the preparation of medicaments. The actions of these groups derive in complex ways from existing practices within the Common Market's member nations, the natures of government control and sanction for the activities of their scientists and professions in this field, the membership constituency for the associations, and, on an international scale, the strength and direction of the thrusts initiated by the international committees of liaison towards the Common Market structure and towards the national governments of the member states.

**Public Authority and Drugs**

Hughes (1952) observes that: 'The great point in the scientist's code is full and honest reporting to his colleagues, and, with it, willingness to submit to full criticism. Since this is so, and since no client is involved, scientists ordinarily do not seek the protection of state license. Informal controls are sufficient.'

In the setting of the pharmaceutical industry, however, scientists and professionals are subject to administrative controls when they act in the capacity of production supervisor or quality controller, and the organization as a whole is subject to product liability claims, as well as the complex of pharmacopoeia and national government regulation. In the 'responsible person' concept is embodied the idea of public regulation and accountability, and in the very nature of the Common Market Directives on pharmaceutical products is close public regulation of the incumbent of the role, whether scientist or professional. That regulation by public authority came to be imposed on the manufacturers of pharmaceuticals because of public health considerations. The process, therefore, that has occurred is one of imposition upon specialities, both scientific and professional, and has become simply another example of what Haberer (1972) refers to as 'politicalization in science'. His concern for the relationships between science and the political order rests upon the well founded assumption that the securing of resources for professional and scientific activities and the acquisition of privileges and status entail obligations or connections with those in power.

In the area of drugs and their manufacture, the involvement of science and professions with public authority has an extensive history in Europe. The first pharmacopoeias within national domains appeared at the end of the eighteenth and the beginning of the nineteenth centuries, in Switzerland, the Netherlands, and France. Elsewhere, such as in Italy, local or regional codes existed. During the eighteenth century, individual authors attempted to encourage unified drug standards through publication of private pharmacopoeias. At a supra-national level, the International Congress of Pharmacy in 1865 aimed to establish standards in the associated countries, and, in 1925, the International Convention of Brussels was signed, the latter following the initiative of the Belgian government. With efforts undertaken under authority of Article 24 of the Pact of the League of Nations coming to naught, further concrete steps did not occur until the World Health Organization in 1946 moved to create *The International Pharmacopoeia* through the efforts of a specially appointed staff composed of experts. The volume produced set standards for drug control, not obligatory upon member nations, but having recommendatory value (Marini-Bettolo, 1969).

Later steps involved efforts through the Brussels Treaty Organization and the Western European Union, and these were followed in 1960 by efforts of the Council of Europe (Partial Agreement), consisting of Belgium, France, Federal Republic of Germany, Italy, Luxembourg, the Netherlands, and the United Kingdom. In 1969, there was published the *European Pharmacopoeia*, issued under the auspices of the Council of Europe (Partial Agreement). The significance of this was anticipated in 1964 by the European Economic Community when it noted

> the need for establishing general standards for the quality of drugs (standards of purity, stability, etc.) has been underlined in different instances. Thus, parallel with work undertaken by certain international organizations such for example as the World Health Organization or the Council of Europe, the Commission has undertaken work with a view to establishing a European Pharmacopoeia. It seems opportune, on the other hand, that the Commission should take the initiative, in collaboration with the competent authorities of the member states and with the help of scientific bodies in the community, to seek standardized methods for carrying out the various tests on drugs (physico-chemical, biological, micro-biological, pharmacological, toxicological and clinical tests) and for their evaluation. In the public health fields ... the advantages and guarantees ... [of] standardization ... [for] the scientific bodies, and ... the fact that it will enable drug manufacturers in the community to profit from the most advanced scientific knowledge [have undoubted importance]. (EEC Commission, quoted in Marini-Bettolo, 1969, pp. 13–14)

These objectives were stimulated by the expectations of the European Economic Community that 1968 would see the free exchange of drugs and unification of national legislation concerning them within its member states. The Council of Europe undertook the initiative for a pharmacopoeia, and in 1963 the European Pharmacopoeia Convention was created. In the following year, a Commission to create the *Pharmacopoia* was brought into being and the efforts of the experts selected, who were organized by a technical secretariat into some 15 groups by the Commission, ultimately bore fruit.

The work of the expert groups had begun in 1965 when the first five groups, charged with preparation of 'general methods of tests and analysis', assumed responsibility for developing the list of reagents, physical and physico-chemical methods, nomenclature and editing, chemical methods, and biological and statistical methods. When this was completed in 1966, additional groups of experts began to deal with the 'study of substances and preparations used as medicines'. That broad category included biological products such as antibiotics, surgical dressings and ligatures, inorganic chemicals, synthetic and natural organic chemicals, galenical compounds, radioactive compounds, and sera, vaccines, and blood products. Documents produced by the groups of experts were reviewed by the Pharmacopoeia Commission, by national pharmacopoeia authorities, and then again by the Commission for approval and adoption. Concluding his summary of this complex of administrative, technical, scientific and political events, the Chairman of the Commission hailed the 'new climate of opinion favourable to the realization of a common pharmacopoeia which, for a hundred years, has been the wish of all those scientists, pharmacists, doctors, industrialists and analysts who are concerned with the development of drugs and which has an important place in the continued protection of public health' (Marini-Bettolo, 1969; *European Pharmacopoeia*, 1969).

The involvement of the World Health Organization in this sector has been manifold. It rests upon the conception of 'national drug policies' which within the umbrella of public health covers the following areas: health problems and drug legislation; pharmaceutical research and development; drug information; production; drug distribution systems; legislation; 'good manufacturing practices'; pharmaceutical inspection and analytic control; registration; lists of essential drugs; monitoring; and problems of drug use (World Health Organization, 1975, 'National drug policies'). While the range is extensive, the restricted focus in this study on production and the responsible person nevertheless permits several general points regarding WHO efforts.

First, the material covered in the WHO summary underscores the statement contained within it that 'Governments are becoming increasingly interested in industrial production, and particularly in pharmaceutical production, since they are concerned both with economic growth and with obtaining products for which there is a need' (World Health Organization, 1975, 'National drug policies', p. 339). Further detail is provided in the subsequent formulations dealing specifically with pharmaceutical production, with legislation, and with 'good manufacturing practices', such as the following:

> The production of finished dosage forms (tablets, injectable fluids, and other pharmaceutical presentations) from half-finished or intermediate products requires quality control measures as well as manufacturing expertise in order to ensure that the final products are of an adequate standard . . . . Adherence to good manufacturing practices and quality control are of course indispensable for meeting international standards.

Synthetic drugs are described as forming the bulk of the drug market while drugs derived from vegetable or animal sources comprise the remainder, and the former require a high level of technology and a large scale production capacity, occurring mainly in countries with well developed fine chemical industries.

The World Health Organization formulation of 'national drug policies' notes that

> The policy followed for the quality control of pharmaceutical products has evolved over the years. Because of the increasing number and volume of products on the national and international markets, it became evident that adequate quality could not be ensured merely by carrying out random checks on samples of finished products. The new approach is to control all stages of production and it is already reflected in the regulations of several countries, which have recognized that adequate pharmaceutical quality control systems should include:
> —control of all stages of manufacture by the producer
> —inspection of manufacturing establishments by the health authorities
> —random checking of samples of products in an analytical control laboratory by the health authorities. (World Health Organization, 'National drug policies', p. 343)

Going further, the World Health Organization has published a series of guidelines on production control which, it states, 'have been established by WHO for manufacturers and inspecting authorities'. Known as 'Good practices in the manufacture and quality control of drugs' (World Health Organization, 1971), these recommendations cover in depth the many aspects of production, including personnel. Concerning the latter, the following recommendations were provided:

> Experts responsible for supervising the manufacture and control of drugs should possess the qualifications of scientific, education and practical experience required by national legislation. Their education should include the study of an appropriate combination of (a) chemistry (analytic chemistry, biochemistry, physical chemistry, etc.); (b) chemical engineering; (c) microbiology; (d) pharmaceutical sciences and technology; (e) pharmacology and toxicology; (f) physiology and histology; and (g) other related sciences. They should also have adequate practical experience in the manufacture and control of drugs. ... The scientific education and practical experience of experts should be such as to enable them to exercise independent professional judgement, based on the application of scientific principles and understanding to the practical problems encountered in the manufacture and control of drugs. (World Health Organization, 1971, 'Good practices in the manufacture and quality control of drugs', p. 100)

Other recommendations include the sphere of quality control for which the following aspects are most important in the context of this presentation:

> Every establishment that manufactures pharmaceuticals should have a quality control department that is autonomous in the areas of responsibility assigned to it. It should control all starting materials, monitor the quality aspects of manufacturing operations, and control the quality and stability of drugs.
> A quality control laboratory must also be available. The laboratory should:
> (1) Be adequately staffed and fully equipped for performing all quality control tests and analyses required during and after manufacture [to which an appended footnote adds that, should animal tests be necessary, the use of outside independent laboratories may be advisable for specialized and complex analytical and biological procedures that require the use of costly equipment and that can be performed only by technicians with specialized training, such laboratories to be adequately staffed and fully equipped]; (2) be supervised by a qualified expert [an insert refers to the earlier listing of appropriate educational fields quoted above], who should have the final responsibility for approving or rejecting all materials tested; (3) be promptly informed of all changes and modifications in the manufacturing procedures and written instructions. (World Health Organization, 1971, 'Good practices in the manufacture and quality control of drugs', pp. 105–106).

The principal duties of the quality control department as a whole are then reviewed and cover control and release of materials and products at every stage and the evaluation of storage, stability, and shelf-life.

The key most relevant to the analysis undertaken here is contained in the following passages of the document:

> Manufacturing procedures and written instructions for each drug must be prepared under the direct supervision of experts ... who have the necessary authority. ...
>
> A separate batch manufacturing record should be prepared for each batch of drugs produced, and should include the following information: ... (7) a duly signed record of each step followed, precautions taken, and special observations made throughout the manufacture of the batch; ... (11) signature of the expert responsible for the manufacturing operations, and the date of his signature; and (12) a full analytical report showing whether the batch complies with the prescribed specifications for the drug (this report should be duly signed and dated, and endorsed by the expert responsible for quality control, to permit the batch to be released). ...
>
> The quality control department should maintain adequate analytical records concerning the control of each batch of drugs manufactured. Such records should include: ... (3) the signature(s) of the person(s) who performed the quality control procedures; and (4) a final review and dated endorsement by a duly authorized expert. (World Health Organization, 'Good practices in the manufacture and quality control of drugs', pp. 104–106)

These formulations clearly require an assumption of personal responsibility by an expert in both manufacturing and quality control to ensure that the materials produced conform to the full to specified standards deemed necessary for public health. This expectation that there will be one or more responsible persons is put forth as part of an authorized document of the World Health Organization, and this in turn is at bottom a recommendation by WHO to the appropriate authorities of government of its member nations. The force and saliency of the concept of the responsible person require adherence by the member governments.

Referring to the WHO 'Good practices in the manufacture and quality control of drugs' statement of 1971 as a 'significant stimulus', Mr C. A. Johnson of the British Pharmacopoeia Commission was later paraphrased in the British journal, *Chemist and Druggist*, as saying 'these were but advisory recommendations having no binding character on member states' (Johnson, 1975). Still, he added, 'Undoubtedly, however, they have been influential in affecting and informing decisions made at national levels in many countries. The establishment of such informatory guidelines at a time when many national authorities had still to publish their national advice on the subject is a model for future international work of this kind' (p. 321). And, in alluding to the WHO-sponsored work of experts, released as technical reports in such areas as teratogenicity, clinical evaluation, carcinogenicity and bio-availability, Johnson is paraphrased to observe that these enunciate 'desirable principles' which represent 'a pooling of the views of a limited number of experts ... and did not necessarily represent decisions of policy of the organization itself'. Such principles were said to be 'advisory guidelines only and had no legal force, national or international', and Johnson further stated that 'Under such circumstances it is often rather easier to achieve a degree of agreement than when recommendations made are to be invested with the force of law' (Johnson, 1975, p. 319).

However noncompelling these recommendations emanating from an international agency may be for the actions of national governments towards the pharmaceutical industries of Europe, their implications for particular professions exist, especially in view of the fact that representatives of them are to be found in the responsible person role. In commenting on analogous issues confronting the pharmacy profession in the United States, Selden (1974) clearly states the importance of events such as these in the following terms:

> Such conflicts between and among the professions have developed in the past and after painful periods of readjustment have generally been resolved without involvement of representatives of the public interest. But economic and social factors external to the professions and changes within them are causing transformations. With increasing dependence of society on the services performed by members of the professions and with greater public funds being directed to the education of future members of the professions, the public has begun to express and is expecting to exert more active interest and involvement in the policies and conduct of the national health professional associations, including the definition of their professional fields of jurisdiction and the resolution of the conflicts among the professions and within the professions.[2]

Such events highlight what Jamous and Peloille (1970) refer to as the 'legitimacy of monopoly, the definition and the function of an activity' which they see as 'perpetually objects of confrontation and conflict', adding that

> the evolution and the changes in a profession do not usually take place continuously and according to any self-regulated process, but by the successive formation of systems which seek to close themselves off and to maintain and perpetuate themselves; they achieve this in the course of a certain period, then they are themselves called in question by the very elements which they themselves have helped to make. These elements, bearers of a new definition extolling openness and leaning on forces external to the profession, will try, when victorious, to perpetuate and keep for themselves, in their turn, the privileges, rules and codes which are the basis of this triumphant definition. (Jamous and Peloille, 1970, p. 118)

And so the presence of chemists, of pharmacists, of other specialists, within the responsible person role can seen as an example of complicated interprofessional exchanges occurring within the diverse contexts of industry, of national government, of international advisory bodies, and of international authority.

That these exchanges among professions are of critical importance rests in some measure upon what Cowen (1970) refers to as 'the major significance of the pharmaceutical industry', adding

> Vast resources of scientific knowledge and engineering skills are required for the preparation, synthesis, physical production, and quality evaluation, not to mention clinical testing of drugs. Without these resources the therapeutic revolution could never have occurred.
>
> All this has placed upon the industry a tremendous social obligation. The products of the industry are virtually *sui generis* and so much more indispensable to social well-being than the ordinary commodities of the market place that the industry has found itself under close public and official scrutiny.[3]

## Authority and Professions in National Settings

Confronted by the Common Market's mandate for harmonization of the responsible person in the manufacturing of pharmaceuticals, the various national associations of specialists sought to exercise influence on public policy within the individual countries in which they were situated and to express their views to the appropriate units of the European Economic Community itself. We shall turn first to the individual nations.

An understanding of the efforts of the national associations within their own political domains must begin with a review, at least to a limited extent, of the basis of the authority for their existence. A cross-national questionnaire distributed to the professional organizations in pharmacy in all but Ireland and the United Kingdom among the member states of the Common Market by the Groupement Professionel des Pharmaciens de l'Industrie Pharmaceutique de la Communauté Économique Européenne provides information on this point (personal communication, 6 February 1973). Response to two questions shall be summarized.

The first was as follows: 'Is membership automatic through the agency of an association? Or is it a matter of an obligatory affiliation? Or through an affiliation freely authorized?' Five associations reported voluntary joining by members, while two others reported that obligatory membership exists. For Germany, membership in the chamber of pharmacists of each Land is obligatory and an automatic affiliation of German pharmacists with them exists; while in France pharmacists have an obligatory affiliation with the Ordre National des Pharmaciens. Second, 'Is the association directed in an absolutely independent fashion?' To this, the German association reported 'no' without supplying clarifying details, while the French group noted that 'the functioning of the Council of the Order of Pharmacists is regulated by the Code of Public Health, Articles L520 and following'.

Regarding the United Kingdom, a spokesman for the Pharmaceutical Society expressed its relationship with the government as follows:

> The Pharmaceutical Society in this country is in a unique position in Europe because we are the registering body for pharmacists and the body which controls the education of pharmacists in this country; so we have statutory obligations which allow us to go direct to the Commission. [The Society is unique in comparison with] any other pharmaceutical society. ... Normally, the government is the registering authority. In this case, the Pharmaceutical Society is the registering authority and therefore has a pseudo-governmental function. (personal interview, Pharmaceutical Society, May 1975)

A parallel point applies to other statutorily registered professions in the main, as was noted in Appendix 9 of the Report of The Monopolies Commission (1970a) in the following terms: 'responsibility for laying down requirements for registration and maintaining the register (normally accompanied by regulatory and disciplinary powers) has usually, though not invariably, been entrusted to a separate body rather than being the direct responsibility of a government department; though a department or officer of State has certain general supervisory powers over the registration body'. It is further indicated in that Appendix that the Crown does participate directly though to a limited extent in affairs of the Pharmaceutical Society. Of 24 members of the council of the Pharmaceutical Society, three are appointed by the Crown, the remainder elected or appointed by the profession. The overall point, however, remains clear, that independence or semi-independence characterizes the relationship of the Pharmaceutical Society and the government of the United Kingdom.

Chemists constitute the other major group to be examined here. Concerning this area of specialization, Chiltz (1973) observes that

> Each of the Common Market countries has a higher education system that produces four different types of chemists: (i) graduates and Ph.D.'s who generally go on to teaching and research; (ii) chemical engineers who receive a fairly theoretical training and go on to be consultants; (iii) chemical engineers who have a more vocational training and intend to enter industry; and (iv) senior technicians who collaborate directly with the other three. However, there are considerable variations from one country to another between the standards of chemists having the same designations.[4]

In the sense of the first category, chemists also of course work in industry. The Monopolies Commission (1970b) presents data, in Table IX of the Appendices volume, which show that 97 per cent of the Royal Institute of Chemistry membership work as 'directors or employees of companies, central or local government departments, etc., not primarily rendering professional services'. It is further noted by Sir Frederick Dainton, President of the Chemical Society, that 'about two-thirds of RIC members [in 1971] are employed in industry';[4] some 6·8 per cent specifically report employment in the pharmaceutical industry (Dainton, 1973). Some 25,487 persons were Fellows or had other membership status in RIC, according to the 1970 Monopolies Commission Report.

Whatever the education or employment of chemists, it appears that societies or associations of chemists are learned in nature and are voluntary. Within Europe, the Federation of European Chemical Societies is described as 'a voluntary association ... of non-profit making learned societies in the field of chemistry whose membership consists largely of individual qualified chemists' (Parker, 1973).[4] For Britain, the Chemical Society and the Royal Institute of Chemistry adhere as one body to this international group. Further, British practice does not require chemists to be members of the RIC (Dainton, 1973); and the President of the Royal Institute of Chemistry, Dr F. A. Robinson, noted (1973) that 'unfortunately [sic], a foreign chemist would encounter no obstacles except economic ones should he wish to secure a job in this country'.[4]

Unlike the pharmacists, therefore, chemists are not statutorily obligated in Great Britain to join an association. For chemists, however, there is activity or function which is reserved to members either of the Royal Institute of Chemistry or of the Pharmaceutical Society of Great Britain, one relevant to the topic of manufacture. The supervision of the manufacture of certain poisons is required by the Poison Rules of 1966 to be performed by a member of either body (The Monopolies Commission, 1970c); Robinson (1973) indicates that the status of Fellow in the Institute is required for any who wish to 'manufacture substances that fall within the scope of the Old Therapeutic Substances Act'.[4]

The mechanism of contact by chemists with their government takes a somewhat different pattern in Belgium. The arrangement was described as follows, by a Belgian chemist:

> We have in Belgium ... for chemists, ... for engineers, Société Chimique de Belgique. That's a society mostly for science, though they are now defending the rights of chemists ..... For the moment, we have a very important problem. You know, there are very many chemists working in the pharmaceutical industry, and a chemist may not sign for a given product. It must be done by a pharmacist or a doctor. And, we must battle, fight, to defend our rights, the rights of our colleagues, and there are many in Belgium in this industry.

Asked how the society had acted in this matter, he commented further:

> First of all, they have fought it at the level of the Community. I read a few days ago, there will be Directives of the Community saying that a chemist may sign for a pharmaceutical product, that the rights of chemists specialized in pharmaceutical chemistry are identical with those of the pharmacist. That is very important, because now they will be obliged in Belgium to do it. In Belgium, we have to go to the Ministère de Santé Publique to obtain that the rules should be changed. (Personal interview, 1975)

The organized structures of scientists and of professionals can thereby exist either as units of public authority or as independent entities with public sanction. Registration or membership can be either mandatory or voluntary. Generally, pharmacy bodies appear to have greater ties with government in the member states of the Common Market, at least in Germany and in France. British practice is quite different, with the Pharmaceutical Society remaining largely independent of government. By contrast, chemists can freely choose to join or not to join their associations under relatively few restrictions, and the bodies themselves, while regulated, exist for the most part independent of national governments.

## Cross-national Groups of Scientific and Professional Associations

A variety of cross-national committees or confederations exist in Europe which draw together for different purposes the associations of scientists and of professionals that exist within the several nations. This has been the result of moves towards international scientific co-operation and regional scientific efforts (King, 1967), and of the development of scientific, professional, and educational communalities of interest (Friedrich, 1969), and generally, as well, is part of the trend described by Beck and his co-authors as Europeanization and the integration of people and institutions within Europe (Beck *et al.*, 1970).

The development of the European Economic Community served to stimulate further growth in international committees' representatives of various scientific, professional, and industrial interests. An infrastructure of consultative and co-ordinating committees comprised of delegates from national associations has developed in a significant number of the 'liberal professions' within the nine member states of the Common Market. These have developed with the encouragement of the institutions of the Community which attempt to deal with each profession, cutting across national lines, on a unitary basis. Communication, information, approval and response from and to chosen professional associations occur through such consultative committees. The committees in turn have functioned as co-ordinative bodies, seeking in some instances to develop common strategies for influencing national governments towards desirable policies and for interceding directly and in consultative capacities with the international body and its units.

For the fields involved with pharmaceutical products, the 1969 publication of the Community's Commission, *Repertoire des organismes communs créés dans le cadre des Communautés Européennes par les associations industrielles, artisanales, commerciales et de services des six pays; associations de professions libérales; organisations syndicales de salariés et groupements de consommateurs*, listed the following bodies:

> Groupement International de l'Industrie Pharmaceutique des Pays de la CEE;
> Groupement Pharmaceutique de la Communauté Européenne; and
> Groupement Professionnel des Pharmaciens de l'Industrie Pharmaceutique de la Communauté Economique Européenne (Commission des Communautés Européennes, 1969).

Such groups and committees had come into existence as well for other fields and liberal professions, the latter including agricultural engineers or agronomists, architects, barristers, financial counsellors, dentists, engineers, physicians, medical specialists, nurses, opticians, and veterinarians. The *Repertoire*'s list of these specialities provides details concerning the *groupes* themselves and information about the various national associations or federations which are the member organizations subsidiary to the international bodies.

As the involvement of the Common Market in pharmaceutical matters extended and broadened, other international *groupements* or committees of liaison were created, and existing bodies increased their concern with the implications of the Market's propositions for their field. The following are among these groups of scientists and professionals:

European Community Biologists Association, described as having been formed by the associations of professional biologists in the member countries of the European Economic Community (*Pharmaceutical Journal*, 24 January 1976); Association of Medical Advisors in the Pharmaceutical Industry, said to have been formed about 1957 and concerned in 1972 with drug approval procedures in the light of Community Draft Directives (*Lancet*, 29 April 1972); a 'joint EEC chemistry committee with direct access to Brussels' was formed (Lee, 1975). A 'common move' by representatives of the chemical societies of the Community countries in regard to the pharmaceutical products Directives was said earlier (Fritsche, 1973) to result from 'close contact between representatives of the chemical societies of the EC countries, through an EC chemistry committee inaugurated in March, 1973 in London'. Writing as General Secretary of the Gesellschaft Deutscher Chemiker, Fritsche observed that 'chemists will meet the challenge of the present and of the future and will contribute their share in building a humane and peaceful world', adding that 'National efforts in this respect will become multinational among neighbouring countries and ultimately European'.[4]

Lee, who is Vice-president of the Royal Institute of Chemistry and was Chairman of the Professional Services Committee, identified the objective of the EEC chemistry committee as follows:

> Keeping a close watch on policies being developed by the EEC commission as they affect chemists, both through government departments and also through a new joint EEC chemistry committee . . . . This committee was formed by direct contact between the RIC and sister organizations in the other EEC countries. The position of the chemist as a controller in the pharmaceutical industry could have been badly affected had the Institute not taken action, although this problem is still unsolved, there is hope for the future. Considerable influence is being exerted on the negotiations relating to the mutual recognition of qualifications.[4]

Another comment relevant to this emergent organization was made two years earlier in 1973 by the President of the Royal Institute of Chemistry, F. A. Robinson, when he was discussing at the Swansea Congress the matter of 'professional dilemmas'. One entails EEC and chemistry, especially, he noted, in view of the fact that

> the main problem presented by membership of EEC is that professional bodies, as we in this country understand them, do not exist in any of the Six. In these countries the only qualifications that are recognized are those awarded by the universities and technical institutes in the form of degrees and diplomas, and the universities and the degrees they confer are controlled by the state in each instance. (Robinson, 1973)[4]

In that context, he noted further that

> the professions cannot be represented directly on the EEC Commission. Those who represent Britain will be civil servants nominated by various government departments. In the second place, a British group acting on its own cannot influence the Commission and we must therefore enlist the support of chemists on the Continent. This we have already started to do and we have now made contact with seven Chemical Societies in Europe, with whom we hope to have discussions on the problem of reconciling chemical qualifications.[4]

This international body of chemical societies came to be known as the 'EEC Chemistry Committee ($E_2C_3$) . . . comprising the major chemistry societies and institutes in the European Communities' and was described as 'a body formed on the initiative of the RIC some two years ago' (Royal Institute of Chemistry, 1975).[5] It filled a vacuum, for R. E. Parker, its Chairman in 1976, later indicated:

> When this country [the United Kingdom] entered the European Communities at the beginning of 1973 we discovered that no organization existed to look after the interests of chemists within the Community, although such organizations did exist for many other professions. . . . It is this Committee that has been principally concerned with the European legislation affecting the position of chemists in the pharmaceutical industry.
> . . . We immediately took up the cudgels on behalf of chemists, both directly from the Committee to the European Commission and through the national societies to their own Governments. In this country the Royal Institute of Chemistry had

meetings with officials of the Government Department (the Department of Health and Social Security) and we also carried out a survey showing that positions of responsibility were more commonly occupied by chemists than by pharmacists. (Parker, personal communication, 2 August 1976)

The creation of the European Community specifically entailed, therefore, the occurrence of problems affecting the various sciences and professions and led directly to the formation of new linkages in each of the discrete fields. Their impact on the steps taken by the Community and the consequences of these actions for the sciences and professions remain to be outlined.

**Common Market Directives**

In essence, the Draft Directive required that the responsible person had to be a pharmacist. In essence, the Directive that was finally adopted identified as qualified persons for the position a series of individuals with competence in a variety of scientific and professional fields. Pharmacy was but one such field so listed.

This was construed by many as a loss or defeat for the pharmacists and a gain or victory for the other specialists, chemists in particular. This change was the consequence of a long period of discussion, negotiation, the exercise of influence upon governments and upon various units of the EEC structure. The final decision was made at the level of the Council of Ministers preceded most closely by the work of COREPER, the Committee of Permanent Representatives. These latter settings provided the scene for the efforts of the various scientific and professional groups through the presentations, rebuttals, and discussions by the governmental representatives privileged to participate. Much of what occurred there can only be guessed. The detailed log of the exchanges there has not been made public. However, the concrete results can be seen, as certain participants summarized the events there in personal interviews and hints of the nature of the discussions have been publicized. The major arguments of the various groups have been laid out in the scientific and professional press, in presentations at meetings, in comments during interviews conducted with spokesmen for the groups, by government personnel and by EEC officials.

The arguments put forth on the various sides of the complex issues can initially be illustrated through the comments to the Nottingham Branch of the Pharmaceutical Society in February 1973 by Mr W. M. Darling, head of the United Kingdom delegation to the Groupement Pharmaceutique, as these were summarized in *Chemist and Druggist* (Darling, 1973):

> within the directive was an article, supported by the Society but opposed by the Association of the British Pharmaceutical Industry, requiring that the person responsible for manufacture and quality control should be a pharmacist. It also said, however, that someone with another scientific degree can become a pharmacist with a supplementary course.
>
> Mr Darling opposed this 'topping up' procedure on the grounds that every pharmacy degree must be broadly based with a properly integrated course.[6]

A very different kind of criticism was voiced by D. F. Lewis, Secretary and Registrar of the Pharmaceutical Society, in his summary in spring 1976 of the 'pharmaceutical consequences of the EEC', presented to the American Pharmaceutical Association. Noting first that the Draft Directive stipulation of the pharmacist as the reponsible person was 'in fact ... already the law in two at least of the original member countries but it was not a legal requirement of the United Kingdom', he went on to say:

> and regrettably the point was contested by the United Kingdom Government under pressure from the pharmaceutical industry. It is easy to understand their opposition. A pharmacist in such a position would be a very important person, or at least equal in status to a director of the company. Indeed, his power would be not far short of that of the managing director. . . . the public should be . . . protected when a medicine ... [is] manufactured on a large scale. A pharmacist should be in such a position of authority as the person recognized as being responsible for its manufacture and quality control.
> Regrettably, the opposition won. A new second Directive was drafted and has now been adopted. . . . The concept of a single 'responsible person' who had to be a pharmacist has gone. The new Directive says that a manufacturer must have at his disposal the services 'of at least one *qualified* person'. The principle of 'divide and rule' has been invoked. The qualified person must have completed a minimum period of four years' theoretical and practical study in one of the following scientific disciplines—pharmacy, medicine, veterinary medicine, chemistry, pharmaceutical chemistry and technology. Additionally the Directive lays down the scientific subjects which that person must have studied.
> Pharmacy still retains one advantage. It is only a pharmacist who has studied all the subjects listed and it is probable that it is only a pharmacist who is fully answerable to his professional body for any negligence or misconduct which has been committed in the course of his employment.
> As a profession we have lost a battle but we are still fighting a war. Another battle looms on the horizon. As noted, the other scientific disciplines mentioned in the Directive are deficient in the study of one or other of the necessary subjects. They are demanding that some instruction in these subjects be made available to them and on the easiest possible basis. Suddenly it seems everybody wants to become a pharmacist.
> The pharmacists in the Community and certainly those in the United Kingdom are violently opposed to any form of 'topping-up' education, a short course which would convert a member of another scientific discipline into a pharmacist within the meaning of this Directive. . . . This battle has started but I do not think that it has yet been clearly won and the danger remains. (Lewis, 1976)[2]

This extensive array of arguments states that a gain in the pharmacists' power within industry would result from their exclusive recognition as the responsible person. Hence, goes the argument, the industry opposes this position. Mr Lewis believes that it is still the pharmacist who has the most appropriately comprehensive education in scientific subjects. The other fields, he contends, do not match pharmacy in the degree to which the individual practitioner is 'fully answerable' to his professional body for negligence or misconduct. This dismissal of the professional bodies in medicine and veterinary medicine is not further explained.

From the vantage point of the international organization which is representative of the pharmacy associations of the EEC member nations, the Groupement

Pharmaceutique de la Communauté Européenne, its views on the matter were put forth in the 1969 publication, *Livre Blanc*, or White Book. The salient points follow:

> In the interest of the infirm, medicaments require the presence of the pharmacist at all stages, from their manufacture until their issuing dispensary. . . .
>
> The pharmacist is the expert on medicaments, from their manufacture through their distribution in the dispensaries.
>
> From the moment at which chemical research and clinical experimentation have established the therapeutic value of a substance, it falls to the pharmacist to move on from that, to create the medicament in the most adequate, most active and most stable pharmaceutical forms.
>
> The role of the pharmacist in industry consists then in directing the manufacture and above all the controls inherent in that. . . .
>
> The responsibility for the pharmacist in industry covers:
>
> (a) the control of the materials initially prepared;
> (b) the surveillance of manufacture;
> (c) the control of the finished products.
>
> That responsibility comprises on the one hand, the strict observation of the legislation on the topic of medicaments, through the requirement for registration by the authorities, and, on the other hand, a guarantee of good conclusion with respect to the owner of the factory, possessors of the authorization for the market place.[7]

These assertions concluded with the observations that they reflected the unanimous views of the *groupement* and of the six national associations participating in it in 1969, that they were being sent to the Commission, the Council, the Parliament, and the Economic and Social Committee of the Community as well as the six member governments, because of the unshakeable desire of the dispensing pharmacists to edify the Community in these matters following the prescriptions of the Treaty of Rome, and that public health required that the propositions and proposals be realized within the member states 'dans l'intérêt supérieur de la Communauté'.

It is apparent from Mr Lewis's comments that the Pharmaceutical Society supported at least this claim to monopoly by pharmacists proposed in *Livre Blanc*. Disagreements existed in other areas, but on the question of whether pharmacy alone should provide the responsible person, the British Society stood with their continental colleagues and counterparts.

Arguments on behalf of the chemists did not in effect ask for exclusive dominance in the same fashion as did the pharmacists. The chemists' views took two approaches. The first was to argue on the basis of the putative *status quo* that chemists were in fact employed in these roles, should not be forced out, and should not be prevented from securing new employment opportunities in such positions. The second concentrated on the nature of the work itself and on the skills deemed necessary for the performance of the tasks, emphasizing therefore that the work often demanded the knowledge and the ability of persons educated in chemistry. The clear implication was that the interests of the public at large could best be served by keeping the chemists in charge of either production or quality control where that would be made necessary by the inherent characteristics of the tasks themselves.

T. D. Whittet of the United Kingdom Department of Health and Social Security, himself the Chief Pharmacist of the Department in 1973, expressed such views at a meeting of medical officers to review all the health professions in the light of the Common Market. Whittet's statement follows:

> In the United Kingdom about 60 per cent of the persons responsible for supervision of production have pharmaceutical qualifications (although they are not necessarily on the register) whereas about 80 per cent of quality controllers have chemistry qualifications. We believe that the person's experience may be more important than his basic qualification. A pharmacist might well be the best person for supervising the manufacture of formulated pharmaceutical products whilst for the chemical synthesis of a drug an organic chemist would be equally or more suitable. For biological products a biologist may be the most suitable person. For quality control a chemist with experience in the pharmaceutical industry would be at least as suitable as a pharmacist. (Whittet, 1973)[1]

Such an emphasis on the assumed natures of the tasks and the appropriateness of the skills of various specialists to carry out those tasks paralleled the comment of an industrial 'pharmacist and chemist' who stated he was 'concerned' about the requirement for pharmaceutical supervision of manufacturing. He was quoted in *Chemist and Druggist* (19 February 1973) to the effect that many who were not pharmacists carried out their production and quality control function as well as any pharmacist. In response, the Pharmaceutical Society's spokesman, head of the United Kingdom delegation to the Pharmaceutical Groupement, observed that the 'increasing diversity of medicines needed the "panorama" of the pharmacist's training'.

That diversity implies the necessity of a pharmacist's competence rather than that of a chemist or of another specialist was challenged in the comment of a Department of Health and Social Security official familiar with the issue:

> what constitutes a medicine by any definition? Now many products under our Medicines Act are medicines which a member of the lay public would not normally consider a medicine. In fact, they are not the type of product for which, even in the pharmacist's training, he is educated to think of as a medicine. And, when we think of the total scope of manufacture as it exists in Britain, it embraces a large number of products for which a pharmacist is not trained. Therefore it is illogical to demand that a pharmacist be responsible. For example, a medicine could be, shall be, a plastic polymer which is used to cement bones together in surgery. (Personal interview, May 1975)

The skills of the chemists, the activities of the Royal Institute of Chemistry, and the efforts of the British government relative to the modification of Directives pertinent to the matter, were then counterposed to the assumptions of pharmacists in the following manner by the same official:

> The pharmacists were proposed as essential by the Common Market. AND THAT POSITION WAS ARGUED BY WHOM? By the Pharmaceutical Society. I think it was the Society's main argument. . . . I think the Society said in the main they supported the views of the Six, and . . . the basis of their support could be summed up by saying it is because the training of the pharmacist is the only graduate training which is specifically directed to the making and testing of medicines. AND THE POSITION PUT FORTH BY THE GOVERNMENT? Well, the alternative

accepted by the Directive, that it is accepted that other graduates were recognized. ... The presentation of the alternative had to be done ... here, at Brussels, and in the expert committees, and we were successful after a long time in persuading the others that this was a desirable, a necessary change. ...

The position developed within the Department. Obviously, there was consultation with the industry, with the Pharmaceutical Society, and with one other big profession, the Royal Institute of Chemistry.

That the pharmacists and chemists were the major groups involved in the consultation process, aside from the industry itself, he explained on the basis of the nature of the work.

There are minorities of other graduates, like microbiologists, but in the main you can say that the controversy was between the pharmacists and chemists, between the two big professional bodies. The reason [is] ... that particularly in the larger manufacturers, it was very common to have a chemist in charge of quality control. This stemmed from the fact that the companies were dealing in complex synthetic drugs which required quite a high level of chemistry to develop and carry out analytic methods, and gradually and I think possibly partly due to the fact that there are more chemists available, and the firms were chemical firms, it got to be a kind of strong hold of the chemistry profession to be in charge of the control of the quality of manufactured medicines. And therefore they are decidedly upset by the possibility of all these people being rendered unacceptable because they were not pharmacists.

... They came here, representatives of the Royal Institute of Chemistry, before Britain came in. That professional body had a strong interest and they developed their arguments that it was both logical and practical to recognize chemists as a suitable person.

And, returning specifically to an argument formed from a conception of the nature of the work, this person added:

originally ... the package ... involved the pharmacists' training and the acceptability of pharmacists. Then the thing was split and the training of the pharmacists was considered an entirely separate matter, and the argument was centred on whether it must be a pharmacist or someone else who was allowable. Then of course we concentrated on arguments to convince people that other graduates were competent to take charge of the manufacture of medicines.

They were already doing it. In fact, in some manufacturers, it was more logical that it should not be a pharmacist, for example, the manufacture of vaccine or blood. It was logical perhaps that a microbiologist should be in charge, or a doctor in charge, because pharmacists have nothing to do with that particular type of manufacture.

... We claim, the government in putting forth its case, it seems far more logical to ask that the authority to manufacture takes into account the type of product to be made in relation to the person. It does not just say, it must be a pharmacist and that takes care of everything.

... Just as now it says that the person in charge of the national authority will decide if the person in charge of manufacture is competent, as opposed to saying he must be a pharmacist.

The situation as it was seen to exist in the United Kingdom by the government there reflected then a perception of the nature of the tasks, and further rested upon an awareness that British practice included chemists along with pharmacists and others in the relevant roles in the manufacturing establishments. Dr Whittet's observation that some 60 per cent of the production supervisors were pharmacists and some 80 per cent of the quality control supervisors were chemists is also relevant. The latter data need, however, some clarification, for another source within the Department of Health and Social Security provided the following, somewhat discrepant, data: of responsible persons with qualifications who supervised production, some 40 per cent were said to be chemists, and 60 per cent pharmacists, whereas for quality control, the reverse obtained, as 60 per cent were chemists and 40 per cent were pharmacists. It was also pointed out that some 29 per cent of the manufacturers of pharmaceutical products employed persons in the responsible person roles who did *not* have qualifications in any field, whether chemistry or pharmacy or any other appropriate field. Such persons apparently acquired experience in industry considered appropriate for the positions they occupied.

An important occurrence was the splitting of the 'package'. The early consideration within the Common Market of the proposals concerning pharmacy focused on the right of establishment. This refers to the ability of individual specialists in the liberal professions to move across national boundaries within the Common Market terrain to engage in their work without handicap because of nationality, and because of diversities among the member states either in registration requirements or in educational prerequisites for entry into the profession. Such movement would occur when a person recognized in one nation as having fully met the requirements for entry into the profession and fully entitled therefore to work in his or her field might decide to migrate on a permanent basis to another member state. Each nation has developed in the course of time its own procedures for regulation of entry into practice and for recognition of what it considers to be the appropriate standards of educational preparation.

Provisions to effect freedom of movement within professions and across national boundaries have been in process of negotiation within the Common Market framework on a profession by profession basis. Thus, the medical doctors, accountants, architects, opticians, nurses, veterinarians, chemists, pharmacists, and dentists and other specialists have separately been the object of discussion and negotiation towards the end of reaching particular formulations that would sanction (1) the right of establishment for those wishing to migrate permanently, (2) the right to provide services for those who wish to or are called upon to practice their skills on a short run basis while maintaining the locus of their work in their nation of origin, and (3) the mutual recognition of diplomas.

Negotiations dealing with these issues with regard to the discrete professions have become protracted, and by 1975 agreement in the form of Council Directives had been reached for the medical doctors alone. Pharmacy proved somewhat intractable along with the other professions. For pharmacy, what occurred when the 'package' was split was that the emphasis changed from a focus on the various rights of individual pharmacists to an emphasis on pharmaceutical products. The movement of products rather than the movement of people turned out to be an easier area for negotiation among the member states. The discussion then centred on qualifications necessary for the manufacture of products and opened up the whole question of whether a monopoly for a single profession ever existed or was indeed desirable for that purpose. The qualifications and characteristics associated with individuals, and their equivalence or lack thereof in the context of internation comparisons, were dropped or rather deferred to the future, and the wide range of questions connected with the attempt to remove barriers to the cross-national migration of individual members of the 'liberal profession' of pharmacy was put off to the future.

Resistance to the split of the 'package' was deep-seated but proved to no avail. As early as 1972, a spokesman for the French Service Centrale de la Pharmacie et des Médicaments, Ministère de la Santé Publique et de la Sécurité Sociale, H. Nargeolet, forecast a great step forward which was in fact not to be taken as he observed: 'A great step will be taken meanwhile, when it will be admitted, in each of the countries of the Community, that the medication, from its manufacture to its delivery to the infirm person, must always remain placed under the surveillance and the responsibility of the pharmacists' (Nargeolet, 1972). Such a concern for the 'responsible person' was clearly one of the matters for discussion which delayed the agreements necessary within the Common Market for the free market flow of pharmaceutical products. This was noted in 1967 by the President of the German Pharmaceutical Manufacturers' Federation when he observed that, although the German delegation held a different view, 'other delegations insist that the free traffic of goods can only be considered after harmonization of legal regulations in the following ...: harmonization of regulations concerning the responsible person in charge of manufacture'. His summary also included other areas, such as advertising, patent law, issuance of prescriptions, price fixing, and the granting of manufacturing licences, which also served to delay agreement in what he described as 'a major Community industry' (Engelhorn, 1967).

The delays came to an end as the Council of Ministers finally agreed to push ahead with the free circulation of pharmaceutical products and to lay aside those other considerations related to the pharmacy profession itself. In May 1973, M. de Crayencour, who was then head of the administrative unit within the Common Market Commission that was responsible for regulations concerning the right of establishment, described to the Congrès National des Pharmaciens de France the state of affairs at that time. These views were particularly important as they emanated from the organ of the European Economic Community which formulated the initial Draft Directives and had responsibility for making proposals to the Council. Further significance is attached to these formulations, in as much as the Commission staff both sought and received communications from the associations of liberal professionals in the Common Market nations and from other interested parties, during the entire period of preparation and drafting of the Draft Directives. M. de Crayencour summarized the state of deliberations and decisions as follows in his presentation to the National Congress of French Pharmacists:

> It will be too long to explain to you the different Community positions necessary in order to bring about the free circulation of products: conditions of putting on the market, norms of protocols, publicity, mutual recognition of the record of putting on

the market. ...

All these arrangements can, in principle, be realized without the application of the free circulation of persons. It is however, a point which must be regulated in order to obtain the free circulation of products: the mutual recognition of the conditions of education of the person responsible for the control of manufacture. ...

As is known, the free circulation of products brings into play considerable interests.

The political desire, at least by certain member states, to lead in this domain, is certainly greater than the matter of the free circulation of persons.

The Council of Ministers has taken, in this matter, an important decision: that free circulation of products must be realized, at least in essentials, before the end of the month of next June.

M. de Crayencour concluded this section of his forecast by observing that the Council of Ministers would be led to the following resolution:

the objective will be to determine the minimal conditions for the education of the professional charged with the control of manufacture in his unique country of origin. ... the conditions for the necessary education for that activity come to be established, the conditions can be satisfied either by a pharmacist or by another professional.

It is a matter of the exercise of the activity uniquely in the country of origin. That means from a strict juridical point of view we are not in the problem of the mutual recognition of diplomas. (de Crayencour, 1973)

These remarks clearly state that the views of the Commission staff in 1973 had moved to acceptance of the point that the activities of the responsible person could be undertaken equally as well by other professionals as by pharmacists alone. However, the arguments of the pharmacists continued to be firmly expressed. An important example is the document of the Groupement Professionnel des Pharmaciens de l'Industrie Pharmaceutique de la Communauté Economique Européenne (GPPIPCEE), dated 26 April 1974, entitled, 'Submission—on the role of the qualified person proposed in Draft Directive II to be responsible for the industrial manufacture of medicinal products—on the necessary education and training of that person, and—on the pre-eminence of the pharmacist as the person to whom this responsibility should be delegated'.

The argument there formulated was an interesting one, in that it noted that the group on economic questions of the Council had not as yet reached a unanimous decision on the responsible person, and it further contended that the question of qualifications of the responsible person had to be clarified and should take paramountcy over development of machinery to provide for the free circulation of medicinal products. The question, then, of alternative qualifications, seen by others to be a block to the move towards more free trade for pharmaceuticals, was seen by this *groupement* as vital before any such steps should be taken.

Its detailed views on the point of pharmacy's imputed pre-eminence were clearly stated, as follows:

the pharmacy graduate is pre-eminent for recognition as the qualified person. ... the effect of formulation on the biological availability of drugs cannot be divorced from the study of pharmacology nor indeed can a knowledge of chemical structural relationships. In practical terms, this means that a pharmacist considers quality control, safety and efficacy, as applied to a medicinal products, not as isolated factors but as a complete entity.

The pharmacist's understanding of the principles of the chemical, physical and biological sciences also enables him to communicate readily with his colleagues in a wide range of other disciplines and with governmental health authorities. His ability to evaluate and interpret the important implications of information provided by specialist departments in the industrial company cannot be matched by the graduate in any one of the scientific disciplines which form an integral part of the pharmacy course.

... a pharmacist has an adequate knowledge of every aspect of science that relates to the preparation, control and action of drugs and medicines.

... the basic first degree has the necessary broad base which, given appropriate experience in the pharmaceutical industry, ideally equips the pharmacist to discharge the responsibility of qualified person.

That position went beyond the scope of the original Draft Directive published in 1969 which required a pharmacist but permitted physicians, veterinarians, chemists or biologists also to serve as responsible persons if they secured further training which would provide the equivalent of the pharmacist's education. Article 10 of Proposition II of the 1969 proposals for the test Draft Directive as presented by the Commission to the Council for its deliberation expressed the point as follows:

All professional holders of the diploma of pharmacist and of a certificate attesting to the completion of a year of preparatory training in the activities in question, are qualified, as well as all other titled professionals, in addition a university diploma of physician, veterinarian, chemist or biologist, holder of a certificate provided by the competent organisms of the Member State of origin or of birth, certifying to the securing of an equivalent proof as much theoretical as practical of a nature to supply, in that Member State, an education equivalent to that of the pharmacist. (Communauté Economique Européenne, 1969).

The counter contention of the chemists attacked the requirements outlined in the 1969 Draft Directives and the even more restricted views of the pharmacists. The European Communities Chemistry Committee recently voiced their objections as follows:

The limitation to pharmacists (or the equivalent) conflicted with established practice. In some member states, for example, where there was no such restriction about 50 per cent of such posts in the pharmaceutical industry were in fact held by chemists. ... It is the Committee's view that the academic knowledge and experience to be demanded of the 'qualified person' must be related, to some extent, to the particular requirements of the sector of the pharmaceutical industry in which he is to be employed and that the emphasis to be placed on each subject of study, individually, will vary accordingly. Whatever his original discipline, therefore, the 'qualified person' will in almost all cases need to expand his academic knowledge by extending either its range or its depth. It is likely, too, that a major emphasis, for the great majority of such appointments, will be on quality control, requiring an extensive and detailed knowledge of chemistry. (European Community Chemistry Committee, 1975)

Interchanges of viewpoints such as these between the organized bodies of scientists and professionals seem likely to continue, based as they are in disagreements regarding the scope and limits of professional expertise. These distinctions between ways in which scientific chemists and professional pharmacists look at their worlds and carry out their tasks provide the bases for the activities of their associations. Confronted by differences in how tasks are performed in different national settings, and the necessity imposed upon them by a supra-national authority of resolving those differences, the associations have had to accommodate by creating new international structures. Thereby, they hope to influence public policy on a broad scale.

**Governmental Actions on Scientific Disciplines**

The final stages of development of the text of the Directive depended upon a search for agreement by representatives of the nine member states of the Common Market, sitting as the Council of Ministers. Extensive effort by the Commission staff, detailed consideration by technical and scientific experts, debates in the working groups and the Committee of Permanent Representatives, deliberations by the European Parliament, and the Economic and Social Committee, preceded the movement to the item of the proposed Directive on to the agenda of the Council itself. The issue and the divisions at the level of the Council to which has been given primary importance here concerned the definitions of the 'responsible person' and the 'qualified person'. Whether pharmacist or chemist, or physician, veterinarian, or biologist, proved to be subjects of prolonged debate. The governments of Europe took positions on these matters and voted finally on them, as they did on all the various phrases, clauses, and sections of the text as a whole. These underwent detailed scrutiny and analysis, modification and replacement, deletion or addition.

During the year preceding the Council approval of the Directive, changes occurred as consensus developed on the final text through negotiations among the governmental representatives who finally had the authority to act. The votes of governments on the inclusion or exclusion of particular scientific and professional fields in the text of the Directive constitute an unusual, indeed rare, situation. The action entailed political spokesmen dealing with matters normally outside their purview, and, at least in this form, almost an intrusion into a domain beyond their competency. A description of how the nine member governments of the Common Market voted on the inclusion or exclusion of scientific fields and subjects in the Directive, and a summary of their arguments, is worthy of record. The details are contained in the accompanying tables.

Table 1 contains a comparison of the 1974 text of the Draft Directive and of the Directive that was approved in 1975. The list of scientific fields did not change, although the field of biology was questioned by the Belgian government which indicated that 'the term "biology" needs amplifying'. Comparison of the list of subjects required in the course of study for the various scientific fields shows that most subjects remained. Some deletions and one addition were made. Basic human anatomy, botany, and zoology were deleted. The addition consisted of the phrase 'study of the composition and effects of the natural substances of plant and

TABLE 1  Disciplinary requirements for qualified persons in 1974 Draft Directive and 1975 Directive[8]

| Draft Directive | Directive |
|---|---|
| *Scientific fields* ||
| pharmacy | pharmacy |
| medicine | medicine |
| veterinary medicine | veterinary medicine |
| chemistry | chemistry |
| pharmaceutical chemistry and technology | pharmaceutical chemistry and technology |
| biology | biology |
| *Subjects required in the course of study for scientific fields* ||
| applied physics | applied physics |
| general and inorganic chemistry | general and inorganic chemistry |
| organic chemistry | organic chemistry |
| analytic chemistry | analytic chemistry |
| pharmaceutical chemistry including analysis of medicinal products | pharmaceutical chemistry including analysis of medicinal products |
| general and applied biochemistry (medical) | general and applied biochemistry (medical) |
| physiology [and basic human anatomy] | physiology |
| microbiology | microbiology |
| pharmacology | pharmacology |
| pharmaceutical technology | pharmaceutical technology |
| [botany] | |
| [zoology] | |
| toxicology | toxicology |
| [pharmacognosy (Medical aspects)] | pharmacognosy (medical aspects) (study of the composition and effects of the natural substances of plant and animal origin) |

Square brackets indicate the delegations disagreed about the inclusion of the subjects so marked and about whether they should be required components of the degree courses necessary for qualification.

animal origin' which was introduced to provide parenthetical clarity to 'pharmacognosy (medical aspects)'.

Votes on inclusion of specific scientific fields as requisites for study are recorded in Table 2. Denmark did not cast a recorded vote. Concerning deletions, Ireland and Italy voted four times to delete particular fields; France and the United Kingdom each voted three times for deletions; Luxembourg voted twice to delete; and the Netherlands and Belgium each voted once to delete. For retentions, Belgium and the Netherlands each voted three times to retain particular scientific fields; Luxembourg voted twice for retention; and France voted once to retain a field in the text. Germany was recorded as having an 'open mind' on the four fields.

TABLE 2  Governmental positions on inclusion of sciences in Directive[8]

| | | |
|---|---|---|
| biology [a] | 'the term "biology" needs amplifying' | Belgium |
| basic human anatomy [b] | in favour of deletion | France<br>Ireland<br>Italy<br>Luxembourg<br>United Kingdom |
| | in favour of retention | Belgium<br>Netherlands |
| | 'open mind' | Germany |
| botany [c] | in favour of deletion | France<br>Italy<br>Ireland<br>Netherlands<br>United Kingdom |
| | in favour of retention | Belgium<br>Luxembourg |
| | 'open mind' | Germany |
| zoology [c] | in favour of deletion | Belgium<br>France<br>Ireland<br>Italy<br>Luxembourg (possibly)[e] |
| | in favour of retention | Netherlands |
| | 'open mind' | Germany |
| pharmacognosy (medical aspects)[d] | in favour of deletion | Italy<br>Ireland<br>United Kingdom |
| | in favour of retention | Belgium<br>France<br>Luxembourg<br>Netherlands |
| | 'open mind' | Germany |

a  In the Directive that was adopted, biology was included as a scientific field which would serve as qualification.
b  In the Directive that was adopted, basic human anatomy was deleted. In the Draft Directive, it was listed as a phrase modifying the subject of physiology.
c  In the Directive that was adopted, botany and zoology were deleted as subjects required for study by those qualified through acquisition of a university diploma.
d  Pharmacognosy (medical aspects) was included in both Draft Directive and Directive. The Directive adopted added the following in parentheses: 'Study of the composition and effects of the active principles of natural substances of plant and animal origin'.
e  This apparently indicated that the delegation required further consultation at the time of the key discussions. The delegation did state its tentative position in favour of deletion.

This episode in public policy is unusual in the evolution of sciences and professions. Governmental departments and ministries of education, health, industry, and social services often make judgements concerned with budgetary allocations, credentials, and competency which have consequences for sciences and professions. Conflicts between specialities may sometimes be adjudicated, resolved or worsened by such events. Career patterns, public support, public service obligations, recognition, and registration may be affected by actions of governmental authorities. Such actions are often indirect and do not entail the kind of overall approval or disapproval of particular fields of competency which occurred in this instance. Further, the interchange among governments on this kind of phenomenon and their voting on assumed merits or demerits of given fields of scientific and professional knowledge constitutes an unusual occurrence.

And so public policy recording the production of pharmaceuticals useful for health care has taken new shape within modern Western Europe. The refinements of institutional arrangements of each of the countries in the European Economic Community have become clarified and the sciences and professions have been challenged by these efforts to integrate the economies of nations through actions by governments. New cross-national organizations of sciences and professions have developed towards the end of permitting their national associations to confront and cope more effectively with the heightened political and economic linkages among nations. Governments have broadened their involvement with scientific and professional systems and have sought both to protect national interests and to provide accommodation for products, persons, and services from abroad. The flow of medicaments from the industrialized plants where their quality and potency are assured through to the hands of the dispensing professionals for distribution to the public continues.

Public health and greater economic integration are the intertwined objectives of public policy which is developing on an international scale. The emergent public policy and the complex processes whereby that policy takes form have far-reaching impact on the performance of scientific and professional tasks, and touch on the assumptions, distinctions, and claims associated with the efforts of scientific and professional associations in their particular domains.

**Acknowledgements**

This study was substantially aided by support from Rutgers University, through various Research Council Grants, including travel funds, as well as its award of a Faculty Academic Study Leave, and the opportunity provided through a Travel Fellowship from the World Health Organization. The hospitality and kindness of many individuals associated with scientific and professional bodies in Europe, the openness and interest of staff members of the Common Market units in Brussels, and the facilities of Astor College of Middlesex Hospital, of the Ciba Foundation, and of the Social Research Unit of Bedford College, all in London, and of La Fondation Universitaire in Brussels, were of critical value, as were the facilities of the British Library, the Rutgers University Libraries, Harvard University's Countway

Library and Baker Library, the Library of the Massachusetts College of Pharmacy, and the European Economic Community Information Office in New York.

## Notes

1. Reproduced by permission of Dr T. D. Whittet.
2. Reproduced by permission of the American Pharmaceutical Association.
3. © The Johns Hopkins University Press.
4. Reproduced by permission of The Chemical Society.
5. Reproduced by permission of the Royal Institute of Chemistry.
6. Reproduced by permission of Benn Brothers Ltd.
7. Reproduced by permission of J. A. Verreydt.
8. The source of this material is the following: 'Drug manufacturers in the EEC: new Draft Directive', *Pharmaceutical Journal*, **213**, 5796, December 1974, 547–551. This contains the text of the Draft Directive described as the product of the Committee of Experts formed by the Committee of Permanent Representatives (COREPER) for the purpose of reaching agreement at a technical level. Upon approval by COREPER, the Draft was placed on the agenda of the Council of Ministers for final action.

   Materials in the Tables are derived from the footnotes contained in that article which were said to 'indicate how the various national delegations thought about certain aspects' of the 'qualified person'.

   Various informants attested to the veracity of the details in the article.

## References

Beck, Robert H., *et al*. (1970), *The Changing Structure of Europe: Economic, Social, and Political Trends*, Minnesota, University of Minnesota Press.

Chiltz, G. (1973), 'Some are more equal than others', *Chemistry in Britain*, **9**, 12, pp. 550–555, December.

Commission des Communautés Européennes (1969), *Repertoire de organismes communs crées dans le cadre des Communautés Européennes par les associations industrielles, artisanales, commerciales, et de services des six pays; associations de professions libérales; organisations syndicales de salariés et groupements de consommateurs*, Brussels.

Communauté Economique Européenne (1969), 'Draft directives and recommendation of the council fixing the procedures for the realization of freedom of establishment and freedom of services for certain non-salaried activities in the pharmaceutical field', *Journal Officiel*, 12 année, no. C.54, 28 April (my translation).

Cowen, David L. (1970), 'The role of the pharmaceutical industry' in John B. Blake (ed.), *Safeguarding the Public: Historical Aspects of Medicinal Drug Control*, Baltimore, Johns Hopkins Press, pp. 72–82, especially 81–82.

de Crayencour, J. P. (1973), 'Remarks to Congrès National des Pharmaciens de France', typescript, Le Touquet, May 1973 (my translation).

Dainton, Sir Frederick (1973), 'Whither chemists and chemistry?', *Chemistry in Britain*, **9**, 1, 306–311, January.

Darling, W. M. (1973), 'Latest on the EEC—but the effects on British pharmacy are "conjecture"', *Chemist and Druggist*, **199**, 4848, 213, 17 February.

Engelhorn, Curt (1967), 'The German pharmaceuticals industry in the EEC', mimeo, Opera Mundi-Europe no. 431, 19 October.

European Communities Chemistry Committee (1975), 'Qualified persons in the pharmaceutical industry', mimeo, London, Royal Institute of Chemistry, October.

*European Pharmacopoeia* (1969), vol. I, published under the direction of the Council of Europe (Partial Agreement), Maisonneuve S. A., Sainte-Ruffine.

Friedrich, Carl J. (1969), *Europe: An Emergent Nation?*, New York, Harper and Row.
Fritsche, Wolfgang (1973), 'A role for tomorrow', *Chemistry in Britain*, **9**, 12, 541–543, December.
Groupement Pharmaceutique de la Communauté Européenne (1969), *Livre blanc de la pharmacie européenne*, Bruxelles (my translation).
Groupement Professionnel des Pharmaciens de l'Industrie Pharmaceutique de la Communauté Economique Européenne (1974), 'Submission—on the role of the qualified person proposed in Draft Directive II to be responsible for the industrial manufacture of medicinal products—On the necessary education and training of that person, and—On the pre-eminence of the pharmacist as the person to whom this responsibility should be delegated', mimeo, Brussels, 26 April.
Haberer, Joseph (1972), 'Politicalization in Science', *Science*, **178**, 713–724, 17 November.
Hallstein, Walter (1962), *United Europe*, Cambridge, Mass., Harvard University Press.
Hughes, Everett C. (1952), 'Psychology: science and/or profession', *The American Psychologist*, **7**, 441; reprinted in Everett C. Hughes, *The Sociological Eye: Selected Papers on Work, Self, and the Study of Society*, Chicago, Aldine-Atherton, 1971, p. 360.
Jamous, H., and B. Peloille (1970), 'Professions or self-perpetuating systems? Changes in the French university-hospital system', in J. A. Jackson, *Professions and Professionalization*, Cambridge, Cambridge University Press.
Johnson, C. A. (1975), quoted in, 'Quality control of medicines', *Chemist and Druggist*, **204**, 4980, 319, 321, 323, 6 September.
King, Alexander (1967), 'Science and technology in Europe' in Stephen R. Graubard (ed.), *A New Europe?*, Boston, Beacon Press.
Lancet (1972), 'Drugs in the EEC', *The Lancet*, **1**, 944–945, 29 April.
Lee, Henry (1975), 'Chemistry as an organized profession', *Chemistry in Britain*, **11**, 1, 65–69, January.
Lewis, D. F. (1976), 'Pharmaceutical consequences of the European economic community', *Journal of the American Pharmaceutical Association*, **NS16**, 7, 406–411, 7 July.
Marini-Bettolo, G. B. (1969), 'Preface', *European Pharmacopoeia*, vol. I, published under the direction of the Council of Europe (Partial Agreement), Maisonneuve S. A., Sainte-Ruffine, pp. 9–19.
The Monopolies Commission (1970a), Appendix 9, The Registered Professions, 86–93, in part II, *The Appendices, A Report on the General Effect on the Public Interest of Certain Restrictive Practices So Far As They Prevail in Relation to the Supply of Professional Services*, London, HMSO, reprinted 1971.
The Monopolies Commission (1970b), Table IX, part (a), 'Breakdown of members of professional bodies and registered practitioners ... by status of employment', part II, *The Appendices* ..., pp. 163–169.
The Monopolies Commission (1970c), Table VIII, 'Reservation of Functions and Titles to Specified Practitioners', Part II, Appendices, 155–161.
Nargeolet, H. (1972), 'Evolution of the efforts of the European economic community in the domain of pharmacy', *Annales Pharmaceutiques Françaises*, **30**, 3, 183–186 (my translation).
Parker, Eric (1973), 'Chemists into Europe', *Chemistry in Britain*, **9**, 12, 546–547, December.
Pharmaceutical Journal (1974), 'Drug manufacturers in the EEC: New draft directive', *Pharmaceutical Journal*, **213**, 5796, 547–551, December.
Pharmaceutical Journal (1976), 'European Community biologists association formed', *Pharmaceutical Journal*, **216**, 5853, 73, 24 January.
Robinson, Dr F. A. (1973), 'Professional dilemmas', *Chemistry in Britain*, **9**, 1, 312–317, January.

Royal Institute of Chemistry (1975), *Professional Bulletin*, no. 17, London, Royal Institute of Chemistry, 1 April.

Selden, William K. (1974), 'Forces affecting the health professions', *Journal of the American Pharmaceutical Association,* **NS 14,** 608–610, November.

Whittet, T. D. (1973), 'Pharmaceutical Directives, remarks to meeting of medical officers', typescript, 16 April.

World Health Organization (1971), 'Good practices in the manufacture and quality control of drugs, Appendix 70 of Specifications for the Quality Control of Pharmaceutical Preparations', *International Pharmacopoeia*, 2nd edn., supplement, Geneva, pp. 99–107.

World Health Organization (1975), 'National drug policies', *WHO Chronicle*, **29,** 9, 337–349, September.

# 5

# NATIONALISMS AND NATIONALIZATION OF THE SCIENTIFIC FIELD IN QUEBEC

## Marcel Fournier and Louis Maheu

With the enhanced development of the sociology of science in recent years, the status of the various factors explicative of the expansion of scientific activity have had to be modified. It is no longer original to claim that science is not the arbiter of its own development. The paradigms and the discoveries of science are not produced solely by evolution, entirely turned in on itself, in a natural history of scientific ideas: a 'cognitive islet' within a society. It is now well established that scientific activity is open to a multiplicity of social influences which are external to it to the extent that they are precisely not components of a natural history of scientific ideas (Ben-David, 1971; Blume, 1974).

It may be argued with some force, however, that the notion of external social conditions as stimulating scientific progress has given rise to a variety of perspectives on the identity of the relevant social conditions which particularly harmonize with the development of science. For some, among the external stimulants to the progress of science must be set the multiple networks of relationships and social organizations within which scientists are located (Crane, 1972; Mullins, 1973; Cole and Cole, 1973). One might add also the various scientific and para-scientific markets on which, impelled by the laws of competition, and the search for professional legitimacy and recognition, the producers operate. The various forms of gratification or reward which appropriately signify first membership, then eminence and success, in the scientific milieu then constitute so many nodal points in these markets (Bourdieu, 1975).

For others, the whole question of the social conditions of scientific progress is seen as a function of the institutionalization of specialized scientific activity within a society (Clark, 1972; Ben-David, 1971; Merton, 1974). It is as if a successful process of institutionalization would consecrate two distinct forms of scientific activity: downstream of this process, scientific activity would be sufficiently developed itself largely to determine, through the weight of its organizational and institutional structures, those conditions of its own development which had previously largely inhered in a social world outside science.

One ought therefore to anticipate that the emergence, then the expansion and the full output of the processes of science, are very closely related to those ideologies and values which dominate a given society. The cognitive and intellectual instruments, with which social actors form their relationships to matter which they thereby vest with conceptual intentionality, structure the various forms of knowledge with which a social collectivity is successively engaged. To be sure, as Moscovici (1968) has shown, these forms of knowledge prove more or less accommodating to scientific activity as one means of understanding matter.

One must therefore seek to understand how the place and the functions of an educational system, and notably of its highest rung, the university system, become determinant within a social structure. Well and good in so much as the educational apparatus provides means of production and reproduction of ideologies, values, modes of understanding, which may be more or less adequate and functional for scientific activity. The various social actors evolving in the wake of this apparatus do indeed produce functions and social roles from which scientific activity is not easily distinguished. Not only are these specialized social actors dependent upon a precise area of production, but in so far as they are themselves an element of society with specific political and economic goals, the various types of intellectuals and of scientists occupy social positions from which emerge important stimuli to scientific progress. In brief, the relationship which a scientific domain has with the religious and intellectual (if not symbolic) domain are a mark of its own development. Moreover, the social and political positions which the scientists and intellectuals occupy are a first crystallization of the relationships between the scientific and other domains.

Even if the scientists and intellectuals make up a social group whose aspirations and interests are of particular importance for scientific activity, they are far from being the only significant group in this respect. Other social groups, classes or elements of social classes, such as the ruling or rising classes, or the *petite bourgeoisie*, also pursue social objectives, and must take account of those values and forms of knowledge open to influences from science as well as of the various more material circumstances of scientific progress. Their social route, the positions which they seek, appear dependent upon the production of new knowledge or on the rationalization of the forms of political and social control. One cannot be sure that the relationships which link a scientific domain to the totality of constraints within the domain of politics weigh but slightly on the evolution of the former.

To be sure, and there is no need to linger on this point, more or less well refined and implanted organizational structures of science can mediate the effects of such external social conditions upon scientific progress. Or better still: they can legitimate that which they declare consonant with the ethics of science, and by the same token they can repudiate contrary aspects of society. But whatever they might do, and however established they might be, they cannot escape entirely from these social conditions, nor render them ineffective.

Outside the central and fully institutionalized scientific systems, in which well structured scientific organizations and the rhetoric of the neutrality of science readily prosper, there exist scientific systems which might be termed 'peripheral' and which allow one to expose more clearly the social conditions of scientific progress. It is not that central systems are totally insulated from such influences; it is rather that a peripheral situation is less adapted to the 'reinterpretations' which a central system (and therefore a more developed and stronger system) can effect according to its own inherent logic. However, in order that analysis of the development of a peripheral scientific system yield results of this kind, it is necessary to reconsider the notions of periphery and peripherality.

One must therefore leave the privileged ground of Ben-David (1971): that of the relationships between one (or a small number of) scientific centre(s) and scientific domains termed peripheral through being less determinant, and thereby less useful, for the most innovative and advanced modern science. Clearly the notion of periphery includes a reality of this kind. But analysis of such an external relationship (between one scientific domain and another), a relationship which is moreover immutable in the short and medium term, rapidly proves to be without more substantial power of enlightenment, if it is not accompanied by consideration of other phenomena relating to the development of a local scientific domain.

A small number of scientific positions, of modes of legitimation and reward within a peripheral scientific domain: are these the indicators of 'colonized science', to adopt Bassala's formulation (Bassala, 1967)? Is the periphery of a given local scientific activity in its institutional forms and in its subject-matter necessarily correlated with its complete dependence upon external scientific systems, whether or not these are central to world scientific production? Under the yoke of such a dependency, scientific activity would be in a way doubly peripheral: not only would it not be central to international production, but within its own society its marginality and isolation would be most apparent (Shils, 1972).

But it is possible to conceive also of peripherality of a less dependent kind. Still peripheral in its external relationships with other scientific systems, a scientific activity can become, or might even be in process of becoming, a social activity more central and developed within a given social structure. Thanks to an enhanced social valuation of science and of its socio-political relevance for various social groups occupying key structural positions, a scientific activity can gradually acquire the means of its own independence. And, as Bassala has stressed, such an evolution most commonly accompanies a cultural and political nationalist movement which unites, in the specific context of a given society, all the social conditions of scientific progress.

This is precisely the clarification needed in order to illuminate the development of the scientific field in Quebec and to systematize its characteristics.[1] We would learn little in qualifying it as peripheral with regard only to its relations with other scientific systems more central to current scientific production, and it is scarcely more satisfactory to treat Quebec science as a subregion of a broader scientific domain—that of Canada—which is itself peripheral at the level of international production. This is unsatisfactory principally because the scientific domain in Quebec, in terms of its existence and of its evolution, depends upon the multiple facets of a socio-political nationalist movement and then, in a way, upon the 'nationalization' of its links with the social conditions of its development. In the light of this it becomes clear that the Quebec scientific field belongs, first and above all, within the social structure of Quebec; even though the organizations and institutional structures of Canadian science provide support of a significant (though far from sufficient) kind for its development.

**ACFAS: a Scientists' Movement**

Before the end of the nineteenth century, truly autoindigenous scientific activity did not exist in Quebec: Quebec was a 'terrain' which European researchers visited to study its flora and fauna, and to collect specimens. As G. Bassala emphasized in his study of 'The spread of Western science' (1967), during this initial phase, scientific researches as generally conducted in disciplines such as botany, zoology, and geology, to some extent in astronomy, in geophysics and in the various geographic sciences, were carried out not only by specialists but also by amateurs visiting the country as explorers, diplomats or missionaries. Some educators, members of the clergy who taught in secondary schools and colleges, had received a scientific education in Europe. But they did not carry out research: occupying hierarchically inferior and marginal positions in their institutions, they tended to confine their activities to the popularization of science.

The first few indigenous men of scientific learning appeared only at the end of the nineteenth century: these were mainly naturalists whose education derived from the study of European works of science. An attempt to create a scientific consciousness or milieu in Quebec may be seen in the establishment, in 1869, of the journal *Le Naturaliste Canadien*. There was also some social scientific research activity principally associated with Léon Gérin who, after a short stay in France, and inspired by the model of Le Play and his disciples, undertook a series of monographic studies of peasant families. These diverse scientific activities might be regarded as 'colonial' in the sense that there was no local scientific education, diffusion, or commitment, and that the problems to which the few indigenous researchers addressed themselves were most commonly defined by those outside the francophone academic community. Quebec's francophone universities, largely controlled by members of the clergy, limited their activities to the education of priests, doctors, and lawyers. Theology and (Thomist) philosophy were of paramount importance among the intellectual disciplines, theology was truly 'queen of the sciences'. Moreover, those students who had access to university studies all came through the *collèges classiques*, where they received a humanistic education, characterized by an emphasis on the teaching of Latin and Greek. To be sure, in 1833 the École Polytechnique of Montreal had been established, but this school, which recruited some European professors, received few students, and produced only 'civil engineers'. Some years later (1915) the professors and ex-students of the school established a journal, *La Revue trimestrielle canadienne*. However, in order to assure regularity of publication for the journal, the founders were obliged to allow contributors from a wide range of non-scientific disciplines (for example law, social science, business studies, literature, etc.) and to treat matters as diverse as architecture, the art of the engineer, social-political economy, finance, history, etc. Study of the articles published between 1915 and 1921 suggests that the most important section was not 'The art of the engineer' (18·5 per cent of articles), nor that of 'Industry/finance' (19·36 per cent), nor 'Science/mathematics' (15·2 per cent), but that of 'Social and political economy' (24·5 per cent). As well as the diversity of issues treated, the educational backgrounds of contributors is an additional and useful indicator of the heterogeneity as well as the difficulty—if not the impossibility—of publishing a journal devoted wholly to the sciences and engineering in Quebec. Thus, it appears that graduates and faculty of the École Polytechnique represented less than 40 per cent of contributors.

It is very tempting to equate the appearance of a Quebec scientific 'community', independent of the American and (anglophone) Canadian scientific community, with the creation in 1923 of the 'Association canadienne-française pour l'Avancement des Sciences' (ACFAS). This event, which followed by a few years the establishment of a School of Surveying and of an École Supérieure of chemistry at Laval University (Quebec) and after the complete reorganization of the University of Montreal (creation of a Faculty of Science, a Faculty of Social Science, Politics and Economics, etc.), certainly stimulated the development of more frequent contacts between the few learned societies, or groups of francophone researchers, which then existed in Quebec. However as C. Ouellet (1964, p. 18) has noted: 'members of societies of amateurs or young people, teachers absorbed by the tasks of instruction, are rarely researchers with valuable works to present'. Moreover, it was not until ten years later that the first annual conference was organized, during which researchers from different regions of Quebec and from different disciplines (biology, physics, chemistry, natural history, philosophy, and social sciences) presented scientific communications.

The intention of the organizers[2] was to participate, by the organization of public lectures, the awarding of prizes and scholarships, etc., in the 'propagandization and the popularization of all the findings of science', and to persuade their co-citizens and the public authorities of the importance of science. It was in a sense a 'scientific movement', i.e. 'a group of people who believe in science as a valid way to truth and to effective mastery over nature as well as to the solution of the problems of the individual and his society' (Ben-David, 1971, p. 78). Use of the term 'movement' signifies that the group of scientists and intellectuals sought not only to spread their point of view, but also to mobilize a much greater number of individuals and also of social groups who recognized the value of scientific research. It was above all the members of the younger generations whom those who organized ACFAS sought to involve in order to inculcate them with the 'taste for science'. For example, between 1925 and 1935 they organized nearly two hundred lectures in the *écoles normales*, in the *collèges classiques*, and in the universities, as well as setting up numerous scientific exhibitions.[3] In addition, the Society of Natural History, affiliated to ACFAS, and which brought together both amateurs and professionals, established a vast network of young naturalists' clubs and created a popular journal for the young. This desire to reach a large and youthful public and to transmit to it some rudiments of science appeared finally in the debate initiated by the scientists, and which aimed to assure the teaching of science in secondary and collegial educational institutions. This 'crusade', aimed at convincing those responsible of the need for scientific instruction at the secondary level, succeeded far beyond all other initiatives in stimulating a reaction of the 'Ancients' against the 'Moderns'. It was that the critique of the scientists represented a calling into question not only of the organization of curricula, but also of their conception: thereby attacking the legitimacy and the authority of the members of the clergy and of the religious groups which controlled the educational institutions. Though initially intellectual, the polemic took on a political dimension, demanding a taking up of positions not merely in the educational journals, but in the intellectual and political ones, and even in the daily press. These media, which the scientists frequently used, show clearly that the audience to which they addressed themselves was not confined to members of the clergy and of the liberal professions (i.e. members of the traditional *petite bourgeoisie* who usually occupied the influential positions in the political and ideological apparatus). The scientists addressed themselves also to new categories, new classes which were slowly forming, and of which a few members worked in educational and cultural institutions (radio, journalism, etc.) or laboured in the cause of a variety of social movements (co-operatism, trades unionism, etc.).

Though few in number, ill paid, and inadequately equipped, the francophone Quebec scientists hoped that the value of the cultural scientific capital which they possessed would be recognized, and that the number of posts—principally in academic institutions—open to recipients of a scientific education would consequently expand.

However, some among those to whom the Quebec scientists addressed themselves scarcely felt inclined to accede to demands which entailed a recognition of the inadequacy of the classical education which they had themselves received: an admission of its 'lack of rigour, lack of critical spirit, and the absence of intellectual integrity' (Ouellet, 1938). To an extent the institutionalization of scientific activity represented for the traditional *petite bourgeoisie*—and principally for its intellectuals—a disqualification, a questioning of legitimacy at once intellectual and political, won in earlier struggles.

The illusion of all scientists' movements, and often of those who analyse them, is to believe that the major obstacle to the development of scientific activity is of a cultural order, and that it is enough to modify the dominant values, or more generally the dominant ideology, for development to take place. Of course in any struggle for cultural legitimacy it is first of all the intellectuals (members of the clergy, professors, journalists, contributors to reviews, etc.) who are mobilized: the struggle appears as a conflict of ideas. But principally because the intellectual and scientific field is only feebly constituted, and scarcely has power to translate external demands into the terms of its own rationality, the struggle also has a properly political dimension: challenging as it does the authority of those responsible for the administration of things and of men. Relatively marginal to the university system the scientists were, until the end of the 1950s, constrained to avoid a too direct or too violent attack whether on the ideology or on the policy of the traditional *petite bourgeoisie* (from which, moreover, they had largely sprung). For example, in the face of the rhetoric of members of the clergy who frequently did not hesitate to oppose religion to science, some scientists were even driven in the course of the debate to show their 'good faith': to publicly demonstrate their faith, their acceptance of Thomist philosophy and their submission to the Catholic Church. And if in a way it was impossible even for a scientist to propound 'the religion of the spirit' without being thereby impregnated with 'the spirit of religion' (Pouliot, 1938, p. 57), the reason for it was that philosophic knowledge (theology), so important in the educational system, represented a form of cultural capital greatly valued by members not only of the clergy but also of the traditional *petite bourgeoisie* (lawyers, notaries, administrators, etc.) who occupied a relatively important place in the social structure and who held the major posts in the state apparatus and in the educational system. The subordination of the sciences to philosophy was, at that time, largely strategic, in that it permitted avoidance of criticism both from the university authorities and from the more conservative segments of the ruling class and of the clergy.[4] At the same time it concealed the realization of important changes (progressive specialization of education, recruitment of foreign professors, increasing value of titles and of diplomas, etc.). That is, it was because they did not appear to menace the established social order or to challenge the legitimacy of those who held political and symbolic (religious) authority, that the scientists won the conditions (posts, research funds) necessary for their own internal objectives: for the advancement of specialized and cumulative knowledge, for the creation of a 'scientific community', and for the transmission of a specific and homogeneous education.

However, though it was members of the clergy and of the religious orders who underlined and denounced the dangers of scientific rationalism, the first intellectuals disposed to change career, to undertake a conversion of acquired cultural capital, were also drawn from this group. In effect, nearly half of the 260 students graduating between 1920 and 1932 from the Faculty of Science of the University of Montreal were members of the clergy and of the religious orders (Boucher, 1931). And if among these graduates and among the first professors of the faculty there was a high proportion of brothers, it was because the attraction of this 'capital conversion' was the greater for those who occupied hierarchically inferior positions within the religious domain. Between the lay scientists, marginal to the university system, and the brothers, of low status in the Church and who worked principally at the primary and secondary levels of education, was instituted a sort of alliance, designed to modify the structure of relationships making up Quebec's intellectual and scientific field. This alliance had all the more strategic value since it allowed the defenders of science to avoid being identified with laïcism and with atheism, and thereby defused many of the arguments and fears of the 'Ancients'. In the light of this the importance which men of religion such as Frère Marie-Victorin were able to acquire in the universities and more generally in the scientific and intellectual milieux of Quebec may be better understood. In such men were united philosophical and theological competence with scientific competence, permitting them legitimately to engage in both scientific and religious activities without the two appearing to be in opposition. Consequently, they were able to assist the transformation both of the position of scientific education within the university system and of that of their religious group or order within the religious/intellectual fields (hitherto but slightly differentiated).

To consider only the general and abstract opposition of religion to science is facilely to conclude that the action of ACFAS, until the end of the 1940s, had been relatively ineffective. Since, though it had attained some diffusion of a 'taste for science' among a much wider public, it had scarcely succeeded in substituting 'religion of the spirit' for 'spirit of religion'.[5] It must be noted that a scientist movement is characterized not so much by a simple spread of ideas in a diffuse and indistinct audience, as by a restructuring of relationships between groups or fractions of classes already vested with some cultural capital, consequent upon the introduction of a new form of such capital. In this regard the activities of the francophone scientists, and of their association ACFAS, were strategically determinant. Their alliance with religious groups seeking a greater religious/intellectual (these having been undifferentiated) legitimacy—and who thus interested themselves in science—contributed to a modification of the structure of relationships between groups of intellectuals and clerics, and thereby of the structure of relationships between the diverse fractions of the traditional *petite bourgeoisie*.

**Nationalist Rhetoric: Well-being (of the Nation) through Science**

As important as the popularization—mobilization—work of a scientist movement might be, its presence alone seems insufficient to ensure the institutionalization of scientific activity. On the contrary, as Ben-David points out, it is necessary that the movement disappear, or at least that there comes into existence a 'scientific community' of specialists different from and autonomous of the scientific movement. However, this differentiation is possible only on condition that, on the one hand there come into being a network of institutions contributing to the formation of a body of specialists, and on the other that there are social groups or classes prepared directly (through financial aid, creation of industrial laboratories) or indirectly (principally through the mediation of the state) to support scientific research and its applications (Oberschall, 1972).

Now, in a social formation such as that of Quebec, in which economic development depends largely upon foreign (English-Canadian and American) initiatives and capital, there is little incentive to the development of a scientific activity fully articulated with industrial production or to technological innovation. At the very most there is room for scientists who devote themselves not to scientific discovery but to tasks of popularization, translation, or 'transfer' of work done elsewhere, or who move rapidly to posts of supervision or management. Further, for Quebec's francophone scientists, the probability that they might accede to such posts as are available is still smaller partly because they lack both the linguistic competence and the cultural capital of the anglophones, and partly because the scientific competence, or capital, which they have acquired, and which is frequently 'European' (or more precisely 'French'), tends to be devalued by comparison with that available in the United States. As one commentator noted at the beginning of the

1930s, 'Education cannot absorb all the young people in search of scientific culture. One would like to see many of them occupying posts in industry, the public services, State scientific organizations. Almost all doors are closed against them' (Boucher, 1931, p. 402).

Faced with the double danger of disqualification and relegation, the scientists have two alternatives: to 'Americanize' themselves (i.e. to 'recycle' in the American research and higher education system), or to 'invest in their nationality'. Even if the former strategy is largely criticized by francophone Quebecois intellectuals as contributing to the Americanization of French Canada,[6] it is nonetheless adopted by a certain number of scientists who spend study visits in the United States or who actively participate in the meetings of the American learned societies.[7] Such activities are often described, as the botanist Pierre Dansereau has underlined, as the attempt 'to facilitate the passage of certain information and values from one culture (the French) to another (the English)', that is, as interpretation (Dansereau, 1964, p. 286). However during the years following the economic crisis of 1929, and which were characterized in Quebec by the rebirth of nationalism, Quebecois scientists were more often led to borrow the 'nationalist' rhetoric, and also the strategies, of the intellectuals among the traditional *petite bourgeoisie*. For the slogans 'Let us take possession of the soil' and 'Let us take possession of industry' the scientists substituted the slogan 'Let us take possession of the summits' (Pouliot, 1938). In addition, to counteract the Anglo-Saxon (American or English-Canadian) influence, university professors were recruited in France and, after the creation in 1926 of a francophone scientific institute in Quebec, closer institutional links with scientists in France were established. Thus, beyond various divergences of opinion, of which the most important was the value accorded to scientific nationality, Quebecois scientists and the traditional *petite bourgeoisie*, and in particular its intellectual element, agreed on the view that the well-being or indeed the survival of French Canada lay in education, or more broadly, in the acquisition of competence, of skills. 'Nothing is possible without the school; with the school all is possible', Édouard Montpetit, Secretary of the University of Montreal and Director of the School of Social Sciences, affirmed in 1935. 'We will build something solid only on the basis of knowledge: knowledge of the elements of our national life, of the milieu in which we live, of the history which unifies our traditions . . .' (Montpetit, 1935, p. 38). This argument was in fact that which, in the course of the 1930s and 1940s, attracted the majority of scientists who occupied senior positions in the university system, or who achieved the presidency of ACFAS. Thus the Quebec scientist Frère Marie-Victorin, who maintained regular exchanges with American and English-Canadian scientists, did not restrict himself to denunciation of the deficiencies of French-Canadian culture (emphasis on popularization at the expense of true science, misunderstanding, fear, and scorn of science, etc.): he devoted his (1938) presidential address to the theme 'Science and National Life'.

There was then a substantial resemblance between the statements of these scientists and the nationalism of the political party (Union nationale) controlling the provincial government in the 1930s. Rather progressive at that time, the

Union nationale enacted a few policies with regard to the use of the natural sciences and the development of schools, related to the expansion of mining, lumbering and agriculture (Duchesne, 1975). The political support given to that government by many francophone scientists and intellectuals crumbled when it became apparent in the following years that two very different schemes of development were proposed for Quebec. The Quebec government led by Mr Duplessis neglected the struggle against the dictatorship of the great corporations; it wanted to enhance French-Canadian control only over the agricultural sector, and to preserve the existing forms of patronage. It failed to modernize or rationalize the state apparatus and finally, scarcely favoured the development of higher education or of university research. The scientists and Quebecois intellectuals offered a perspective of society, admittedly not wholly systematized, but characterized essentially by an enlargement of the place of science in secondary collegial and university education as well as in the management of social problems and conflicts.

But that the scientists affirm, for example, that 'the well-being of the nation depends upon the development of science', or that 'economic problems are first and foremost scientific problems', and that they adopt a 'nationalist' position in an important political debate, is not explicable simply in terms of the resentment or feelings of inferiority which the intellectuals of a 'dependent' country may have with regard to the culture and the power of the foreign metropolis. Our view here is opposed to that of Shils (1972, p. 400). In fact, the intellectuals and the scientists of such a country have an objective interest in resorting to 'nationalist' 'measures' and in borrowing the strategy of 'falling back'. In providing themselves with the instruments of diffusion, of exchange, and of gratification, while at the same time trying to define themselves, and for themselves, norms of scientific production and criteria of scientific worth, the scientists assure themselves of a more effective monopoly over the range of positions open to those with scientific training. Moreover, the French-Canadian scientists could thereby avoid so direct a competition with their anglophone or American colleagues, whose departments by then had much greater resources of manpower and research equipment. All the same, the constitution of a national scientific domain was scarcely possible without considerable enlargement of the number of scientific posts: without establishment of industrial laboratories and research centres; without development of scientific education within educational institutions; and without more frequent recourse to the services of scientists on the part of government. As Bassala (1967) has accurately noted, transformations such as these require a modification of the relationships existing between science on the one hand and the state (and the ruling class more broadly) on the other: this is particularly true of 'dependent' countries. To a certain extent, indeed, the 'national-ization' of the scientific domain in such a country requires its 'nationalization' (i.e. take over by the state): or at least more frequent and more regular intervention by government in the educational and research sectors.

Thus the claims of ACFAS in the 1930s and the 1940s were mainly submitted to the provincial government. However, those requests, occasionally granted, did not reduce the scientific backwardness of Quebec. By the beginning of the 1950s, Quebec had not gained in Canadian science a position corresponding to the importance of its population, its natural resources, its degree of industrialization (ACFAS, 1954).

Many of the public interventions of the francophone Quebecois scientists threw that backwardness into relief. Although 'nationalist', these interventions were, in the context of the political and constitutional issue of federal grants to the provincial universities, opposed to the views of other intellectuals. The traditional *petite bourgeoisie*, and mainly its intellectuals, discredited 'as traitors' those francophones who supported the policies of the federal government about the financing of provincial universities.

However, ACFAS refused to consider the problem of financial aid solely from the constitutional point of view, arguing that 'the lack of federal grants more enfeebled the powers of the Province in matters of education than their acceptance would challenge these powers': it thereby opposed the 'autonomist' policy of the provincial government. The propensity to adopt an 'autonomist' point of view was much slighter among francophone scientists in Quebec than among those groups and fractions of social classes which were in a sense struggling to maintain the value of their cultural capital (the classical humanities), and who scarcely felt disposed to recognize the importance of a properly scientific competence. To be sure, the scientists, whose object then was less to constitute a scientific domain more independent of that existing in the rest of Canada than to modify the ethnic division of scientific labour—thereby facilitating the access of francophones to higher positions in Canadian science—recognized the provincial government as a privileged interlocutor: hoping even that it might become their 'principal benefactor'. In the absence of an industry which could offer large numbers of jobs to graduates of the science faculties, only government intervention could stimulate employment and induce expansion of scientific higher education. The provincial government was of particular importance, since by virtue of its constitutional control of education, it could create teaching posts at the secondary level: it could also award scholarships and make additional funds available for research. However, faced with the inertia of the conservative elements of the traditional *petite bourgeoisie*, Quebec's francophone scientists, who continually called the conservatives to order—i.e. invited them 'to fulfil their responsibilities to the nation'—had little choice other than to continue to solicit more generous federal aid for research and for scholarships. They could only accept the few posts in federal research organizations made available to them, and integrate themselves in Canadian science by publishing articles in English in Canadian journals, by participating in Canadian scientific conferences, and by recognizing the legitimacy of the Royal Society of Canada.[8]

## State Control and the Institutionalization of Scientific Activity

Far from being determined by the inherent nature of the scientific disciplines, as Ladd and Lipset (1972) suggest, the 'apoliticism' of scientists is only the expression of the modification of their position within the university system and of the transformation of the structure of relationships between the scientific and intellectual domain on the one hand, and the religious, economic, and political domains on the other.[9] As paradoxical as it may seem, it was at a time when Quebecois scientists were least forced to respond to a variety of social demands, and when they were least tied, through the receipt of financial aid, to the state, that they most often spoke out and intervened in political debates. The period in which the francophone scientists could most easily intervene publicly in order to politicize debate over the development of scientific research was certainly that in which the scientific domain was still scarcely differentiated from the political and the religious: a period in which, for example, it was members of the clergy and the religious orders who controlled the educational institutions, the principal intellectual reviews, and the publishing houses; a period in which men of religion as well as senior officials frequently figured among the presidents of ACFAS. At that time the conditions under which scientists could participate legitimately in political debate, without risking their standing as scientists or the discrediting of their actual scientific work, had not yet been defined. In the absence of any such norms it was perfectly possible for scientists to accept positions and responsibilities outside science, to publish works of popularization, or even of literature—and to take positions in political debate. All the same, in order to account for the diverse activities in which the scientists did engage it is not sufficient to consider only the structure and the functioning of the scientific system of which they were part. It is necessary also to consider their location within the social structure, and more broadly the social functions which they fulfilled (or which science fulfilled) within the social formation.

It is commonly argued that the development of scientific research in Quebec was largely dependent upon the financial support of the federal government. Without being entirely false this view, often expressed by scientists themselves, tends to conceal the fact that this support could only have been effective if articulated with a transformation of the educational system. Now this transformation, which the scientists called for, and to which they contributed, was itself only possible on condition that it responded to the interests of groups and social classes possessing number and weight in the social structure sufficiently great for them to demand replacement of the 'bloc' holding power. In other words, it was only by virtue of the access to (political) power of the new (technico-professional) *petite bourgeoisie*, and subsequently of the modernization/rationalization of the provincial government's modes of management and of the scholastic system in its entirety, that there could occur significant growth in numbers of university students and in budgets for scientific research. It is hardly surprising that Quebec's scientists, for whom 'the highest level of science which a country can achieve is determined by the quality of its universities' (ACFAS, 1962, p. 7), sought reforms of the educational system;[10] or that they contributed by their writing (for example, in the review *Cité Libre*) and by their lectures to the overthrow of the Union Nationale government;[11] or that they participated in the realization of various social and political reforms in the early 1960s.

The progressive transformation which was effectuated in the educational system and its social functions at the end of the 1950s and in the course of the 1960s, was particularly apparent at the university level. For example, it was during those years that the faculties of pure and applied science, the schools of commerce, and the faculties of education opened wide their doors to a student clientele emerging directly from the public educational system (Tremblay, 1954). This clientele thus did not make use of the network of private institutions of secondary education, under the control of the clergy and the traditional *petite bourgeoisie*, which had hitherto been the royal, if not the exclusive, route to higher education. (It is perhaps unnecessary to add that the public system had proved distinctly the more open to the sciences.) Indeed, contributing to the explosion in university student numbers, those students not graduating from the private schools became at the beginning of the 1960s, the most significant group in the whole student population. Parallel to this diversification in clientele, there developed a certain democratization in the student population, to the extent that students of lower and medium socio-economic status families (for example, the children of skilled and semi-skilled workers, office workers, etc.) invaded the university system in increasing numbers.[12] They were particularly to be found in those faculties which were the more open to diplomates of public secondary education (commerce, education, pure and applied science); nevertheless some among them entered the academic streams, such as medicine, which promised especial and foreseeable social mobility (Maheu, 1974, p. 291–293).

For some time, the francophone universities of Quebec seemed almost split between their social function of producing and reproducing the minor local notables of the traditional *petite bourgeoisie*, and their function of mobilizing specific segments of the population in search of greater technico-professional skills outside those of the more traditional professions. Relying heavily on the network of private institutions, the traditional professional faculties thus served a socially and culturally clear-cut clientele, while the other faculties broadened the base of university enrolment. It is thus apparent that the polarization which characterized the francophone university system in Quebec was based in broader social oppositions within the *petite bourgeoisie*, and that therefore the conditions of evolution of the system were in fact to be found in the general social structure rather than in the university itself.

In effect, the social pressures exerted on the Quebec university system in the 1950s only achieve their full significance when their relationships with other, and broader, social phenomena are elucidated. The 1950s and early 1960s were marked in Quebec by a much larger oppositional movement, demanding the modernization and the rationalization not simply of the educational system, but also of the entire system of central political control by which the provincial government operated. It is because demands of this (latter) kind were made that one can identify the specific social classes mobilized by this movement. For it is those social classes making up the new technico-professional *petite bourgeoisie* which tend to express their interest in the effective working of government, and who seek influence upon the central politico-administrative apparatus in a society. This political manifestation of social demand is, in the strict sense of the term, structural: it is by virtue of their social positions within society that these particular elements of the population turn towards the state. Only recently urbanized and educated, those social groups suddenly revealed by a process of industrialization which modified the occupational structure of society had to await a government capable of coping with the contradictions which beset them. Apparent structural identification not only of these social classes, but even of their socio-political aims is certainly clearer cut within a social structure dependent upon external political and economic powers for its industrialization. The elements making up the new *petite bourgeoisie* demanded of the local government, often perceived as symbolic of a national grouping, that it deal with the contradictions of a 'dependent' process of socio-economic development with which their own interests seemed to conflict.

At the very centre of the socio-political claims of these social groups figured the fate of the educational apparatus and thus of the university system. Acquisition of professional competence better adapted to the exigencies of industrialization was seen as the means by which social mobility could best be achieved. In as much as large numbers of intellectuals, of scientists, (notably) of social scientists, of social activists, developed in the wake of the educational system (Maheu and Bélanger, 1972, p. 310), they tended to espouse the social aims of the classes to which they belonged by virtue of their social status. And when a new power bloc supporting this new *petite bourgeoisie* achieved control of the provincial government, the theme of collective national advancement through reform of the educational apparatus accompanied its accession to, and first steps in, the exercise of political power.[13] Thus this period, often referred to as 'the Quiet Revolution',[14] is identified first by its reforms of the educational system, and then of the whole apparatus of political management and control.

This represented a substantial change in 'social issues' for numerous elements making up these social groups. At a blow, from the periphery where they had been when seeking alliances outside the provincial political scene, their socio-political aims had become central to the social structure of Quebec. The essential strategy of social advancement of the new *petite bourgeoisie* thus consisted in the constitution of a new power bloc capable of exerting influence on the apparatus of provincial political control. Outstripping the traditional *petite bourgeoisie*, in a way on its own ground, this social advancement was characterized by a strong nationalist sentiment appealing to a much altered social vision compared to the nationalism of the traditional *petite bourgeoisie*.

It is within this particular political conjuncture that there was conceived, and then realized, the rationalization and the take over by the state of the upper rungs of the educational apparatus: the secondary, the post-secondary, and the university. The Quebec government thus became the principal proprietor of virtually the totality of institutions making up these upper rungs: corresponding to each there developed a network of public institutions controlled directly by the state. Reform of institutions was accompanied by reform of the means of their control by the creation, in 1963, of a Ministry of Education. The decade 1960–1970 thus appeared crucial for the development of the Quebec university system, and in particular for its francophone sector. The general expansion of the student body during this period was unquestionable: even if differing in intensity from one academic sector to another, it was both apparent and massive. Between the end of the 1950s and the mid-1960s, for example, the student population of the principal francophone universities in Quebec grew at a remarkable pace in such fields as social sciences, education, literature, basic sciences and, though admittedly less rapidly here, applied sciences (Ostiguy, 1971). In total, the student population of the francophone universities in Quebec doubled twice between the mid-1950s and the end of the 1960s. The extent of university enrolment in the 20–24 age group of the francophone population rose from 2·94 per cent in 1960–1961 to 7·65 per cent in 1970–1971, even though this proportion remained lower than among the same age group of Quebec's anglophone population (DGES, 1972, p. 27). More significant to our discussion is the development of post-graduate work in the francophone universities. The universities no longer offered simply the first cycle qualifications associated with disciplines of the traditional professions (in which expansion did occur), but, moving strongly into the sciences, social sciences, etc., began to offer higher level qualifications in these fields—graduations being greatest in the basic, applied, and social sciences.

One might add that the real 'take off' of university research in Quebec's francophone universities, first in pure science, then in applied sciences and social sciences, dates precisely from this period. Through the 1960s, their research expenditure grew at an accelerating rate: in fact it multiplied more than five-fold over a period of five to six years. One could argue that from the mid-1960s the research capability of the universities has taken a great leap forward: possessing now numerous centres and research institutes in both science and social science, and still developing at an undiminished rate. And finally, the provincial government has established a programme for the finance of university research which, since about 1965, has been principally available to the francophone universities in order that they might make good their backwardness in research output.

For the social sciences in particular these were decisive times, marked by a concatenation of circumstances distinctly favourable to the development of these disciplines. Increasing numbers of students were attracted into the area at the same time as those social conflicts in which large numbers of the early pioneers of the social sciences in Quebec had participated resulted in the access to power of social groups dedicated to rationalizing and dynamicizing the governmental apparatus and the political administration of society. After this *coup*, the social legitimacy won by the social sciences, their articulation with the socio-political interests of specific social classes, favoured their development and institutionalization (Fournier, 1973a, 1973b). Subsequently, modernization of the government bureaucracy and a renewal of the processes of political administration opened up new professional horizons for graduates and specialists in the social sciences. The civil service itself, applied research projects, as well as a demand for professional expertise on the part of the state and its various ministries, commissions, and specialized committees, have all produced an enlargement and a diversification in the practice of these disciplines.

One might thus stress that the development of the social sciences has been a function of a range of specific structural changes in Quebec society. This contention is supported by noting the extent to which provincial funds are now made available for research in these subjects. In fact it is within the social sciences alone that provincial support for university research has for some years been more or less equivalent to that made available in Quebec by federal agencies disbursing funds of a similar kind (Maheu and Menard, 1975). Inclusion of intramural government research expenditure would not affect this conclusion: federal intramural research carried out in Quebec is almost exclusively concentrated in the natural sciences. Scarcely more than 2 per cent of all federally employed professionals, scientists, and engineers carrying out research and development (R & D) in Quebec came from the social and human sciences (in 1972–1973): in terms of federal intramural R & D expenditure in Quebec this amounted to less than 1 per cent (Conseil de la Politique Scientifique du Québec, 1975, p. 20–28). (Admittedly contract research financed by the federal government and involving specialists in the social sciences could slightly affect this picture.)

The development and the institutionalization of the social sciences are thus clearly rooted in the evolution in Quebec society which has occurred over the last decades. Their development may also be seen as having been a function of changing relationships between the scientific and the political domains, and between the political domain and other domains such as the religious and the intellectual. Hence structural incentives remained dependent for their effects upon the range of social positions then occupied by scientists, since relationships with other domains were significantly characterized by norms relating to the occupancy by scientists of political and administrative positions.

It is most commonly argued, with respect to the fundamental (natural) sciences, that their development in Quebec has depended upon scientific activity in Canada generally, particularly by virtue of federal involvement in the finance of research in this sector. Beyond the research-funding structure, there did develop various modes of legitimation and rewarding of research within Canadian science, specifically relevant to academic research in the basic sciences. Under the active patronage of the federal government, since the Second World War, there has slowly formed a 'republic of science' particularly flourishing within these disciplines (Comité Senatorial de la Politique Scientifique, 1971, 1972). Such structural and organizational incentives could not be entirely unrelated to the development, within the francophone universities of Quebec, of certain activities and research structures in the basic sciences. They have also favoured the (unanticipated) trend towards professionalization of university personnel in this sector, as measured, for example, by such classic attributes of professionalization as possession of the doctorate or receipt of academic tenure.

But such a view sees the conditions of the development of scientific activity as inhering solely within the scientific system itself: its structure and its organization. Such legitimation of the 'republic of science' ideology thus tends to mask the fact that in Quebec this development was a function of the transformation of the educational system (notably of its highest rungs) and of its relationships with various social classes and strata. The effects of such a structural and organizational model could only be determinant at a time when the science faculties of the francophone universities had achieved an increased institutional visibility by virtue of a student clientele progressively greater than that which had previously come from the private secondary education sector. Contrary to the common view this clientele, which in a sense 'belongs' to the science faculties only to the extent that it does not branch off towards a professional training, say in the health field, after a few years, has been characterized by rates of academic success and perseverance equal or superior to those of students coming traditionally from the private sector (Maheu, 1974, pp. 246–255; 293–295).

As with the development of the social sciences, that of the basic sciences seems to depend closely on the transformation of the Quebec social structure: a transformation which demanded and provoked the explosion of the francophone university system, as well as the reorganization of provincial government, and a restructuring of relationships between the scientific, religious, and political systems. The acquisition for scientific activity of a more central place within Quebecois society thus depended less upon the continuous financial investments of the federal government than upon these various structural mutations. It was as a result of this that promotional strategies, strategies of access both to higher positions and greater resources pursued by the francophone scientists and researchers, became of increasing complexity. The markets for research and for professional success functioned to a considerable extent in concert with the 'take off' of research within the francophone university system and the intervention of the provincial government in terms both of investment in, and legitimation of research. In as much as for all scientists and researchers within the Quebec scientific domain, and particularly for those among them whose interests were essentially a function of their location within the Canadian scientific community as a whole, nationalization of the Quebec university system, the existence of the social conditions for scientific progress within that system, opened the way for nationalist strategies of an interest-defending and promotional kind. Claims made of the Canadian scientific system thus became more frequent and more apparent: the attempt was made to secure better treatment for francophone scientists in Quebec universities, as well as a more profound awareness of the particular difficulties associated with the (still recent) development of research within these universities (Dugal, 1969; University of Montreal *et al.*, 1969; ACFAS, 1972). These demands were accompanied by a scarcely veiled threat: that of a turning in on itself of Quebec science, associated with a constitutional insularity in Quebec's modes of finance and legitimation of research, in the possibilities of supporting research on behalf of the federal government, and of decision-making relating to expansion and growth of local scientific activities and to local scientific institutions generally (Garigue, 1968).

One might, however, wonder if the Quebec scientists will not hesitate for very much longer than their colleagues in the social and human sciences before adopting this strategy of withdrawal: before attempting the complete 'nationalization' of the Quebec scientific system. In fact, despite changes in the traditionally marginal position of the natural sciences in Quebec, these remain more dependent upon the federal government than are the social and human sciences in terms both of posts and of financial resources. Thus, if one considers only those research posts in the federal and in the provincial civil services held by natural science and by social science graduates, it appears that at the federal level natural scientists are a much higher proportion of all researchers employed (84·9 per cent) than at the provincial level (56·2 per cent) (Conseil de la Politique Scientifique du Québec, 1975, p. 86). A similar difference exists with respect to R & D expenditures: the sums expended by the federal government on research in the natural sciences are greater not only absolutely, but as a proportion of all scientific expenditure, than is the case with the provincial government.

These differences are not explained simply by the greater resources of the federal government, nor by the fact that in comparison with the provincial government it is more interested, more open, in the natural sciences. Account has to be taken also of the historical division of labour in matters of policy-making between the two governments; of the gradual loss of provincial responsibility for economic development and confinement of the provincial government to the planning and management of human resources (education, health, social affairs). In this context, it seems that little possibility exists of profoundly modifying the ethnic division of scientific labour in Canada without first transforming the existing demarcation of political responsibilities between federal and provincial governments and consequently the social and power relationships between the French and English-Canadian ethnic groups.

Hitherto, scientists in fields such as biology, chemistry, physics, etc., have limited themselves to expressions of discontent or, better, of resentment at the science policies of the federal government. It is foreseeable, however, that as the nationalist movement develops in Quebec, groups of francophone scientists (perhaps first those occupying lower positions in the university and research systems, and those working in the provincial bureaucracy and in semi-public organizations) will adopt the general political perspective of this movement. In imitation of their colleagues in the social and human sciences they might then seek the 'nationalization' of their disciplines. Nationalist measures to which they would have increasing recourse (relating, for example, to take over of means of scientific production, management, diffusion, and reward) would then have significance only to the extent to which they were articulated with, or supported, the general political strategy of other social groups or classes.

## Conclusion

Studies of the development of the sciences, and of the periodicity of this development, which are not simply the histories of ideas, are generally limited solely to description of changes within the scientific domain itself. That is to say, account is not usually taken of transformations in the structure of relationships between the scientific and intellectual systems, and the political, religious, and economic systems: transformations which are themselves correlated with the changing structure of relationships between social classes. And even when such studies do make reference to external social conditions, they generally avoid only with difficulty the danger of reducing the development of the sciences to the double process of differentiation/specialization and progressive insulation of the scientific disciplines from external social demands.

To be sure one cannot deny that, in parallel with the institutionalization of scientific activity, the scientists (who increasingly work in specialized institutions) gradually lose on the one hand the possibility of mastering a diversity of skills, on the other the right to express views on matters external to science and the possibility of simultaneously occupying a variety of social positions. However, it does not seem that this evolution in the scientific role is a linear process, or that it depends solely on the momentum of science itself or on the will of the scientists themselves. On the contrary, analysis of the development of the social and natural sciences in Quebec indicates that passage from one phase of development to another depends largely upon the interest of various groups and fractions of social classes in the sciences (or more broadly in scientific rationality), and on the social support which these offered. It was only, for example, by their success in convincing of the importance of scientific rationality, in mobilizing, other intellectuals and academics, members of the liberal professions, as well as of the clergy and the religious orders, that some francophone scientists achieved posts in higher education and obtained resources for research and for training researchers. But it became rapidly apparent that this support, which the scientists had gained through the dissemination of information on the sciences (especially through the medium of ACFAS and its constituent societies), was insufficient to alter the inferior position of scientists in the educational system, or to permit them to achieve parity with their anglophone colleagues within Quebec and the rest of Canada. But even if the activities of ACFAS, which constituted a kind of 'scientific movement', had permitted the scientists to acquire greater social visibility and to develop an 'academic science', the sciences themselves (which were still attempting to differentiate themselves from other intellectual disciplines to which they were subordinate) had not acquired any centrality within Quebec society at the levels of economic production or of political administration. In order that training in science might become something more than a complement to the professional training received by doctors and engineers, and that scientists might attain more numerous and more senior positions within the Quebec social structure, certain changes were necessary. It was essential that after modernization of the economic infrastructure, profound transformations took place both in the total educational system and in the system of political management and administration. This in turn depended upon the accession to political power of new social groups. It was thus only through participation in, and support for, the 'Quiet Revolution' that Quebec's francophone scientists (notably those in the social sciences) gained the means to pursue and to intensify their production and dissemination of scientific knowledge. Far from being incompatible with the pursuit of scientific activities, politicization of the scientists[15] appeared, at the end of the 1950s and the beginning of the 1960s, as a crucial condition of separation between the scientific domain in Quebec and the intellectual, religious, and political domains.

It is not necessary to conclude from this, however, that there was thus constituted a scientific system in Quebec independent of that of Canada.[16] To differing extents according to discipline, Quebec's francophone scientists maintain close links with their English-speaking colleagues, as well as continuing to urge the federal government to participate more actively in the process of levelling disparities, equalizing opportunities, between the two ethnic groups. If state control of scientific activity, in a dependent society such as Quebec, is an important determinant of the emergence of a national scientific system, it is no less the case that complete 'national-ization' of this system (i.e. its independence of the Canadian and American systems) is scarcely feasible without a transformation in the relationships obtaining between English- and French-Canadians. The struggle of the Quebec scientists to take control of the means of scientific production, dissemination, and reward then appears inherently political, in the sense that not only is it not independent of nationalist rhetoric or of a nationalist stance, but also and above all because it seeks, and necessitates, the mobilization of social groups whose economic and symbolic interests lead them also to 'invest in nationality'.

## Notes

1 In the context of the present article we restrict our 'scientific domain in Quebec' principally to its francophone element (institutions, scientific groups). There will thus be little reference to McGill University and to the groups of anglophone professors and researchers in Quebec whose contribution to the development of the sciences in Canada has been so outstanding.

Until the early 1970s, McGill University had awarded many more higher degrees in the sciences than all the francophone universities together, and had also received far greater research subvention largely financed by the federal government. These English-speaking scientists were rapidly integrated into the Canadian scientific domain, of which they were a major element. It does appear, that the anglophone scientists in Quebec have not been very responsive to Quebec nationalism, or that they have contributed to the constitution of a truly Quebec scientific system. At this stage of our research we are defining 'Quebec scientific field' to exclude them.

2 In its beginnings, ACFAS united scientists and intellectuals with few common characteristics. Thus, among its early leaders, one finds intellectuals as different both in their social positions and in their intellectual orientations as the doctor Léo Parizeau, the botanists Frère Marie-Victorin and Jacques Rousseau, and the professor of political economy Edouard Montpetit.

3 To these various activities one should also add the participation of scientists in numerous radio broadcasts, as well as in the publication, in 1936, of an encyclopaedia, *La Science pour tous* (8 volumes).

4 The relations which the scientists enjoyed with philosophers were not simply of a subordinate kind: often there was collaboration or alliance. This was the case, for example, in the involvement of scientists in the foundation of the Société de Philosophie de Québec. Similarly, at the annual congress of ACFAS, there were regular presentations in the 'philosophy and moral sciences' section.

5 In fact, it was only at the beginning of the 1960s that Quebec's francophone scientists dared publicly to criticize the monopoly which the Church had acquired in the education and health sectors and in trades unionism (Dansereau, 1960).

6 This anti-Americanism had much support from Quebec intellectuals at that time, who devoted numerous lectures, articles, and books to it. The universities were obliged to avoid any imitation of the American university system: the founder of the School of Social Sciences in the University of Montreal, Edouard Montpetit, preferred to take his inspiration from the 'great model' of the School of Political Science (École des Sciences Politiques) in Paris. Similarly, the University of Montreal in 1920 turned down a proposal from the École Polytechnique (Montreal) to establish a school of engineering and applied science, in favour of the establishment of a faculty of pure science. As in France, this provided courses in physics, chemistry, and the biological sciences, for students of medicine.

7 This was the route followed, for example, by the first French-Canadian to specialize in anthropology. Thus, after a period of studies in England and in France, Maurice Barbeau, who entered the service of the National Museum of Canada in 1910, established frequent and regular contacts with American researchers. (He was a member of the American Folklore Society, the American Anthropological Association, the Washington Academy of Sciences, and of the editorial board of *The Journal of American Folklore*.) The same was true of many whose scientific careers began in the 1930s.

8 A number of Quebec social scientists, in the course of the 1940s and 1950s, showed a desire to integrate themselves in the Canadian scientific system, principally by publishing most commonly in the *Canadian Journal of Economics and Political Science*, and by participating in the activities of the Canadian Political Science Association (of which two francophones, G. H. Lévesque and J.-Ch. Falardeau, became presidents). As for the possibilities of publishing a French language social science journal, these proved to be slight: the *Cahiers de l'école des sciences sociales, politiques et économiques de l'Université Laval* soon became *Cahiers du service extérieur d'éducation social*, and began to address a non-specialized audience through popularized articles, or articles sensitizing to current social problems (Fournier, 1973a, pp. 677–681).

9 To these structural changes corresponded also a change in the social and educational characteristics of those achieving scientific posts. There was, in effect, a growth in the number of students within the science faculties from the middle and popular classes who had not followed the traditional route to the university, i.e. through the private *collèges classiques*. Now, a reasonable hypothesis is that this new student population, whose subsequent success depended largely upon educational attainment and the diplomas awarded, were more dependent on the university system, and that thus they readily assimilated all the 'dogmas' of the scientific community and readily internalized the norms making up the scientific ethos. If this was the case, we have a means of explaining the distance which scientists kept from politics and from those interested in politics, compared with their colleagues from other disciplines.

10 On this, see also 'L'Anarchie de notre système d'enseignement' in *L'Université dit non aux Jésuites* (Montreal, Éditions du Jour, 1964). This work, with a preface by Léon Lortie, was published by the Association des Professeurs de l'Université de Montréal, with the participation of Michel Brunet (historian), Pierre Dansereau (botanist), Abel Gauthier (mathematician), Jacques Henripin (demographer), Maurice L'Abbé (mathematician), André Morel (jurist), and André Raynault (economist).

11 Editor's note. Maurice Duplessis had led the Union Nationale from 1935 when it was formed till his death in 1959, and had been provincial premier from 1936–1939 and from 1944–1959. For an account of Duplessis' policies of 'conservative nationalism' see Herbert F. Quinn, *The Union Nationale—A Study in Quebec Nationalism* (Toronto, University of Toronto Press, 1963).

12 At the beginning of the 1950s the student clientele coming from these lower socioeconomic strata represented less than a quarter of the total student population of the francophone universities in Quebec. In the course of the 1960s this proportion rose to

40 per cent for the same institutions (being higher in those situated outside the major centres of population). So far as McGill, the major anglophone university, was concerned, it never proved so receptive to lower stratum students (Maheu, 1974, pp. 320–321).

13 At a time when he was covering the province in order to gain public support for the establishment of a Ministry of Education (which would 'deprivatize' the control of the educational system), the minister responsible affirmed

> it is necessary, in effect, to understand that there will never exist, any more than in the past, a superman or a supermachine to regulate all the problems, and the future, of the nation. On the contrary, it is necessary to recognize that the ministry is an essential condition of our well-being, of our progress, of our individual and collective opening up, of our economic emancipation, of our political advancement. This is why I have already said 'Give me a great ministry of education, a population awakened to the essential importance of educational problems, an army of teachers aware of their responsibilities and ready to make a great effort over several years, and everything becomes possible'. (Gerin-Lajoie, 1963, p. 123)

14 Editor's note. The 'Quiet Revolution' is an expression often used to designate the period of reforms introduced by the Liberal government of Jean Lesage, which overthrew the Union Nationale in 1960.

15 This politicization of scientists, i.e. their participation in political debates and struggles, is also closely related to the unionization of significant groups of scientists.

16 One index of the feeble organization of the scientific domain in Quebec is the importance acquired by the popular review *Québec Science*, not only among students of science, but among teachers and scientists themselves (Delisle, 1975). The impact of this periodical, which is very different from the impact of similar ones, say, in France (Maldidier, 1973), can only be explained by Quebec's lack of major scientific journals, and more generally by the feeble networks of information exchange (whether formal or informal) between Quebecois scientists. Moreover, a large proportion of scientists in some disciplines (for example, physics) write their articles in English, and publish them in Canadian and American journals (Blume and Chartier, 1974).

## References

ACFAS (1954), *Mémoire présenté à la Commission Royale d'Enquête sur les problèmes constitutionnels*, Montreal, January, p. 30.

ACFAS (1962), *Mémoire présenté à la Commission Royale d'Enquête sur l'enseignement*, Montreal, June, p. 18.

ACFAS (1972), *Quelques commentaires sur le rapport du Comité senatorial de la politique scientifique*, Montreal, June, p. 16.

Association des Professeurs de l'Université de Montréal (1964), *L'Université dit non aux Jésuites*, Montreal, Éditions du Jour.

Bassala, G. (1967), 'The spread of Western science', *Science*, **156**, 5 May, pp. 611–622.

Ben-David, J. (1971), *The Scientist's Role in Society*, New Jersey, Prentice-Hall.

Blume, S. S. (1974), *Toward a Political Sociology of Science*, New York, Free Press.

Blume, S. S., and M.-J. Chartier (1974), *The Effects of Biculturalism on Science in Canada*, unpublished report to the Science Council of Canada, University of Montreal.

Boucher, E. (1931), 'Les Anciens de la faculté des sciences', *La Revue trimestrielle canadienne*, *XVII*, pp. 398–411.

Bourdieu, P. (1975), 'La Specificité du champ scientifique et les conditions sociales du progrès de la raison', *Sociologie et societes*, **VII**, I, May, pp. 91–119.

Brazeau, J., J. Dofny, G. Fortin, and R. Sevigny (1962), *Les Resultats d'une enquête*

*auprès des étudiants dans les universités de langue française du Québec*, Montreal, Department of Sociology, University of Montreal.
Clark, T. N. (1972), 'Les Étapes de l'institutionnalisation scientifique', *Revue international des sciences sociales*, **24**, 4, pp. 699–714.
Cole, J. R., and S. Cole (1973), *Social Stratification in Science*, Chicago, University of Chicago Press.
Comité Senatorial de la Politique Scientifique (1971, 1972), *Une Politique scientifique canadienne*, Ottawa, Information Canada.
Conseil de la Politique Scientifique du Québec (1975), *A.R.E.Q., Inventaire de la R.D au gouvernement du Québec, 1972/73*, Document synthese, Éditeur officiel du Quebec, January.
Crane, D. (1972), *Invisible Colleges*, Chicago, University of Chicago Press.
Dansereau, P. (1960), 'Lettre à un seminariste sur l'alienation des intellectuels', *Cité Libre*, **XI**, 32, December, pp. 14–17.
Dansereau, P. (1964), 'Lettre de New York', *Liberté*, **33**, May–June, pp. 222–234.
Delisle, M. A. (1975), *Les Fonctions sociales de la vulgarisation dans un champ scientifique dependant: le cas de Québec Science*, Department of Sociology, University of Montreal.
DGES (1972), *Statistiques de l'enseignement supérieur: évolution de l'enseignement supérieur au Québec, 1961–1971*, Quebec, Ministère de l'Éducation.
Duchesne, R. (1975), *Le Développement de la communauté scientifique quebécoise et ses relations avec le gouvernement provincial (1920–1968)*, Montreal, I.H.S.P.S., University of Montreal, 51 pp.
Dugal, L. P. (1969), 'Le Gouvernement fédéral et l'aide à la recherche' in J. B. Macdonald et al., *Le Gouvernement fédéral et l'aide à la recherche dans les universités canadiennes*, Ottawa, Imprimeur de la Reine.
Fournier, Marcel (1973a), *Institutionnalisation et différenciation de disciplines dans une situation de double dépendance*, EPHE, thèse de doctorat de 3e cycle, Paris.
Fournier, Marcel (1973b), 'L'Institutionnalisation des sciences sociales au Québec', *Sociologie et sociétés*, **V**, I, May, pp. 27–59.
Garigue, P. (1968), 'La Recherche au Québec et les problèmes constitutionnels', *Science Forum*, **2**, April.
Gerin-Lajoie, P. (1963), *Pourquoi le bill 60?*, Montreal, Éditions du Jour.
Ladd, E. C., and S. M. Lipset (1972), 'Politics of academic natural scientists and engineers', *Science*, **176**, 9 June, pp. 1091–1100.
Maheu, Louis (1974), *Enseignement supérieur et structure sociale: les fonctions sociales de l'Université québécoise francophone*, EPHE, thèse de doctorat de 3e cycle, Paris.
Maheu, L., and P. Bélanger (1972), 'Pratique Politique étudiante au Québec', *Recherches sociographiques*, **13**, 3, September–December, pp. 312–313.
Maheu, L., and J. Menard (1975), *Les Études supérieures en sciences humaines à l'Université de Montréal*, Rapport soumis à la Commission d'Enquête sur les études supérieures dans les sciences humaines (Conseil des Arts), Montreal, University of Montreal.
Maldidier, P. (1973), *Les Revues de vulgarisation, contribution à une sociologie des cultures moyennes*, Paris, Centre de Sociologie de la Culture et de l'Éducation.
Marie-Victorin, Frère (1938), 'La Science et la question nationale' (1938), *Annales de l'ACFAS*, **5**, 1939, pp. 130–155.
Merton, R. K. (1973), *The Sociology of Science*, Chicago, University of Chicago Press.
Montpetit, É. (1935), 'Quinzième Anniversaire de l'École', *Annuaire de l'École des Sciences Sociales, Politiques et Économiques*, Montreal, University of Montreal, pp. 37–39.
Montreal, University of, Laval University, and University of Sherbrooke (1969), *Les Politiques scientifiques au Canada*, mémoire soumis au Comité spécial du Sénat, Montreal.

Moscovici, S. (1968), *Essai sur l'histoire humaine de la nature*, Paris, Flammarion.
Mullins, N. C. (1973), *Theories and Theory Groups in Contemporary Sociology*, New York, Harper and Row.
Oberschall, A. (ed.) (1972), *The Establishment of Empirical Sociology*, New York, Harper and Row.
Ostiguy, H. (1971), *Statistiques détaillées relatives à l'enseignement supérieur: les inscriptions étudiantes*, Montreal, Department of Sociology, University of Montreal.
Ouellet, C. (1938), 'Les Sciences dans l'éducation', *Les Idées*, **8,** 1–2, July–August, pp. 60–72.
Ouellet, C. (1964), *La Vie des sciences au Canada français*, Quebec, Ministère des Affaires culturelles.
Pouliot, A. (1938), 'Le Salut par l'éducation', *Les Idées*, **VIII,** 1–2, July–August, pp. 48–59.
Schneider, W. G. (1968), 'Letter to the editor', *Science Forum*, **3,** June.
Shils, E. (1972), 'Intellectuals in the Political Development of the New State' (1960) in E. Shils, *The Intellectuals and the Powers*, Chicago, University of Chicago Press, pp. 386–424.
Tremblay, A. (1954), *Les Collèges classiques et les écoles publiques: conflit on coordination?*, Quebec, Presses de l'Université Laval.

# 6

# TOWARDS A RELEVANT SOCIOLOGY OF SCIENCE FOR INDIA

### Radhika Ramasubban

Among the many influences upon the formulation of an approach to science and its role in society, those of Karl Marx and Max Weber may be taken as the most significant. Of these two, Weber's general theory of society which later evolved into the modern functionalist school of sociology—academic sociology—constitutes the paradigm of the Mertonian sociology of science. It is this functionalist paradigm which has dominated the sociological study of scientific activity in the West. In the underdeveloped countries, too, the functionalist school holds sway over the minds of sociologists as a result of the continuing cultural and economic dependence of these countries on the West even after they have formally ceased to be colonies. This paper attempts to critically evaluate the Mertonian model and show that, particularly in a developing country like India, the Marxian sociology of science is relatively more relevant to an understanding of the general developmental problems faced by Indian society, and of the anomalies and distortions presented by Indian scientific development in particular.

Marx's contribution was that he brought out for the first time the social character of science, and the corresponding necessity of science to society. Modern science for him was inseparably connected with the controlling of nature for human benefit and with the understanding of nature only in so far as it can be used to change it. This does not diminish in any way the speculative value of science but only imposes the check of material test and utility to establish the position of science at any point of time. Weber (1962) in his eloquent essay 'Science as a Vocation' dealt not so much with the place of science in society as with the 'inward calling' for science. In his other works,[1] however, he was concerned with relating the development of the rationalist economic ethic, as embodied in the capitalist system, to the sets of values embodied in other areas of social activity, particularly religious. The interest in science, though not specifically articulated, is there by implication, as part of the rational scheme of values.

The third decade of the twentieth century was the heyday of the social interpretation of seventeenth-century science. In fact science as a social activity had not been analysed in any great detail by earlier social theorists. Being close to the heart of Marxist sociology, however, it is easy to see why Boris Hessen (1931) took up the theme and presented a Marxist critique of seventeenth-century science, with its central figure of Newton, at the 1931 Congress of the History of Science and Technology. Hessen attributed the creation of the new science to the economic needs of the rising bourgeoisie; he saw science as essentially subservient to the socio-economic forces of capitalism. Zilsel, another Marxist, in a later study (Zilsel, 1941) suggested that a dramatic lowering of the class barriers which had prevented any dialogue between the scholar and the craftsman in medieval and ancient society resulted in a fusion of empiricism and rationalism and the birth of a new science.

Hessen's thesis of the dependence of science upon the socio-economic structure forced back into prominence an approach to society and social institutions which had been carefully exorcised from sociological theory and discredited in the prevailing social philosophy after Marx. Although Hessen's thesis made an impact upon a few leading progressive scientists in Britain, in academic sociology, and in the embryonic sociology of science, the response to Marxist social theory continued to be negative. Here it was Merton, the founding father of the functionalist sociology of science, whose thesis was influential.

It is quite possible, although it is nowhere recorded (or it might be a case of 'simultaneous discovery'), that Hessen's critique provoked Merton to undertake a study of seventeenth-century science, in the tradition of academic sociology which has been shaped, consciously and unconsciously, by its polemic against Marxism. He attempted in his first study (Merton, 1938) to apply Weber's hypothesis of the importance of the Protestant Weltanschaung in aiding the development of capitalism in Europe, to the emergence of science in the same culture area, and concluded that science as a social activity was meaningfully and historically related to the Calvinist way of looking at the world, and that Puritan values had been important in seventeenth-century England in concentrating a great deal of attention upon the study of the natural sciences. Merton did not pin down the causal factor (or factors) responsible for the emergence of modern science. By implication, however, his conclusion that religious values were a strong factor predisposing the adherents towards experimental science, made *values* rather than material factors the primary focus of investigation.

Merton's study of the emergence of modern science as a social institution fostered by a particular value-complex, emphasizing the interrelatedness of the systems of ideas, found uncritical and enthusiastic response in Western academic circles and became the basis for future work in the sociology of science.[2] The new sociology of science now came to be characterized by its functionalist method of analysis. With Merton's first study, the deeply ingrained prejudice against the Marxist theories of society and social change reasserted itself with the result that, towards the end of the 1930s, any attempt at the 'holistic' study of science in the total social reality was abandoned as was the sociology of knowledge, both of which had become prominent areas of interest after Marx included them in his comprehensive study of society. Merton's study of science in seventeenth-century England was also his last major work on the social contexts that influence the substantive output of scientific knowledge; he turned next to the 'social structure' of science, defining science as a subsystem of society.

## The Functionalist Approach

As developed by Merton the sociology of science concentrates attention on the way in which science as a system of social relationships operates. This approach emphasizes the social rules, the norms of science, and the rewards that are built into the social system of science in order that it should work efficiently. The basic premise of this approach is that scientists are organized into a social system and, like all social systems as analysed by functionalists, the values and norms or rules of the system are such as to ensure that the system continues in roughly the same way as before. When things happen that might have the effect of disrupting the system, then the mechanisms of social control built into the system and legitimized by the underlying values are exerted upon the disrupting elements and they are either destroyed or contained, or the system changes in some way to accommodate them.[3]

Given the preoccupation of the Mertonian sociology of science with mechanisms of social control, it is not difficult to see the reason for the large literature on the reward system of science which forms the core of the discipline and constitutes the bulk of the writings by Merton and his students. The issues taken up are generally the question of priorities in scientific discoveries (Merton, 1957), the ubiquity of multiple discovery (Merton, 1961, 1963a), the attitudes of scientists towards the circumstances and consequences of achievement (Merton, 1963b, 1968).

Central to the model itself are the norms and values upon which the social system of science is supposed to rest, and which are generated by the needs of science as a social institution. The observance of these norms, according to Merton, is the key to scientific progress as a social process. The norms are expressed in the form of prescriptions, proscriptions, preferences, and permissions and are legitimized in terms of institutional values. The 'affectively toned complex' of these values, and norms, Merton calls the ethos of science (Merton, 1942, pp. 268, 269).

As is well known, Merton lays out four sets of institutional imperatives—universalism, communism, disinterestedness, and organized scepticism. An associated value which Merton includes in his scheme is the autonomy of science. For the effective functioning of science, a primary requirement is a large degree of freedom from restrictive external controls, which confers on the scientists what Bernard Barber (1952) calls 'an essential autonomy'. The external controls may be of various types, religious, economic (i.e. utilitarian), or political; where these controls exist they function as obstacles to unfettered scientific activity, placing limits upon the 'free play' of the scientific imagination, or vitiating the direction of scientific research.

Merton's approach to science as a social activity is based upon his conception of science as an intellectual pursuit, as the disinterested search for knowledge and truth. Hence when Merton formulates his sociology of science, it is pure science alone that he is concerned with.

In keeping with the functionalist perspective, the Mertonian sociology of science restricts its analysis of science to its internal functioning. The conception of science accordingly is that of an independent subsystem of society. The functionalist postulate is that the patterns of interaction among the two or more participants in a social system, and consequently the social system itself, are maintained because the reaction of the participants to one another's behaviour is mutually rewarding. This makes the reward system a core element in this approach to social behaviour.

Of crucial importance to the successful pursuit of science as a social activity is conformity to the 'ethos of science' or to its institutional imperatives. What ensures this conformity is the internal reward system of science, which recognizes excellence and rewards originality. To be rewarded and recognized for their efforts is essential to scientists. Creativity being a natural human drive, the competent response of others to one's creations is needed before the creative act is really felt to be completed; therefore the scientist's need for recognition stems from this basic drive. The social system of science, however, would provide a structure within which the scientist may obtain the competent response he desires only if he supports the 'ethos of science'. Hence the function of the reward system is that of a social control mechanism in order to ensure that the social system of science operates successfully and maintains a certain measure of stability (Storer, 1968).

However, the scientist being embraced by the reward system is contingent upon his conformity to yet another institutional norm accorded great importance by Merton, i.e. originality. The manner in which the institution of science rewards those who variously live up to its norms are several. Eponymy, the practice of affixing the name of the scientist to all or part of what he has found is one; the Nobel Prize, and the place accorded to scientists of distinction by historians of science, are yet other ways in which recognition is allocated.

A striking feature of this model is that in spite of the stimulus of Merton's first work, it has become more and more bound up with the inner workings of the social system of science and less and less interested in the relations that exist between scientific activity and the historically determined social and political environment in which it takes place. The approach is individualistic in tone—its main focus being on such matters as the scientist's desire for recognition through publications; the reward system of science; the question of originality, etc. (Storer, 1966, chapter 4; Stein, 1962; Merton, 1957; Price, 1962; Storer, 1968).

This approach to science has several consequences. The kinds of issues which are taken up for analysis are atomized, exceptional ones. On the basis of this, generalizations are made for the total role of science. For example, Merton's essays on 'Priorities in scientific discovery', 'Behaviour patterns of scientists', 'Singletons and multiples in science', 'The ambivalance of scientists', etc., deal with eminent men of science—Newton, Einstein, Bacon, Mendel, Darwin, etc. While this special area in the sociology of science is interesting, and can be fruitful, it would be wrong to believe that what is true of these exceptional cases would be true of all participants in scientific activity. For the bulk of the working scientists are not those who give their names to scientific phenomena or after whom whole epochs are named (see also Sklair, 1973). This approach in sociology is the counterpart of that approach in history which sees leaders as making history.[4]

The rationale for this approach is probably the belief among Mertonians that the study of science begins with its product, i.e. scientific knowledge, 'rather than simply with those individuals who occupy the social position of scientists'. This, Storer rationalizes, is probably why there is a dearth of sociological studies focused on 'run-of-the-mill or unproductive scientists: so long as science is defined by its research product, those who contribute little directly to the product, are difficult to fit into the picture' (Storer, 1975). In the Mertonian scheme of things, therefore, the working norms of the great majority of scientists, who do not conceive of their work in heroic terms and who do not win Nobel Prizes, are quite inconsequential. This derives directly from the excessive emphasis placed upon the norm of originality and conversely the virtual absence of any interest in the working climates of the rank and file of scientists. The Mertonian sociology of science would seem opposed to studying the objective reality underlying the process of scientific development in itself, and *then* placing the scientists in that objective reality.

Science is not just a body of esoteric knowledge in which stand out a few phenomenal figures, but is a body of organized knowledge whose most important claim to being 'socialized knowledge' is its social role aiding society in the process of change and transformation. Therefore the norms, activities, and working conditions of every scientist who contributes to this endeavour, however ordinary and unproductive he may be, should be worthy of study for the sociology of science. Hence a social psychology of the scientific elite cannot pass for a sociology of science.

Another limitation of the Mertonian sociology of science is that it refers only to pure science or 'academic' science. Hence by definition, and at other times by implication, large sections of modern science are excluded from the analysis resulting in the 'fallacy of generalization from unrepresentative samples'. To use Sklair's phraseology again, the Mertonian sociology of science might perhaps be more aptly termed the sociology of pure science or sociology of academic science (Sklair, 1973, p. 161). This is one of the major weaknesses of this model, in that it fails to explain how the entire scientific world operates; and is hence misleading to this extent. Merton himself says little about applied scientists or technologists in terms of the norms he sees as relevant for pure science. But generally Mertonians have looked upon technologists and applied scientists as instances of limited ability to live up to these norms (see Barber, 1952, p. 95), or as peripheral. To quote Storer (1966, p. 18): 'To be sure the applied scientist does sell his expertise, but the application of knowledge is not the central concern of science and the applied scientist is in this respect somewhat removed from the "center" of the profession.' In his role as 'scientist'; the individual is seen as undertaking activities not because they will be of benefit to anyone who may be considered a client, but because they will result in more 'knowledge'. The main factor which distinguishes the applied from the pure scientist is that while the latter is concerned primarily with increasing knowledge and in communicating with his colleagues, the former earns his livelihood by performing 'esoteric service' for the organization for which he works. This relationship puts certain restraints on the researcher's role and is reflected in—

(1) Limited communalism, whereby he can share his research results only with his company until the process/product is patented.

(2) Focused truth whereby, unlike the scientists who can pursue any problem regardless of its utility or practicality, the industrial researcher has to focus his interest upon a particular process/product.

(3) Selflessness—which implies that often the researcher has to put forward his ideas but leave it to the administrator to make the final decision about its further development.

(4) Communication with lay personnel—implying that his reference group, unlike the scientist's, will perforce be non-scientific personnel who are in decision-making positions with whom he must communicate in non-technical terms.

Additional complications are created by the employee aspect of his role which entails certain other attitudes which are expected of him (Stein, 1962, pp. 334, 335).

The Mertonians, therefore, in so far as they look into the situation of scientists and technologists in industry, and government, generally explain the norms of technology in two interrelated ways. The technologist/applied researcher feels frustrated by his inability to conform to the 'ethos of science'. Then as a response to this frustration, these technologists give up the attempt to be *real* scientists and switch to different, usually professional or managerial norms. Hence technologists adopt an administrative status system and operate by the appropriate norms. These, the argument goes, are antagonistic to the Mertonian norms of pure science and this is used to explain the 'fact' that certain types of industrial scientists are said to have problems at work and low job satisfaction (Sklair, 1973, p. 69).

Recent criticism of the functionalist conception of the 'ethos of science' has come from several quarters. The main thrust of the criticisms is that it is unacceptable both empirically and theoretically. On the one hand, it cannot be taken to mean that without the norms science would not progress. For instance, even if scientists are motivated to do research for the purpose of personal gain rather than of increasing knowledge, there is no evidence to show that thereby the basic *direction* or *nature* of scientific activity is affected.

On the other hand, scientists do not necessarily behave in accordance with the Mertonian norms. For instance, Michael Mulkay (1972) has shown how originality is no doubt valued, but originality which remains within limits imposed by the existing 'style of thought'. If originality takes the form of challenging and requiring reformulation of the frameworks and paradigms hitherto held by scientists and which have attained a quasi-moral commitment, the originality is likely to be rejected 'without regard for the putative ethical restraints imposed by the scientific ethos'. Using the Velikovsky case as an illustration, Mulkay tries to demonstrate the inadequacy of the functionalist view that scientists function in conformity with the normative controls. His thesis is that scientific theory and methodological rules operate as the dominant source of normative controls in science and in fact as a basic hindrance to the development and acceptance of new conceptions. Mulkay is here applying the Kuhnian view that a large measure of scientific activity is a product of intellectual and social 'closure'; that scientific activity most of the time consists in the 'attempt to force nature into the conceptual boxes supplied by professional education . . .' (quoted in Mulkay, 1972). Scientific *advance* is a result of 'revolutionary science', i.e. when radical innovations challenge the very basis of the accepted paradigms, whereas in the case of 'normal science' research will be guided by the accepted paradigm and professional recognition will be gained primarily by means of contributing to the further articulation of the paradigm within the limits provided by established technical and cognitive norms.

Further, the prescriptive norm of originality, if it has helped scientific growth, to a certain extent has deleterious consequences as well. For example, the continued growth in the number of scientific papers being published in the West every year (Hirsch, 1968, p. 124) is a reflection of the economic pressures which force scientists to go for bulk rather than quality of publication, which is, in Bernal's words 'dictated by the need of establishing priorities, itself an indication of the unnecessary struggle for existence that goes on inside the scientific world' (Bernal, 1937). Merton, however, does not see the dispute over priorities in terms of this publish or perish norm. On the contrary, he views it as evidence of the enthusiasm of scientists for publishing their work. The tendency to jealously guard their claim to priority is, according to Mertonians, only a reflection of this interest in extending knowledge.

Another dimension of the normative aspect is the conception of science as an autonomous, non-utilitarian subsystem. This derives from the general functionalist notion of the various spheres of social activity as individual social systems which can be studied independently of their interconnections; and also from the conception of 'science' as pure science, basically non-utilitarian, and *therefore* enjoying an essential autonomy. To quote Merton (1975, p. 270):

> one sentiment which is assimilated by the scientist from the very onset of his training pertains to the purity of science. Science must not suffer itself to become the handmaiden of theology, economy or the state. The function of this sentiment is to preserve the autonomy of science. For if such extra-scientific criteria of the value of science as presumable consonance with religious doctrines or economic utility or political appropriateness are adopted, science becomes acceptable only insofar as it meets these criteria. In other words, as the pure science sentiment is eliminated, science becomes subject to the direct control of other institutional agencies and its place in society becomes increasingly uncertain. The persistent repudiation by scientists of the application of utilitarian norms to their work has as its chief function the avoidance of this danger, which is particularly marked at the present time.

This assertion is supported by the distinction made between pure and applied science: a neo-Aristotelian conception of different kinds of knowledge—theoretical, practical, and productive. The Mertonians have preferred to focus their attention only upon pure science and its goal of a disinterested search for truth. 'The very existence of a distinction between basic and applied research', says Storer (1966, p. 16) 'suggests that the utility of knowledge is not its raison d'être so far as most scientists are concerned.'

Merton argues that in its early days, before modern science had acquired a 'substantial autonomy' as an institution, it needed extraneous sources of legitimation. This was provided by the emphasis upon the institutionalized value of utility. 'However, science gradually acquired an increasing degree of autonomy, claiming legitimacy as something good in its own right, just as much so as literature and the other arts, as the quest for physical well-being or for personal salvation' (Storer, 1966, p. 185).

Historical analysis of science, however, does not seem to support this notion of the evolution of science as an autonomous non-utilitarian activity. In pre-capitalist society the skills and experience of artisans were far removed from the theoretical pursuits of scholars. It was also the period prior to the emergence of what we know as modern science, when science was stifled by the religious world-view. It needs to be emphasized that the beginning of the modern period, i.e. the Renaissance and Reformation, also coincided with the rise of capitalism in Western Europe. The emerging class of merchant capitalists raised the slogan of freedom in all walks of life, including science and scholarship, because unless and until science was liberated from religious constraints, it could not be utilized for commercial purposes. Thus science became 'autonomous', not in the sense of being free from the fetters of feudalism. If one traces the emergence of modern science in the context of the development of capitalism one finds that the autonomy of science was achieved precisely in order that science could be utilized by the progressive capitalist class for rapid expansion of what Marx calls commodity production. The barriers between craftsmen and intellectuals broke down and made way for experimental science, for the utility of things took on a new value in the eyes of a class which made the profit motive its driving force. The autonomy of science which Merton stresses was only an illusion and even this illusion disappeared with the emergence of industrial capitalism, the characteristic features of which were socialization of production and interdependence of all spheres of human activity including the so-called disinterested search for knowledge. In twentieth-century capitalism science has been completely stripped of any veneer of non-utilitarianism and autonomy, and has become fundamentally dependent upon the politico-economic aspirations of corporate industrial enterprises.

The ideological bias in the Mertonian norms supposedly governing scientific activity becomes clear from Barber's assertion that these norms can be guaranteed only in a 'modern liberal democratic society'. The social conditions characterizing such a society, which are particularly favourable to a high level of scientific activity, are delineated by him as 'a highly developed division of labour, a social class system which permits of considerable climbing, a political system in which the autonomy of many diverse activities is respected'. These social conditions are particularly congruent not only with science but also with all the cultural values that are characteristic of the 'modern world'; 'rationality, utilitarianism, universalism, individualism, progress and meliorism'. Such a social order conducive to science may be contrasted with other 'restrictive' kinds of societies such as feudal Europe, Nazi Germany, and Soviet Russia—the first with its supreme religious authority, the latter two with their 'hierarchical political organisations' (Storer, 1966, p. 67).

On account of its prescriptive conclusion, the Mertonian sociology of science has limited validity. On the one hand, it can hardly explain the progress of even pure science in Soviet Russia where (according to the Mertonians) scientific enquiry cannot be autonomous and, being governed by utilitarian considerations, it cannot therefore progress. (Its original sin, of course, is that it lumps together the three social orders with no concern for their fundamental economic and historical differences.)

On the other, it could not explain why even in a liberal democracy like the United States of America pure science and 'disinterested' university scientists have become subservient to the military–industrial complex. The fact that twentieth-century science is in large measure team-oriented, requiring expensive equipment and a perennial flow of funds, has reinforced the interdependence of scientific activity and politico-economic processes in all economic systems. The research goals of the scientist are not uninfluenced by the presence of and accessibility to large funds. If this is the case, not only does his become a 'service' profession albeit of a different form from the applied scientist; he is also irrevocably tied up with the needs and approach of funding bodies. Hence Storer's (1966, p. 90) discussion of the economic system and the scientific system as if the two were independent of each other is unrealistic.

This two-fold inadequacy of the Mertonian sociology of science arises from the fact that it mistakes what it considers desirable to be real. Because Mertonians believe that scientific activity as a search for knowledge ought to be autonomous, they conclude that it is in fact so. It is true that scientists strongly desire to be free of extra-scientific constraints, but scientific activity historically, in any economic system, is not governed, by the wishes of scientists, but by the social environment of which they are an integral part and which bears the cost and derives utility from the scientists' search for knowledge. As Marx had observed in the context of the bourgeois democratic revolution, one cannot judge the basic economic realities underlying a revolution from the slogans of those who carry it out.

A society in which science is not autonomous cannot grant autonomy to scientists. It is to prevent their conscious awareness of the extent of their alienation, which derives from the objective conditions governing scientific activity, that the myth of autonomy is nurtured and sustained. In this manner scientists believing fully that as free agents they have helped to enhance human knowledge, have made handsome contributions to the success of the production and military technology of their respective countries. Some take the view that the question of what uses their work will be put to is beyond their legitimate interest. For most scientists, however, the decision to accept funds is not very simple as the government departments provide generous funds for *basic* research which creates in the scientist the conviction (and illusion) that he is after all being faithful to his calling.

To quote Hirsch (1968, p. 147): 'It takes little moral and intellectual effort to subscribe to the ethos of science in abstract terms. The real test of the operative power of specific values takes place when scientists are faced with involvement in a project whose sponsors retain the ultimate control over the uses to which the research will be put.'[5]

**The Marxian Approach**

The Marxian sociology of science derives from Marx's wider theory of society, which attempts to examine the social system as a whole and in the context of the stages of its historical development. While, for the functionalists, social equilibrium is both a norm and a reality and 'value-consensus' among all the members of society the basis of this equilibrium, for Marx society is a dynamic concept, it is a social *formation,* and the basis of this formation is the material conditions of life. Deriving from this base is the division of society into antagonistic classes, each with its own values, beliefs, and cultural products, and the value-conflict arising out of this division is the characteristic feature of social relationships. The major themes of Marxian sociology are (1) the mode of production and the corresponding class structure, (2) the ideological 'superstructure', and (3) social revolution or the means by which social formations historically progress from one stage to another. Put in a nutshell, the Marxian sociology of science is as follows: Science or knowledge of nature is social knowledge, a tool which man progressively perfects to enhance his own material development.[6] In this approach there is no place for a reified conception of science as abstract, pure knowledge. The premise that the only value of knowledge is that it can be applied for human benefit, makes a rigid distinction between pure and applied science unnecessary in the Marxian scheme except in relative terms. Further, by asserting that the state of science in any period is critically influenced by the given level of development of the material forces of production, the corresponding relations of production, and the superstructure of social ideas, the Marxian approach does not see science as autonomous of extra-scientific considerations but rather as essentially subservient to historically determined social forces. This historico-relative approach to the development of science is the defining characteristic of the Marxian sociology of science.

In the functionalist approach the term 'knowledge' is interpreted very broadly to encompass virtually the entire gamut of 'cultural products'—ideas in general, i.e. arts, literature, social value-systems, juristic and ethical beliefs, philosophy, science, technology, political ideologies, etc. However, Marx expressly distinguishes natural science from other spheres of knowledge or 'cultural products' which constitute the ideological superstructure corresponding to a historically determined mode of production (infrastructure).

> With the change of the economic foundation the entire immense superstructure is more or less rapidly transformed. In considering such transformation the distinction should always be made between the material transformation of the economic conditions of production *which can be determined with the precision of natural science* and the legal, political, religious, aesthetic or philosophic—in short ideological forms in which men become conscious of this conflict and fight it out (Marx, 1904, p. 12).

The superstructure in any social formation at any stage in history consists of the prevailing *social ideas*, i.e. the conscious social relations and attitudes which may be subsumed under the rubric social consciousness. *Knowledge* in the sense of exact knowledge of natural phenomena—objective laws and precise prognoses—which arises out of man's interaction with nature and his need to master his natural and social environment, is essentially the foundation upon which technology develops, progressively developing the productive forces, and thereby conditions the mode of production which in turn moulds a certain superstructure of ideas. This does not mean that the prevailing ideology has no bearing on the development of the natural sciences, for the process is a dynamic one[7] and there is a kind of circular relationship between the superstructure of social ideas and the development of scientific knowledge in the sense that the latter's direction, pace, and aims are subject to the influence of the superstructure of social ideas in so far as social ideas constitute a part of the total social formation. For instance, the conceptual phrasing of scientific problems is often influenced by the economic, cultural, and social context of the scientists, for example Darwin's theory of selection was modelled after the prevailing notion of a competitive social order, which in turn was grounded in the economic reality of capitalism, just as in the seventeenth century Newton's quantitative epistemology could be linked to the development of commerce in Europe, which necessitated a new quantitative mentality able to calculate accurately quantities of goods bought or sold, investments made, profits to be gained, etc.

Marx's theory of knowledge is centred on the problem of theory and practice (praxis). Theory, he believed, must evolve an adequate interpretation of the world before it will be able to change it. In fact the history of philosophy is the continuous search for such an adequate picture of the world. He came to understand practice, therefore, in the sense of a concrete, conscious effort to remould the existing reality through human action and thereby change the course of history. This self-creation of man is a social development based upon the human mastery over nature. 'Nature builds no machines, no locomotives, railways, electric telegraphs, self-acting mules etc. These are products of human industry; natural material transformed into organs of the human will over nature, or of human participation in nature. *They are organs of the human brain, created by the human hand;* the power of knowledge objectified ...' (Marx, 1973b, p. 706).

The link between science and technology embodies the link between theory and practice;[8] since 'natural science underlies all knowledge' and the value of knowledge consists in its application. The explanation of the unity and difference between the pure and applied sciences (i.e. between theory and practice) is an important feature of the Marxian approach to the study of science.

To quote Bukharin (1931, p. 26), one of the most brilliant theoreticians on this subject:

> there is an objective contradiction between theory and practice, and at the same time their unity; there is their difference as opposite poles of human activity and at the same time their interpenetration; there is their separate existence as functions, as branches of divided social labour, and at the same time their unitary existence as

steps in the 'joint production of social life'. Under the cover of the difficulty of the exact demarcation of the applied and theoretical sciences beats the dialectics of the relationship between theory and practice, the *passing* of one into the other. In reality we have a whole chain of various theoretical sciences, linked up by internal connections. ... These sciences are born out of practice, which first sets itself 'technical' tasks: the latter require in their turn the solution of theoretical problems ... a special (relative) logic of motion being thereby created. Practice in this way grows into theory: the sought-for rule of action is transformed into the search for the law of objective relationship: there arise innumerable knots and interlacings of problems with their solutions: these in turn sometimes fertilise a number of hierarchically lower branches of science, and through technology penetrate into technique—consequently into direct practice of material labour, transforming the world. Here law becomes transformed into a rule of action, the persipient decision is verified by that action, orientation in the surroundings becomes the alteration of those surroundings, the intellect is immersed in the will, theory once again reverts to the form of practice. But this metamorphosis has as its final result by no means a simple repetition of the previous cycle of practice, since practice becomes practice on a more powerful and qualitatively altered basis.

The objective basis of technology is the laws of nature, i.e. technology is the embodiment of the knowledge man has accumulated in his struggle to harness the forces of nature. Technology, however, can develop only to the degree that it corresponds to the laws of natural science, regardless of whether the laws are applied in technology unconsciously, as in the first stages of its development, or consciously as at the present time. However, the achievements of theoretical science constitute only one of the determinants of technology in the sense that theoretical science only indicates the possible solutions for the given technical problems; by itself it cannot determine the direction and pace of development of technology. In fact the advancement or stagnation of theoretical science is influenced by factors external to it. Here we come to the other important aspect of science and technology: the social basis of their development.

What led Marx to this understanding was his historical analysis of the emergence and development of the capitalist system. While in pre-capitalist societies, for example feudal society, theoretical science did not interact in any substantial or critical manner with the productive forces, capitalism built up science as an instrument for the development of the productive forces through advances in techniques, in the period of the industrial revolution. The growth of commodity demand in the later Middle Ages due to the expansion in international trade following the discovery of new trade routes and new continents, necessitated the invention and use of machinery as the only effective way to ensure a growth in production commensurate with the rapidly advancing markets. However, the technological innovations during the period of the industrial revolution became possible only because of capital accumulation that had already taken place during the era of mercantile capitalism. The importance of capitalism is that it is a highly developed stage in the unfolding of man's creative powers of which technology is one of the most important manifestations. These powers would not have come into being had they not been caused by the economic necessity which in turn could have arisen only under specific historical circumstances.

Hence the basic determinant of the development of even theoretical science is to be found in the problems of developing technology which in turn result from the economic forces—the compulsions to develop production capacity—operating in a given social formation. The economic characteristics of feudalism or the feudal mode of production are such that they can do without modern science; it is the development of capitalism which generates the powerful impetus for the development of machine technology and hence the impetus for the advancement of modern theoretical science.

It is the investigation of the combined impact of the mode of production, and the corresponding superstructure of ideas at each stage of history upon the development of science, which constitutes the Marxian sociology of science.

While the general approach of the Marxist sociology of science is fruitful in providing an insight into the working of science as a social process, the relatively stronger emphasis placed on economic factors by Marx and Engels, and their relatively inadequate treatment of some superstructural elements such as individual psychology, leaves certain questions in the sociology of science unanswered. The reference here is specifically to the phenomenon of creativity. The instances in the history of science, of discoveries and inventions totally unrelated to the then existing economic and social organization, make it difficult to see all science as stimulated solely by the prevailing social and economic factors. Generally the Marxian principle of the primacy of social forces holds in the case of 'normal' science; even in those cases of 'revolutionary' science, when new fields of enquiry are opened up and existing theories challenged, it is possible to see the working of a constellation of forces both social and scientific which make it difficult to place any exclusive emphasis on brilliant originality, although the latter is a very important component of the scientific process though not its *cause*. For breakthroughs are part of social processes and a response to the social pressures for the movement of science in a particular direction.

However, where one encounters difficulties in explanation is with regard to those chance observations operating on history which are not determinable by otherwise socially determinable factors; extraordinarily brilliant contributions to science which arise out of no perceptible social needs and which for long remain unabsorbed by the existing stock of knowledge due to the absence of favourable social conditions.

This, however, constitutes the limits of any sociology of science; the functionalist approach and the innumerable studies of creativity alike have so far failed to give a complete explanation of this phenomenon. The inadequacy of the Marxian theory to satisfactorily explain the phenomenon of creativity does not invalidate the overall significance of the theory, i.e. of explaining the general trend of the development of science and technology.

**Science, Technology, and Socio-economic Organization**

Since we hold that the form of social and economic organization largely conditions the pace and direction of the development of science, the discussion here will centre on the specific interaction between science and socio-economic organization in the two vital sectors of the Indian economy—agriculture and industry. These are the spheres in which there has been considerable investment in scientific research by government, accompanied by policy statements to the effect that the objective of this investment is to modernize production in these two sectors in order to make for economic development, meaning thereby both growth and the elimination of poverty. The real test of the development of science rests upon its performance in relation to these two sectors, for although India may continue to expand her scientific apparatus, she remains scientifically sterile on account of the characteristic features of the Indian political economy. Although, apparently, among the Third World countries, Indian science is regarded as having made rapid strides, the facts remain that on the whole scientific research has made only a marginal contribution to whatever economic development has taken place in India after independence, and economic development has exerted little pressure for the development of science. The hallmark of Western capitalist countries and socialist countries is that science is integrated with economic growth. Till such integration takes place there is little hope for true scientific development in India.

It is in agriculture, however, even more than industry, that scientific and technological developments assume greatest importance. The predominant share of agriculture in national income and employment has important implications for economic development. Further, the fact that 40 per cent of the population live below the poverty line, and that 60 per cent of rural and 45 per cent of urban *per capita* monthly consumption expenditure is on foodgrains, makes it imperative that an increase in foodgrain production be effected and that foodgrains be made available at prices which the mass of the people can afford. Most important is the need to increase the flow of the marketable surplus to the cities to be made available to industrial workers at lower prices thereby bringing down the wage costs and raising the margin of profit in industrial production.

Given the importance of raising agricultural productivity, concerted efforts have been made by the Indian government over the last decade to break the vicious circle of stagnation through the much vaunted 'green revolution'. Agricultural backwardness, the problem of hunger and the spectre of social tensions that it tends to generate, have made the question of scientific and technological changes in Indian agriculture a crucial one. The questions that confront us, therefore, are:

(1) What is the nature of changes that are taking place in agriculture?

(2) To what extent are these changes a function of the research-induced 'green revolution'?

(3) What are the prospects for the agricultural research system to grow, and to contribute to a radical alteration of the 'agrarian prospect' of India?

Since 1965 which can roughly be said to mark a watershed in the development of agriculture in India, the country is supposed to be going through a 'green revolution'. This radical transformation of Indian agriculture refers primarily to foodgrain production, and among foodgrains particularly to wheat, where record yields have been achieved. The belief among those involved in agricultural research and policy-making is that Indian agricultural growth since the mid-1960s is qualitatively different in that agricultural production has been brought under the control of science and technology and the foundations laid for its liberation from its traditional subservience to the vagaries of the monsoon.

In order to understand the significance of the green revolution for Indian science and technology (and vice versa), we must trace the changes in emphasis in agricultural policy which culminated in the betting on technological changes to bring about a transformation of Indian agriculture.

At the time of independence, a network of institutions for agricultural research already existed. A heritage of the colonial experience and devoted mainly to cash crops, these research institutes, however, had no contact with production techniques at farm level. After independence, the focus of agricultural policy was not so much on expanding the research apparatus or improving technical efficiency in agriculture, as on undertaking a social uplift of the rural sector, to be embodied in a Community Development Programme, comprising the spheres of health, education, communication, agriculture, etc. It was to be above all a participatory programme introducing 'democracy at the grass roots'. To quote an extravagant statement by Nehru in 1955: 'I think nothing has happened in any country in the world during the last few years so big in content and so revolutionary in design as the community projects in India.'

The real problem of the ruling class, however, was how to leave the existing pattern of landownership and the rural power structure intact, and yet create conditions for agricultural production. In its search for solutions it was obligingly helped by the United States, and the Community Development Programme was launched with the active financial, administrative, and technical guidance of the Ford Foundation and the Technical Co-operation Mission of the United States government.

The Community Development Programme, however, failed to make any impact on production. The officials entrusted with implementation were more concerned with token achievements and 'visible' evidence of money spent. All the studies and assessments of the programme (for instance, Desai, 1969, pp. 611–622) and even the government's own Programme Evaluation Organization Reports (Government of India, 1957) unequivocally state that whatever benefits accrued went to the rural elite to the exclusion of the lower-caste cultivators, landless, and Harijans. In addition it was found that the Community Development Programme gave an opportunity for the landowning elite to further strengthen their positions of authority as the programme was administered through them and expected to percolate to the masses. Practically all the evaluations of the Community Development Programme have exposed the futility of this 'oil-stain' approach.

Coinciding with the evident failure of the Community Development Programme in the late 1950s, was the breakthrough in wheat technology reported by the Rockefeller Foundation. Extensive research initiated in 1943 by the foundation in collaboration with the Mexican government had succeeded in producing, under tropical and subtropical conditions, a 'package' of practices—short-strawed, fertiliser-responsive high yielding wheat varieties which would be non-sensitive to day-length; together with improved cultural practices, better management, and more effective pest control—that would improve productivity.

The technological breakthrough found immediate response in India in the form of a shift in agricultural development policy. The official justification was contained in a report by a group of American experts sponsored by the Ford Foundation (1959). The scientific rationalization was that the 'general practitioner' approach to agricultural development had not been particularly effective as it had attempted to utilize ill-suited agricultural technology in programmes in which primary attention was given to community development, extension systems, cooperatives or other factors. Basing itself on the United States' own experience in modernizing agriculture through 'combining highly specialised competencies' (Moseman, 1970, p. 13), the Ford Foundation strongly recommended a shift in emphasis from the all-embracing Community Development Programme in favour of technological solutions to the problem of agricultural development.

Alongside the import of the new technology, steps were initiated to prepare the capacity of the host country to absorb the new technology. In 1954 and 1959 respectively, two joint Indo-American teams prepared reports which were to lay the foundations of research work in agricultural sciences in India. The proposed structure of agricultural education was to be patterned on the Land Grant institutions in the United States of America. The major foreign agencies involved in the ventures were the Ford and Rockefeller Foundations and the United States Agency for International Development (AID); they committed themselves to providing support to vital segments of the new agricultural strategy. The massive aid for this (not less than 60 per cent of the total foreign aid from different countries received by India between April 1957 and September 1969 has come from the United States alone; 40 per cent of United States' aid directed towards agriculture) was categorized for (Naik and Sankaram, 1972, p. 99):

(1) Establishment of agricultural universities;
(2) Crop improvement;
(3) Supply of fertiliser and pesticides;
(4) Provision of American expertise;
(5) Training of Indians in American universities;
(6) Soil testing and other related programmes out of PL-480 funds.

As regards the infrastructure for research and education, the entire American effort was to be concentrated on a few leading agricultural universities, and research centres which were to be developed into advanced centres of excellence geared to achieve a high level of competence and performance. Indian scientists were sent in large numbers to the United States to obtain their higher degrees, some on shortterm assignments. Administrative personnel of the new agricultural development programme were also taken to the United States 'to observe administrative procedures and institutional organisation and to gain broad perspectives of institutional role and operations'. American architects constructed campuses for the proposed agricultural universities—'... what we see in these institutions today is akin to a physical transplantation of US land grant college campuses to the Indian soil ...'—and American technical assistance equipped research laboratories with a generous supply of all the most modern precision instruments and equipment, and libraries with books and periodicals and photocopying, microfilming and other facilities. The entire administration of American aid was supervised by American experts in India. Between 1951 and 1970 as many as 2,825 American specialists served in India; at any one time about 200 were present in the country assigned for agricultural development in areas such as education, agronomy, soil and water management, entomology, and plant breeding (Naik and Sankaram, 1972, pp. 88, 92, 93, 102).

Foreign influence on Indian agricultural development policy did not end with the introduction of the 'miracle seeds', foundation of agricultural universities, and administrative reorganization of the Indian Council of Agricultural Research.[9] The new technology required massive imports of fertiliser and pesticides and resulted later in the setting up of industries for fertiliser production with foreign technical and capital collaboration. To quote Lester Brown (1970, p. 47):

> The transfer of the new seeds and associated technologies across national boundaries which has made the agricultural revolution possible is impressive in scale. But perhaps even more impressive is the fact that this transfer of technology is being institutionalised. The institutions involved in this transfer include agricultural research centres (supported largely by private foundations), multinational corporations engaged in what has come to be called 'agribusiness', national and international assistance agencies and universities. American experience has played a formative part in the roles each of these institutions has assumed. The conduct and dissemination of agricultural research is becoming institutionalised on a global scale simply because it has proved to be one of the most profitable investments mankind can make.

The above historical background is essential if we are to assess the performance of the research-based green revolution and whether it signifies the 'arrival' of Indian science and technology.

The new technology came into operation on a wide scale by about 1967. The final precipitating factors were the drought years of 1965–1967. The first phase, the Intensive Agricultural Districts Programme (IADP), introduced into three districts in 1960–1961, was part of the extensive trials initiated by the Rockefeller Foundation in the early 1960s in the Near Eastern and South Asian countries with co-operation from the FAO. Supported also by the Ford Foundation, the IADP emphasized 'measures for immediate increase in agricultural production rather than measures for improving the general context for development or immediate welfare' (Mellor, 1968, p. 83). It was a package programme, the most prominent element of which was the provision of new physical inputs and the credit to buy them with, directed specifically to the economically most viable cultivators in areas of assured irrigation. The inputs included fertiliser, new high yielding variety (HYV) seeds, pumpsets for tubewells and a variety of farm machinery which the small peasant could not possibly afford on his smallholding.

In the areas of assured irrigation where the new technology has spread, some striking changes have been effected. In less than a decade the area under HYV seeds of all foodgrains has increased twelve-fold; consumption of chemical fertilisers, numbers of tractors, pumpsets, and tubewells have all grown dramatically, and productivity and total output have risen. However, except in the case of wheat, it is far from clear that growth in output has particularly exceeded pre-established growth rates. Serious doubt has been expressed about the arrival of the green revolution.

Further, despite the dramatic increases in wheat production, it appears that the new research-based technology has not been able, so far, to liberate Indian agriculture from its traditional subservience to the weather. The decline in output in 1971–1972 due to serious deficiency of rainfall in several parts of the country and the drastic drop to 95 million tonnes in 1972–1973 (the mark reached in 1967–1968) due to severe drought demonstrate the instability of Indian agriculture in the face of uncertain weather.[10] All this is in spite of the new technology, expansion of area under HYV, and increase in the volume of fertiliser consumption. The pattern of yearly fluctuations in production levels which has not changed substantially between 1950–1951 and 1973–1974 shows that agricultural production is even today largely governed by the vagaries of the weather.[11] The Report of the Agricultural Prices Commission feels constrained to remark: 'There seems to be little basis here for inference that the foodgrain output of the country has moved away to a higher growth path . . .' (Government of India, Agricultural Prices Commission, 1968b, p. 2). 'The prolonged dry spell during a good part of . . . 1972–73 . . . coming as it did after the experience of 1971–72, only served as a rude reminder of the fact that with an irrigated area still short of ¼ of the total cropped area, the agriculture of the country continues to be dependent on the vicissitudes of the weather' (Government of India, Agricultural Prices Commission, 1972b, p. 2).

The bumper harvest of 1970–1972 seems to clinch the issue. The bulk of the increase in output occurred, not in the states where the development programmes have been making rapid strides but in those with low irrigational facilities and high dependence on rainfall. Of the increase of 8·3 million tonnes, as much as 4 million tonnes came from Rajasthan alone; another 2·7 million tonnes were realized from Madhya Pradesh, Gujarat, and Bihar where again available irrigation facilities are meagre and where the contribution of additional acreage brought under the HYVs would not seem to account for very much in the foodgrain output increase. On the other hand a state like Punjab where the development programmes have been making impressive headway, registered only a moderate increase of less than 10,000 tonnes (Government of India, Agricultural Prices Commission, 1971, p. 4). The bumper crop, therefore, would seem to be only fractionally attributable to the new technology and almost entirely the result of favourable weather. In fact, with the exception of 1971–1972 and 1972–1973, all the green revolution years have enjoyed exceptionally good weather which makes it difficult to estimate precisely the impact of the new technology. The conclusion which emerges is a drastic one—that science and technology have made no revolutionary impact upon Indian agriculture and that the much vaunted green revolution has been due not so much to the 'miracle seeds' evolved in the research laboratories, as to the blessings of the weather gods.[12]

The apparent reasons for this are technical in nature. For one, only 15 per cent of the total cropped area is under the HYVs, of which wheat constitutes 39 per cent, rice—19·3 per cent, bajra—15·6 per cent, maize—8·7 per cent, and jowar—5·4 per cent (Rao, 1975, pp. 9, 10). Of this the only HYVs which are of some significance are those which have been evolved for wheat, a *breakthrough* having occurred only in relation to this crop. It is this which gives the green revolution its character; in fact it might more appropriately be called the 'wheat revolution'. Hence the new technology is not only limited in extent of application (the wheat-growing regions forming only 12 per cent of the total cropped area) but is also regionally concentrated.[13]

Two factors operate to set limits to the further spread of the wheat technology. For one, the area under wheat cannot be extended indefinitely due to constraints of suitability of soil conditions and other technical factors. For another, the area under assured irrigation is limited—only 21·8 per cent of the net sown area—which exposes Indian agriculture to the fluctuations of the weather. An added problem here is that energized minor irrigation with its controlled water supply, which makes for the most efficient exploitation of the new techniques, covers only about one-third of the irrigated area. This seriously inhibits the spread of the new technology even in the wheat regions, as controlled water supply is an indispensible ingredient of the modern 'package' of techniques.

There are other technical factors which also operate. Rice and coarse grains are relatively more important than wheat both in terms of area and production.[14] However, rice technology labours under serious constraints and has been unable to evolve effective varieties. In the case of coarse grains, which form an integral part of the diet of the rural poor (and the poor man's substitute for wheat, which is a superior cereal), very few concerted research attempts have been made to increase productivity. The new technology has reached some high yields in maize, some new varieties have also been evolved for bajra; but their effectiveness has been diluted by the absence of assured and controlled water supply as all coarse grains are grown entirely under rain-fed conditions. The prospects for increasing these facilities are not too bright; but even when provision for irrigation is made where feasible, the sown area often tends to shift away from coarse grains to more lucrative crops like wheat. Jowar and small millets have demonstrated a distinct lack of progress approximating to stagnation.

The important point is that these technical constraints derive from socio-economic realities. That the new technology has remained confined to wheat and is concentrated in areas of assured irrigation is due to the operation of factors outside the technical sphere. The new wheat technology was evolved in Mexico and the new varieties had only to be acclimatized to local conditions and pests. On the other hand, despite the fact that for high yielding maize the fundamental research was done in the international institutes, and for high yielding bajra the basic genetic material also came from the Rockefeller scientists, research in coarse grains has required a greater amount of applied work to be done at home than was required for wheat.

The reason for this, which is also an important factor responsible for the failure of even whatever technology has been evolved for bajra and maize, has been that coarse grains are mainly grown in unirrigated areas and the new varieties for these cereals are defined by the same integrated package of inputs (assured water supply, fertilisers, pesticides) as for wheat. In the unirrigated, dry-farming areas under these cereals, therefore, increase in crop-productivity has no prospects unless either high yielding varieties for dry-farming conditions are evolved or irrigation facilities are extended.

As regards the first alternative, i.e. evolution of HYVs for dry-farming conditions, some obstacles exist. So far the Indian research apparatus has been mainly involved in adaptive research, working largely upon the know-how already developed in the International Research Institutes which in turn have drawn on the experience of agricultural development in the developed countries. Borrowing wholly or adapting with minor variations, technological changes suited to the factor-endowments of the developed countries, the Indian research structure has been ineffective where it has had to innovate for indigenous problems and conditions. Assured and regulated water supply not being a problem of agriculture of the developed countries, the innovations embodied in the modern inputs also take controlled water supply as given. Naturally application of the same technology to unirrigated regions in India or irrigated regions lacking in efficient methods of water control has yielded no results. An important socio-economic factor responsible for the fact that research is mainly directed towards wheat and rice is that coarse grains enter into the consumption of only the poorer sections and hence do not constitute a profitable area of agricultural production.

The problem of increasing irrigation facilities is a complex one. While up to 1961 government had undertaken several major irrigation works, after 1961, due to scarcity of capital for such huge outlays, the strategy was to play down direct public investment in irrigation and make credit available to economically viable farmers to undertake such investment themselves in the form of minor irrigation works. The result was that while between 1951 and 1961 the sown area as well as the irrigated area registered a significant increase, between 1961–1962 and 1969–1970, the net sown area under irrigation increased from 18.3 per cent to a mere 21.8 per cent (Rao, 1975). The main reason would appear to be that minor irrigation through private investment being a costly enterprise, progress in this direction has come to depend entirely on its profitability to the investor. This in turn depends upon how high the product prices are. Hence in the sporadic cases where creation of irrigation facilities has been undertaken in the unirrigated regions, acreage has immediately shifted from coarse grains to wheat. The main reason for this is that the ruling prices for wheat are high which makes irrigated wheat farming profitable. In unirrigated regions, therefore, the returns from the new technology with all its constraints and uncertainties would have to be enormously high if farmers have to be induced to invest in minor irrigation works.

From the above discussion it is clear that it is the criterion of profitability which determines the direction of research efforts and the success or failure in implementation of research results. This, however, is not the way the problem is viewed by most observers of the Indian agricultural scene. The general lament is that the new techniques have not spread to the extent that would be desirable. Some are optimistic that India's food problem can be solved in the foreseeable future provided progress continues in the technical field towards the solution of problems of soil conditions, water control, entomological problems of HYVs, etc. Others see the greatest obstacle to the spread of the new techniques in the limited area under irrigation which exposes Indian agriculture to the vagaries of the weather. However, the area under assured irrigation will continue to remain limited in extent as long as those who have the resources to invest in minor and private irrigation works, i.e. the big farmers, do not find it profitable to do so, and the small farmers who want to invest in minor irrigation cannot because they do not have the resources.

The reasons for the constraints on the new technology must be sought both in the nature of the new technology and in the complex pattern of interaction between land and labour. The defining characteristic of the new technology is that it is an *integrated* package of modern inputs, like HYVs of seeds capable of doubling and even trebling yield per acre with adequate fertiliser inputs; assured water supply through tubewells, pumps (electric or diesel); tractors and other mechanical implements, and pesticides. Hence the new seeds are effective *only* if water supply is assured both in *quantity* and *timing* and they benefit *only* those who use large inputs of fertiliser of the right kind. The new seeds, being hybrid varieties and the result of a process of genetic manipulation in research laboratories, have been found to be highly susceptible to pests and diseases and therefore require certain types of pesticides. (The tradition varieties, although not as high yielding, were nevertheless sturdier and better able to withstand the ravages of weather and pests.) Given all these inputs, the new seeds are capable of expressing their yield potential; it is when all the variables are under control that weather ceases to be of overriding importance. However, if the 'package' is incomplete, the new technology may prove infructuous to the cultivator and may even prove counterproductive.

Being 'intensive' in character, with the effect of raising productivity per unit of land, it can be applied with equal gains on small as well as large farms; it is in this sense size-neutral. However, as it is complicated and requires simultaneous fulfilment of so many conditions, the new technology creates the need for credit to invest in tubewells, pumps, pesticides, fertilisers, etc. If this investment is made, the new technology is considerably profitable. In other words, it is capital-intensive and hence can be adopted only by those who have the wherewithal to invest in the modern inputs. It is this factor which makes the prevailing social structure a crucial condition, either providing a climate for the rapid advance of the new technology or acting as a constraint on its further spread.

The new technology has been introduced into an agrarian structure based on the private ownership of the means of production; it is only those who control an adequate quantum of these means who can go in for the modern techniques. Land is the only productive asset for three-quarters of the population, and its ownership confers a wide range of alternatives and a considerable degree of flexibility in decision-making. On the other hand, a high degree of concentration of landed property, uncertain employment opportunities for wage-labour, excessive pressure of population upon land, and the absence of alternative avenues of employment opportunities, limits to a considerable extent the choices open to those who do not possess land or whose holdings are uneconomic. Hence the initial resource position of the participants in production activity affects their bargaining position and the character of their market participation. It is this complex relationship between land and labour which determines whether the new technology will be adopted at all and by whom, and once it is adopted, what forms its impact on the rural social structure will take. From this, although it is difficult to make generalizations, it might be possible to draw out a tentative hypothesis of the possibilities for the new technology to spread without radical changes in the existing pattern of agrarian relations.

Certain general observations may be made regarding the agrarian social structure in India. The basis of this structure is the highly skewed pattern of landownership. Twelve per cent of the rural households own no land at all; 30 per cent of the households own holdings of 0·5 acre or less; another 25 per cent own between 0·5 and 2·5 acres. Thus 55 per cent of the total owners own less than 2·5 acres and their share in the total cropped area amounts to only 7 per cent. The holdings of three-quarters of the landholders, i.e. 72 per cent, is less than 5 acres and they control only one-fifth, i.e. 20 per cent, of the total cultivated area. As against this, those owning 10 acres and above constitute only 14 per cent of the total landowners. They, however, control 60 per cent of the total cultivated area. Of this 14 per cent, about 4 per cent own holdings of 25 acres and more, their control of the total cultivated area being as high as 28 per cent. The total picture, therefore, is one of acute concentration of landownership (Government of India, Ministry of Agriculture, 1962).

The fact that 30 per cent of the agricultural households own below 0·5 acres of land and 55 per cent own less than 2·5 acres, and the additional fact that for a holding to be economic it must be at least 2·5 acres in irrigated areas and 4·5 acres in dry areas, precludes over half the agriculturists from adopting the new technology. For those holding between 2·5 and 5 acres (i.e. 17·2 per cent of the households) and between 5 and 10 acres (i.e. 14·5 per cent of the households), whose holdings cover 43 per cent of the total area, size is not 'neutral' but becomes an important constraint as they lack both the strength of resources to buy the new inputs and the risk-bearing capacity which the new technology requires. Hence the majority of the small and middle farmers have remained outside or on the fringes of the new technology for economic reasons though not for technical ones.

Small farmers may be classified into two categories—owner cultivators and tenant cultivators. One of the major disabilities standing in the way of this section adopting the new varieties is lack of institutional credit. A field study of small farmers conducted by the Reserve Bank of India in 1967–1968 found that in eleven out of the twelve districts surveyed,

> in the issue of agricultural credit, the record of cooperatives was dismal.... The bulk of the credit requirements of small farmers in 11 out of 12 districts was met by private credit agencies ... consisting of landlords, professional moneylenders, agriculturist-moneylender, agriculturists-cum-traders, traders and commission agents and relatives ... commercial bank credit was conspicuous by its absence in 10 districts.

The survey found that small farmers were as eager to adopt the new technology as were the large farmers but were prevented from doing so by lack of credit facilities. On the one hand the co-operative credit societies are dominated by large landowners who discourage small farmers from enrolling as members, and who corner the major part of the funds; on the other hand the insistence of the credit societies on the security of assets (although this is against the basic principles of co-operative finance) rather than the purpose for which credit is sought, and the poor creditworthiness of the small farmers, again result in a major proportion of co-operative credit going to the large landowners who already have substantial resources of their own (Government of India, Reserve Bank of India, 1974a).[15] What is significant is that these funds, which are theoretically meant for the small farmers, find their way into the hands of rich farmers and are not used for the purpose of capital investment and of augmenting agricultural production, for which they are intended; rather, more than 40 per cent of them are diverted to unproductive uses (All India Rural Credit Survey, 1963–1964). Thus the small farmers, who are also poor, for whose benefit the co-operatives were set up in the first place, are excluded from the sphere of co-operative credit. Further, the loans are not available in the quantity, and at the time when the small farmers need them most. Hence they have no alternative but to fall back on private credit agencies because of the timely availability of the loans and the fact that they are given against personal security. What is significant about borrowing from private agencies is that it results not in the improvement of the economic condition of the small farmer but in his further impoverishment. This is on account of the usurious rates of interest which result in the perpetual indebtedness of the small farmer.

The major obstacle to tenant farmers adopting the new technology is the prevailing tenurial system. About a quarter of the cultivated land in the country is under tenancy; in some regions its incidence is as high as 40 per cent; and about 80 per cent of these tenancies are insecure, operating on oral or informal leases (Appu, 1975). Insecure tenancy is yet another system by which the economic position of the weaker sections of the cultivators is undermined. The number of small farmers and peasants with uneconomic holdings being very large and the uncertainties of the employment market not being sufficient incentive for these sections to hire themselves out as full-time wage labourers, leasing out land becomes extremely profitable for the landlord. On the one hand, he can reap the benefits of agricultural production without engaging in agriculture himself, while the tenant bears the entire risks of cultivation. On the other, the rents on these holdings are extremely high, usually paid in kind, and on an average 50 per cent of the produce, but they can be raised arbitrarily by the landlord on threat of eviction.

For purposes of production and also to see him through till the next harvest the tenant is compelled to borrow money, generally from his landlord. The peasant typically borrows at a time, a few months after the harvest, when the current market prices are very high, while his repayment is extracted from him just after the harvest when current market prices are at their lowest. Between paying his rent, repaying his debt, and keeping himself alive, he remains perpetually indebted. This peculiar relationship (which may also require him to commit his own and sometimes even his family's future labour) of the peasant of being perpetually indebted to the same person from whom he leases his land more or less ties him to a particular landowner in the manner of a serf (see Bhaduri, 1973; Prasad, 1973).

Hence, in appearance, free markets in land and free choices of occupation exist, but in reality the pattern of landownership and income distribution so severely restricts the choices of the economically weak sections, that the choices are virtually non-existent. 'Such interpenetration of markets not only increases the exploitative powers of the landlord but also has certain dynamic consequences. The freedom to take decisions or the area of feasible choices for the economically vulnerable sections shrinks and this may over time mean the perpetuation of bondage whose form is not so obvious' (Bharadwaj and Das, 1975, p. 223).

Given his acute poverty and perpetual indebtedness, therefore, it is rare to find a sharecropper who has the desire and capacity to invest in modern inputs. On the other hand, since the landlord is assured his income from the high rents and moneylending he has no incentive to invest in the new capital-intensive technology. To quote from the fourth Five Year Plan:

> It has been observed that under the present arrangement of informal tenancy and share-cropping the landlord considers it unwise to invest in improving his land; likewise the sharecropper or the tenant is either unable or reluctant to invest in inputs like fertilisers. The insecurity of tenancy has not only impeded the widespread adoption of the HYV's but in some cases led to social and agrarian tensions. (Government of India, Planning Commission, n.d. 2, p. 177)

Not only have the small farmers not had the facilities to avail themselves of the new technology, the latter has served as an instrument for the worsening of their socio-economic condition. The new technology is confined to irrigated areas. The demonstrated profitability of the new techniques has greatly enhanced land values in these areas thereby increasing the demand for land. This has led to increased purchases of land by large landowners, dispossession of land of small farmers, and threat of eviction of tenants and therefore their greater insecurity, resulting in even further concentration of landownership.[16] Rents have also increased in some areas to two-thirds of the output, particularly in the case of tenants growing HYVs (Sau, 1972, p. 362; Raj, 1972, p. 261; Rao, 1975, p. 157).[17]

From the above it is clear that it is the big farmers who are the beneficiaries of the new technology. However, this is no accident, given the pattern of landownership and the fact that the new strategy was implemented through the agency of the big farmers as the quickest and most assured means of increasing the marketable surplus. The government's policy for foodgrain prices has also been in favour of the big farmers. Since the new technology is expensive, the price at which government offers to buy the wheat stocks has to be high enough to make the adoption of the new technology lucrative for the politically powerful big landowners. However, the procurement prices have remained unjustifiably high. The Agricultural Prices Commission feels constrained to remark that 'There is an obvious oddity in the situation in which prices undergo a spurt in the face of increasing production and mounting stocks of the cereal. That the producers have benefited from the wheat revolution is only as it should have been. But there must come a time when the benefit starts percolating to the consumer too . . .' (Government of India, Agricultural Prices Commission, 1972a, p. 3). 'It [also] generates an impression even though unwittingly, that government policy is discriminating in favour of the big farmers and traders' (Government of India, Agricultural Prices Commission, 1968a, p. 10).

Although rice is the most important crop, agricultural research has made a very limited impact on this crop. There are two kinds of constraints which operate here—technical and socio-economic.

In the first place, although the first HYV for rice—IR8—was released by the International Rice Research Institute in 1966, a technological *breakthrough* in rice has as yet failed to occur. In fact international rice research experts are themselves not very optimistic about the possibility of even a future breakthrough (Barker, 1971, pp. 117–130). The problems of absorption have been several. First, the modern production techniques used for the new strains provide environments which are not only good for plant growth but also provide ideal conditions for the development of diseases and harmful insects which were previously unknown or unimportant. To fully exploit the potential offered by the semi-dwarf plant types, therefore, a high degree of resistance to different plant parasites must be incorporated in the new varieties. This requires much investment in research. Apart from the fact that these varieties can be effective only in sufficiently irrigated areas and can make little headway in poorly irrigated or rain-fed areas, even in irrigated areas problems of water control and soil conditions constitute an important reason for the poor performance of these varieties.

An additional problem is that of the acceptability of the new varieties. In terms of milling and eating quality and appearance these varieties are considered to be inferior to the traditional varieties. A major influence on eating quality is the amylose content of the rice which influences the degree of stickiness. The new varieties IR8 and IR5 are high in amylose content; therefore cooked rice is dry and flaky but tends to become hard when allowed to cool. Because of the above factors the new varieties, though high yielding, sell from 10–20 per cent below the traditional varieties and in India are classed as coarse rices (Barker, 1971, p. 126). This has certain socio-economic implications for the big farmers who are the major beneficiaries of the new technology. A survey (Mencher, 1974, pp. 309–323) conducted in Tamil Nadu has found that big farmers, who were the ones encouraged to grow the new rice in the first place, have begun switching back to traditional varieties which require little or no modern expensive inputs and which do not require such careful supervision in the fields during the growing season, while fetching a higher price. On the other hand these farmers have largely benefited from the infrastructure created by the government for the absorption of the new technology in the form of loans for tubewells and pumpsets which guarantees them a secure second or even third crop. They are thus better off than before even with the traditional varieties.

What is interesting here is that the small farmers, who are the principal consumers of the new cheaper varieties, and who have generally evinced a desire to use the new HYVs, have, by virtue of their economic conditions, been unable to do so for, although the price of the new rice is low, the cost of investment in fertilizers, pesticides, and water resources is beyond their reach. Neither has their resource position been improved by institutional credit agencies which by their very definition of creditworthiness exclude the small farmers.

In the wet rice-growing areas both in the Southern and Eastern regions, the landlord derives high, risk-free income from feudal rent and moneylending. Not only must any new technology, if it is evolved, be effective, and profitable, but the gains from it must exceed the risk-free gains described above, if the HYVs are to spread.

Any change which weakens the system where the economic and political power of the landowner is largely based on his being able to keep the peasant constantly indebted to him, will naturally be resisted if the gain in his income from the risks of increased productivity consequent upon technological change falls short of his loss in risk-free income from usury and rent due to the improvement in the economic circumstances of the peasant. This is illustrated by the fact that in the region irrigated by the Kosi river valley project, the big landowning class exercising economic and political control over the sharecroppers and labourers, has no interest in encouraging the direct producers to adopt the new technology as it would liberate the latter from servile bondage even though, on economic grounds, it would be profitable to the landowner as well. On the other hand, for the tenant, having to bear the costs of production, lack of resources make it impossible for him to do so (Appu, 1975; Prasad, 1973).[18]

Where tenants have used the new seeds they have had to labour under constraints which neutralize whatever high yielding virtues the seeds might possess. A study conducted in some canal-irrigated villages in Orissa (Bharadwaj and Das, 1975) found in the case of tenants who adopted HYVs of paddy, that the rents continued to be exhorbitant. In order to raise the rents every season, the landlord found it to his advantage to make the lease contract short—either giving it over to new tenants or treating it as a separate lease even with the old. Insecurity of tenants has thus increased as, in order to counter the threat of eviction, they are forced to pay higher and higher rents, in addition to rendering labour services. The only change in the nature of the rent is that, in the case of tenants cultivating HYVs, the rent has to be paid *in cash, in advance of the harvest*. This compulsion may, however, lead the tenants into yet another cycle of indebtedness.

From the foregoing discussion it is clear that the agrarian social structure has so far not provided the conditions for the spread of the new technology among the majority of the cultivating population. Although this is officially attributed to technical problems such as the limited area under irrigation, problems of evolving suitable dry-farming technology or effecting a breakthrough in rice technology, we have seen the socio-economic constraints which operate to perpetuate the technical problems. Where it has been absorbed at all, it is only by 7 per cent of the cultivators and its spread accounts for only 10–15 per cent of the cropped area.

There is one question which arises at this point. If the prevailing social structure dictates that only the big farmers can have access to the new technology, do they as a class have the dynamism to bring about a radical transformation of Indian agriculture and make for rapid economic development? Framed in Marxian terms the question may be put as follows—does the new technology imply the advent of capitalism in Indian agriculture and can the farmers who use the new technology be called capitalist farmers? The rapid pace of technological progress in the West has always been in response to the needs and vigour of the capitalist mode of production in those countries. Since agricultural production in India is based on the private ownership of land, it seems logical to enquire whether the mode of production which prevails in Indian agriculture, particularly after the infusion of the new technology, is also tending towards capitalism; and the implications of this for scientific and technical progress here.

The new seeds have been likened to the role of the steam engine in Europe and the beginning of industrial capitalism there (Brown, 1970, p. 12). The industrial revolution, however, was neither the beginning of capitalism nor its culmination; rather it was made possible by the process of capital accumulation which preceded it, in the period of mercantile capitalism. The development of machinery or technology was essentially in response to the need for profitable investment of this capital in order to ensure a corresponding growth in production. In the Indian case we have seen how the agrarian structure characterized by dominant feudal features received its first major impetus to modernization only with the new agricultural strategy begun in 1965. Unlike in Europe, the prior socio-economic conditions did not evolve to a point where they themselves made technological innovations necessary. Rather the motive force for the so-called capitalist development was exogenous in nature, i.e. the new strategy and the inputs for it, the new technology, were of foreign origin. Moreover, the new seed technology, as evolved in the developed countries, is capital-intensive and more suited to the factor-endowments of these countries than to the capital-scarce economies such as India. The implications of this capital-intensive technology are that it necessitates continued dependence on the multinational corporations which, either by themselves or through technical collaborations with local industrialists, supply the fertilisers and pesticides, tractors and pumpsets indispensible for the success of the new technology, resulting in the perpetual dependence of the agricultural sector of the Indian economy on massive doses of foreign financial and technical aid. In such a situation the prospects for local science and technology to develop along an independent growth path appear remote. There are today 23 national and central research institutes and laboratories, eight soil conservation research, demonstration and training centres and 19 agricultural universities. The rapid increases in agricultural education has already resulted in an estimated 14,000 and 2,500 agricultural graduate and post-graduate job-seekers respectively (Government of India, Council of Agricultural Research, n.d., p. 76). However, the path of dependent development with its emphasis on quick, visible results has resulted in the wholesale and continuous import of the basic genetic material for the new seeds from the International Research Institutes while the Indian research institutes confine themselves mainly to adaptive research. The National Commission on Agriculture has reported the virtual absence of any basic or long-term applied research in both the central research institutes and agricultural universities and has deplored the exclusive emphasis on short term adaptive research which would yield quick results (Government of India, National Commission on Agriculture, 1971).

The choice of this path of dependent development, which leaves only a marginal role for Indian science and technology was inevitable since the ruling class did not want to effect any major changes in the agrarian social structure. Effective implementation of land reform measures could have provided security to tenants and regulated rents, broken concentration of land, increased the size of the uneconomic holdings, and perhaps created the conditions for co-operative farming, and released the social energies of three-quarters of the cultivating population who are now subsistence farmers.

Land reform legislations directed towards abolition of zamindari, security of tenure for tenant cultivators, and imposition of ceilings on landholdings were passed in the period following independence. But the nature and strength of resistance rendered these ineffectual.

Given the historical dependence of the Indian economy upon the advanced capitalist countries on the one hand and the strategy of increasing the marketable surplus of foodgrains without changing the pattern of agrarian relations on the other, technological change appeared to be a substitute for land reforms. We have shown that the agrarian social structure poses a grave impediment to the widespread implementation of these technological changes and thereby constitutes a fetter on the development of indigenous science and technology.

Scientific research related to industrial development was non-existent during British rule. Soon after independence huge expenditure was incurred in setting up national research laboratories for industrialization. However, with the second Five Year Plan and the pronounced emphasis on speedy industrialization and the strategy of building basic and heavy industries requiring highly advanced technology, any dependence on indigenously developed science and technology had to be postponed. Given the choice of development strategy it was logical that the 'technological gap' could be filled only by large scale import of technology.

The policy of the government with regard to foreign collaborations had already been spelt out in 1949. It was explained that foreign capital should be utilized in a manner most advantageous to the country. Indian capital needed to be supplemented by foreign capital not only because domestic savings would not be enough for the rapid development of heavy and basic industries on the desired scale, but also because in many cases scientific, technical, and industrial knowledge and capital equipment could be quickly secured only through inflow of foreign capital. It was made clear that there would be no discrimination between foreign and Indian enterprises; that foreign interests would be permitted to earn profits subject to regulations common to all enterprises and that they would be normally permitted to remit profits or withdraw capital subject to considerations of foreign exchange scarcity. As regards equity participation by foreign capital, it was indicated that 'as a rule, the major interest, ownership and effective control of an undertaking should be in Indian hands'. However, it was clarified that this was not a hard and fast rule and that government would not object to foreign capital having control of a concern for a limited period if it was found to be in the national interest (Government of India, Planning Commission, n.d. 1; Government of India, Ministry of Industrial Development, 1969, p. 14).

Between 1948 and 1958 the numbers of collaborations entered into were relatively small and in addition India's sterling balances provided the necessary foreign exchange for the import of machinery and equipment. Later, towards the close of the 1950s with increasing foreign exchange stringency, foreign capital participation became the main vehicle through which import of machinery and equipment could be effected. A number of tax concessions favouring foreign enterprises were introduced and industrial licensing procedures streamlined to avoid delays in approvals of foreign collaboration. Hence, while during 1948–1958 recourse to foreign collaboration was limited to an average of only 50 approvals a year, after 1958 the numbers have been on a constant increase. From 284 in the period 1948–1955, it rose to 796 between 1956 and 1960, while in the period 1960–1973 the total number of collaborations have been 3,242 (Government of India, Reserve Bank of India, 1974b, p. 1).

The significance of the role of foreign collaboration in Indian industry cannot, however, be fully assessed merely from the *number* of foreign collaborations. It is the share of the foreign collaboration sector in the total industrial output which is significant. For instance, although out of a total of over 12,000 manufacturing units, only 620 or 5 per cent have entered into foreign collaborations, they cover nearly 40 per cent of the total value added of all the companies. To illustrate further, the major industrial groups with collaboration, manufacturing electrical goods, chemicals, machinery and machine tools, etc., cover 15–25 per cent each of the total number of companies, but cover around 70–90 per cent each of the total value added of their individual groups (Government of India, Reserve Bank of India, 1974b, p. 97). This data clearly shows the substantial dependence of Indian industry on foreign technology and know-how.

Notwithstanding the wholesale dependence on foreign technology, the scientific structure was continually assured that it, too, was important. A Scientific Policy Resolution was announced in 1958 (see Government of India, Administrative Reforms Commission, 1970), which, however, deliberately avoided any operational definition of the objectives, or specifying how a forward-looking, self-reliant science policy would be dovetailed into an economic plan which admittedly relied on advanced technology imported from the developed countries. In the period which has followed the Scientific Policy Resolution, industry and the scientific establishment have remained independent of each other. Alienated from industrial activities because of lack of sufficient demand from the industrial sector for locally developed technologies, science has become largely, what Cooper calls, a 'consumption' item (Cooper, 1974, p. 5). Between 1956 and 1971 seven committees were instituted to work out how programmes of research and programmes of industrial development could be co-ordinated. The fact that they were all ineffective, repeated the same recommendations which were never followed up, and that in the case of some of the committees not even published information on their functioning is available, is sufficient to show the ineffectiveness of science policy.

In the event of their alienation from production activities, some of the research establishments have remained on the periphery of industrial development. In the absence of any pressures from the economy, research efforts have gone into the evolving of processes for improving the quality of ice-cream, vanilla essence, bug-poisons, lustre of artificial pearls; manufacture of consumer products catering to the middle classes in the urban areas such as dehydrated peas, 'instant' food products, expensive protein biscuits; or products for export such as pigs' intestines and high quality leather for sophisticated leather garments, handbags, and other accessories. In the absence of any specific policies in the majority of the national laboratories, the main determinants of research orientation are the individual decisions of research workers. This in conjunction with the absence of pressures from industry results in expenditure on areas of research which may be solely in keeping with the aspirations and training of the individual research worker rather than making any tangible contribution to industrial innovation. In those cases where individual scientists have evolved import-substituting processes, either industry has been reluctant to 'risk' adopting them or the laboratories or the National Research and Development Corporation (which was established for precisely this purpose) have lagged in their efforts to scale up the processes to pilot-plant level and prove their commercial viability.

It might be argued that in itself there is nothing wrong with foreign technology. Given the high levels of scientific advancement reached in the developed countries, it would be wasteful to expend time in repeating what has been accomplished elsewhere. Further, local production capacity can be strengthened by the imported technology and the host country enabled to 'take off' into rapid industrial growth. With the gradual transfer of technology from the developed to the underdeveloped countries the latter will in course of time achieve technological sophistication and independence.

However, in effect this is not how the system has worked. Not only does most of the technology come tied to foreign capital through foreign subsidiaries and joint ventures; even those which come as part of pure technical collaboration agreements are replete with restrictive clauses which do not permit technology assimilation by the host country but rather perpetuate its technological dependence.[19]

Examples of such restrictions are those on the use of know-how by the Indian collaborator. This involves the stipulation that Indian ventures are to keep in secrecy all technical information and not to transfer, assign or sublicense the right to know-how to any third party (Subrahmanian, 1972, p. 144).

Another restriction takes the form of limiting the freedom of the Indian collaborator to introduce change (either modifications or improvements) in the product/process design and know-how (Government of India, Reserve Bank of India, 1974b, p. 117). A recent survey found that in some cases, it was stipulated that even in the event of any improvement being invented/discovered/evolved in respect of the concerned product by the host company or by any of its employees, the former must promptly disclose the full details thereof. If the foreign collaborator so wished, the host company may join the inventor in applying for patent protection in any country of the world. It was also stipulated that any patent so obtained would be the property of the foreign collaborator although the Indian company would be entitled, without royalty or premiums, to the non-exclusive use thereof *during the duration of the agreement in the manufacture of the concerned product* (Government of India, Reserve Bank of India, 1974b; Subrahmanian, 1972).

This restriction of the Indian collaborator's freedom to introduce changes in the product design retards the assimilation of the imported know-how. This is generally aided by yet another stipulation that raw materials, spares, components, and services must also be imported directly or indirectly through the foreign collaborator. The latter being the single source of supply, he has unfettered freedom to decide what is to be imported in what quantity and at what price in addition to exercising technical control over the production in the Indian venture.[20]

The control over the Indian collaborator by his foreign counterpart extends in other areas as well, the most prominent of which are control over local sale and export restrictions. The former manifests itself in the foreign collaborator's dominance in the pricing and sale of the product in the domestic market. The latter is also a very important feature of foreign collaborations and complementary to the former. Although several collaboration agreements are sanctioned by government because of their export potential, the collaboration agreements are generally so riddled with export restrictive clauses that they clearly indicate that the intention of the foreign collaborator is to manufacture mainly for domestic consumption in India and not in order to enable the Indian counterpart to export the product. One major reason why foreign firms are interested in entering into collaborations in India is that, with the existing import restrictions, the only way in which they can have a foothold in the Indian market is through collaborations. On the other hand, having their own interests to pursue in the markets provided by other countries, they would not be interested in encouraging exports from India which might clash or compete in the foreign markets. In order to safeguard these interests, therefore, most foreign collaborators impose export restrictions in the collaboration agreements with regard to the area of exports.

Between the two Reserve Bank of India survey periods, there was a rise in the number of such export restricting classes—from 455 in 1963–64 to 956 in 1969–1970. In fact in the latter period the export clauses constituted the bulk of the restrictive clauses—nearly three-quarters (Government of India, Reserve Bank of India, 1974b, pp. 102, 117) despite the government's export promotion drive.

Given the above described dynamics of foreign collaborations and import of technology therefore, it is clear that the prospects of the economy to reach a stage of self-reliant growth are bleak. Although, motivated by tax concessions, more and more companies in the private sector are setting up their own research and development laboratories,[21] the main emphasis in these is not product/process innovation or import substitution in production process, but only development, adaptation, and modification in the product/process supplied by foreign patent holders. Even here these laboratories admit that although their foreign collaborators had no explicit restrictions on improvement/modification of the imported technology, there was either an understanding or indirect stipulation that the Indian firm should not make any alterations without the foreign collaborator's consent (Government of India, Reserve Bank of India, 1974b, p. 137).

To conclude, the main reasons for the rush on the part of Indian entrepreneurs for foreign collaborations is that there is minimum risk involved in establishing plants based on proven technology; combined with this is the desire to acquire a share with the foreign firm in the advantages of monopoly position and utilize foreign brand names.[22] What makes the situation highly attractive to the foreign collaborator is that it gives them a secure position in the sheltered Indian market and facilitates export of know-how and/or capital on unilaterally determined terms, the terms of payments being agreed upon in such a complex manner that they can reap maximum returns with minimum commitments. Further, collaborations take place mainly in those areas where the rate of technological progress in the developed countries is relatively fast. An important reason for such collaborations is that it offers for the foreign monopolies a market for obsolete machines, equipment, and know-how which in turn facilitates the continuation of technological progress in the home countries. The impact of this upon Indian industry is that the 'technological gap' becomes a self-perpetuating reality and foreign dependence the keynote of Indian industrial development.

Some national laboratories claim that they have successfully sold their processes to small-scale industries which lack access to foreign technology and resources for inhouse research and development facilities. Taken at face value, this claim, combined with the fact that the share of the small-scale sector in total industrial production is one half, may appear to be a progressive and encouraging sign. But that section of the small-scale sector which will take recourse to the newly evolved processes in the national laboratories, i.e. the progressive section, is inevitably marginal. Being economically weak, small-scale entrepreneurs prefer traditionally proven and easily accessible technology and traditional products. In an economy where even big entrepreneurs are reluctant to take risks with indigenous technology, it is unrealistic to expect the small-scale industrialist to experiment with indigenous newly evolved technology.

In industry, therefore, the overall position is one where the dominant hold of foreign capital and foreign technology does not leave much scope for indigenous science and technology to make an impact on the Indian economy.

From the above discussion it is clear that in a non-communist developing country like India, the 'dependent' path of economic development has marginalized the importance and relevance of indigenous science and technology in the spheres of industry and agriculture. On the other hand, the fact that scientific institutions have proliferated and scientific personnel have increased at a phenomenal rate[23] has led to uncertain fortunes for a large, growing infrastructure for scientific research which cannot and does not produce any tangible results for economic development. The 'science' advisers to the economic planners have so far worked on the assumption that in order to make science an instrument for economic development all that is required is to create an apparatus and train personnel; that if such programmes have failed to produce expected results it is only because they were not well planned or well administered, or well financed or properly utilized. In keeping with this approach, solutions to the problem of changing the socio-economic reality through the development of science have been sought in factors internal to the scientific apparatus, such as machinery for streamlining the administrative structure of the research institutions, payment of higher salaries for scientists, increasing the budgetary provisions for the creation of facilities for scientific research, according to 'national recognition' to scientists, etc. However, these remedial measures have failed to integrate science with the mainstream of Indian life.

One problem which has been receiving a great deal of attention in public debates as well as in policy-making is that of the 'brain drain', i.e. the progressively increasing number of scientists migrating to the West. Related to this is the problem that those who return after being trained abroad become dissatisfied with the working conditions and the insufficient opportunities to utilize the advanced skills they have acquired abroad.

As a solution to this problem, an apparatus for esoteric science, however irrelevant it may be to the problems of economic development, is created with a view to provide an outlet for the expertise of this minority of highly specialized foreign-trained scientists. This is clearly illustrated by the fact that in 1972–1973, the expenditure on atomic energy and space research exceeded that on agricultural, industrial or medical research.[24]

The basic cause of the problem of the 'brain drain', however, is not contained within science but in the fact that the peripheral role of indigenous science and technology coexists with institutes of advanced studies in science and technology, which, being sponsored by foreign agencies, are geared to keeping pace with scientific and technological developments in the advanced countries and hence turn out scientists who are over-specialized for local conditions. Thus the brain drain is a result of two causes: (1) a foreign-dependent development policy, and (2) scientists mainly come from the middle class/upper castes, whose aspirations for quick success draw them abroad.

The other problems of scientific activity in the country are also seen as arising from the scientific structure, for example the hierarchical structures prevailing in research laboratories, nepotism and favouritism in the selection of personnel, dissatisfaction with pay scales on the part of scientists, the pirating by senior scientists of the work of their junior colleagues, all resulting in an atmosphere of frustration and politicking in research establishments.

However, even these are not organizational problems arising from within 'science' but are a projection of the problems prevailing in the wider society which is governed by feudal, authoritarian values and hierarchy. Because economic conditions do not favour the advance of science, science has not in turn made any impact upon the social structure in the sense of laying the basis for rational values and a reward system based on merit and efficiency. Caste, linguistic, regional and religious afiliations being still strong in the social environment surrounding science, they have inevitably encroached upon the scientific community which cannot in any country insulate itself from the value-system governing the wider society.

It is not hard to understand why the functionalist sociology of science with its ahistorical, fragmented perspective is an unreal analytical framework within which to analyse Indian science. It is only the Marxian sociology of science, with its historical perspective and relating science to its economic basis, which provides the necessary insights into the functioning of science as a social activity.

## Acknowledgements

I should like to thank Professor J. V. Ferreira of the Department of Sociology, University of Bombay, and Dr S. S. Blume for their encouragement; A. N. Oza of the Economics Department, St Xavier's College, Bombay, for helpful discussions of economic aspects of this paper; the library staff of the Indian Society of Agricultural Economics and the editorial staff of the *Economic and Political Weekly* for making material available to me.

## Notes

1. See especially his *Protestant Ethic and the Spirit of Capitalism*, and the application of his central thesis in *Society and Religion in India*.
2. The thesis, however, has not lacked critics in recent years. See, for example, Rattansi, 1972, pp. 2–3.
3. A detailed discussion of this is given in Sklair, 1973.
4. The great man in history has an important role. He is an individual, and being an outstanding individual is also a social phenomenon of outstanding importance. However, to quote Carr,

   the view (that must be discouraged is that) which places great men outside history and sees them as imposing themselves on history by virtue of their greatness, as 'jack-in-the-boxes who emerge miraculously from the unknown to interrupt the real continuity of history'.... What seems to me essential is to recognise in the great man an outstanding individual who is at once a product and an agent of the historical process, at once the representative and the creator of social forces which change the world and the thoughts of men.' (Carr, 1961, pp. 54–55)

5. Although Hirsch provides a more empirical understanding of science in American society than any of the neo-Mertonians, theoretically he remains within the systems framework, defining science after the Parsonian manner as a 'set of institutionalised relationships functioning to implement goals that are held in common by specified members of society'. (Hirsch, 1968, p. 16).
6. Marx's conception of society and nature as parts of a single system led him to declare

that 'Natural science will one day incorporate the science of man just as the science of man will one day incorporate natural science; there will be a single science' (Marx, 1973a, p. 143).
7 It is this model of a society composed of different levels which has been the crucial point of difference between Marxists and non-Marxists, the controversy centring on the question of the hierarchy of the levels and the mode of their interaction. While the mode of production and its corresponding social relations have been regarded as primary by Marx, nowhere does he see a one-to-one correlation between this 'base' and the ideological superstructure. His assertion is that it would be erroneous to see the ideological forms *independent* of the base, i.e. they are not 'pure' phenomena but have a material basis. Hence the economic situation is not *the* cause or is alone active while everything else is only passive. 'Rather there is an interaction on the basis of economic necessity which in the last analysis always prevails' (Engels to Mehring, 1893), quoted in Bottomore and Rubel, 1956, p. 34). Engels elaborates further: although the economic situation is the basis, the various elements of the superstructure—the international circumstances; political conditions; political, juristic and philosophical theories; religious views; the further development of all these into systems of dogmas; 'even the traditions that haunt human minds'—also exercise their influence upon each other and upon the base (see Althusser, 1970, p. 112).
8 F. Engels elaborates on this key concept in Marxian theory (Engels, 1974). A good discussion of the concept and its forerunners is also to be found in Avineri, 1970, pp. 124–149.
9 On the recommendations of the two teams—the Second Joint Indo-American Team (1959) and the Agricultural Research Review Team (1963) which was again Indo-American in composition, under the chairmanship of a USDA official—the Indian Council of Agricultural Research was completely overhauled. Research activities previously scattered among commodity committees, research stations, State Government Departments and central institutes were now centralized and co-ordinated and pay scales of agricultural scientists were raised.
10 The index of foodgrain production, which had increased from 90 in 1965–1966 to 134 in 1970–1971, declined to 131 in 1971–1972 and to 119 in 1972–1973 (source: Directorate of Economics and Statistics, Ministry of Agriculture).
11 An examination of the fluctuations in foodgrain output over the past 18 years reveals that two out of every six consecutive years have experienced a fall in production compared to that in the preceding year; in some years the decline has been even larger than 7% of output. Irrespective of the impact of the HYV's and other inputs it appears somewhat impossible that this pattern will soon be reversed (Government of India, Agricultural Prices Commission, 1968b).
12 Oza (1976) was particularly useful in formulating the arguments on Indian agriculture.
13 There is a tremendous regional concentration in foodgrain output increase in three states alone—Punjab, Uttar Pradesh, and Haryana. Between 1969–1970 and 1971–1972 the relative shares of these states in wheat production were 22.1 per cent, 30.6 per cent, and 9.6 per cent respectively (source: Directorate of Economics and Statistics, Ministry of Agriculture). There has been considerable disparity also in the rates of growth of foodgrain output as between the individual states. In a few states such as Punjab, Haryana, and Tamil Nadu the rate of growth has been above 3 per cent per annum; as against this in Uttar Pradesh, Assam, Madya Pradesh, Maharashtra, and West Bengal, the rate of growth has been barely 1 per cent or less (Government of India, Agricultural Prices Commission, 1968b).
14 Rice accounts for about 25 per cent of the cropped area; coarse grains (i.e. jowar, bajra, maize, and small millets) 25 per cent; pulses 15 per cent; and wheat 12 per cent.
15 What is significant about this study is that the villages were selected purposefully, the existence of the High Yielding Varieties Programme or the Intensive Agricultural Areas Programme being an important consideration. The report specifically states that

'the high yielding varieties programme had not made any significant impact on the small farmers in any of the districts; whatever improved seeds were adopted by the farmers were mostly those other than the high yielding varieties' (Government of India, Reserve Bank of India, 1974a, p. 79).

16 In Punjab and Haryana where the green revolution has scored its greatest successes, even in 1961, 49·32 per cent of the households owned less than 2·5 acres of land and accounted for only 0·69 per cent of the total area, while those owning between 10 acres and 30 acres constituted 20 per cent of the total households accounted for 81·66 per cent of the total land (Dandekar and Rath, 1971, p. 111). Recently a research study has reported that the land owned by the big farmers in Punjab increased by about 9·5 per cent between 1955–1956 and 1967–1968, mostly through purchase. Farms of the size group 20–25 acres expanded only by 4 per cent whereas those in the size group 100–150 acres increased by about 14 per cent (Rudra, Majid, and Talib, 1969, p. 145).

17 P. S. Appu found the same situation prevailing in the Kosi region of Bihar.

> Prosperity in the wake of the new technology has resulted in landowners buying more land and increasing the size of their landholdings. Small farmers have been displaced and sharecroppers evicted. However this further concentration of landownership has not served to discontinue the earlier pattern, for the landowners still find it more lucrative to have the land cultivated through new sharecroppers. (Appu, 1974)

Patnaik has also shown a high incidence of sharecropping in the areas of technological change (Patnaik, 1972).

18 This under-utilization of irrigation capacity is true not only of the Kosi region. Even official sources admit that 30 per cent of the total irrigation capacity of the country remains under-utilized.

19 The actual content of foreign collaboration as permitted by the government is in contradiction to the guidelines of its foreign collaboration policy. To give a few examples of stipulated guidelines: the Indian party should be free to sublicense the technical know-how/product design/engineering design under the agreement to another Indian party on terms to be mutually agreed to by all the parties concerned; arrangements or clauses which in any manner bind the Indian party with regard to the procurement of capital goods, components, spares, raw materials, pricing policy, selling arrangements, etc., should be avoided; to the fullest extent possible there should be no restrictions on freedom to export to all countries; the use of foreign brandnames will not be permitted for internal sales; and so on (Government of India, Ministry of Industrial Development, 1975).

20 The second survey of the Reserve Bank of India found that on the estimates provided for the companies for the 4-year period 1970–1974, a steady and sizeable increase in imports from Rs. 429 crores in 1969–1970 to Rs. 650 crores in 1973–1974 was definitely indicated as well as a steady rise in royalty and technical fees. To quote from the report: 'The rise in imported inputs required for production within the existing capacity as well as for anticipated expansion would seem to indicate the continued reliance by companies on imports from the country of the collaborator' (Government of India, Reserve Bank of India, 1974b, pp. 29, 117).

21 Of the 877 private sector companies and 41 government companies in the RBI survey sample, 308 and 31 respectively had R & D departments.

22 Nearly 70 per cent of the private sector companies entering into collaboration agreements have a specific clause assuring exclusive or monopoly rights to the licencees to the use of the know-how. This manufacturing licence generally includes the right to use the foreign patent and/or trade mark. The implication of this is that technology once imported into the country by one entrepreneur can neither be assimilated by him due to the restrictive clauses, nor by any other Indian entrepreneur due to the monopoly rights. One result of this is the phenomenon of multiple

collaborations, i.e. several Indian firms entering into collaborations with several foreign firms for the manufacture of the same product, for example there are ten firms having collaboration for manufacture of refrigerators.

23 There are 95 universities imparting higher learning in science and providing facilities for research; five national institutes of technology with facilities for a high level of education and research in engineering and technology; five big research agencies (Department of Atomic Energy, Council of Scientific and Industrial Research, Indian Council of Agricultural Research, Indian Council of Medical Research, Defence Research and Development Organisation, and Department of Space); 30 national laboratories (there were 200 in 1947); a network of more than 200 other laboratories and research institutions. The total number of scientific and technical personnel exceeds 1,000,000. Expenditure on scientific research has gone up from Rs. 4·7 crores in 1950–1951 to Rs. 255 crores in 1973–1974. Official agencies claim that the science and technology components of the fifth Five Year Plan will be a total of more than Rs. 2,380 crores (including centre, state, private sector and non-plan expenditure) (Government of India, Ministry of Information, 1975).

24

|  | 1972–1973 (Rs. in crores) |
|---|---|
| Department of Atomic Energy and Department of Space | — Rs. 43·39 |
| Indian Council of Agricultural Research | — Rs. 29·91 |
| Council of Scientific and Industrial Research | — Rs. 24·66 |
| Indian Council of Medical Research | — Rs. 2·40 |

(Government of India, Ministry of Information, 1975).

## References

All India Rural Credit Survey (1963–1964), *6th Follow-up Report*. Quoted in *Economic and Political Weekly*, special number, August 1975, p. 1228.
Althusser, L. (1970), *For Marx*, New York, Vintage.
Appu, P. S. (1974), 'Agrarian structure and rural development', *Economic and Political Weekly*, Review of Agriculture, September.
Appu, P. S. (1975), 'Tenancy reform in India', *Economic and Political Weekly*, special number, August.
Avineri, S. (1970), *The Social and Political Thought of Karl Marx*, Cambridge, Cambridge University Press.
Barber, B. (1952), *Science and the Social Order*, New York, Free Press.
Barker, R. (1971), 'The evolutionary nature of the new rice technology', *Food Research Institute Studies*, **10**, 2.
Bernal, J. D. (1937), *The Social Functions of Science*, London, Routledge. Quoted in L. Sklair, *Organized Knowledge*, London, Granada, 1973.
Bhaduri, A. (1973), 'A study in agricultural backwardness under semi-feudalism', *Economic Journal*, March.
Bharadwaj, K., and P. K. Das (1975), 'Tenurial conditions and mode of exploitation; a study of some villages in Orissa', *Economic and Political Weekly*, annual number, February.
Bottomore, T., and M. Rubel (eds) (1956), *Karl Marx: Selected Writings in Sociology and Social Philosophy*, Harmondsworth, Penguin.
Brown, L. R. (1970), *Seeds of Change: the Green Revolution and Development in the 1970s*, New York, Praeger.
Bukharin, N. (1931), 'Theory and practice from the standpoint of dialectical materialism' in *Science at the Crossroads*, London, Kniga.
Carr, E. H. (1961), *What is History?*, Harmondsworth, Penguin.
Cooper, C. (1974), 'Science, technology and production in underdeveloped countries' in C. Cooper (ed.), *Science, Technology and Development*, London, Frank Cass.

Dandekar, V. M., and N. Rath (1971), 'Poverty in India', part II, *Economic and Political Weekly*, **6**, 2.
Desai, A. R. (1969), 'Community development projects: a sociological analysis' in A. R. Desai (ed.), *Rural Sociology in India,* Bombay, Popular.
Engels, F. (1974), *Dialectics of Nature*, Moscow, Progress Publishers.
Government of India (1957), 'Evaluation report on working of community projects and national extension service blocks, vol. I.
Government of India, Administrative Reforms Commission (1970), 'Report of the study team on scientific departments', January.
Government of India, Agricultural Prices Commission (1968a), 'Report', March.
Government of India, Agricultural Prices Commission (1968b), 'Report on tariff policy for kharif cereals for 1968–9 season', September.
Government of India, Agricultural Prices Commission (1971), 'Report', September.
Government of India, Agricultural Prices Commission (1972a), 'Report', March.
Government of India, Agricultural Prices Commission (1972b), 'Report for kharif cereals for 1972–3 season', September.
Government of India, Council of Agricultural Research (n.d.), 'Present state of research and education in agriculture, animal sciences and fisheries, and approach to the future development during the fifth plan period.
Government of India, Ministry of Agriculture (1962), 'NSS report', no. 144, 17th round, September 1961–July 1962.
Government of India, Ministry of Food, Agriculture, Community Development and Cooperation (1959), 'Report on India's Food crisis and steps to meet it'.
Government of India, Ministry of Industrial Development (1969), 'Report of the Industrial Licencing Policy Enquiry Committee. Main report', July.
Government of India, Ministry of Industrial Development (1975), 'Guidelines for industries 1974–5'.
Government of India, Ministry of Information and Broadcasting (1975), *India—A Reference Annual.*
Government of India, National Commission on Agriculture (1971), 'Interim report on some aspects of agricultural research, extension and training'.
Government of India, Planning Commission (n.d.1), 'First Five Year Plan'.
Government of India, Planning Commission (n.d.2), 'Fourth Five Year Plan'.
Government of India, Reserve Bank of India (1974a), 'The small farmers (1967–69)—a field study', November.
Government of India, Reserve Bank of India (1974b), 'Foreign collaboration in Indian industry, second survey report'.
Hessen, B. (1931), 'The social and economic roots of Newton's Principia' in *Science at the Crossroads,* London, Kniga.
Hirsch, W. (1968), *Scientists in American Society*, New York, Random House.
Marx, K. (1904), *A Contribution to the Critique of Political Economy*, Chicago, Charles Kerr, 1904 ed.
Marx, K. (1973a), *Economic and Philosophical Manuscripts of 1844,* London, Lawrence and Wishart, 1973 ed.
Marx, K. (1973b), *Grundrisse: Foundations of the Critique of Political Economy,* Harmondsworth, Penguin, 1973 ed.
Mellor, J., T. Weaver, U. J. Lele, and S. L. Simon (1968), *Developing Rural India*, Ithaca, N.Y.
Mencher, J. (1974), 'Conflicts and contradictions in the "Green Revolution": the case of Tamil Nadu', *Economic and Political Weekly,* annual number, February.
Merton, R. K. (1938), 'Science, technology and society in seventeenth century England', *Osiris,* **4,** 2.
Merton, R. K. (1942), 'The normative structure of science,' reprinted in R. K. Merton, *The Sociology of Science—Theoretical and Empirical Investigations.*

Merton, R. K. (1957), 'Priorities in scientific discovery', reprinted in R. K. Merton, *The Sociology of Science.*
Merton, R. K. (1961), 'Singletons and multiples in science', reprinted in R. K. Merton, *The Sociology of Science.*
Merton, R. K. (1963a), 'Multiple discoveries as a strategic research site', reprinted in R. K. Merton, *The Sociology of Science.*
Merton, R. K. (1963b), 'The ambivalence of scientists', reprinted in R. K. Merton, *The Sociology of Science.*
Merton, R. K. (1968), 'Behaviour patterns of scientists', reprinted in R. K. Merton, *The Sociology of Science.*
Merton, R. K. (1975), *The Sociology of Science—Theoretical and Empirical Investigations*, Chicago, University of Chicago Press.
Moseman, A. H. (1970), *Building Agricultural Research Systems in the Developing Nations*, New York, Agricultural Development Council.
Mulkay, M. J. (1972), 'Cultural growth in science', reprinted in B. Barnes (ed.), *Sociology of Science*, Harmondsworth, Penguin.
Naik, K. C., and A. Sankaram (1972), *A History of Agricultural Universities*, OUP India and IBH Publishing Company.
Oza, A. N. (1976), chapter on agriculture in D. S. Namjoshi, S. P. Malapur, A. N. Oza, and G. M. Rajarshi, *An Introduction to Indian Economy*, India, Macmillan.
Patnaik, Utsa (1972), 'Development of capitalism in agriculture' parts 1 and 2, *Social Scientist*, **2,** 3, September, October.
Prasad, P. (1973), 'Production relations: Achilles' heel of Indian planning', *Economic and Political Weekly*, **8,** 19, May.
Price, D. J. de S. (1962), 'The exponential curve in science' in B. Barber and W. Hirsch (eds), *Sociology of Science*, New York, Free Press.
Raj, R. N. (1972), 'Some questions concerning growth, transformation and planning of agriculture in the developing countries' in Indian Society of Agricultural Economics, *Comparative Experience of Agricultural Development in Developing Countries of Asia and the South East since World War Two*, New Delhi.
Rao, C. H. H. (1975), *Technological Change and Distribution of Gains in Indian Agriculture*, New Delhi, Institute of Economic Growth.
Rattansi, P. M. (1972), 'Social interpretation of science' in P. Mathias (ed.), *Science and Society 1600–1900*, Cambridge, Cambridge University Press.
Rudra, A., A. Majid, and B. D. Talib (1969), 'Big farmers in Punjab', in *Economic and Political Weekly*, **4,** 39, September.
Sau, R. (1972), 'Indian economic growth; constraints and prospects', *Economic and Political Weekly*, annual number, February.
Sklair, L. (1973), *Organised Knowledge*, London, Paladin.
Stein, M. (1962), 'Creativity and the scientist' in B. Barber and W. Hirsch (eds), *Sociology of Science*, New York, Free Press.
Storer, N. (1968), 'Sociology of science' in Talcott Parsons (ed.), *Knowledge and Society*, Washington, Voice of America.
Storer, N. (1966), *The Social System of Science*, New York, Holt, Rinehard and Winston.
Storer, N. (1975), 'Introduction' in R. K. Merton, *Sociology of Science*, Chicago, University of Chicago Press.
Subrahmanian, K. K. (1972), *Import of Capital and Technology*, Bombay, People's Publishing House.
Weber, M. (1962), 'Science as a Vocation', reprinted in B. Barber and W. Hirsch, *Sociology of Science*, New York, Free Press.
Zilsel, E. (1941), 'The sociological roots of science', *American Journal of Sociology*, **47,** 1941–1942.

# 7

## CONTRARY MEANINGS OF SCIENCE—INTERACTION BETWEEN CULTURAL AND PERSONAL MEANINGS OF RESEARCH IN A DEVELOPING COUNTRY SCIENTIFIC RESEARCH INSTITUTION

Stephen C. Hill

**Introduction**

Contemporary analyses of science in developing countries (LDCs) are spread across writings in a range of disciplines. There is not a consistent literature developing a focused sociology of science in LDCs. We find, first, a plethora of analyses—produced most often by natural scientists or engineers—based on 'experience' of science in LDCs. These largely put science and technology on the centre stage of underdevelopment and deal with questions of technology transfer, adaptation, and developing science communities in the image of those in industrialized nations. Such analyses are largely atheoretical, are often couched in normative terms and projected as appropriate policy to overcome science underdevelopment and underdevelopment *per se*. Second, there is a small statistically empirical literature which examines science in LDCs largely by comparison against developed countries. Again, this literature remains atheoretical on the basis that explanation will follow preliminary statistical observation. Third, there is a literature derived from development economics but, as Nelson (1974) observes, the economists' concern with the causation of underdevelopment largely in terms of 'investment' has generally relegated science as 'residual factor' into the wings of explanation.[1] Fourth, there is a small literature on the history of science and science institutions in some LDCs, but these studies are largely specific and not related into general theory development. Finally, there is a literature, the focus of which could be loosely classified as political sociology of science in LDCs (though not always written by social scientists).

These various literatures have remained largely unconnected. This leads to a variety of explanation bases of LDC science organization and behaviour of researchers within these organizations. Essential interaction between these explanations and complexity within remain unrecognized, so that they convey conclusions which may well be far too simplistic. A great deal of the literature is also dominated by an assumption—expressed in a variety of ways and depths of subtlety—that what is right for science in the industrialized West must be right for LDCs: that as scientific knowledge is 'universal' thus, too, must scientific activity and its organization be everywhere the same. Derived from this is a further assumption that once science is organized as in advanced Western countries, it will therefore be effective in producing social and economic development in LDCs.[2] Here, the literature is often confused. Questions concerning impingement on science *organization* and scientist behaviour are not separated from analysis of the role of science organizations in LDC development. Unconnectedness yields poorly developed theory.

Thus, in presenting a case study of science organization in a developing country, I must first draw together what seem to be the most relevant threads of explanation from this variety of sources. Towards a sociological focus, the literature can be very broadly classed as embodying either structural or interactionist perspectives; 'structural' literature most frequently embodies the assumption of connectedness of science to development. As this assumption is open to some question (Bell and Hill, 1976), I shall attempt to separate literature which directly makes this assumption from that which does not.

## 'Structural' Literature

Within the literature which broadly pays attention to structural impingement on LDC science is a range of explanation bases.

First, there is that literature which deals with scientific communities and viability of science institutions within the 'arid' political and intellectual climate seen to characterize many developing countries. Focus of this literature is on individual motivation and behaviour and its contention most frequently is that structural conditions of support for science in LDCs lead to problems such as isolation of individuals and brain drain. See, for example, Dedijer (1963); Salam (1966); Thomas (1967); Grubel (1968), and Moravcsik (1966, 1971). Science organization within LDCs is usually seen as problematic unless a mirror of accepted Western practice; structural problems of developing country economies remain unexamined; but the assumption remains that implantation of Western science organization will lead to local economic and social development. For example, Moravcsik (1964, 1966, 1971), Piel (1964), Haskins (1964) and the general thrust of many United Nations reports on LDC science and its organization (such as Unesco, 1970, 1974; UNIDO, 1970, 1973) all embody this assumption. Even within more formal sociology of science, such an assumption is evident. For example, Norman Storer (1970), in turning a Mertonian view of science towards developing countries, relates only to the building up of a 'self-sustaining scientific community', arguing that basic research will lead to a nation's 'scientific capability for domestic progress and international influence'. And Ziman (1971) argues that the 'utilitarian reason for doing research is powerful and respectable', that is must draw support for LDC universities from practical men, and 'helps directly in the great task of social development'. Such an assumption is supported by studies which leave even more of the internal dynamics of science organization, and linkage with industry unexamined, drawing simplistic international parallel between national science expenditures and measured 'development' level (e.g. Dedijer, 1962, 1964).

Second, there is a literature which locates LDC scientist goals and values in an *international* structural context. On the basis of international science expenditures and some observation of behaviour, the Sussex Group (1969, 1971) suggests that advanced country science expenditures (and associated political, economic, and social goals) have structured the goals and values of science organization and researchers in LDCs (see also Sachs, 1971). So that, as Sagasti (1973, p. 54) summarizes, 'prestige is conferred on researchers who work on exotic and sophisticated advanced topics, choice of which is often dictated by scientific fashion or novelty. Most of these have nothing to do with the more pedestrian scientific and technical problems faced by underdeveloped countries.' I establish later in this analysis ways in which international science perspectives may set a context for behaviour, not just of fundamental but also applied researchers, but the connection is not quite so simple as the above studies suggest.

Cooper (1972) demonstrates a *process* of connection between international research orientations and behaviour of individual LDC researchers via consideration of the structural context of underdevelopment. He argues that LDCs are characterized by technological dependence. Income distribution is skewed in favour of urban middle and upper classes, so favoured consumption is for the same products as used overseas. Demand by this sector is thus for the same technologies as used overseas. The traditional sector generates no effective demand for science-based technologies. Consequently, he argues, there is little pressure on science by the indigenous economy, and science becomes a consumption rather than an investment item. Cooper concludes that research orientations are more likely the individual decisions of research workers who take their lead from international orientations of research. Thus precisely *because* there is a poor linkage between production and LDC science—as a condition of underdevelopment—LDC science goals are not primarily oriented towards genuine integration with the state of underdevelopment. Herrera (1973) throws further light on the relationship between LDC science institutions and surrounding *social and economic structure* in setting science underdevelopment into its political context. Relating his observations primarily to Latin America, Herrera distinguishes between 'explicit' and 'implicit' science policy; 'explicit' policy is the 'front'—a formal prestigious facade for 'progressive' or modernizing governments presented as panacea for curing urgent material problems of underdevelopment without necessitating change in the social system. The *real* science policy, he argues, the 'implicit' policy, is in service of the ruling classes. Its purpose is to create a science and technology system which is *not* fully autonomous (for this could lead to fundamental questioning of the social system), but which presents the façade of liberal modernity in solution of minor problems. Neither Cooper nor Herrera claim (as do earlier quoted authors) that science is the motor of social and economic progress. Both articles assume that science *can* contribute to solution of underdevelopment problems, not that it necessarily will.

*'Interactionist' Literature*

These studies do not deal directly with connectedness of science with economic development, but focus more on its internal organization. Nayudamma (1973, p. 516) continues from Rahman's (1970) observation of interaction with government organizational practice and relates this to traditional society: 'Being done under the auspices of government, it tends to be administered in the same way as any other government department or office. In a traditional society [he observes], hierarchical attitudes, respect for age, and a belief that questioning is inappropriate, serve to reinforce similar tendencies which are codified in civil service rules and conventions.'

Parthasarathi (1969a) further observed the effect that interaction between local Indian culture and international science had on science organization and researcher behaviour. He claims that this saps local scientists' self-confidence, negatively affects their capacity for independent thought, and injects a 'caste system' in science (based on overseas versus local education) into the local science community. He also stresses the manner in which home background and socialization in the local university context (with emphasis on humanistic tradition, social and intellectual conservatism, and rote learning rather than free enquiry) influences scientist behaviour. Thus, Parthasarathi (1969b, pp. 1388–1389) concludes that traditional cultural forms have subsumed international science: 'the value system and culture of science have proved to be inadequately robust while the "archaic" social structure has proved maddeningly resilient'; indeed, 'Indian society has demonstrated time and again its inexhaustible capacity to dilute and devour the most potent of injected cultures'.

Important qualifications must be added to both structural and interactionist perspectives. From analysis of structural context, it is clear that the condition of underdevelopment *per se* (and perhaps of relationships to international science) sets conditions within which LDC research organization may be fashioned. But when scientific research is not separated from technological activity, and when the process of linkage between research and social-economic development remains unquestioned, the mechanism of structural influence over research behaviour is not yet clear. As we have argued elsewhere (Bell and Hill, 1976) when LDC industrial context is carefully examined, scientific research may be only marginally integratable with LDC development. From interactionist perspectives, the contemporary organization of LDC science and behaviour of researchers (both towards scientific and technological goals) is located in historic and cultural contexts. Consequently, science organization may be influenced by the specific history of research institutions in that country, by cultural, religious, and wider administrative values and practices, by cultural and educational background of researchers, and by interaction of these with international science perspectives and meanings. But this literature generally implies one local culture and one international science culture and set of values: interaction is between the two. I believe that our own case study demonstrates that this interaction is important in fashioning science organization and researcher behaviour in LDCs, but that neither the influence of local nor international science cultures may be unitary, and that interaction between them may also be strongly influenced by the structural context of underdevelopment.

Our case study is about a major applied scientific research institution in Thailand, to which I here attribute the pseudonym, the Thai Research Centre (TRC). It commenced in 1963 as a model of Western science organization—derived from the Australian Commonwealth Scientific and Industrial Research Organization (CSIRO)—and was based on the assumption that scientific research would lead to local social and economic development. By the time we observed the organization (mainly from 1970 to 1973)[3] its organizational form and researcher behaviour closely resembled that characterizing most other Thai bureaucracies—with, for example, emphasis on centralized structure and patrimonial behaviour. The surface explanation appeared to be that of international science and local Thai cultures in conflict, with the institution being transformed by Thai society's 'inexhaustible capacity to dilute and devour the most potent of injected cultures'.

However, on more detailed analysis, it was clear that an adequate explanation of organization behaviour was more complex than this. Specifically, we found—
(1) The international science culture imported into TRC embodied assumptions that were highly conducive to Thai cultural meanings taking over; that the covert goals[4] of international experts who established the organization led them to develop organizational practices—in the name of Western science—which seemed identical with what would otherwise appear to be Thai organizational practices: so, maybe what appear to be peculiarly Thai practices are not necessarily so.
(2) We became increasingly aware that *unitary* concepts of international Western science and its institutions and of Thai institutional practice were inadequate for analysis. Not all Western experts who were involved in TRC saw the organization in the same way. For some this was a scientific institution, for others (or even for the same people at different times) it was a technological research institution. At the same time, some organizational practices became somewhere *en route* neither Thai nor particularly Western. Yet a context presented by a translated and, at times, disembodied meaning of 'Western' science had a persistent influence on organizational behaviour.

On the other side, much of what was apparently Thai (particularly patrimonial) practice that pervaded the institution could be traced to the influence of one particular individual. In the interests of his own personal (covert) goals, the Thai executive who took over the organization capitalized on accepted Thai bureaucratic practice and thus *promoted* this, and pushed the organization further towards Thai practice than many other thoroughly Thai participants might have done. Indeed, we discovered instances of Thai originated behaviour which were

strikingly inconsistent with what we would have expected from most analysts of Thai institutional behaviour. Some aspects of organizational change introduced by Thai participants were more consistent with Western practice in research institutions than that originated by the Foreign Special Governor.
(3) The external environments of TRC also directly influenced organization behaviour. Its structural relationship to other organizations and its own 'clients', as well as to government power structure, all impinged heavily on TRC. The very structure of underdevelopment as it existed in Thailand confounded workability of the concept TRC expressed.

Thus the organizational form observed was, I would suggest, the result of a highly complex set of interactions. The meaning of research within the institution was subject to continuing negotiation; it moved, and was different for different participants at the same time—as a result of interaction between cultural, personal, and structural conditions within which it was set. As such, this article hopefully contributes to an evolving 'interpretive' perspective in mainstream sociology of science literature (see Law, 1974; Law and French, 1974). To develop this case I will first present a focused summary of the history of TRC, and then observations that initially appear to explain organizational behaviour of dominant features of Thai organizations. These same features appeared in TRC but, as our evidence moves on to demonstrate, were not simply transported in from Thai culture.

**The Thai Research Centre: Its Original Concept**

The conditions of TRC's establishment were that it be an autonomous body, funded primarily by the government, and controlled by a Board reporting to the Prime Minister. It was seen as the principal research agency of Thailand and was established with substantial United Nations assistance officially 'to provide research and related services to government and industry' (Nicholls and Pradisth, 1969, p. 75).

Initiation of the project was based on a report prepared by a UN adviser to Thailand in 1961 which, following an earlier World Bank mission, outlined the need for scientific research in Thailand and promoted the formation of an Australian CSIRO-style science organization. The UN adviser had been seconded from CSIRO. The analytical base for decision was drawn from three sources: (1) demonstration of *paucity in the scientific activities* conducted currently within Thai bureaucracy, government institutes, and universities; (2) statements (rather than independent analyses) drawn from the earlier World Bank report on Thailand (see International Bank, 1959), which contended that there existed a small-scale private sector which was growing and would need to grow more rapidly; and (3) a *belief* that 'research leads to social and economic development'. No analysis was conducted of the actual need in industry or agriculture for scientific research or of ways in which science could be integrated with industrial or agricultural practice. Indeed such analysis had not been attempted by the end of the tenth year of TRC's life, when our study period concluded.

The assumption that well organized research must lead to socio-economic development was carried unquestioned from the original report, through implementing documents, into the form of the organization. The development of science was seen as the first priority; changes in the economy and society would follow. The CSIRO-based concept of TRC[5] meant it was to be an indigenous 'centre of excellence' in research. For the sake of autonomy it needed to be separate from government departments and procedures, and as a viable 'centre' had to be an 'empire' collecting together the scattered remnants of all major scientific activity within the nation.

Focus of applied scientific activities was vested in a substantive UN assisted Technological Research Institute (TRI) and a subsequent Agricultural Research Institute (ARI). Other institutes were shortly established, namely the Environmental and Ecological Research Institute (EERI) and the Institute for Development Studies. Other centres were also collected into the corporation: the Thai National Documentation Centre, the Centre for Thai National Reference Collections, the Centre for Thai National Standard Specifications, the Instrument Repair and Calibration Centre, the National Building Research and Development Centre, and the Computing Service Centre.

Institutes within TRC were headed by research directors who were responsible to the organization's Research Director General (RDG) and Governor; the planned organizational structure was that of a 'matrix' form—organized into disciplinary groups from which researchers were drawn to work on problem-focused projects; project groupings were notionally flexible and would change as project demands required it. Administrative and technical services were provided by a Central Service Facility. 'Economic evaluation' of research was to be provided by an Economic Evaluation Group established separately from discipline-based research groups. Though there have been changes in the internal organization of institutes (for example, moving of research units from one group to another, elimination and creation of others), change in the name of one, and in incorporation (post 1972) of public relations and business management units into the Governor's office, the actual organization still (as at June 1974) remained much as it was. The organization chart moved from presentation of emphasis on areas of science to one which partly emphasized problem areas. But the substance of activities changed very little.

To establish the organization, the UN Advisor who proposed TRC (and also drafted its form and establishing Act) was appointed as Special Governor; his counterpart, formerly Assistant Director General of the National Research Council, and by this stage Director General, was appointed as Research Director General (RDG) of TRC: this was a half-time position. The National Research Council was the science policy and administration arm of the government, and so, with TRC ultimately reporting through it to the government, the position of the Research Director General of TRC was powerful. In effect he was his own boss (though between his two roles stood the TRC's Board).

From its inception to the end of our observations, the development of TRC organization went through three identifiable stages. The first stage in its development was under the control of the Foreign Special Governor (to 1969) who acted essentially as entrepreneur: his power was virtually dictatorial and it was his drive which got the organization off the ground over the five year period from 1964. The organization was his concept; his move from the role of Special Governor to Advisor, thence his departure, left a decision-making vacuum. Following the Special Governor's departure from office (at the end of phase 1 of UN involvement), the Thai Research Director General (RDG) stepped into direct control, while still holding office as head of the National Research Council. A Governor was appointed but initially appeared to have little real power and ambiguous definition of responsibilities. During this period (primarily 1969–1973) and particularly in 1971, TRC was subjected to very severe financial constraint. Out of its earlier period very little had been produced in the way of demonstrable economic or social change in the Thai productive sector; United Nations funding was being phased out, and pressure was mounting from the Thai government to produce more applied results. During the previous period there was little such pressure, as the argument was generally accepted that a new science organization would need some time to be established and for its research to come to fruition.

Towards the end of the second period (May 1972), the Thai RDG was asked to resign from TRC (along with the Secretary and another senior member of staff). A UN management expert reviewed the organization in October 1972, and with his directive of better rationalization of TRC, 'selling' and contracts, the organization moved on into a third stage of development with an RDG (Number 2) in charge. External pressure to produce technical change in the economic sector continued.

Before analysing in some detail the structure of the organization and behaviour of people who worked there, I will demonstrate briefly what organizations tend to be like in Thailand, particularly government organizations. It is into this context, and the supporting pattern of cultural values and expectations, that TRC entered. To the extent that social relations in traditional organization forms and in wider society are at variance with those assumed of TRC's design, one would expect some interaction between them.

**The Patrimonial Form of Social Order in Thailand**

The dominant form which analysts attribute to social organization in Thailand is that of hierarchy (e.g. Siffin, 1966, pp. 191–196) of relationships based on vertical integration, and of access to resources within bureaucracies being primarily determined by vertical status (pp. 169–178). The patrimonial character[6] of the vertical chain of organizational relationship is expressed by Wilson (1962, p. 161):

> A Minister, when he steps into his ministry, possesses the traditional authority of his office, and he can expect to get the deference, respect, and obedience from his subordinates which tradition demands. He is obligated by tradition to look out for these subordinates, however, in order not to disturb his authority and perhaps that of the whole clique, he must look to this obligation.

Siffin (1966, pp. 217–221) thus observes that action by subordinates and promotion of them is more based on serving superiors than fulfilling prescribed function.

As a consequence management of prescribed activities in Thai bureaucracies is seen more as 'system maintenance' (Siffin, 1966, p. 207), form taking precedence over function (p. 204): though administrative paper work is seen as essential and extremely time consuming, it bears little relation to function (p. 236), and provides little feedback on which functional evaluation *could* be based (p. 208). In addition, horizontal relationships between government departments tend to be weak: co-ordination tends to occur only at the top of organization hierarchies (Hanks, 1967, p. 6; Siffin, 1966, pp. 168–178) while relations between government departments 'vary from indifference through guarded deals to outright hostility' (Hanks, 1967, p. 6).

Not only are monopolistic patrimonial organization chains pervasive through bureaucracy; they are deeply set into Thai culture. As Siffin observes, bureaucracies have a long history of such forms of control; Shor (1960, p. 69) finds depth of patrimonial construct in 'ancient hierarchical traditions' which orient social interaction towards deference to superior status. Hanks (1962, p. 1249) demonstrates that hierarchical relationships are an *indispensable* condition for group existence in Thailand: 'Groups themselves are tiny hierarchies with a superior showering benefits on his nearest inferior, who in turn relays a portion to someone standing beneath him'. The linear organization remains evident though 'the leader must see that even the lowliest member is adequately cared for'. Indeed 'groups form only when a man has gathered resources and can distribute them as benefits to others', so, as Hanks thus claims, 'the coherence of Thai society rests largely on the value of becoming a client of someone who has greater resources than one alone possesses'. Kirsch (1967, p. 17) thus observes 'there are virtually no social roles nor interactions among Thai which do not carry some connotations of hierarchical difference in status'. Certainly status differentials are continuously reinforced in Thai language and forms of greetings: Thai pronouns constantly keep social status of relationship in mind; greeting ritual requires increasingly extreme deference as social status distance widens.

Indeed it would appear that there is a deeper belief system context as well for a general patrimonial social order. Thai religious beliefs and practices are predominantly Buddhist. Within the *secular* expression of central Buddhist values, and particularly within the ritual that joins the layman to Buddhist philosophy, Buddhist moral hierarchy underscores the layman's social hierarchy (see Kirsch, 1967, and Hanks, 1962, p. 1248).[7] This contextual connection is parallel to the analysis by Weber (1958) of the way a Protestant (particularly Calvinist) ethic underscored competition in nineteenth-century Europe. In Thailand, 'merit' and 'merit-making' become intimately related within social hierarchy to achievement of religious rewards (or punishments) within the moral hierarchy. These provide ritualistic forms by which the thoughts and motives of individual laymen are joined to the sophisticated Buddhist world view. A rich man, or a man of high status (who thus has access to more resources for distribution) is (counter to Christian philosophy) more effective and able to be more generous than a poor or low status man, and is freer from 'suffering'. Thus in a country strongly influenced by Buddhist religion, there is close isomorphism between the role of, and aspiration towards, patrimonialism (and generosity required of increasing status) and the ritualized social expression of religious hierarchical values.

**Organizational Behaviour within the Thai Research Centre**

With the depth of meaning attributed by analysts to vertical structure of social relationships in Thailand, and pervasiveness of form-oriented patrimonial behaviour in bureaucracies, we would expect these to interact with an implanted organizational form. In keeping with this expectation, we found evidence of the importation of external culture into TRC. The organization *was*, at the time of our observations, characterized by highly centralized, strongly administration-oriented decision-making, by elements of patrimonial form and attachment of status (for both individuals and in their presentation of the organization) to this. Hierarchical integration was virtually non-existent; 'form' of how things were done apparently assumed priority over the functional content of activities. However, detailed analysis of behaviour which, on the surface, appeared to be characteristically Thai, demonstrates the complexity of interaction that produced this apparent Thai form.

*Centralization of Decision-making*

At the time we observed TRC all decision-making was centralized at the top of the organization, including approval for very minor financial expenditures and visits to industry. Information dissemination was controlled centrally: 'contact notes', which were supposed to be filled in after every contact with industrial or outside personnel, were sent up the organizational hierarchy to the Secretary, who then controlled distribution. In several cases that we know of the contact notes sent from the Economic Evaluation Group were not passed on to Group Directors with a direct potential interest in the 'contact'.

Such massive over-centralization with its consequent effect on staff time spent merely on administration appears a far cry from the decentralized concept of CSIRO's decision-making (see Peres, 1963). It appeared to be very similar to administrative form in Thai bureaucracy. A Western-based 'matrix' organizational form was presented as TRC's initiating concept, and this embodied a *dual* hierarchy of project and discipline organization. But the Foreign Special Governor had gathered all decision-making unto himself. Thai managers reported that his control of senior management decision-making during the first phase of the organization's development was virtually dictatorial. On his departure, there was a decision-making vacuum—more a state of confusion than of planned change. The context was not only set for Thai organization practices and expectations to intrude into the organization; but practices which stressed central administrative control—a character of Thai bureaucracy—had been established in the name of international science practice.

*Patrimonialism*

Set within an outside Thai cultural context and an internal centralized administration, the development of patrimonial social order in TRC was to be expected. Indeed we found some evidence for its existence. But much of what we observed in the organization could be attributed to the Special Governor's influence. We would expect with a Thai patrimonial form to find not only vertical control of relationships but also the head of the organization and its senior management acting as patron to subordinates, looking after their welfare, expecting in return allegiance even before functional competence. We would expect subordinates in general to see such a system of relationships as appropriate rather than merely an imposition from above. We would also expect, in a Thai context, more attention being paid to growth of the organization, therefore providing a greater resource base for control by patrimonial favour.

Indeed, during the time when we observed TRC we found concern for staffing was paramount over virtually all other organizational activities. The total numbers of people in the organization increased rapidly from its inception until UN Management Review at the end of 1972—to a total of 378 people. These included 16 Research Officers (ROs); 102 Experimental Officers (EOs), 86 Technicians, 41 Administrative Service Officers, and 133 ancilliary and assisting staff. *Numbers* of people employed appeared to be more important to TRC management than rational balance of capabilities. As financial crisis became increasingly evident, looking after those employed assumed a top priority. As a consequence, between 1971 and 1972 the salaries proportion of the total budget rose by 6·5 per cent from 61 per cent to 67·5 per cent while the proportion of money available for equipment and support facilities fell from 20 per cent to 16·4 per cent. But the initiative for such an empire came from the Foreign Special Governor.

Action was almost certainly coloured, though, by concern for subordinates' welfare, for this seemed to be a covert—perhaps patrimonial—priority of the organization. The importance of organizational obligations to staff was demonstrated in the attention paid at a senior level to minor staff considerations rather than to overall policy and finance. For example, the Board did not discuss TRC's 1972 submission to the Bureau of the Budget. Instead it was primarily concerned with staff appointments, punishments, salaries, welfare, and provident funds. The policy of executive attention to staff *evaluation* and *encouragement* was inherited from CSIRO practice (cf. Peres, 1963). But executive attention to staff moved from functional evaluation to *care for subordinates*. This shift could not be directly related to the Special Governor's control. Indirectly, perhaps, it could because he appeared to have left the Board little firm direction as to what they should do.

In addition, a senior managerial committee (involving the RDG, the Governor and institute heads) made *all* staff appointments to TRC, including those of the lowest level secretarial and support personnel. However, the Special Governor had established this committee, interestingly enough, in an attempt to *prevent* patrimonial favour entering into the organization.

A character of senior management patrimonial behaviour was clearly demonstrated in behaviour of the RDG. As against the amount of time he spent on administration, the RDG spent *no* time visiting junior personnel apart from those within a group, the head of which was his wife. However, he spent a full night helping one M.Sc. student employee in the United Kingdom pass an exam, by writing a supporting reference: the student had come to the RDG over the head of his own middle-management boss, and the RDG had responded to the student (counter to centralized procedure) without reference to the student's immediate superior. Significance of the incident appears when we found that the student apparently never wanted or expected 'advice' from the RDG. The request was seen by other Thais in TRC as a convenient means of bringing himself to the RDG's notice, implicitly acknowledging 'loyalty', respect and so on, in the realization that future career prospects are determined by the RDG, not his immediate supervisor. Tighter patron control was exercised through a small circle of trusted compatriots who were given increased power and resources. The wife of the RDG was appointed a head of one research group of TRC: the unit was given the strongest *research* manpower, the highest proportion of overseas training scholarships, and (until the rather desperate rush for contracts following UN review in 1972) received the greatest number of *exclusive contract* research projects (the majority of which had been invited by the RDG from among his industrial friends).[8]

Similarly, when middle-management positions became vacant, responsibility was passed up to either the RDG or a close subordinate, never delegated down.

Action by the RDG on replacement of middle-management was, however, severely constrained by the presence of very few people who could have assumed the responsibility. This was a direct product of the Special Governor's concern with spreading the organization as an umbrella over as many areas of Thai science as possible, with inadequate attention to strength in any one of them. We should qualify the Special Governor's influence, however, by pointing out that TRC had a small pool of capable local research people to draw from: the organization found it difficult to attract top graduates from local universities in any field as these students were attracted to the established traditional status of government, or to more lucrative industrial employment. Graduates directly from Thai universities were generally trained in a system which emphasized status distance between lecturers and students, fairly rigid curricula within which achievement was more a product of rote learning than critical questioning (see for example, Guskin, 1966). However, apart from particular people known to management, neither the Special Governor nor subsequent Thai management introduced any serious recruitment programme overseas.

This pattern of observations of the RDG's patrimonialism suggests something of its particular expression in this organization. As Research Director General of a range of supposedly semi-autonomous institutes, the RDG would find tight vertical control and sustenance of subordinate obligation rather difficult. Thus to the extent he was acting to promote a patrimonial system, he was doing so via a small number of trusted immediate subordinates. Included among these was his wife, through whom he could call on obligation of her immediate subordinates. It was this group to whom greatest favour was shown.

That the RDG was not *only* continuing centralized practices created by the Special Governor, but was attaching to them a somewhat Thai specific meaning, is perhaps reflected in his strong response to particular threats and in the issues he found threatening. The most acrimonious conflict we observed during his term of office was with a Manager of Administrative Services. Conflict arose on separate occasions, over the manager's attempts to appoint three poorly qualified juniors to TRC and change formal employment procedure to aid them. In each case, as well as in two incidents involving purchase of an office refrigerator and attempt to gain access to the airport tarmac to 'receive visiting dignatories' (through direct appeal to high level associates outside TRC), the manager attempted to promote and enhance his own senior status. The RDG's response was to effectively reduce this status, by creating a new position and appointing another administrator (an ex-army colonel) from outside the organization over the manager's head. The manager was formerly a minor Thai diplomat; with general social status attached to ex-government status designations in Thailand, the appointment of a colonel over his head caused him severe loss of face. It is worth adding that this conflict finally led to widely expressed charges by the manager of the RDG's financial 'corruption', and to attempts by the manager via external political allies to have the RDG removed from office.

To the extent, however, the RDG did abuse his position of power for personal ends, the context for his patrimonialism was established both by the Special Governor's example of autocracy, and the Governor's allowance of a counterpart thence executive head of TRC who still retained the position of head of the National Research Council. This put the RDG in a position, as we observed before, of being effectively his own boss.

While our observations so far suggest close attention to vertical organizational relationships and statuses,[9] horizontal integration was virtually absent. The Special Governor's autocratic administration set the pace for subsequent centralization of decisions and administration. By gathering decision-making unto himself he eschewed the matrix organization form he espoused in organization charts he designed. With its emphasis on horizontal linkage and shared or shifting allegiance to superiors as functional demands of projects changed, it was an anathema to external Thai expectations of social relationships. Thus later when the foreign head of the Economic Evaluation Group brought a case of two teams in separate institutes (of TRC) working on the same subject to the attention of both groups and to the head of TRC (the RDG), parallel redundancy was allowed to continue.

However, we found evidence of behaviour by some senior managers who were attempting to change their inherited organizational form *towards* more rational function-oriented perspectives. As examples, when the new Thai Governor assumed office once the Foreign Special Governor left, he immediately sought, but failed, to establish serious project evaluation. He also introduced some budgetary discretion for lower level management and removed the necessity for phone calls and up-country trips to be approved by himself. Both centralized procedures had been instituted by the Special Governor. *But,* with apparent organization failure and increasing economic pressure from outside, centralization even of minor expenses had to be reinstituted. TRC literally had virtually no money in 1971 to do anything much except pay the salaries to which the organization was committed. Thus, one must conclude that although a wider than organization pattern of social expectations influenced organizational behaviour, this influence was by no means unitary. Closer analysis of the form of relationships within TRC thus does demonstrate a character which can be attributed to its 'Thai-ness'. But the organization was set by the Special Governor, who initiated it, in an organizational mould that was highly conducive to values of Thai bureaucracy becoming TRC values. To the extent that the RDG *capitalized* on Thai expectations and on his position of power in the organization, he pushed TRC even further towards a vertical patrimonial organization form.

*Priority of 'Form' over Function: a Legacy of Confusion*

The Special Governor's influence extended further than just the injection of centralized practice. In the interests of creating a science 'empire', he set in motion a comprehensiveness of research programmes which sapped TRC's ability to focus on any one of them; he initiated functional evaluation procedures, but with insufficient strength for them to remain on his departure. In the interests of maximum funding of *different* activities under TRC's umbrella, he allowed major (particularly military) funding sources to seriously distort areas of TRC research activity and staffing structure. The interests of a science 'empire' created a vital context for the apparent priority given to the form of how things were done rather than their functional content—an observation made by others of Thai bureaucracy. This, together with overstaffing, and non-integratability of organization activities with its industrial milieu (an issue we deal with shortly), helped to create a situation of confusion and financial trauma. Attention to form was at least partly a direct consequence for Thai management of not quite knowing what else to do.

I will first present what happened to the organization's research activities: research projects conducted in TRC were largely set into the original portfolio of programme and project headings established by the Special Governor at the outset. Within one year of starting operations, the organization had 36 research 'programmes' on its books. After three years, 231 projects, and after eight years, 380 projects (organized under 60 'programmes'), had been approved.

In addition to these 380 projects approved under formal programmes, however, there were another 130 'miscellaneous' and 'confidential' projects, 'studies' and 'appraisals' 'on the books', making a total of 510 separate projects. The diversity of these projects was enormous. They ranged, for example, across studies of agricultural products, studies of food processing and handling, perfumes and fragrances, cotton, paper pulp from kenaf, cotton husk, cornstalks, bamboo, industrial clays, gypsum; concrete and laminated timber; studies of smelting, ceramics, casting, zinc refining and tinplate; studies of crabs, migratory animals, and primates; studies of transportation, science policy, housing; attempts to develop climatology, soil, physical and human resources inventories; studies of power systems, computerized structure analysis, hydrology, and solar flares; and an exposure testing programme for assessing Thai military goods.

The portfolio of research projects consequently was very large indeed. Even though many were currently inactive or suspended, they had *drifted* into this status (usually due to lack of manpower, of interest, or with departure of a foreign expert) rather than been assigned by conscious decision. At least 145 projects were registered and had never been started. When it is realized that there are only 13 research officers (in research or research-administration positions) together with a roughly equivalent number of short term foreign counterparts to conduct, orient, and administer this research, then it is clear that there was very great diversification of senior researcher activities or responsibilities; that effort was expanded on at least starting a very large number of new activities during any particular time; and that consistent and concerted research effort was possible in only a very few areas of application. Direction of effort was also governed by staffing. Sixty-six staff, or 17·5 per cent of total, were involved in National Reference or Documentation Centre Studies; only eight (of the 13 people in *research* positions) or 2·1 per cent of total were involved in industrially oriented research. Though an *applied* research organization, only *one* person was employed as an engineer to engage in development work.

To evaluate the vast range of projects, the Special Governor established centralized procedures for research approval, evaluation, and termination. These procedures were used, though rather irregularly and inadequately by the Special Governor. But by the time our participant observation of TRC started, the procedures had fallen into functional irrelevance; all that remained was a disembodied form.

Towards the original approval of research projects, for example, proponents had to submit a project outline for decision by the corporation Board. If this document *stated* that there were no manpower problems or equipment needs, it was invariably approved—hence there was growth in numbers of projects to about 500. No evaluation was carried out of effect on other projects, or resources or relevance of the work. No senior staff member was ever called before the Board to defend a research proposal. In spite of formality required of approval procedures, we found at least a dozen projects that were implemented at least twelve months before approval was given.

Progress reports on research programmes were required every three months. During the Special Governor's period of office, progress reports not submitted were pursued by an assistant to the Special Governor—interestingly enough, not from central administration but from the Computing Section. After the Special Governor left, progress reports were still 'required', but some researchers submitted them only occasionally, having realized nobody checked them any more. Response often simply followed an occasional revitalization of the requirement by senior management. The RDG, when in charge of TRC, kept no copies of progress reports; even the centralized files were misplaced for over two years; he reported evaluating research programmes from their technical reports. These were produced sometimes up to 18 months after projects had finished, and only from relatively successful research. In the ten years from establishment of TRC's research, serious evaluation seems to have occurred only in three cases (out of approximately 500 candidates): these were conducted during the Special Governor's term.

Ongoing project evaluation was formally guided by a senior management steering group. Apart from early meetings when the Special Governor controlled TRC, this group did not meet. One of the very few projects that we found had been formally terminated was one on solar flares, a highly abstract piece of pure research being conducted in liaison with a local university. This project was stopped, however, early in TRC's history when the expatriate Special Governor actually held the steering committee meetings. Apart from one or two exceptions such as this, projects which stopped simply died either because participating staff left the organization (usually foreign experts) or because attention of group activities moved elsewhere. In one case where a project was stopped, awareness of the actual research seemed to have completely escaped management. The researcher had worked for eight years planting many strains of one agricultural product and conducting chromosome counts in preparation for breeding. No conclusions, recommendations or changes in breeding strategy had been arrived at. The project stopped because TRC needed to build new workshop facilities and these were located on the test area where the agricultural product was growing.

Project proposals rarely had any time scale attachment: it seemed ex-ante or ex-poste that it did not matter if a project took six months or six years. Meanwhile the *minutes* of staff time were carefully controlled by an elaborate procedure—checking 'clocking in' and 'out' times—for *all* staff. Before industrial contact, time-card forms had to be completed and approved by senior management though, as one senior Thai researcher pointed out, 'no one knows where you are during the day anyway, so you can go and do a job privately if you want to'. Each of these procedures was, however, established by the Special Governor. Non-evaluation of project duration appeared a product of his belief in a notion that research would eventually lead to results, but the length of time could not really be predicted. Time-cards were established specifically in an attempt to *prevent* practices the Special Governor saw in other Thai institutions—i.e. 'moonlighting' for personal gain and coming to and from work as personnel chose rather than according to a formal workday. The Special Governor sought to establish this as principle by applying the procedure to all staff including senior management, foreign experts, and himself.

With the stamp of validity having been put on proliferation of projects, with totally inadequate research initiation capability, with centralization of all decision-making and with a half-time RDG at the top, it is not really surprising that attention to research function slipped into a second order priority. Consequent attention to form was a product partly of confusion, and partly of Thai response to this confusion, where attention to form was commensurate with traditional Thai bureaucratic practice. When, after the first six years or so, pressure started to build up from outside the organization to produce the applications by now expected, one management solution which demonstrated both concentration on form and confusion as to what else to do was the exhortation to researchers that they should 'work harder'. As financial crisis came to dominate TRC, and in absence of knowing what else to do, senior management became increasingly dependent on the Thai Government Budget Bureau. TRC was allowed to lose its previous relative independence, and eventually was following standard budgetary procedure for Government ministries. This required the submission of a 200-page foolscap document which listed, in detail, items as minor as small quantities of individual chemicals ten months prior to the subsequent financial year, i.e. 22 months before its use.

## *Relationships with External Environment: Consequences of Empire Building*

There were two other major influences on TRC's subsequent behaviour created originally by the Special Governor's quest to construct a science empire. The first—behaviour that sought funds first and examined consequences later—was a direct continuance of the Special Governor's approach to eliciting external funding. The second—behaviour that emphasized the 'face' of the organization—was necessitated by conflicts established with other government bureaucracies arising from the apparent poaching of functions by TRC. The need to distinguish its role and do virtually anything to obtain funds observed during its second stage was also a product of a desperate financial situation, particularly towards the end of 1971. This was in large part a result of the organization's apparently inherent non-integret*ability* with its industrial milieu, an issue I return to shortly, and, of course, its ungainly size. As crisis closed in, what else could be done but respond as managers and participants best knew how? Thai organization practice provided the experience and social meaning of organization in general, the 'Thai' way was perhaps the only recourse for TRC personnel.

First, I will demonstrate what I mean by the effect of the Special Governor's approach to external funding. Within the first few years of TRC's existence, funds were accepted from ARPA, the United States Advanced Research Projects Agency (an extension of the United States Defense Department), to build up a large Resources Inventory Group. Its stated purpose was to map key Thai resources and so aid their exploitation. In fact, its role involved only the drafting of new maps based on data which were already available. The composite maps, for example, of radar shadow zones in the south-east, of cross-country tracked vehicle manoeuvrability, hole diggability (time according to terrain for a standard man to dig a standard hole), had direct military relevance but gave little economic insight. Training was promised but in practice the only competences developed were in draughtsmanship. An American ARPA man was in charge of the group for most of the project. The Washington-based project manager even commented at a TRC seminar that the main reason the project was conducted in Thailand was that it was cheaper than employing people in Washington to do the same job. When

ARPA money ended TRC was left with a large group of draughtsmen with job tenure and no function. On accepting funds, no carefully formulated decision was made on long term consequences.

Another project was implemented on ARPA military funds on 'exposure testing'. The project consisted of monitoring military uniforms and software deterioration in a jungle. Primarily in order to find continuing funding for staff inherited from such as the ARPA Resources Inventory Project, TRC management were prepared to do organizational handstands. Within two months of hearing of a NASA earth resources satellite programme, the National Research Council and TRC (both of which were headed by the RDG) had set up a National Earth Resources Satellite Committee (ERTS) comprising 22 government agencies, had formed an interdisplinary task force of 17 Thai scientists, had formulated the proposal and achieved government backing for its submission to NASA. In addition, they had approached UNIDO and USAID for assistance in training Thai personnel for data interpretation. In another instance, the name of one institute was changed three times in less than as many years, as new potential sources of funding appeared and a shift in presented emphasis appeared appropriate.

TRC's political position with respect to other government agencies made its dependence on government funding increasingly tenuous also. As a multipurpose research institution, its function often overlapped—certainly in name and appearance—with research and testing done in a number of government departments, for example in the Ministry of Industry; Department of Science; and Ministry of Agriculture. The Special Governor had chosen to take over their functions in the belief, perhaps justified, that very little *scientific* research of consequence was happening there.[10] None of these departments was prepared to let go established areas of formal responsibility and staff.

In context of such competition, TRC was in a weakened political situation. First, the organization had been established to be independent of direct government control. Chiefly because of the early joint appointment of the one man as head of the National Research Council and Research Director General of TRC, it became established practice for TRC to submit its budget to the National Research Council. TRC's 'items for financial support' (worth approximately $(US)1·1 million) were then attached to the end of NRC's budgetary proposal to the Budget Bureau. Consequently, TRC did not (as do government departments and NRC) have its own code in the Budget Burea. As recently as 1974 the Governor or TRC sought, from the Ministry of the Prime Minister, *direct* financial support from the Budget Bureau. The Ministry allowed the organization to correspond (officially to other government offices) independently rather than through NRC, an action not previously permitted.[11] But it would not break the budgetary link of the organization with NRC.

The nature of TRC as a research organization then further weakened its political position. Other government departments at one level or another had power over allocation of resources to different groups in the society—thus enhancing their own power. TRC produced a 'research' product, it then had difficulty 'selling'; it had no power to coerce or control. And, it was a new instrumentality competing with the firmly established patterns of funding of other government agencies (see Eisenstadt, 1965).

TRC had to have *something* to which could be attached a status intrinsically worthy of support and separate from that of competing government departments. The original concept of the organization was that it should be a *scientific* 'centre of excellence'—this was established by the Special Governor and continuously presented as such to the outside world by himself, United Nations funding agencies, and senior management of TRC.[12] Thai management consequently hung on to this presentation of a surface reality. On several occasions TRC management separated TRC's status from competing government research departments, stressing its own 'scientific quality' and *their* more routine testing functions. TRC constantly resisted pressure from the Thai National Economic Development Board to 'co-ordinate' with competing departments.

Such behaviour, which presents the scientific 'face' of the organization, was to some extent a perceived means of the organization surviving. 'Scientific' status was validated by the organization's original concept. But the consequence of these conditions seemed mainly to provide reinforcement for a value intrinsic to meaning in the organization—that of 'status'. Presentation of the intrinsic 'status' of TRC characterized much of the pattern of its relationships with industry. Status of researchers who were permitted to contact industry was centrally controlled. For example, at the December 1971 TRC meeting to discuss industrial contact, current practice was reinforced that there were no general staff rules governing industrial contact: any TRC member contemplating industrial contact had to ask the RDG or Governor for a *specific* policy on that one contact. Note, however, that this was *established* practice originating in the Special Governor's previous dominance over all organization practice and his apparent, perhaps at times justified, lack of faith in the competence of lower status researchers to handle presentation of TRC in industrial liaison. However, this concept of industrial contact, as a *special* activity, continued. In March 1972, it was agreed to let *someone* (one person) 'visit firms and identify problems'. This did not apply to a range of people in different research areas, but to one person who would act *for* TRC across all types of technical problems.

It appeared also, however, that at least one meaning of the organization to Thai participants was more or less as a 'patron' which presented completed research results for industry's *benefit*. Deference was expected in return. For example, at a senior executive meeting in December 1971—a time when financial crisis was paramount and industrial financial sponsorship the more attractive—senior management noted the presentation of TRC's 'prestige' and concluded 'contact by the researcher does not mean we go out and sell. Mostly industry comes to see the researcher'. The effect of an individual researcher breaking this norm is shown in the following example: the researcher (a relatively low status experimental officer) had been interviewing a senior member of the Ministry of Industry and in passing comments suggested that perhaps TRC could do some product testing for them. He reported this in the subsequent contact note. The result was severe sanction of the experimental officer and devious response by TRC to the Ministry of Industry representative: the *Deputy* RDG sent a letter to the Ministry of Industry person asking if he wanted to know TRC's capability, and directing him to tell the organization the types of parts to be tested. In a meeting prior to sending the letter, it was decided the letter should come from the Deputy RDG because if the RDG were to write, it would commit TRC to a positive response to any forthcoming request. It was seen that if the Deputy RDG wrote, he could always blame a subsequent refusal on his superiors not supporting him.

Even foreign 'experts' visiting the organization for a period usually of about two years or so often found themselves enclosed from initiating close relationships with industry. In general, experts were not given counterparts with whom they could work. In the few cases where counterparts were available during the expert's stay, they were usually committed to other activities and not committed to the expert's research or technological interest. Frequently, facilities such as interpreters, transport, and even equipment were just not made available in time for the expert to be able to function properly. For example, one relatively junior foreign expert joining an industrial technology-oriented group was positively *dis*couraged from going out into industry to conduct a general survey. The Group Research Director told him 'what the problems were'; the foreign researcher was given no counterpart to work with, and could rarely gain access to a car or interpreter. When he finally did visit several firms he found the Director (who, apart from firms run by acquaintances, had conducted no such survey previously) had seriously underrated the sophistication of some sectors of the industry.

Consequently, a number of foreign experts made the observation to us of their apparent 'enclosure'. Partly this could perhaps be attributed to potential threat by irremovable non-Thai individuals to, by now, established status-oriented ways of doing things in the organization and in relation to its industrial environment. But then again, absence of counterpart integration, scant attention to the industrial milieu, and definition of research in absence of knowledge of industry, had all characterized the Special Governor's period of office.

*Interaction between Thai and Universalistic Perspectives in the Organization: Consequences for Organizational Effectiveness*

From the analysis of our observations presented above, it *is* clear that the organization we observed, though based on, and presented as, an example of international research practice, became very like other Thai government bureaucracies. Behaviour of organization participants appeared to be commensurate with those values ascribed to Thai organizational form by observers of Thai society quoted earlier. Relationships were ordered vertically not horizontally; decision-making was highly centralized; there appeared to be elements of patrimonial concern for subordinates and obligations from them; preservation of personal and organizational status was an organizational priority; the organization appeared to be viewed to some extent as itself, 'patron' to the potential 'clients'; activities within were dominated by a 'system maintenance' approach to administration, and the form of the way things were done appeared to have priority over function—indeed it often got in the way of whatever intrinsic function (research or application) management may have chosen to pursue. In absence of traditionally ascribed sources of patronage relationships to clients, the presented image of TRC was to some extent guided by the fashioning of a new image in the name of the ascribed 'internationally validated' image of science. As a multifaceted organization (containing a range of separate institutes) patrimonial control appeared to be handled selectively rather than ubiquitiously.

In view of the apparent pervasiveness and depth of commensurate social forms observed by others in wider Thai society, and even within other government science departments, such a shift in meaning of the organization is to be expected. Decentralized control and horizontal integration would appear to come into direct conflict with social form that is likely to be the baggage of organizational practice and expectations brought into the organization from wider Thai experience.

*However*, as appears from more detailed analysis of what actually happened, the apparent Thai form of the organization was influenced by the covert personal goals for the organization of two people—the Foreign Special Governor who established it and the Thai Research Director General who took it over. Entry of patrimonialism probably took a more extreme form than it otherwise might have done because of the Thai RDG's influence. It is worth noting that exertion by him of patrimonialism within TRC was, however, set in context. He was originally appointed to NRC, thence to TRC, at least partly because of his relationship (though relatively removed) with a still powerful major political-family group, the Phin-Phao clique.

As most observers of Thailand would acknowledge, such major family cliques (though they themselves move in and out of favour, in the 1950s and 1960s particularly via involvement in political coups) have a persistent influence over Thai political appointments. Within this context patrimonial behaviour is perhaps an expected response.

Although there was some shift away from the organizational form and procedures the Special Governor established, a posited 'Thai' pattern of expectations was entirely commensurate with the 'empire' he created. What he did to create this empire not only put a stamp of 'international' validity on such practices, his autocratic control left in its wake a decision-making vacuum, conflict with government departments, an intrinsically unworkable system within, and generally pervasive confusion. Ironically, many of the procedures he established sought to circumvent entry of traditional Thai practices into TRC; the difficulty he confronted in getting Thai scientists to take over responsibility in the organization was as much a problem of there being very few competent people around as of his autocratic style. Thus, it was at least partly a product of Thailand's underdevelopment particularly in production of competent analytic university graduates. The unintended consequence of the Special Governor's action, however, was an organizational mirror to the rest of Thai bureaucracy, but robbed of its support base and established connection into the wider bureaucratic system.

Most fundamentally at issue was what the organization was supposed to be successful at doing. The Special Governor acted in the best of motives in establishing a *science* organization to try and achieve technological change in the productive sector. Here we come the full circle back to the literature with which we started this paper. In the literature, as I noted, there has very often been confusion about the role of science in development. Particularly throughout the period of the Special Governor's influence on TRC, the literature just did not question the 'obviousness' of linkage between science organized along Western lines and development results which could be expected to follow. As I argued earlier, this assumption appears to be a fundamental premise of the implantation of science in an LDC context. However, as we demonstrate in some detail in other publications,[13] the industrial context in underdeveloped countries may just not be ready to *receive* research results (or even technology embodied in specific techniques) from a research-oriented organization like TRC. In many LDC contexts (and, we believe, in some advanced country sectors as well) *technical change* in industry does not depend on technology *transfer*, but on the creation of an endogenous technological capability which allows firms (1) to move from just operating existing techniques to understanding, thence changing them, and (2) to develop technological decision-making abilities in management and an organization capability to absorb technical change. Consequently, to the extent its function embodied creation of technical change in industry, we believe the TRC concept was doomed from the start. Producing knowledge for others to absorb and use is not enough when these 'others' cannot absorb and use it.

The result of ineffectiveness strongly influenced what happened in the internal social organization and behaviour of TRC. By its second phase, the organization was *expected* to have produced identifiable changes in its environment and by and large it hadn't. This expectation was a practical reinforcement of the unexamined belief that science must (at least after seven or eight years) lead to development. Response to this extrinsic pressure was to rely increasingly on TRC's surface reality, to reinforce its PR image of 'science' to leave little room for management to manoeuvre except towards traditional Thai ways of coping with organization. Practices already established in TRC reinforced this approach. These served to emphasize the definition of problems worthy of attention in *scientific* terms; to effectively insulate research activities from the industrial milieu; and to relegate industrial study and liaison to the end of development-directed activities. Projects were usually formulated on the basis of what looked like good research ideas, with no reference to economic evaluation. The emphasis was on doing research first then checking out if the results could be applied. Programme No. 1, for example, was on utilization of kenaf: project 1/1 analysed the anatomy of the kenaf stem, projects 1/2 and 1/3 analysed the physical and chemical properties of kenaf fibre ... project 1/10 was on economic studies of kenaf. Thus, the industrial environment was thought of at the *end* of projects, not in project formulation. The concept underscoring integration with industry was that of 'selling' products of research to industry, while there was little understanding of who the customer was or of his needs.

The 'internationalist' or 'cosmopolitan' perspective of TRC's initiation established an important context for subsequent social meaning of its range of activities. Though research was spread across a range of fundamentalness—from plotting of sunspots to counting of spots in toilet bowls—emphasis remained on creation of 'knowledge'. As the organization came under increasing pressure to produce technological change, this 'knowledge' was to be 'sold' through better PR. Based largely on their advanced country experience, UN management review experts reinforced the validity of this practice.

The 'centre of excellence' concept remained and reinforced self-definition of the organization in its relations with industrial milieux. Pressure created the need for polishing the image of TRC in the mirror of its origins—for turning inward towards reinforcement of 'scientific' status. Thus, although the activities may have varied in formal definition across fundamental-applied orientations, their context, expectations, perceived surrogates of success (for example in technical reports) were all set within a pattern circumscribed by 'internationalist' perspectives. The *activities* were not necessarily 'internationalist' but their validity was informed by a translated skeleton of this orientation. When this skeleton was set into a local Thai meaning of 'activity' within the organization (partly, at least, in service of social goals), it developed a meaning of its own while appearing on the surface to maintain an internationalist orientation. This applied equally to counting spots on the sun as it did to counting them on china lavatory bowls!

The general role of foreign scientific or technological experts in the organization often reinforced a surrogate of 'internationalism' quite unintentionally. The surrogate was the production of technical reports, which—quality unexamined—was often all that remained once the expert left after a two-year period. Technical reports—within this perspective—are a necessary stage in the research-to-application continuum; they also provide a somewhat disembodied reflection of 'publication', the Mertonian 'communality' norm of scientific enquiry. Absence of counterparts to train was a serious and persisting problem, so often there was no one to carry on where the expert left off. Indeed projects of industrial relevance conducted by experts usually lapsed once the expert left. But the attitude of many (but not all) experts that research must lead to application and development reinforced non-integration and set a pattern for Thai researchers to emulate. One visiting expert on building research, for example, showed to us a detailed critical path analysis of work he was to do while in Thailand: the end category was 'write report'! Experts' career concern for research on the 'novel' also reinforced the research-only focus of TRC. Some experts (usually those trained in more technological disciplines) were overtly committed to industrial relevance. But the concept and character of the organization circumscribed their ability to be effective. Those whose experience was more centred in research sometimes were not at all committed to wider relevance. For example, experts sent by the United Nations to aid the development of TRC's organic chemistry research were interested only in Thai raw materials which were different from those so far reported in the literature.

## Concluding Remarks

*Interaction between Meanings of Research*

Presentation of this case study seeks to show how observed local institutionalization of research was a product of interaction between at least five meanings of TRC's research activity—that attached to social expression of science's perceived 'internationalism'; the covert meaning of the organization's research activities to the Foreign Special Governor; the covert meaning of TRC research activities to implementing UN agencies; the meaning of organizational activities in wider Thai society; and the covert meaning of organizational activity to the Thai head who took over from the Special Governor. Interaction between these various meanings attached to what was apparently the same research activity was set in an external (to the organization) structural context of Thai government bureaucracy as well as that of Thai industrial and educational underdevelopment.

Imported into Thailand were 'internationalist' or universalistic notions about science. These were primarily expressed (1) by the view that scientific research would lead to social and economic development—which thus set the form of project selection, and the form of relationship to the Thai productive milieu (involving economic evaluation and 'selling' of research products at the *end* of organization activities); (2) in the organization concept which, based on a model of a developed country 'centre of excellence' (Australia's CSIRO), requiring (a) an 'umbrella' organization that collected remnants of Thai science under one 'empire', (b) set a discipline-based internal organization structure (with horizontal integration around particular projects expected to follow), (c) set a primary role for the organization's executive as paying attention to TRC personnel, and (d) validated a training policy that was based on building up scientist-education with no attention to developing managerial capability because this, too, was expected to follow. The *overt* function of this form was rational scientific-based enquiry.

Notions of the universalistic nature of science were translated into action by a Foreign Special Governor whose own covert goals attached a separate meaning to the organization's overt function—the conduct of scientific-based enquiry. His apparent concern for visible success of the institution resulted in the creation of an 'empire' without due concern for external impingement on (and consequent hostility from) other government research agencies, or internal impingement on balance of staff capabilities, priorities of activities, and evaluation of programme of activity; in centralization of all decision-making to ensure the institution *worked*, but with unintended negative consequence to Thai decision-making capability, internal horizontal integration, and relationships to TRC's industrial milieu. In an attempt to ensure the organization was not subsumed by more general Thai bureaucratic practice, the Special Governor established a range of preventative procedures: he established TRC separate from government bureaucracy to prevent impingement of bureaucratic procedure: he allowed its Thai head to hold a superordinate government position so that TRC's political position *vis-à-vis* the Thai bureaucracy would be enhanced. Ultimately the Special Governor's action was oriented towards fulfilment of a meaning of LDC science to him, in terms of its extrinsic value to personal career and prestige goals. The unintended consequence of each procedure he implemented, or failed to give priority to, was, however, the generation of an organization form—and confusion within it—that provided a context entirely commensurate with the meaning attached to organization and social order in wider Thai society.

United Nations impingement on the organization was guided by wider acceptance within its various component institutions of the meaning of LDC science to them. Overt function of LDC science to UN implementers and reviewers was also guided by universalistic assumptions that science would lead to development and that its organization should be modelled along developed country lines. United Nations agencies thus accepted a concept that evaluated the apparent vacuum of scientific capability in the nation but not the industrial milieu into which science was set or mechanisms of linkage between institution-based science and its industrial use. Review of the organization assumed utility of *concept* and emphasized better selling of its research products, an approach believed to work universally within developed countries. Procedures for ongoing review first allowed implementing UN agents—with vested interest in presentation of its surface success—to provide the main source of feedback. With each UN agency dependent on higher level approval, apparent successfulness of TRC was presented increasingly positively (via selective editing of reports) the further up the UN organizational tree the reports went. Consequently, the concept of TRC activities was not questioned; its ineffectiveness was seen as a product of poor on-site management—measured against developed country criteria. Ineffectiveness was not attributed to either inapplicability of concept or to its interaction with other—particularly local—meanings of TRC research activities.

TRC was imported into a Thai cultural context which has a long history and wide contemporary pervasiveness of particular forms of social relations and organizations. These especially appear to emphasize a patrimonial form of vertical hierarchy; a meaning of organizational activity as primarily serving extrinsic social location and status rather than overt functional ends; a system-maintenance procedure designed to ensure bureaucratic survival as major priority; presentation of success in terms primarily of *apparent* 'surface' reality. The context set for organizational form and behaviour by the Foreign Special Governor's implementation (via his own covert goals) of universalistic assumptions applied to LDC research, rather than being an antithesis for entry of Thai meanings attached to research, actually reinforced it. However, though the colour of wider Thai social values could be observed in TRC, all Thai participants did not fully subscribe to such meanings attached to the organization. Particularly once TRC's survival was threatened by its apparent ineffectiveness and external pressure to be effective, some members of Thai management sought to implement *more* function-oriented procedures than formerly existed under the Special Governor. Their action was constrained by inherited confusion, the deadweight of established organizational size and shape and an inherent (but internationally unquestioned) inapplicability of the organizational concept.

The context for entry of Thai meanings and attachment to already established procedures was set also, however, by the external context of the organization. Impingement was evident first from structural conditions of underdevelopment: an industrial milieu of undeveloped technological sophistication that was unable and unwilling to accept research products presented to them from TRC; and an education system which was unable to feed TRC with the analytic and appropriately trained capabilities on which the organization's functioning depended.

Second, there was impingement on internal organization from external relations with TRC's government milieu. Established in conflict with established government departments, and with a tradition of non-integration between government agencies, with no power base for established government funding, TRC was forced to find a means of distinguishing its role; 'scientific' status assumed this role, and the need to present this surface reality helped insulate TRC further from its industrial milieu. In a context of organizational confusion, Thai management could see little alternative but to become increasingly dependent on Thai bureaucratic budgetary procedure as a means of obtaining government funding; thus wider bureaucratic formalism increasingly entered the organization as context for research activity.

Consequently, what initially appears on the surface a relatively straightforward process of acculturation was on finer analysis very complex indeed. Acculturation normally refers to the process of two previously separated meaning systems coming into contact with adequate force to produce change. Here, the meaning systems coming into contact appeared to be that of a universalistic culture of science as attached to applied research, and that of a traditional Thai culture. But this interaction was mediated through the covert meanings attached to research activities of the organization by individuals involved. Interaction between meanings of research was set in the organization's interaction with its structural milieux. Research clearly had a constellation of meanings; with its institutionalization came confusion. It assumed all of these meanings at once, and was able to functionally satisfy none of them.

*Contributions to an 'Interpretive' Sociology of Science*

Consequently, the analysis demonstrates something of an 'interpretive' perspective in the sociology of science advocated by Law (1974) and Law and French (1974): meaning of research in this LDC science institution is clearly subject to continual negotiation. The case demonstrates the way science, rather than being isolatable from, or corruptible by, other forms of social life, was 'one aspect of a situated system of activity' (Law and French, 1974, p. 582). In an LDC context, science and its institutionalization served a variety of overt, covert, cultural, and personal ends. Meaning of research activity was in constant negotiation with impingement on and from the institution's transactions with its external structural and cultural environment.

This brings me back to the literature with which I began. To assume *a* normative role of science in LDCs as most of the 'structural' literature does can be seriously misleading, not just because the linkage between science and its structural impact (its relation to 'function') is highly questionable, but also because it assumes an acultural 'form' of research itself—it assumes a single 'meaning' for research. To stop as even the more perceptive 'interactionist' literature on LDC science does with the assumption of interaction between two cultural forms—that of international science and that of local cultural tradition—is also inadequate. In the above case study the appearance of a Thai culture 'diluting and devouring' an international science culture, was on more detailed analysis far too simple. This is particularly so when one realizes the extent to which the Foreign Special Governor, in translating 'universalistic' assumptions into Thailand, actually created the base for Thai cultural impingement. Also, the meaning of research was not only subject to a process of cultural interaction, but this process was in continuing transaction with the research institution's external structural environment.

*A Perspective on Interaction between Science and Indigenous Culture*

As a first stage in attempting to relate this case study to what may happen in other LDC research institutions, it is worth examining something of the dimensions of *cultural* interaction within which the process we observed was set. Even without the Special Governor's particular influence, there is evidence that a similar research institution in Thailand would interact similarly with local cultural meanings of activity. Although observations of other science institutions were by no means as detailed, it appeared that in Thai government science departments, in an FAO generated research institution in southern Thailand, and in a Japanese-managed research institution in north-eastern Thailand, similar cultural interactions were being played out. Like any other cultural symbol or set of symbols the forms within which science's 'universalistic' meaning is embodied are bound to interact with local cultural forms and meanings. To attempt internal reorganization of TRC along 'Western' lines—rationalizing organizational relations without reference to depth of cultural attachment to, for example, vertical hierarchy and against horizontal integration—seems bound to lead to failure. Thai organizational culture has a long history and appears to be deeply embedded in wider social meanings.

In other cultural settings (where depth of existing organizational culture varies) one would expect different products from the interaction between an implanted research culture and that of local society. To elucidate a range of possible differences, below are some basic hypotheses covering possible results of such interaction. I must emphasize, however, that I am dealing only with one (albeit important) dimension of an interaction or interpretive perspective on LDC science institutions. As the case study demonstrates, understanding the *process* of interaction in each case requires detailed historic and empirical analysis of interactions between cultural/personal meanings; overt/covert goals; transactions between institutionalization and its structural context.

Given these major qualifications of *process*, it could be expected that, in general, when research institutions modelled on Western lines are introduced into non-Western cultures, without firm consistent managerial and organizational training (or *en*culturation of organization members), the form of the resulting organization will interact with local organizational values, meanings, and traditions.

Consequently, the stronger and deeper are these values in extant institutions, the greater will be the movement of the research organization and its embodied meaning of research activity away from Western universalistic assumptions and towards indigenous meanings and forms.

Although referring to business organizations, Onyemelukwe (1973, p. 14) in contrasting African with Japanese experience provides an example which broadly supports this contention. He notes that in Japan contemporary 'modern' business is strongly influenced by, and had incorporated, distinctly Japanese values of overall responsibility to the Japanese society; responsibility to employees; the need to be successful. Thus organizations are very paternalistic and offer comprehensive lifelong security to their members, are very attentive to age and seniority, while individual decision and personal ambition are sublimated to the interests of the group.[14] 'The weaker is indigenous organization and less secure is its meaning, the higher is the chance that universalistic science organization and (therefore, research) activity forms will be imitated, but divested of any depth of meaning.'

Science in this case generates a genuine cargo cult: build the institution like in (for example) the United States, perform the rituals on its staging area, and natural benefits will follow.[15] Onyemelukwe's (1973, p. 57) observations of African business organizations demonstrate a parallel example of this hypothesis. He notes that in the movement of these organizations from their former colonial models, imitation resulted in African managers 'like other African elites' having 'difficulty in distinguishing between "form" and "substance" in the new Westernised society in which they find themselves'.

Personal and institutional identity is thence more likely to be associated with this ritualistic imitation rather than with its function. An impoverished meaning of research activity would allow a very weak connection to its (Western) function. 'The closer are universalistic science (and therefore, research) forms to local established organization and activity meanings, the more complete will be the *enclosure* of universalistic science meanings into local cultural meaning.'

Comparative analysis of cultural interactions between industrializing nations could elaborate what is generally assumed to be a single meaning and form of modern research activity and organization. Graham's (1975) study of the historic origins of Russian research institutes provides one case study of such an analysis. He demonstrates their basis in pre-revolutionary Russia, the influence of particular foreign models and discusses the uniquely Soviet innovations which were introduced after the Revolution and the way these reflected the characteristics of the Soviet social and political milieu.

A variant of this hypothesis would be worth exploring in Latin American nations, for as Herrera (1973) observes, in Latin American nations there is strictly speaking no indigenous culture: even in those Latin American countries with a high proportion of indigenous population, dominant classes and cultural patterns are European.

On the surface, the case of India appears a direct parallel to that of Thailand. But there are some important differences worthy of exploration: (1) Indian research institutions have a long history of growing out of British colonial organization forms; Thailand has no such tradition. (2) India has an ancient history of its own indigenous science, whereas Thailand has not. (3) Indian culture is presently set in far greater poverty than is that of Thailand. (4) Indian culture is a great deal more diffuse than that of Thailand, where, for example, social and moral hierarchies come together in the monarchy and polity. (5) There are parallels between Indian and Thai religious contexts of hierarchy, but important differences particularly *vis-à-vis* individual status mobility.[16]

The histories of many LDCs are characterized by sharp discontinuities—as with social revolution or invasion (and consequent change of values and social forms), or with the mainly recent ejection of colonial powers. Social revolution may, of course, take radically different forms, so may have varied consequences for subsequent growth of research institutions, their form, function, and meaning. For example, Herrera (1973) observes that the Mexican and Bolivian revolutions which aimed to transform and modernize the most archaic structures in Latin America except for pre-Revolutionary Cuba, were staged by predominantly indigenous sections of the population (Mexican peasants and Bolivian miners respectively) and not by the presumably more dynamic and open-minded 'modern' sectors. The new powers had little interest in science. Counter to this is the case of China. A fundamental consequence of the 1947 Revolution was the extension of elementary science education across the whole society, the overt function of which was to introduce 'scientific' attitudes of scepticism and rationality in place of 'superstition' and traditional authority (Dean, 1974). In ex-colonies there is pre- and post-independence impingement of colonial powers and even competition between them. These 'Western' nations may have left quite different forms of research organization and attitudes. For example, Pereira (1971) observes that Britain, France, and Belgium exported to Africa conflicting research philosophies for universities versus economic development—resulting in little contact or community of thought between those who set up African universities and agricultural pioneers in the colonial government services. As a result, although universities existed, the colonizers had to set up research institutes to serve the economy, thus creating a dual research system. Then, with independence, the majority of experienced overseas staff departed long before adequate African scientists could take over. Pereira concludes that though the French system—with its base in specially built laboratories in France—has been more durable, 'precarious maintenance by a discontinuous series of short-term visitors under bilateral government aid or United Nations aid schemes has maintained the form rather than the function of these laboratories in many territories under former British or Belgian administration'. As in the present case study, it can be seen here how detailed analysis of *process* is essential to an understanding of cultural interaction expressed in LDC research organization.

Thus, I would suggest that analysis of the contemporary meaning of research in LDCs and its organization ideally requires highly detailed case study, and this would include study of historic development, interaction with wider social tradition, belief systems, and change. However, hopefully a broad interpretive theoretical framework might provide both some leads for questions to analyse, as well as a structure for future theory into which such detailed empiricism could be fitted.

### Acknowledgements

This paper is one outcome of a larger research project conducted by the University of Sussex's Science Policy Research Unit (SPRU) between 1970 and 1973 in Thailand. The project would not have been possible without the initial financial support of a generous grant from the Ford Foundation. It would not have been as exhaustive or lengthy without the continuing support from the Science Policy Research Unit's own scarce resources. The paper would have been very different if the Nuffield Foundation and the University of Wollongong had not provided a Small Research Grant and travel support respectively, that enabled the author to rework preliminary analysis with staff at the Science Policy Research Unit, in particular with Martin Bell. As consequence of this reworking important changes occurred in the perspective of this analysis. The case study presented in this paper was the result of research and close collaboration with Martin Bell of SPRU. Data collection was supported by the assistance of Wit Satyarakwat. Mike Howes contributed much to the theoretical perspective. Martin Bell was of invaluable assistance, however, in conducting research, in the development and reformulation of theoretical frameworks for analysis, and in detailed editing. However, responsibility for the final analysis is my own; it does not necessarily reflect the views of the Science Policy Research Unit.

### Notes

1 This particular imbalance is, it would appear, being redressed. Contributions by, for example, Vaitsos (1974), and those which we discuss shortly by Cooper (1972) and Herrera (1973, demonstrate insights to economic theory derived from somewhat more perceptive analysis of interaction between social, economic, and political conditions of underdevelopment and science. In a forthcoming book on our work in Thailand, additional empirical support will be presented for the nature and dynamic of linkage between science, technology, and economic development.
2 Both these assumptions and their connectedness appear to be a product of an implicit acceptance of Mertonian (1937) norms of science and the transport of these into their *social* expression. Specifically, we would suggest that the assumption of Mertonian 'universalism' embodies an assumption of usefulness of science knowledge; the pure normative statement of universalism by Merton, is that because natural phenomena are everywhere the same, so social, cultural, and political contexts are irrelevant to objective evaluation of the truth of scientific statements. But such 'truth' has more than philosophic value as it can form explanation of everyday experience and can become embodied in objects of our everyday experience. Thus, 'truth' can be recognized outside a science circle of adherents. As a norm, universalism, as other

posited norms of science, assumes a social system. There is no basis for science as a social system supported by society unless scientific truth is perceived as of value to society. Thus, within the 'normative' scientist's world view of science, usefulness is not the goal of scientific enquiry; but usefulness is seen to follow certification of knowledge and operation of other internal norms that ensure its validity. Without this assumption, science as a social system has no contemporary basis. When science is turned towards developing countries (either by scientists or analysts of science), the utilitarianism which often remains implicit within the scientific community's meaning system while in advanced countries becomes explicit. Thus, the assumption reads, 'valid knowledge must result from universalistic science practice, and this knowledge must be useful in LDCs'. This assumption is *explicitly* stated by Dedijer (1963, p. 64): 'Every aspect of national development policy depends on research conducted within the country, although it must, of course, be based on the achievements of, and conform with, the standards of international science.' Consequently, my use of 'universalism' is similar to Merton's, but not coincident with it. As our paper goes on to demonstrate, universalism as a norm of science when transformed into its social expression within LDCs (in particular) becomes the basis for institutional action—for building a 'centre of scientific excellence', and expecting social/economic development to follow.

3 The research was conducted primarily by Martin Bell and myself. In this article I draw on the work of both of us. Together, our research included, (1) interviews with key personnel (both in the TRC and in CSIRO) in 1965 immediately after the organization was established; (2) participant observation and recording over a three-year period, together with preview and review visits (covering the five-year period from 1969–1974); (3) interviews with all senior management, the majority of scientific advisers to the corporation, interviews and informal conversations with staff in all divisions of the organization; (4) interviews with senior UN officials, officials in related Thai government departments, institutions and Thai universities; (5) extensive visiting of industrial firms and observation of other government research institutions; (6) analysis of quarterly reports on all research projects over the ten-year period 1964–1973 (inclusive); (7) analysis of 'contact notes' formally reporting external contacts by corporation staff; (8) review and analysis of UN, corporation and Thai government documents pertaining to the establishment and review of the organization; (9) analysis of technical reports and publications of the corporation.

4 I am using 'covert' and 'overt' goals and functions throughout the text as expressions to emphasize the existence of two quite distinct systems—one which is the stated and partly fulfilled purpose of the organization (i.e. good quality scientific research, thence industrial application of research), or of individuals, and the other which is the purpose of the organization for individuals or separate groups as expressed in behaviour and attitudes. In TRC, 'overt' organizational goals changed over time; there was a variety of 'covert' organizational and individual goals and these interacted.

Overt and covert differs from Merton's (1937, p. 51) use of 'latent' and 'manifest', because 'latent' refers to unintended consequences of the manifest goals and organization. The covert system expressed by individuals associated with TRC can hardly be called unintended. Our use of overt and covert embodies an essential 'motivation' component to action whereas Merton's concepts ostensibly do not.

5 Peres (1963) presents an analysis of the organizational form of CSIRO and, in particular, the role of the Executive, from evidence collected at approximately the same time as its concept was transferred to Thailand.

6 It is worth noting that patrimonialism has a somewhat culturally specific meaning in Thailand. Care must be taken in transferring the same term applied in a Western context into an explanation of Thai society. Dalton (1959), for example, in discussing vertical cliques in a Western business firm refers to patrimonialism. He sees vertical cliques as being either *symbiotic* (where the top manager gives patronage to juniors in return for information about possible rumblings of discontent) or *parasitic* (where sup-

port exists for juniors because of a family or friendship link—he also notes that these relations will be eventually discovered and are then damaging to the participants). Dalton's views are, however, anchored in Western cultural assumptions: he sees patrimonialism as a response which is intended to decrease subordinate threats to position; this is quite different to the Thai context where patrimonialism/obligation are more a *basis* for organization. Dalton sees the nepotistic links as being organizationally embarrassing whereas in the Thai context they are taken somewhat more for granted.

7 I am very aware here of the danger of logic in connecting complex and sophisticated patterns of Buddhist philosophy to contemporary social behaviour. As Kirsch (1967) reflects, searches back from social values to Buddhist philosophy such as conducted by, for example, Embree (1950), Mosel (1957), Ayal (1963, 1969), Wilson (1964), have always been successful. I rely here on Kirsch and to a lesser extent, Hanks (1962) however, for they start *in* the philosophic basis of Thai Buddhism, and demonstrate isomorphism to social order. Kirsch, in his discussion of ritual, provides a link between philosophic Buddhism and its secular expression; he thus provides a theoretical base for the validity of his correlation. Strength is added to correlation of religious context with vertical form in social life in observation of the relatively classless base of stratification in Thai society. Wilson (1962, p. 76) notes, for example, 'The fact that the observable practices associated with these ... ways of thought are a part of the everyday life of a large portion of the Thai nation, without great distinction of social class or even of education is adduced here to support the main contention, that the world view of the Thai is an elaboration of the idea that the cosmos is a moral unity.' However, I do not carry this coincidence of religious philosophy and social form very far. I extend no further than to justify the claim that secular Buddhist form and ritual provide a basic *context* for a general acceptance of patrimonial social order (see Riggs, 1966, pp. 324–325, who also accepts this context). I do this in order to demonstrate that the social form observed in TRC may have deep contextual roots in the general belief system of the society. It is not a form which can be easily replaced by unaware new management practice.

8 This observation needs to be tempered by the knowledge that TRC was having great difficulty eliciting research money from industry. I explain the most central reasons for this later when discussing organizational effectiveness.

9 I will present further evidence of vertical control of status a little later in discussing the pattern of relationships established with organizations and people outside TRC.

10 Reports outlining projects from at least one such department, for example, often embodied no more extensive a statement than 'project completed': no results were presented or published. All government research departments were characterized by the bureaucratic formalism and status orientation that the Special Governor sought to avoid.

11 This change in procedure may, on the surface, appear rather trivial. But in the context of Thai bureaucracy, where communication between agencies is handled at the top, it was important. Formerly, TRC could only contact other government departments on a formal basis through the head of NRC—who coincidentally was also Research Director General of TRC. Thus the RDG had high level power in controlling integration between TRC and its government milieu. This change occurred after he had left TRC, but still retained control of the National Research Council, so it represented something of a shift of power back into TRC.

12 United Nations attached personnel (including those within TRC) 'sold' the organization to the Thai Prime Minister, to visiting dignatories, to the international community of academics, and to the public as 'the best industrial research institute in the region ... organized according to accepted world practice'. These remarks were publically reported from a meeting in February 1969 between two UNDP representatives and the Thai Prime Minister. Similar glowing praise about TRC is presented to a general

academic community (see Nicholls, 1968, and Nicholls and Pradisth, 1969). When Robert McNamara, Head of the International Bank of Reconstruction and Development, visited the TRC in November 1972 his briefing documents informed him that the organization was 'one of the best scientific organizations in the developing world'.

In addition, the need to continually 'present' the organization seriously hampered ongoing work by senior management. In support of TRC's international contacts and status, a great deal of time was devoted to entertaining visiting missions. A senior UN expert did an analysis at the beginning of 1972 of use of his own time over the previous six months: over a period of 120 working days, 50 man days (42 per cent of his time) had been taken up talking with visiting missions—the majority of which were from international or other host national agencies (for example, from the United States Overseas Mission). As most senior management were involved in these visits, the amount of time devoted by senior management to international agency liaison was enormous.

13 See Bell and Hill (1976). Presentation of more detailed evidence from large and small scale industrial and agro-industrial sectors will be presented in a forthcoming monograph from the SPRU team who worked on Thailand.

14 The Japanese case is particularly interesting in relation to our example from Thailand. Japanese research organizations can be highly effective, but still in organizational form express singularly Japanese cultural values. In the case of Thailand, we attribute ineffectiveness of the research institution primarily to inappropriateness of its original concept to relationships with its industrial milieu, and to confusion of meanings of research activity within. But a non-Western culture *does not have to be* in conflict with effectiveness of research organization towards whatever function it is designed to fulfil. To assume it does, assumes a monolithic culture of research. Recent mainstream sociology of science literature puts such an assumption into serious question.

15 This also, by the way, appears to have characterized the science-centred approach to development within UN thinking transported into many LDC research institutions such as the one we observed in Thailand (see also Hill and Bell, 1974).

16 Buddhist religious ideology developed from Hindu philosophy: both share central doctrines of *karma* and *multiple rebirths* and, as consequence, moral hierarchy. But in Hinduism, moral hierarchy is expressed in caste membership and unchangeable (in this lifetime) birth status; Thai Buddhism locates mobility of religious status in the individual, a doctrine which is socially reinforced through ease of upward moral projection by becoming a monk. In secularized expression of Thai Buddhism, social hierarchy reflects moral hierarchy. Thus to the extent that religious values set a context for hierarchical order in the societies, we would expect a fundamental difference between India and Thailand. For example, in Thailand, science may provide social status but remain completely commensurate with religious context; in India, perhaps such social status can only be achieved by rejecting religious values and hierarchies. Note, however, as Rahman (1970) observes, Indian scientists may well express the definitions of reality embodied in religion or indigenous knowledge systems within the *content* of scientific activity: 'Belief in astrology and its practice is not uncommon among scientists and some even seem to practice it to propitiate results of experiments.' Rahman more significantly notes an eminent Indian scientist, Professor Seshadri (FRS), President of the National Institute of Science of India: 'A complete definition of science should include the idea of higher knowledge of the Vedanta and allow the scientists to move into more subtle and more difficult planes of study' (Special Convocation Address, Banaras Hindu University, 1968). See Potter (1967) for a discussion of the bases in Indian philosophy for integration with scientific definitions of reality.

# References

Ayal, Eliezer B. (1963), 'Value systems and economic development in Japan and Thailand', *Journal of Social Issues,* **19,** 35–51.
Ayal, Eliezer B. (1969), 'Value systems and economic development in Japan and Thailand' in Robert O. Tilman (ed.), *Man, State and Society in Contemporary South East Asia,* London, Pall Mall Press.
Bell, R. Martin, and Stephen C. Hill (1976), 'Research on technology transfer: some limitations and new directions' in F. Bradbury, P. Jarvis, R. Johnston, and A. Pearce (eds), *Transfer Processes in Technical Change* (forthcoming).
Cooper, Charles (1972), 'Science, technology and production in the underdeveloped countries: an introduction', *Journal of Development Studies,* **9,** 1, October, 1–8.
Dalton, Melville (1959), *Men Who Manage,* New York, Wiley.
Dean, Genevieve (1974), 'Science and politics in China: reflections on *One Hundred Thousand Questions',* review in *Science Studies,* **4,** 93–96.
Dedijer, Steven (1962), 'Measuring the growth of science', *Science,* **138,** 3542, 781–788.
Dedijer, Steven (1963), 'Underdeveloped science in underdeveloped countries', *Minerva,* **2,** 61–81.
Dedijer, Steven (1964), 'International comparisons of science, *New Scientist,* **379,** 20 February, 461–464.
Eisenstadt, S. N. (1965), *Essays on Competitive Institutions,* New York, Wiley.
Embree, John F. (1950), 'Thailand—a loosely structured social system', *American Anthropologist,* **52,** 181–193.
Graham, Loren R. (1975), 'The formation of Soviet research institutes: a combination of revolutionary innovation and international borrowing', *Social Studies of Science,* **5,** 303–329.
Grubel, Herbert G. (1968), 'The reduction of the brain drain: problems and policies', *Minerva,* **6,** 541–558.
Guskin, Allen E. (1966), 'Tradition and change in a Thai university' in Robert B. Textor (ed.), *Cultural Frontiers of the Peace Corps,* Cambridge, Mass., MIT Press.
Hanks, Lucien M. (1962), 'Merit and power in the Thai social order', *American Anthropologist,* **64,** 1247–1261.
Hanks, Lucien M. (1967), U.S. military aid and social disequilibrium in Thailand', Bangkok, Thailand, ARPA Research and Development Centre, mimeo.
Haskins, Caryl P. (1964), *The Scientific Revolution and World Politics,* New York, Harper and Row.
Herrera, Amilcar (1973), 'Social determinants of science policy in Latin America—explicit science policy and implicit science policy' in Charles Cooper (ed.), *Science, Technology and Development,* London, Frank Cass, pp. 19–37.
Hill, Stephen C., and R. Martin Bell (1974), 'Paradigms and practice: innovation and technology transfer models—their unexamined assumptions and inapplicability outside developed countries', paper delivered to the Conference on Technology Transfer, University of Stirling, July, SPRU, mimeo.
International Bank of Reconstruction and Development (1959), *A Public Development Program for Thailand,* Baltimore, Johns Hopkins Press.
Kirsch, A. Thomas (1967), 'The Thai Buddhist quest for merit', paper delivered to American Anthropological Association, Washington, D.C., 30 November, 3 December.
Law, John (1974), 'Theories and methods in the sociology of science: an interpretive approach', *Social Science Information,* **13.**
Law, John, and David French (1974), 'Normative and interpretive sociologies of science', *Sociological Review,* **22,** 581–595.
Merton, Robert S. (1937), *Social Theory and Social Structure,* New York, Glencoe Free Press (revised ed., 1968).

Moravcsik, Michael (1964), 'Technical assistance and fundamental research in underdeveloped countries', *Minerva*, **2**, 197–209.
Moravcsik, Michael (1966), 'Some practical suggestions for the improvement of science in developing countries', *Minerva*, **4**.
Moravcsik, Michael (1971), 'Some modest proposals', *Minerva*, **9**, 55–65.
Mosel, James N. (1957), 'Thai administrative behaviour' in William J. Siffin (ed.), *Toward the Comparative Study of Public Administration*, Bloomington, Indiana, Indiana University Press, pp. 278–331.
Nayudamma, Y. (1973), 'Decentralised management of R. & D. in a developing country', *Minerva*, **11**, 516–536.
Nelson, Richard R. (1974), 'Less developed countries—technology transfer and adaptation: the role of the indigenous science community', *Economic Development and Cultural Change*, **23**, 61–77.
Nicholls, Frank G. (1968), 'Science in development in Thailand', *University of Melbourne Gazette*, **24**, 2, 10 April, 4–6.
Nicholls, Frank G., and Cheosokul Pradisth (1969), 'Harnessing science to development in Thailand', *Impact of Science on Society*, **19**, 1, 75–84.
Onyemelukwe, C. C. (1973), *Men and Management in Contemporary Africa*, London, Longman.
Parthasarathi, Ashok (1969a), 'Sociology of science in developing countries—the Indian experience', *Economic and Political Weekly*, **4**, 2 August, 1277–1280.
Parthasarathi, Ashok (1969b), 'Sociology of science in developing countries—the Indian experience—a sequel', *Economic and Political Weekly*, **4**, 23 August, 1387–1389.
Pereira, H. C. (1971), 'The integration of research agencies for African agricultural development', *Minerva*, **9**, 38–45.
Peres, Leon (1963), 'Research organization and the control of incentives: the case of an Australian scientific organization', *Public Administration*, **22**, 4, 330–349.
Piel, Gerard (1964), 'Role of science in India's self recovery', *Nature*, 20 June, 1154–1155.
Potter, Karl (1967), 'Attitudes of Indian philosophers toward science' in Ward Morehouse (ed.), *Understanding Science and Technology in India and Pakistan*, New York, Foreign Area Materials Center, Occasional Publication no. 8, pp. 43–53.
Rahman, A. (1970), 'Scientists in India: the impact of economic policies and support in historical and social perspective', *International Social Science Journal*, **22**, 54–79.
Riggs, Fred (1966), *Thailand—the Modernization of a Bureaucratic Polity*, Honolulu, East-West Center Press.
Sachs, Ignacy (1971), *La Decouverte du Tiers Monde*, Paris, Flammarion.
Sagasti, Francisco (1973), 'Underdevelopment, science and technology: the point of view of the underdeveloped countries', *Science Studies*, **3**, 47–59.
Salam, A. (1966), 'The isolation of scientists in developing countries', *Minerva*, **4**, 461–465.
Shor, Edgar L. (1960), 'The Thai bureaucracy', *Administrative Science Quarterly*, **5**, 1, 66–86.
Siffin, William J. (1966), *The Thai Bureaucracy—Institutional Change and Development*, Honolulu, East-West Center Press.
Storer, Norman W. (1970), 'The internationality of science and the nationality of scientists', *International Social Science Journal*, **22**, 80–93.
Sussex Group (1969), Charles Cooper, Christopher Freeman, Oscar Gish, Stephen Hill, Geoffrey Oldham, and Hans Singer, 'Science, technology and underdevelopment: the case for reform, draft introductory statement for the United Nations', *World Plan of Action for the Application of Science and Technology to Development*, UN Economics and Social Council, EIAC, 52/L.68, 19 October.
Sussex Group (1971): Charles Cooper, Christopher Freeman, Oscar Gish, Stephen Hill, Geoffrey Oldham, and Hans Singer, 'Science in underdeveloped countries', *Minerva*, **9**, 101–121.

Thomas, Brinley (1967), 'The international circulation of human capital', *Minerva*, **5**, 479–506.
Unesco (1970), 'Manual for surveying national scientific and technological potential', *Science Policy Studies and Documents*, no. 15, Paris.
Unesco (1974), 'National science policies in Africa', *Science Policy Studies and Documents*, no. 31, Paris.
UNIDO (1970), *Industrial Research Institutes*, New York, United Nations.
UNIDO (1973), 'Seminar for the stimulation of industrial research in developing countries', Singapore, 21 November–2 December, Final Report, ID/WG, 132/13/Rev. 1, 24 January.
Vaitsos, Constantine V. (1974), *Intercountry Income Distribution and Transnational Enterprises*, Oxford, Clarendon Press.
Weber, Max (1958), *The Protestant Ethic and the Spirit of Capitalism* (trans. Talcott Parsons), New York, Charles Scribner's Sons.
Wilson, David A. (1962), *Politics in Thailand*, Ithaca, New York, Cornell University Press.
Wilson, David A. (1964), 'Thailand' in George McTurnan Kahin (ed.), *Government and Politics of Southeast Asia* (2nd ed.), Ithaca, New York, Cornell University Press.
Ziman, John (1971), 'Three patterns of research in developing countries', *Minerva*, **9**, 1, 32–37.

# INDEX

Acculturation, 220
Advisory bodies, 6, 56, 63
Age in science (*see also* Generations), 15, 77, 81, 82, 86, 88, 92
Agricultural research, 169, 170, 173, 179, 210
Agriculture, 16, 63, 140
  in India, 168–182
  production and productivity, 168, 169, 172, 175, 181, 189
Alienation, 163
Althusser, L., 189, 191
Andrews, F. M., 21, 49
Appu, P. S., 180, 190, 191
*Association Canadienne–Française pour l'Avancement des Sciences*, 134, 135, 138, 139, 140–141, 142, 147, 150, 152
Australian Commonwealth Scientific and Industrial Research Organization, 199, 200, 201, 204, 205, 225
Authority
  in organizations (*see also* 'Thai Research Centre'), 29, 73, 187
  in science, 11, 13, 26, 29, 33, 43, 44, 46
Autonomy of science, 4, 5, 6, 46, 52, 72, 75, 79, 146, 157, 161, 162, 163, 164, 197, 201
Avineri, S., 189
Ayal, E. B., 226, 228

Barber, B., 2, 18, 157, 162, 191
Barnes, B. S., 11, 18
Bassala, G., 133, 134, 140, 152
Belanger, P., 144, 153
Bell, D., 51
Bell, M., 198, 224, 225, 227, 228
Ben-David, J., 1, 2, 18, 131, 133, 135, 138, 152
Benveniste, G., 8, 18
Berger, B., 77, 93
Bernal, J. D., 1, 161, 191
Bernstein, B., 9, 18
Bhaduri, A., 178, 191
Bharadwaj, K., 178, 180, 191
Bhaskar, R., 25, 48
Bitz, A., 22, 24, 28, 32, 33, 34, 36, 37, 38, 48, 49
Blume, S. S., 4, 6, 7, 18, 81–82, 92, 93, 131, 152, 188
Böhme, G., 12, 18
Boucher, E., 139, 152
Bourdieu, P., 12, 13, 17, 18, 31, 32, 44, 48, 131, 152
Brandt, Willy, 57, 58
Brown, L. R., 181, 191
Bukharin, N., 165–166, 191
Bush, G., 92, 93

Cahn, A. H., 7, 18
Cancer research, 37, 46
Capitalism, 51, 53, 155, 156, 162, 166, 181
Caplow, T., 92, 93
Cargo cult, 222
Carlsson, G., 92, 93
Carr, E. H., 188, 191
Carr, I., 37, 38, 49
Carson, Rachel, 57, 58, 59, 60, 61
de Certaines, J., 36, 48
Chartier, M.-J., 152
Choice of research problem, 23, 66, 80, 81, 87, 88, 197, 216
Cichomski, B., 89, 93
Citation analysis, 22, 76
Clark, T. N., 152, 181
Clergy (in Quebec) (*see also* Religious values), 134, 136, 137, 142, 143
Coates, C. H., 90, 94
Cognitive structure of science, *see* Science
Cole, J. R. and S., 2, 6, 19, 131, 152
Cole, S., 89, 93
Collaboration in science, 28, 33, 34, 37, 40, 86, 88, 92
*Collèges classiques* (Quebec), 134, 135
Collins, H. M., 12, 19
Colvin, P., 45, 48

231

Community Development Programme (India), 169–170
Competition in science, 30, 32, 42, 72, 81, 140
Cooley, R. A., 57, 69
Cooper, C., 184, 191, 224, 228
Cowen, D. L., 108, 127
Crane, D., 2, 19, 22, 48, 83, 88, 89, 93, 131, 152
Cultural capital, 31, 32, 43, 44, 45, 136, 137, 138, 141
Culture. 12, 15, 16, 17, 73, 74, 162, 198, 199, 202, 219, 220, 221, 223–224, 225, 227
 production of (*see also* Knowledge), 18, 164

van den Daele, W., 12, 13, 19, 54, 55, 64, 67, 69
Dalton, M., 225–226, 228
Dansereau, P., 139, 150, 152
Das, P. K., 178, 180, 191
Davis, A. K., 78, 93
Dean, G., 223, 228
Dedijer, S., 196, 197, 225, 228
*Der Spiegel* (*see also* Mass media), 58, 59
Desai, A. R., 169, 192
Developing countries, science and technology in (*see also* Economic development, Industrialization, Underdevelopment), 6, 16, 167–188, 195–200, 216, 220, 221, 225
Division of labour in science, 27, 28, 29, 30, 31, 32, 33, 35, 86
 ethnic, 141, 148
Dobrov, G. M., 76, 93
Dolby, R. G. A., 10, 11, 19
Duchesne, R., 140, 153
Dugal, L. P., 147, 153
Dupree, A. H., 54, 69

Ecology, 62, 66
Economic development (*see also* Developing countries, Social change, Underdevelopment), 54, 63, 105, 138, 144, 148, 168, 186, 187, 198, 199, 202, 216, 223
Edge, D. O., 30, 49
Educational curricula, 9, 16, 39, 96, 136
Eisenstadt, S. N., 92, 93, 213, 228
Elites
 intellectual, 16
 rural, in India, 169, 180, 182

 scientific, 24, 28, 30, 31, 36, 38, 43–47
Ellul, J., 51, 69
Employment of scientists (*see also* Recruitment of scientists, Scientific labour markets), 7, 25, 81, 136, 140, 141
Engelhorn, C., 120, 127
Environmental protection, 15, 54, 56, 58, 60, 62, 65, 66
 movements, 57
Environmental research, 60, 66
Erlich, P., 58, 59, 60, 61
European Economic Community, 96, 97, 99, 100, 101, 102, 103, 104, 109, 112, 113, 114, 119, 120, 121, 122, 123, 126
 chemistry committee ($E_2C_3$), 112–113, 122
*European Pharmacopoeia*, 98, 104, 105
Expertise, 8, 16, 32, 36, 37, 46, 54, 61, 63, 98, 123
 foreign (in developing countries), 171, 199, 210, 214, 217

Fafara, R., 92
Falk, G., 86, 88, 93
Faris, R. E. L., 87, 93
Federal German Government, 56, 63, 64, 69
Federation of European Chemical Societies, 110
Ferreira, J. V., 188
Finalization (*see also* Theoretical closure), 12, 64
Financial resources for science, 5, 7, 24, 30, 41, 45, 46, 66, 74, 81, 103, 140, 141, 142, 145, 147, 148, 163, 168, 179, 187, 197, 212, 220
Flash, E. S., 8, 19
Fleming, D., 32, 48
Foodgrains, 168, 169
 high yield varieties (*see also* 'Green revolution'), 171, 172, 173, 174, 175, 179, 180
Fournier, M., 5, 7, 15, 16, 145, 151, 153
Freeman, R., 92, 93
French, D., 12, 19, 22, 49, 200, 220, 228
Frost, P. A., 21, 50

Garigue, P., 147, 153
Gaston, J. C., 2, 19, 33, 48, 85, 93
Generations, 39, 75–82, 92, 135
 ahistorical concepts of, 15, 75–78
 differences between, 77, 85
 historical concepts of, 15, 78–82, 92

in science, 15, 43, 75–82
  roles of, 76–78
Geology, 25, 26, 32, 34, 37
Georgescu-Roegen, N., 25, 45, 48
Glaser, B. G., 21, 48, 91, 93
Gomezgil, M. R. S., 6, 19
Gouldner, A., 91, 93
Government of India, 169, 172, 175, 177, 178, 179, 181, 183, 185, 186, 189, 190, 191, 192
Government of Quebec (see also Union Nationale), 139, 142, 144
Government policy, 53, 56, 58
  educational policy (see also Science policy), 55
Graham, L. A., 8, 19, 222, 228
Greenberg, D. S., 7, 19
'Green revolution', 16, 168, 169, 171, 172, 173, 174, 175, 179, 181, 190
Guskin, A. E., 206, 228

Haberer, J., 103, 128
Habermas, J., 51, 69
Hagstrom, W. O., 1, 3, 11, 19, 22, 48, 87, 93
Hall, O., 78, 84, 93
Hallam, A., 32, 48
Hanks, L. M., 203, 226, 228
Haskins, C. P., 196, 228
Hattery, 92, 93
Health care, 97–98, 100, 102, 126
Herrera, A., 197, 222, 223, 224, 228
Hessen, B., 1, 155–156, 192
Hickson, D. J., 29, 49
Hill, S. C., 16, 198, 227, 228
Hirsch, W., 161, 163, 188, 192
Holton, G., 21, 48, 87, 93
Howes, M., 224
Hughes, E. C., 103, 128

Industrialization, 222
  in India, 182–188
    role of foreign firms in, 182–183, 185, 186, 190
  in science, 30
Industrial research in India, 182, 183, 184, 186
Infeld, L., 75
Intellectual domain, 74, 90, 132, 137, 142, 150, 164
  and scientific domain, 134, 140, 148, 150, 152
Inter-disciplinary research (see also Scientific disciplines), 37, 58, 63, 66, 85

International associations (see also European Economic Community Chemistry Committee, Federation of European Chemical Societies), 96–97, 99, 100, 103, 115, 123, 126
Internationalism in science, 15, 16, 91
Internationalist (universalist) perspectives on science, 197, 198, 199, 204, 214, 215, 217, 218, 219, 220, 221, 224

Jamous, H., 95, 108, 128
Jenkin, P., 45, 48
Johnston, R. D., 13, 14, 20
Journals, scientific, 32, 33, 38, 39, 43, 45, 83

Karlsson, K., 92, 93
Keesing, R. H., 86, 93
King, M. D., 3, 11, 19, 22, 48
Kirsch, A. T., 203, 226, 228
Klima, R., 23, 48
Knowledge (see also Culture, Scientific knowledge)
  production of, 21, 23, 24, 39, 40, 45, 47, 55, 78, 217
  types of, 21, 131, 161
Kröber, G., 9, 19
Krohn, W., 12
Kuhn, T. S., 10, 19, 22, 49, 79, 80, 81, 87
Küppers, G., 51, 66, 69

Ladd, E. C., 141, 153
Lakatos, I., 10, 11, 17, 19
Law, J., 12, 19, 22, 49, 200, 220, 228
Laws of scientific development, 9
Lemaine, G., 28, 36, 49, 67, 69
Lewis, D. F., 115, 116, 128
Lipset, S. M., 141, 153
Lundgreen, P. 51

McAlpine, A., 22, 36, 37, 38, 48, 49
McGee, R. J., 92, 93
Maheu, L., 5, 7, 15, 16, 143, 144, 146, 147, 152, 153
Maldidier, P., 152, 153
Mannheim, K., 92
Manniche, E., 86, 88, 93
Marias, J., 76, 93
Martins, H., 4, 9, 11, 19, 22, 49
Marx, Karl, 155, 156, 162, 163, 164, 165, 167, 188, 192
Marxian sociology of science, see Sociology of science

Mass media (*see also* Popularization of science), 55, 58, 59, 136, 150
Mayntz, R., 53, 69
Menard, J., 146, 153
Mencher, J., 179, 192
Merton, R. K., 1, 2, 3, 4, 11, 17, 19, 22, 76, 78, 81, 88, 92, 94, 131, 153, 156, 157, 158, 159, 161, 162, 192–193, 225, 228, 229
Mikulinski, S. R., 9, 19
Mitroff, I., 3, 4, 19
Mobility of scientists, 73, 80, 81, 187, 196
Montpetit E., 139, 150, 151, 153
Moravcsik, M., 196, 229
Moscovici, S., 132, 154
Mulkay, M. J., 3, 4, 6, 7, 8, 9, 19, 22, 23, 30, 49, 80, 81, 87, 94, 161, 193
Mullins, N. C., 11, 12, 19, 21, 22, 33, 49, 83, 131

Naik, K. C., 170, 171, 193
National Academies of Science, 7, 8
Nationalism, 16, 130, 141, 144, 147, 150
Nationalist movements, 133, 148
Nayudamma, Y., 198, 229
Negotiation (*see also* Sociology of science, interpretive), 12, 17
  over meaning of research, 200, 218–220
Nelkin, D., 9, 20
Nelson, R. R., 195, 229
Newcomb, T., 93, 94
Neyman, E., 15
Nicholls, F. G., 200, 227, 229
Nichols, D., 7, 20

Oberschall, A., 138, 154
Objects of scientific work, 25–28, 29, 34, 35, 37, 39, 40, 42, 43, 44, 45
Offe, C., 52, 69
Onyemelukwe, C. C., 222, 229
Organization of science (*see also* Science, institutional structure of), 16, 62, 83, 196, 197, 198
Organization of scientific work, 14, 21, 23, 24, 25, 26, 27, 28–39, 42, 43–47, 48
Orzack, L., 15
Ossowska, M., 76, 94
Ostiguy, H., 145, 154
Ouellet, C., 135, 154
Oza, A. N., 188, 189, 193

Pantin, C. F. A., 25, 26, 34

Paradigms, 10, 13, 17, 22, 24, 38, 79, 80, 87, 161
Parry, G., 44, 49
Parsons, T., 5
Parthasarathi, A., 198, 229
Patents, 185, 190
Patnaik, U., 190, 193
Patterson, M., 83, 94
Pellegrin, R. J., 90, 94
Pelz, D. C., 21, 49
Pereira, H. C., 223, 229
Peres, L., 204, 205, 225, 229
Peripheral scientific systems, 15, 16, 17, 132–133
*Petite bourgeoisie* (in Quebec), 132, 136, 138, 139, 141, 142, 143, 144
Petoille, B., 95, 108, 128
Peyré, H., 78, 94
Pfetsch, F., 54, 69
Pharmaceutical products, 15, 97, 98, 99, 102, 105, 106, 109, 117, 119
Pharmacists, 99, 102
Pharmacy as a profession, 108, 116, 119, 121
Physics, 27, 28, 29, 32, 40, 41, 66, 75, 87, 88
Piel, G., 196, 229
Pinch, T. J., 44, 49
Planning, 53, 74
  of science (*see also* Science policy), 9, 13, 187
Political action, 51, 52, 54, 55, 56, 62, 63, 67, 69, 89
Political domain (*see also* Intellectual domain), 132, 142, 150
Political issues, 56–61, 66, 67, 69
Political theory, 51
Politicization of science, 7, 61, 103, 142, 149, 152
Pollution, 13, 57, 58, 59, 60, 63
Popularization of science (*see also* Mass media), 16, 57, 59, 84, 134, 135, 142, 223
Post-doctoral fellows, 40, 45, 72
Potter, K., 227, 229
Pouliot, A., 137, 154
Prasad, P., 178, 180, 193
Praxis, 165, 166
Prestige in science, 32, 33, 41, 43, 44, 45, 54, 72, 73, 77, 83, 85, 86, 88, 197
Price, D. J. de S., 158, 193
Priorities in research, 26, 31, 32, 33, 36, 38, 40, 45, 46, 161
Productive relations, 77, 164

Professional jurisdictions, 14, 15, 108, 118, 126
Professional monopolies, 95, 96, 109, 114, 116, 120
Pugh, D. S., 29, 49
Pulsars, 30

Rabkin, Y. M., 9, 20
Radio astronomy, 30, 31
Rahman, A., 198, 227, 229
Raj, R. N., 178, 193
Ramasubban, R., 16
von Randow, T., 57, 58, 69
Rao, C. H. H., 174, 178, 193
Rattansi, P. M., 188, 193
Ravetz, J. R., 8, 20, 22, 30, 50
Recognition in science (see also Reward system of science), 2, 3, 6, 22, 23, 78, 91
Recruitment of scientists (see also Employment of scientists, Scientific labour market), 23, 24, 25, 33, 38, 41, 42, 72, 75
Religious values, 156, 198, 203–204, 223, 226, 227
Renouard, Y., 76, 94
Repertoires of accounts, 4, 6, 8
Research areas (see also Specialities), 11, 12, 21, 32, 33, 37, 39, 66
Research organizations (see also 'Thai Research Centre'), 21, 26, 32, 38, 46, 47, 85, 182, 184, 186, 187, 221
  promotion in, 73, 78, 83, 84, 85
Research problems, 30, 31, 35, 36, 38, 40, 41, 43, 46, 47, 54, 60, 62, 64, 184
  external influences on, 45, 46
  'packaging' of, 39, 41, 42
Research students, 29, 34
Research tasks, 28, 29, 30, 31, 33, 35, 36, 37, 40, 41, 44, 45, 46
Research techniques, 26, 27, 28, 30, 31, 33, 35, 37, 39, 41, 42, 44, 46, 47
Restricted sciences, 14, 25, 26, 27, 28–34, 35, 36, 37, 38, 39–41, 45
*La Revue trimestrielle canadienne*, 134–135
Reward system of science (see also Recognition), 6, 71, 72, 73, 84, 90, 91, 150, 157–158
Riggs, F., 226, 229
Robbins, D., 13, 14, 20
Roe, A., 87, 92, 94
Rose, H., and S., 22, 50

Royal Institute of Chemistry, 110, 113, 117, 118, 129
Ryder, N. B., 77, 92, 94

Sachs, I., 197, 229
Sadler, J., 37, 38, 46, 50
Sagasti, F., 197, 229
Salam, A., 196, 229
Salaries of scientists, 74, 91, 187
Salomon, J.-J., 6, 20
Sankaram, A., 170, 171, 193
Sapolsky, H. M., 8, 20
Sarapata, A., 74, 94
Satyarakwat, W., 224
Sau, R., 178, 193
Scharpf, F. W., 69
Schelsky, H., 51, 69
Schmookler, J., 5, 20
Schroeder, B., 8, 20
Science
  as consumption, 184, 197
  cognitive structure of, 8, 13, 24, 30, 31, 32, 36, 37, 38, 45, 46, 47, 48, 65, 81, 86, 88, 92
  conflict in, 11, 13
  controversies in, 13, 14
  institutionalization of, 6, 11, 12, 16, 131, 136, 138, 149, 156, 162, 220
  institutional structure of, 11, 14, 66–67, 71, 75, 77, 131
  internationalism in (see also Internationalist perspectives on science), 15, 16, 91
  organization of, 16, 62, 83, 196, 197, 198
  professionalization of, 7, 146
  science of, 9
  social control in, 3, 4, 11, 30, 34, 42, 45, 103, 157, 160
  social functions of, 8, 12, 52–55, 64, 142, 159
Science policy, 5, 13, 52, 54, 60, 66, 71, 72, 73, 74, 81, 148, 183–184, 201
  explicit and implicit, 197
Scientific career, 15, 21, 28, 32, 39, 41, 66, 72, 73, 74, 75, 79, 81, 82–93
  'essential', 83–84, 85, 90, 91
  strategies, 84, 89
  types of, 89–92
Scientific change, 7, 11, 12, 22, 23, 24, 47, 66, 77, 81, 87
  internal and external determinants of, 52, 64, 67, 69, 131, 148–149, 166–167

Scientific community, 22, 24, 55, 57, 58, 59, 60, 62, 66, 71, 74, 87, 91, 147, 188, 196, 198, 225
  in Quebec, 135, 137
Scientific disciplines, 35, 36, 44, 45, 47, 65, 74, 80, 124–125
  autonomous and borrowing, 86
  boundaries between, 62, 63
  differences between, 36, 37, 47, 85–88, 148, 150
Scientific knowledge, uses of, 52, 53, 54, 56, 61, 64, 67, 163, 165, 216
Scientific labour market (*see also* Employment of scientists), 15, 23, 46, 71–75, 82, 83, 92
Scientific method, 2, 10
Scientific 'movement', 135, 136, 138, 149
Scientific norms, 2, 3, 4, 6, 16, 22, 38, 140, 157, 160, 161, 162, 217, 224–225
  counter, 3
  governing extra-scientific activities, 142
Scientific progress, 10, 11, 16, 52, 53, 64, 66, 77, 131, 132, 133, 147, 157, 163, 165, 167, 168
Scientific roles, 2, 6, 103, 116, 149, 159
Selden, W. K., 108, 129
Shils, E., 140, 154
Shor, E. L., 203, 229
Siffin, W. J., 202, 203, 229
Sklair, L., 158, 159, 160, 188, 193
Smith, A. Kimball, 7, 20
Social change, 66, 77, 143, 149, 159, 164, 202, 224
  in Quebec (the 'Quiet Revolution'), 144, 149, 152
Social origins of scientists, 72, 82, 151, 187, 198
Social structure, 8, 13, 16, 74, 132, 133, 143, 144, 188, 197, 198
  of India, agrarian, 175–178, 180, 181, 182
  of Quebec, 133, 137, 147, 149
Sociology of education, 9, 23
Sociology of knowledge, 10, 12, 156
Sociology of science
  cognitive, 4, 9–12, 14, 47
  diachronic, 15, 18, 21
  epistemological assumptions in, 5, 12, 22
  externalist, 4–9, 12, 14, 15, 16, 17
  functions of, 18
  interpretive (interactionist), 12, 17, 22, 198–200, 220–221
  Marxian, 9, 16, 67, 155, 164–167, 188
  orientations in, 1–18, 81, 131, 155–167, 195–199
  scope of, 1, 17–18, 22
Sociology of social sciences, 17–18, 75, 145–146
Specialities in science, 11, 12, 13, 21, 32, 33, 37, 39, 43, 47, 65, 80
Stehr, N., 81, 94
Stein, M., 158, 160, 193
Storer, N. W., 3, 8, 20, 158, 159, 162, 163, 193, 196, 229
Stratification, 6, 14, 32, 43, 46, 55
Subrahmanian, K. K., 184, 193
Sundquist, J. L., 57, 70
Swatez, G. M., 21, 50
Symbolic profit, 13

Team research, 40, 85–86
Technicians, 35
Technocracy, 51, 52, 67–68
Technology, 16, 52, 53, 57, 63, 65, 66, 67, 160, 163, 165, 166, 167, 181, 186, 197, 198
  diffusion of, 173, 175, 180
    factors affecting, 173, 175, 177–179, 180
  transfer, 170, 171, 174, 182, 183, 184, 195, 216
Thai bureaucracies, characteristics of, 199, 202–203, 204, 205, 208, 210–211, 214, 215, 219, 225, 226
Thai National Research Council, 201, 202, 207, 212, 215, 226
'Thai Research Centre' (TRC)
  as centre of excellence, 213, 217, 218
  decision-making in, 204–205, 214, 218
  establishment of, 200–202
  evaluation procedures in, 201, 207, 209, 210, 216, 218
  patrimonialism in, 205–208, 214, 215
  relations with government, 212–213, 215, 218, 220, 226
  relations with industry, 202, 206, 213, 214, 216, 217, 219, 220
  research projects in, 208–209, 211–212, 216
Theoretical closure (*see also* Finalization), 27, 35, 37, 42, 161
Third world (Popper), 47
Thomas, B., 196, 230
Training of scientists, 23, 26, 29, 39–43, 45, 79, 149, 218
  in restricted sciences, 39–41
  in unrestricted sciences, 41–43
Tremblay, A., 143, 154

Underdevelopment, structural context of (*see also* Developing countries, science and technology in, Economic development), 197, 198, 199, 200, 218, 220
Unionization of scientists, 7, 152
*Union Nationale* (*see also* Government of Quebec), 139–140, 142, 151
United Kingdom government, 102, 114, 115, 117, 118
United Nations, 196, 200, 201, 217, 218, 219, 226, 230
University systems, 16, 60, 132, 191
  Indian, 170–171, 181
  in Quebec, 134, 135, 136, 137–138, 144, 150–151
    growth of, 143, 145, 147
  in Thailand, 206
Unrestricted sciences, 14, 25, 26, 27, 28, 34–39, 41–43, 45

Vaitsos, C. V., 224, 230

Wandesforde-Smith, G., 57, 69
Watson, J., 31, 50
Weber, M., 155, 193, 203, 230
Weinberg, A., 85–86, 88, 92, 94
Weingart, P., 11, 13, 14, 15, 20, 54, 55, 66, 67, 69, 70
Wesolowski, W., 74, 94
Whitley, R. D., 3, 11, 14, 20, 21, 22, 24, 26, 30, 31, 36, 43, 45, 48, 50
Wigner, E. P., 88, 94
Williams, G., 92, 94
Wilson, D. A., 202, 226, 230
Wilson, R. K., 87, 92, 94
Wolfle, D., 60, 70
Woolgar, S., 30, 49, 50
World Health Organization, 105, 106, 107, 126, 129

Zilsel, E., 156, 193
Ziman, J. M., 92, 94, 196, 230
Zuckerman, H., 2, 20, 76, 78, 81, 92, 94

**LIBRARY OF DAVIDSON COLLEGE**